THE OFFICIAL

MANCHESTER UNITED ILLUSTRATED HISTORY

LIST OF CONTRIBUTORS

JUSTYN BARNES: Former editor of *United*, the official monthly magazine of Manchester United FC. Now a freelance journalist and editorial consultant, he contributed the section covering United's historic Treble triumph of 1999.

ADAM BOSTOCK: Editor of www.manutd.com, the club's official website. His other books about the club include *Access All Areas: Behind the Scenes at Manchester United*, which featured the photography of Roger Dixon, and four editions of the *Official Manchester United Annual* (2002–2005). He contributed chapters 11 and 12 on the 1980s and the new chapter 15.

CLIFF BUTLER: Official club statistician at Old Trafford and the editor of the club's official programme. He has written two books, *Manchester United Official Yearbook 2001* and *Manchester United Quiz Book*, and collaborated with Ivan Ponting on three others. As well as the Glossary, he wrote about the 30 years after World War I.

AUBREY GANGULY: Editorial Director at Future Publishing. He is a Former Editor of *United*, the official Manchester United magazine. He contributed the chapter on the mid-1950s era of the Busby Babes and the section charting Alex Ferguson's league championship and Double triumphs of the early 1990s.

GRAHAM MCCOLL: Freelance sports writer and journalist and a regular contributor to *FourFourTwo* magazine. A Scotsman, he has written seven books, including *Manchester United in the Sixties*, and, with former United legend Joe Jordan, *Scotland in the World Cup Finals*. He contributed the sections on the 1960s and 1970s.

MARK WYLIE: Curator of the Manchester United Museum at Old Trafford. A historian, he has contributed the first two chapters of this book, describing the 40-odd years from the club's formation up to the end of the Billy Meredith era and the outbreak of World War I.

First published in 2001

This revised and updated edition published in 2004

Copyright © 2001, 2004 Manchester United Plc
Text and design copyright © 2001, 2004 Carlton Books Limited

Manufactured and distributed by
Carlton Books Limited
20 Mortimer Street
London W1T 3JW

A CIP catalogue record for this book is available from the British Library

ISBN 0 233 00102 6

Project editor Martin Corteel
Project art direction Russell Porter
Design Simon Mercer
Picture research Daffydd Bynon and Stephen O'Kelly
Production Sarah Corteel & Kate Pimm

Printed in Portugal

The following photographs appear on the opening pages of the various chapters.

Chapter 1 (Page 13) **Main:** Newton Heath, 1889–90. **Inset:** Sam Black
Chapter 2 (Page 23) **Main:** United won the first ever FA Charity Shield in 1908, beating QPR in a replay. **Inset:** Sandy Turnbull
Chapter 3 (Page 39) **Main:** George Mutch (stripes) wins a header against West Ham United's Jimmy Ruffell in 1936. **Inset:** Jack Cape
Chapter 4 (Page 55) **Main:** Jack Rowley heads for goal against Preston during United's run to the FA Cup in 1948. **Inset:** Stanley Pearson
Chapter 5 (Page 69) **Main:** Duncan Edwards clears the ball during the Busby Babes' last game in England, a 5–4 win at Arsenal. **Inset:** Duncan Edwards
Chapter 6 (Page 87) **Main:** Bobby Charlton, in street clothes, shows off his ball control to three young football fans. **Inset:** Dennis Viollet
Chapter 7 (Page 101) **Main:** Denis Law was named European Footballer of the Year for 1964 after scoring 46 goals in the season. **Inset:** George Best
Chapter 8 (Page 125) **Main:** George Best shoots at goal before Leeds United's Paul Reaney (left) and Jack Charlton can intervene. **Inset:** Ian Ure
Chapter 9 (Page 135) **Main:** Sammy McIlroy turns away after scoring against Wolves in the 1976 FA Cup quarter-final replay. **Inset:** Alex Stepney
Chapter 10 (Page 153) **Main:** Mickey Thomas has a shot blocked during the 1979 FA Cup final defeat against Arsenal. **Inset:** Ray Wilkins
Chapter 11 (Page 171) **Main:** Manchester United's first League Cup final was in 1983, but Liverpool won in extra time. **Inset:** Gary Bailey
Chapter 12 (Page 189) **Main:** Brian McClair celebrates his goal against Oldham in the FA Cup semi-final replay of 1990. **Inset:** Paul Ince
Chapter 13 (Page 209) **Main:** Steve Bruce's powerful header gives United a late winner against Sheffield Wednesday in 1993. **Inset:** Peter Schmeichel
Chapter 14 (Page 227) **Main:** Dwight Yorke heads past Ruud Hesp for United's third goal in the 3–3 draw in Barcelona. **Inset:** Dwight Yorke
Chapter 15 (Page 247) **Main:** Ruud Van Nistelrooy goes for goal as United take on Real Madrid in the Champions League. **Inset:** Van Nistelrooy

THE OFFICIAL
MANCHESTER UNITED ILLUSTRATED HISTORY

SECOND EDITION

Adam Bostock

CONTENTS

1901

1922

1935

1948

1957

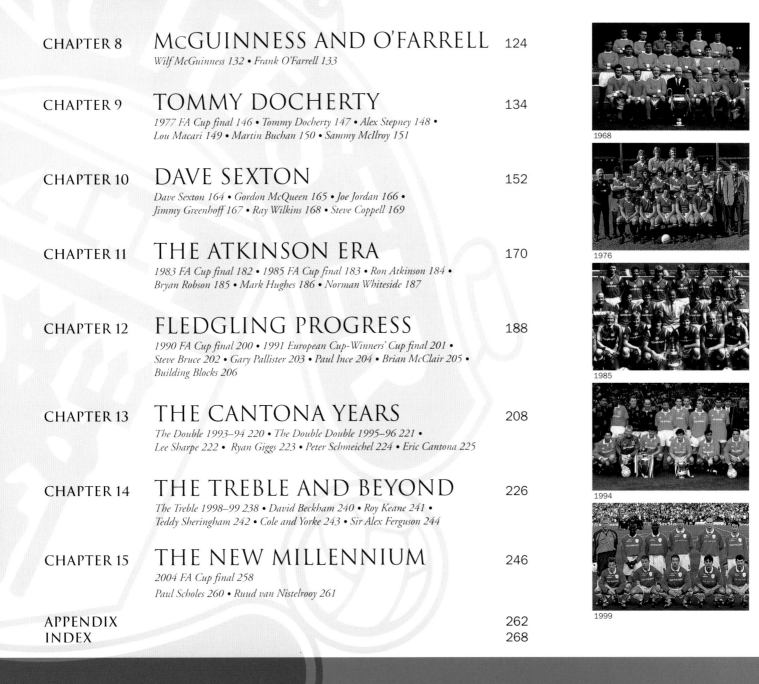

1968

1976

1985

1994

1999

FOREWORD

BY SIR ALEX FERGUSON

ASSOCIATION FOOTBALL is the only game that can lay claim to being truly global. It is played in virtually every nation around the world and I'm convinced that in each and every one of those countries you will find supporters of Manchester United.

Wherever I have travelled in my years as manager of the club I have been staggered by strength of devotion shown by the fans for a sporting organisation which in some cases is thousands of miles from their own shores. It speaks volumes for the club's magical appeal, which has always been strong but has increased hugely since Matt Busby took charge at the close of the Second World War.

Present day Manchester United is amongst the most popular, successful and biggest clubs in football, but it hasn't always been in such a strong position.

The club was founded in 1878, as Newton Heath, in the humble surroundings of the railway yards of north Manchester and for many years struggled in the face of poor funding, shortage of support and less than ideal facilities. In fact, it was financial problems that brought about the name change in 1902, to the title – Manchester United – which is now known all around the world.

The club's fortunes changed in the years that followed with the League championship being won twice before the outbreak of the First World War brought serious competitive football to a halt. The FA Cup also found its way to Manchester during that time, but they were to be the only honours of note for a considerable time.

The years between the two wars brought severe austerity to Old Trafford and not one single major trophy was collected during that period. The club again faced financial strife in the early thirties, but it wasn't long before football was again interrupted when in 1939 the world was once again plunged into war.

There was a new wave of optimism following the end of the Second World War and nowhere more than at Old Trafford. Matt Busby had been installed as manager and, the rest as they say is history.

Manchester United became synonymous with attractive, attacking football and as a result the club's fame spread around the world. The transformation was incredible and in no time the club was winning trophies once again.

Matt Busby's huge contribution to the re-birth of United and his efforts in turning the club into a world famous sporting giant is well documented in the pages of this illustrated history. As indeed are all the other remarkable chapters that combine to make the Manchester United story so fascinating.

I have been privileged to play my part of that ever-changing story; a period of my life that I wouldn't have missed for anything.

Manchester United is now without doubt one of the biggest names in world football and through the pages of this book the long and, sometimes, distressing road it has taken to reach its now lofty status in the game can be charted.

It's one of football's greatest odysseys.

Alex. Ferguson

INTRODUCTION

FROM HUMBLE BEGINNINGS beside an English railway, through tragic scenes on a German runway, to an unprecedented triumph in a Spanish city … the basic thread of the Manchester United story is well-known throughout football.

Yet one sentence such as that cannot begin to do justice to the reserves of emotion, talent and dedication that have been drawn upon during the development of the club. Only in one book such as this can the stature and significance of United truly be reflected on and admired.

The point is there are many great players, managers, matches and moments to remember, and many shorter stories to be told to make up the whole. Only then can the reader appreciate what it has taken for the club to rise out of the railway yard at Newton Heath to the Nou Camp in Barcelona and beyond.

It is the beyond that challenges the publisher and prevents him from presenting "The Complete History of Manchester United" to the world. The story continues, and there is no convenient end (the night in Barcelona would have been perfect, had this been a screenplay for Hollywood).

The best we can do is to tell the story so far, and it's quite an epic, produced on this occasion by six different writers. In most cases, the authors were asked to write about periods in United's history they could vividly remember, but this could not be said for Mark Wylie and Cliff Butler!

Fortunately, as the club's current and former curators, Mark and Cliff were able to use their finely tuned research skills to write authoritatively about events that occurred more than fifty years ago.

Mark begins the book with his opening chapter about Newton Heath, the original team formed beside the Lancashire and Yorkshire railway in 1878.

In Chapter Two, he reflects on how the club won its first League Championship and FA Cup under the name of Manchester United, and recalls its relocation in 1910 to Old Trafford.

In Chapter Three, Cliff Butler reminds the reader that United have not always been successful. But after the threat of extinction in Chapter One, we should be grateful for small mercies!

In Chapter Four, Cliff introduces the reader to Matt Busby for the first time, before passing the baton to co-authors Justyn Barnes and Aubrey Ganguly. Again belying their ages, the pair take us back to the Fifties when Manchester United would have surely dominated like they did in the Nineties, had it not been for the cruel intervention of tragedy in 1958.

Graham McColl then writes about the aftermath of the Munich crash in Chapter Six, and the European Cup-winning side in Seven, which features the so-called holy trinity of Sixties legends – George Best, Denis Law and Bobby Charlton.

McColl continues into the Seventies to record United's struggle to emulate Busby's achievements, under managers such as Tommy Docherty and Dave Sexton. Trips to Wembley were quite commonplace, but success in the League proved elusive.

It was much the same story in the Eighties – a decade described by Adam Bostock in his two chapters on Ron Atkinson and then Alex Ferguson's early years. The team may not have won titles at that time, but it boasted some great players, and Adam had the pleasure of speaking to three in the process of writing this book – Arthur Albiston, Lee Martin and Brian McClair.

The Nineties, of course, saw a plethora of League Championships and other prizes grace the Old Trafford trophy room. It was the happy task of Justyn Barnes and Aubrey Ganguly to recall this recent period when most things seemed to go United's way, give or take the occasional altercation with an abusive supporter and the sporadic rise of Blackburn and Arsenal.

Arsenal's challenge becomes more than sporadic in Chapter Fifteen. Adam Bostock writes about a period in which the Londoners made life difficult for United on the pitch, while, off the pitch, speculation about the manager, certain players and the power-brokers reached new levels of intensity. Thankfully, it ends on a high note with victory in the 2004 FA Cup Final.

The search for Sir Alex Ferguson's successor will no doubt be detailed in a future edition of *The Official Illustrated History*. Whomever he is, he would be advised to read our book, in preparation for the biggest job of his life. The rest of us, however, can forget the homework and just enjoy reading the saga of a remarkable football club named Manchester United.

Opposite: Kings of Europe again, Manchester United players celebrate after their victory over Bayern Munich in Barcelona.

Overleaf: Paul Scholes sends a header towards goal in the UEFA Champions League game against Bayer Leverkusen, November 2002.

CHAPTER ONE

NEWTON HEATH

MANCHESTER UNITED IS ONE OF THE MOST FAMOUS FOOTBALL CLUBS IN THE WORLD, BUT IT WAS NOT ALWAYS SO. THE STORY OF MANCHESTER UNITED BEGINS ON THE OTHER SIDE OF THE CITY ALONG THE RAILWAY LINES OF THE LANCASHIRE AND YORKSHIRE RAILWAY AT NEWTON HEATH.

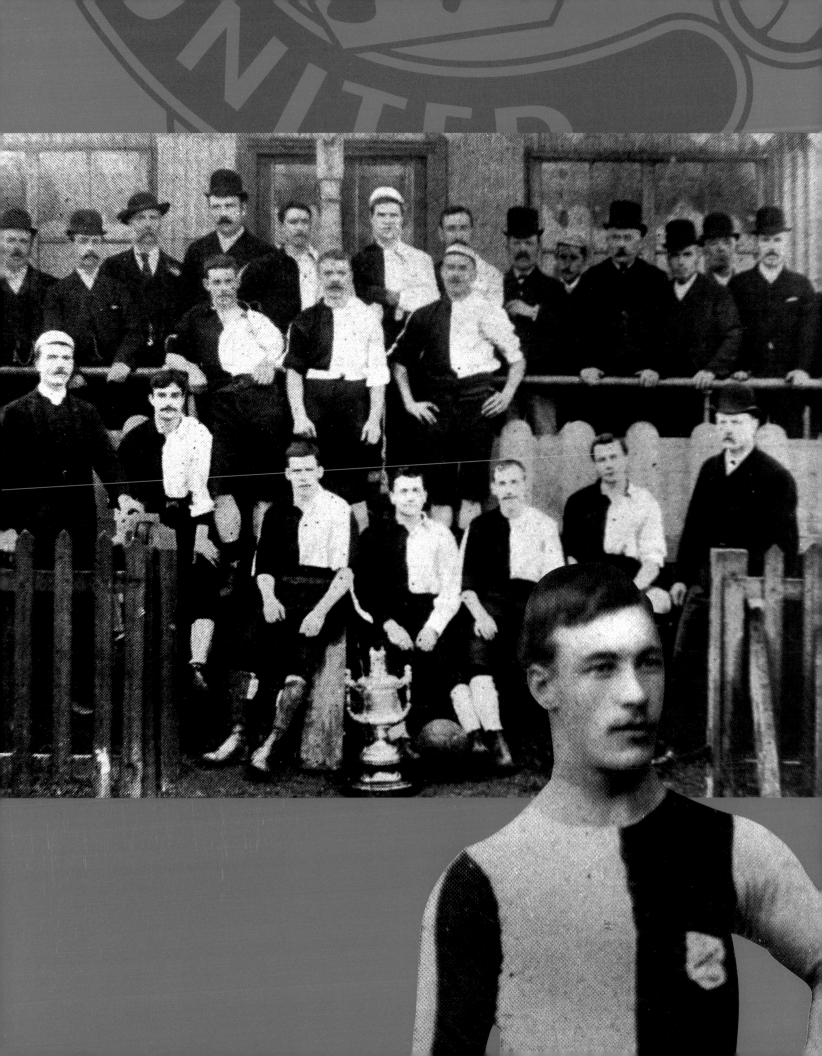

14

I n the second half of the nineteenth century, Manchester was thriving, full of mills, factories and workshops and home to over 400,000 people – a city rapidly expanding and cementing its place as the cotton cloth capital of the world. Even in 1835, a French visitor described it thus:

> The footsteps of a busy crowd, the crunching wheels of machinery, the shriek of steam from boilers, the regular beat of the looms, the heavy rumble of carts, these are the noises from which you can never escape in the sombre half-light of these streets.
>
> From *Journeys to England and Ireland* by A. de Tocqueville.

By the 1870s, there was very little heath left in Newton Heath, an area that had been mainly countryside only 20 years before. The Lancashire and Yorkshire Railway Company had chosen Newton Heath for one of its depots and for a carriage and wagon works. It was at this carriage and wagon works that the team that would become Manchester United was formed.

In common with many other large Victorian employers, the Lancashire and Yorkshire Railway took an interest in the social lives of its employees, probably in an attempt to steer them away from the temptations of alcohol. To this end, the company had organized "classes of improvement". The Dining Room Committee at the works was responsible for these, and swiftly took over the supervision of a proposed cricket and football club, one of a number of sports clubs that were set up by the workmen. The new club, founded in 1878, was called Newton Heath (Lancashire and Yorkshire Railway) Cricket & Football Club.

Cricket and rugby were generally the preferred sports around Manchester, but football was slowly gaining a toehold in the city. A patch of land was found adjacent to the works on North Road and cricketers and footballers shared this ground throughout the year. Never the best of pitches, it was dogged by drainage problems in the winter and the ground became renowned as a mud bath. As the Newton Heath bazaar programme noted in 1901:

> The ground was little better than a clay pit, its surroundings a quagmire. After you had entered the bottom gate, it was quite a work of art to steer clear of pools of water, but when once you got there you were all right, if it didn't rain; if it did rain, you just – well, if you've never experienced it you cannot possibly be enlightened.

Despite the quality of the pitch, which must have caused at least as

many problems for the cricketers if not more, this was to be the home of Newton Heath (L & Y R) Cricket & Football Club into the 1890s. There were no changing facilities whatsoever in those early years, the players having to resort to using a public house on Oldham Road. This pub, The Three Crowns, was over half a mile from the ground, a distance that must have seemed at least twice as far after a bruising match on the terrible pitch. Later the Shears Hotel, also on Oldham Road, served as changing rooms and unofficial club headquarters before an office was rented at 33 Oldham Road.

Information on these early days of football in Manchester is sparse. Football was seldom reported on, even in the many local newspapers. It is likely that the men from Newton Heath played matches against fellow workers at the depot, for instance the engine drivers who went on to form a team of their own, Newton Heath Loco(motive). As a company-approved activity, matches between departments and against other depots would have been the most likely fixtures. Green and gold, the colours of the Lancashire and Yorkshire Railway, were chosen as the club colours and soon these green and gold halved shirts became well known around the Manchester area.

The President of the club was Mr F. Attock, the superintendent of the carriage and wagon works. Around him he gathered some of the most notable men of the day as vice-presidents. These included three local MPs – A.J. Balfour (who went on to become Prime Minister in the 1890s), C.E. Schwann and Sir James Ferguson – and C.P. Scott, the editor of the *Manchester Guardian*.

By the early 1880s, Newton Heath were not only challenging other teams from both their own and other railway company's depots, but also venturing further afield. Teams such as Manchester Arcadians, Hurst and West Gorton became familiar opponents in the multitude of friendly matches arranged throughout the season. Games against the longer established teams of Lancashire were, if truth were told, an aspiration. Newton Heath were one of the best teams in Manchester, but they were no match for even the reserve sides of clubs such as Bolton Wanderers. Two 0–6 defeats against the Trotters reserves confirmed the Heathens place in the game. But visits to places as far away as St Helens, Southport and Crewe became a reality as the club looked further than its local patch.

Tempted away from a continual round of friendly matches, Newton Heath entered the Lancashire Cup in the 1883–84 season, but crashed out 2–7 in the first round to the FA Cup holders, Blackburn Olympic. The club evidently still had a fair amount of progress to make before it could reasonably tackle the Lancashire clubs. However, impressed by the performance of Newton Heath's captain, Sam Black, Blackburn Olympic tried to entice him over to

Newton Heath's fixture list in 1882–83 included Bolton Wanderers and Crewe Alexandra as well as Blackburn Olympic, who would go on to win the FA Cup in 1883.

Blackburn. But Black was determined to remain a Heathen, which he did until he eventually returned to his hometown and joined Burton Wanderers.

The foundation of the Manchester Cup for 1884–85 gave Newton Heath a local challenge and the opportunity to win a trophy. They stormed through to the final where, before a crowd of 4,000 spectators, they met old rivals Hurst from nearby Ashton-under-Lyne. Despite losing just one match throughout the season, a 0–3 defeat left the Heathens licking their wounds, but it was the start of a purple patch for the club in the Manchester Cup. In its first nine seasons, Newton Heath were finalists on no less than eight occasions, going on to win it in 1886, 1888, 1889, 1890 and 1893. The 1886 success brought Newton Heath their first-ever trophy, although the controversial 2–1 victory over Manchester FC on 3 April provoked many arguments in the bars of East Manchester. The Heathens' winning goal was claimed by Manchester to be both offside and a handball.

The Heathens' success did not go unnoticed. Four players won caps as representatives of Manchester District in March 1884. The majority of the players still worked at the wagon works and most lived close by. However, all was not as it seemed. The possibility of gaining a job working on the railway became a major incentive for players from further afield. Professionalism was still illegal, but many of the prominent Lancashire clubs were finding success by adding some talented Scottish players to their ranks. These players were primarily in Lancashire for the football, but were found jobs to keep up the pretence of amateurism. Newton Heath employed similar tactics and in the mid-1880s an influx of Welshmen arrived,

with jobs being found for them at the works. Newton Heath were not a wealthy club, despite having the backing of the Lancashire and Yorkshire Railway Company. It was essentially still a works team, far removed from the semi-professional elite of Lancashire with their wealthy backers. However, the Welsh influx brought some established international players – Jack Powell, from Bolton Wanderers, Joe Davies, Tom Burke, Jack Owens and brothers Jack and Roger Doughty.

Again reaching the final of the Manchester Cup in 1886–87, Newton Heath lost out to West Manchester 1–2. This surprising defeat came after a phenomenal 11–1 annihilation of Gorton in round two, the club that would become known as Manchester City. The same season saw Newton Heath enter the FA Cup for the first time, one of the few clubs from the Manchester area to do so. They drew Fleetwood Rangers in the first round. Two Jack Doughty goals earned a 2–2 draw but, asked to play extra-time, Newton Heath refused and the referee awarded victory to Fleetwood Rangers. It was a sorry end to the Heathens' first attempt to win the FA Cup.

It was in August 1887 that Pat O'Donnell famously walked from Glasgow to Newton Heath in search of a job. He won both a job at the carriage works and, soon after, a place in the team. The *Manchester Evening News* noted the composition of the Newton Heath team on 1 October 1887:

> …Burke, Davies, Powell, Owen and Doughty are all Welshmen, while Tait is a Scotchman and O'Donnell, Irish; in fact with the exception of Wright, we do not recognize a local man in the team.

So many Welshmen were playing for the club that on 10 March 1888, a substantial contingent of five Newton Heath players – J. Powell, T. Burke, Joe Davies and the Doughty brothers – appeared for their country against Scotland in Edinburgh. The Scots were easy 5–1 winners.

Professionalism was making an impact, but in the 1887–88 season, Newton Heath were known to have just two professional players, goalkeeper Tom Hay and full-back Jack Powell. This was far fewer than the Lancashire elite, who were pressing for the formation of a league system. Newton Heath were still the most successful club in the Manchester area and hoped for an invitation to join the elite. However, they were rejected by the Football League. They responded by joining other similarly rejected clubs in setting up their own competition – the Football Combination. Unfortunately, this competition was not as well thought through as the Football League and lasted just one season. The member clubs continued to play round after round of friendly matches. Newton Heath found themselves playing as many friendlies as before, even if one was against international opposition – they lost 0–2 to a Canadian XI.

The problems of the Football Combination were quickly realized and acted upon. For the following season, a new competition emerged, the Football Alliance. Newton Heath struggled to find any consistency, finishing in the bottom half of the table. They entered the FA Cup but again lasted a solitary round. Up against the holders and league champions, the Invincibles of Preston North End, Newton Heath crashed out 1–6. Friendlies were still a major part of Newton Heath's season despite their Football Alliance fixtures. Harsh economic reality made it a necessity despite the obvious effects that too many matches had on the stamina of their players over the season. Friendlies against local opposition often attracted far higher crowds than the Alliance fixtures at a time when Newton Heath's finances were under considerable strain. The costs of professionalism, increased travel costs for Football Alliance matches and the lease of their home ground at North Road all mounted up. Newton Heath had never been a rich club and without a major wealthy financial backer these extra costs forced them to walk a financial tightrope each season.

J. Powell
One of a number of Welshmen playing for Newton Heath in the 1880s.

Desperate to gain entry to the Football League, Newton Heath made an annual application for membership, but season after season they were rejected. Eager to show the Football League their status as the best club in Manchester, in 1891 the committee members went ahead with the construction of two new stands at North Road, able to hold over 2,000 supporters. This followed on from previous construction work in 1887, when the stands at North Road were extended.

A concerted effort was made to win the Alliance as the club's committee members belatedly woke up to the thought that only success would gain the club access to the Football League. For once things ran relatively smoothly and Newton Heath finished runners-up in the Football Alliance. At the same time, the Football League announced its expansion to include a bigger First Division and a new Second Division. For Newton Heath and their fans, this was a dream come true – league football, in fact First Division football.

The promise of league football drastically altered the club. All connections with the railway company were finally severed and, in 1892, a new limited company, Newton Heath FC, was formed. Newton Heath's expenses took a sharp rise and a club secretary was employed for the first time – Alf Albut, signed from Aston Villa. The railway company responded to the formation of the new company by raising the rent of the North Road ground. Furthermore, the bonus of concessionary railway travel vanished. The share floatation was a great disappointment. Share capital in the form of 2,000 £1 shares was promised but not realized.

Centre-forward Bob Donaldson kicked off in the club's first league match, a baptism of fire against Blackburn Rovers at Ewood Park. Rovers quickly went on the attack, rushing into a 3–0 lead. The position looked desperate for the newcomers, but Donaldson scored Newton Heath's first-ever league goal and Coupar added a second to make the half-time score 3–2 to the Rovers. Both teams added a goal in the second half and Newton Heath were far from disgraced against one of the most famous clubs in the country.

All eyes now turned to North Road for the biggest match to have been held in Manchester. Over 10,000 spectators crowded into North Road to see Newton Heath take on Burnley. An exciting match ended in a 1–1 draw with Donaldson scoring another goal to give the Heathens their first league point.

However, league football was of too high a standard for Newton Heath, and despite a small number of fine victories and Bob Donaldson's 16 goals, the team ended the season at the bottom of the table. Strangely enough, Newton Heath's first-ever league victory was against Wolverhampton Wanderers, who in their FA Cup-winning season went down to a 10–1 defeat. This is still a record league victory for Manchester United. The Heathens had a chance to save their First Division status. At the end of the season, Test matches were played, precursors of the present-day play-offs. The top teams in the Second Division took on the bottom teams in the First and Newton Heath were too strong for the Second Division champions, Small Heath – a 1–1 draw and a 5–2 victory meant that the club stayed up.

In the close season there was further trauma at the club. An eviction notice was served on their North Road ground. There were several possible reasons – complaints from the cricketers, who still played at the ground in the summer, and Newton Heath's practice of charging spectators for admission. By charging for admission, Newton Heath hoped to cover their greatly increased costs, but this, it was alleged, broke the terms of their lease on the ground. Rented from Manchester cathedral by the railway company for the use of all their employees, the fact that the footballers had exclusive use of the ground in the winter gave the railway company an excuse for eviction. Newton Heath were ordered to quit before the start of the next football season, despite the railway company gaining "… a very handsome rent from the Newton Heath Club, they, in turn, paying a nominal rent to the Dean and Canons", according to the Newton Heath bazaar programme in 1901.

The severing of links with the railway company probably just hastened the club's move to a new ground. Ordered to leave North Road as they had found it or leave behind their expensive and relatively new stands, the club directors had little option but to leave the stands. Receiving under £100 for them, Newton Heath FC immediately found itself out of pocket.

A new ground had to be found, and quickly. For the club secretary and directors, the summer of 1893 was occupied by the search. The ground had to be ready to receive Burnley in the first home league match of the season. Initial enquiries to the cathedral authorities proved fruitless, but after a thorough search, a new ground was finally found towards the end of June. It was in Bank Street, Clayton, three miles from Newton Heath and their supporters. A rental agreement was quickly drawn up with the Bradford and Clayton Athletic Company.

With stands &c, the ground ought to be a commodious one, and no doubt when the first of September comes it will be fully equipped. The only doubt that remains is as to whether the ground will be convenient from a Newton point of view… Mr Albut, the secretary, and the directors are to be congratulated in having secured the ground. *Manchester Evening News* 24 June 1893.

Bradford and Clayton Athletic Company and their new tenants worked hard throughout the summer to get the ground ready for the football crowds. There was already a stand along one side of the pitch and another behind one of the goals. To increase capacity, a new cinder terrace was built behind the other goal.

Some 7,000 spectators saw Burnley kick off in the first league match at the ground. Newton Heath were soon behind and, with the wind behind them, Burnley added a second. The Heathens kept pressurizing and by half-time, goals from Donaldson and Farman had brought the scores level. A late penalty from Farman gave Newton Heath the lead and a winning start at Bank Street.

The location of Newton Heath's new ground, close to a number of chemical works, gave some visiting fans the excuse that the Heathens players must be used to the foul and toxic smells and therefore gained an extra advantage. It was even alleged that the chimneys belched forth more fumes when Newton Heath were losing in an attempt to put off the opposition!

Despite their winning start to the 1893–94 campaign, Newton Heath were soon in difficulties. The club's directors took exception to an article that was published in the *Birmingham Daily Gazette* on 14 October 1893 after a 4–1 victory over West Bromwich Albion:

It wasn't football, it was simple brutality and if these are the tactics Newton Heath are compelled to adopt to win their matches, the sooner the Football Association deal severely with them the better it will be for the game generally.

The directors sued the newspaper for libel, enlisting the help of the match referee to fight this attack on both their tactics and style of play. With his help the case was won, but feelings of victory were short-lived as the judge delivered his verdict on damages. Each side was instructed to pay their own legal costs and Newton Heath were awarded damages of a solitary farthing. Perhaps the directors had thought this libel case was a way to pay off some of the club debts. Ultimately, it ended up costing money they could ill afford to misspend.

Stories about the financial problems of Newton Heath are plentiful and it is difficult now to separate fact from fiction or even fact from exaggeration. One perhaps mythical story relates how the directors of the club had to meet in a room lit by candles fixed in ginger beer bottles as the Manchester Corporation had cut off the gas supply. A summons was served on the club for the non-payment of their gas bill after Alf Albut had allegedly used the money for the bill to acquire an unsettled player from another club. Short of his wages, the player threatened his club that unless he was allowed to move to Newton Heath he would serve a summons on them to get his wages. Unfortunately, there is no record of which player was acquired in this curious manner. It has also been alleged that another unnamed player was to be paid with a percentage of the gate receipts. On discovering that there was a lower crowd than usual, he announced that he felt a twinge from an injury and changed back into his everyday clothes. A third story tells how one of the Heathens' players, on being given his wages, found that he was unable to redeem his best suit from the local pawnbrokers. His team-mates organized a collection to avoid this embarrassing situation.

For Newton Heath the victory in the court case in 1893–94 was one of the few they achieved that season and they again finished bottom of the First Division. Another end-of-season Test match was their dubious reward. Against a confident Liverpool side that had won the Second Division title by eight clear points, Newton Heath went down to a 0–2 defeat. They never played in the top division again. They made an enthusiastic attempt to win promotion, in their new colours of green shirts with gold trim, during their first season in the Second Division. That same season, Newton Heath's long-suffering fans acclaimed what they thought was a new club scoring record when Walsall Town Swifts were sent back to the Midlands after a 14–0 drubbing. They also hailed new signing Joe Cassidy who, on his league debut, scored four goals on what the newspapers described as a "fearfully heavy" pitch. After the Swifts appealed to the Football League over the state of the Bank Street pitch, a replay was ordered. They needn't have bothered because Newton Heath again ran out convincing winners. This time it was 9–0 with Cassidy scoring two.

Newton Heath 1895–96 Wearing their green shirts with gold trim and with shinguards outside their socks, Newton Heath line up at Bank Street. Back row from left to right: A.H. Albut (secretary), F. Paley (trainer), J.M. Dow, W. Douglas, F.W. Palmer (director), F. Frentz, W.R. Davidson, G. Faulkner (director). Middle row: W. Crompton (director), G. Perrins, J.M. McNaught, W. Stewart, H. Jones (vice president). Front row: J. Clarkin, R. Donaldson, J. Cassidy, R. Smith, J. Peters.

Players came and went throughout the 1890s as Newton Heath continued to strive for that elusive promotion. Walter Cartwright, Harry Stafford, Fred Erentz and the redoubtable Welsh international, Caesar Augustus Llewelyn Jenkyns, all became local heroes for the Bank Street faithful, but the club remained a Second Division team. Second place was achieved in 1896–97 in the new colours of white shirts and blue shorts – or knickers, as they were known at the time. Again the Test matches proved to be Newton Heath's undoing.

A first victory in the Lancashire Cup with a 2–1 win over Blackburn Rovers was almost the only cheerful event at the cash-strapped club as the end of the century drew nearer. The sale of key players to local rivals and rich Southern League clubs was a symptom of their financial problems. Any profits from a consistent promotion challenge or a good Cup run merely served to reduce the existing debt problems. The opening of a social centre in a disused schoolroom in the Institute at Miles Platting was an interesting attempt to provide facilities for supporters on non-match days and some income for the club. Despite the attraction of a billiards table, it ran at a loss. Inevitably, the centre closed, hastened by the loss, or theft, of all the billiard cues and a bailiff's raid in an attempt to settle some of the outstanding debts.

The eagerness of local newspapers to report on Newton Heath's exploits in the Football League did pay dividends. Keen to be the first newspaper to publish the Newton Heath match reports, the *Manchester Evening News* asked if they could erect a wooden hut and install a telephone at the ground. Ever an opportunist, secretary Alf Albut agreed, on condition that he could also use it for club business. So the club's registered office moved to the Bank Street ground when the Institute closed.

At the turn of the century, Newton Heath were even deeper in financial trouble. Alf Albut had resigned as secretary, his place being taken by James West who joined from Lincoln. In February 1901, a fund-raising bazaar was held in the St James's Hall in the city centre. The intention was to raise over £1,000 to secure the club's finances and boost it back to the First Division. Good publicity and support was forthcoming from local rivals Manchester City, but the bazaar was not a financial success, and barely covered its costs.

By February 1902, Newton Heath were £2,670 in debt and in danger of following Accrington, Bootle and Darwen out of the league. One of the club's former directors, building contractor William Healey, had taken the club to court for over £240 he was owed in loans and unpaid bills. He was granted a winding up order, and the future looked bleak.

A meeting of shareholders at New Islington Hall on the 18 March 1902 was crucial to the club's future. Newton Heath needed

Newton Heath 1901–02 Despite the poor quality of this photograph, club captain Harry Stafford can be seen in the back row, second from the left.

financial backing. When team captain Harry Stafford stood up to reveal that this was now available, the audience were astonished. Stafford and four businessmen would each invest £200 in the club to help pay off the debts. But how had he found these benefactors in the club's hour of need?

For the answer we have to go back to the bazaar held at the St James's Hall in 1901. While the event had not been a financial success, it did have one great result. Harry Stafford had brought along his St Bernard dog, Major. Complete with a collection box, the dog roamed around the stalls gathering donations for the club, but it went missing. A search proved fruitless; there was no sign of the animal or the collection box. Both were eventually found by John Henry Davies, a wealthy brewer. Wanting the dog for his young daughter, Davies set about finding out who owned the stray animal. He eventually met Harry Stafford, and was made aware of the plight of Newton Heath. In return for support for the club from the wealthy brewer and a few of his business colleagues, Stafford allowed Davies to keep the St Bernard for his daughter.

Harry Stafford and the four businessmen – Mr Jones, James Bown, James Taylor and John Henry Davies – took control of Newton Heath Football Club as a condition of investing in the company and the previous board all resigned. Now came the thought that a new name would be an appropriate gesture, especially since it had been eight years since the club had been based in the Newton Heath area. Various suggestions were made until on 28 April 1902, with the blessing of the Football Association, Newton Heath FC became Manchester United FC. A glorious new chapter in the history of the club was about to unfold.

CHAPTER TWO

THE MEREDITH YEARS

MANCHESTER UNITED BECAME ONE OF THE POWERHOUSES OF EDWARDIAN FOOTBALL AND PROFITED FROM MANCHESTER CITY'S FALL FROM GRACE BY SIGNING ONE OF THE LEGENDARY FIGURES IN BRITISH FOOTBALL – BILLY MEREDITH.

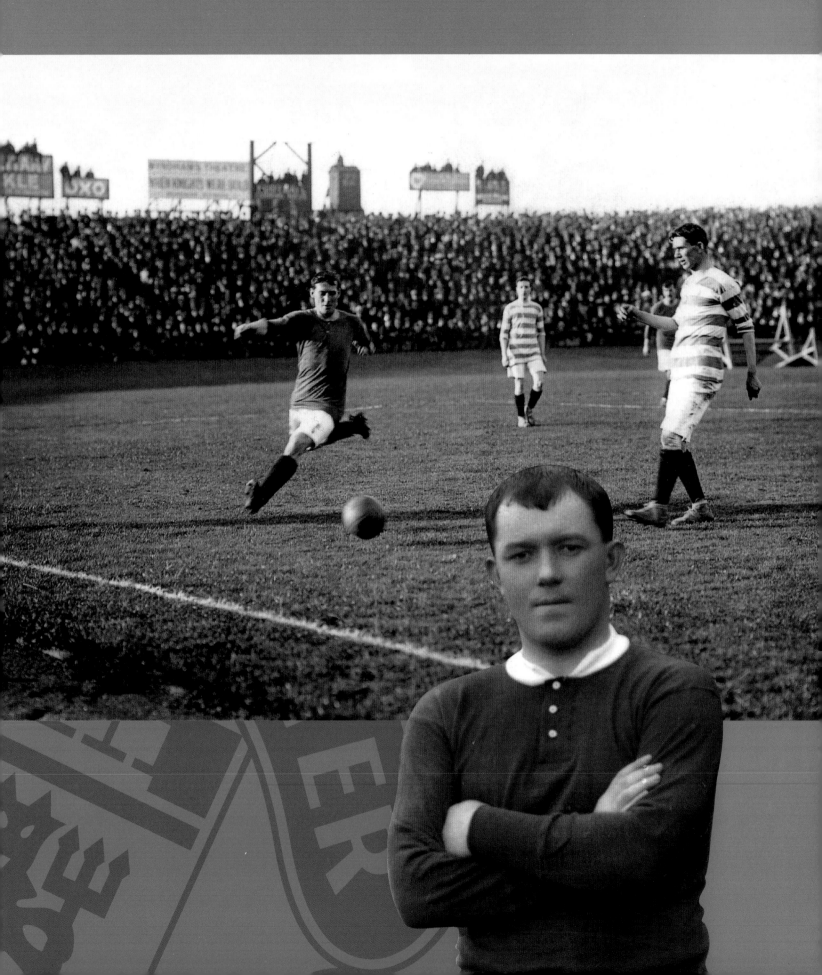

Newton Heath officially became Manchester United on 28 April 1902, less than a week after they had played their final match of the season, a 2–0 win against Chesterfield. The new era brought a change of strip to red shirts and white shorts, and these have remained Manchester United's colours to the present day.

The immense wealth of John Henry Davies soon singled him out as the major benefactor of the club. Davies was a self-made man who had worked as estate agent, innkeeper and brewer. A director and later chairman of both Walker & Homfrays Brewery and the Manchester Brewery Company, he built both these companies into great successes. Davies cared little for football until his meeting with Harry Stafford back in 1901. Before then, he had been known for his support of other sports in the Manchester locality such as bowls and cycling, and for his many gifts to charity. Already wealthy, Davies had married into money. His wife Amy was the daughter of Henry Tate, co-founder of the Tate & Lyle sugar-refining empire. Their combined wealth meant that they could buy almost anything they wanted.

Davies could see there was potential for two large clubs in the Manchester area and, as president of United, set about reorganizing the administration and finances of the club. He recognized that Newton Heath's financial problems dated back to 1893 and their eviction from North Road. Since then the club had been without a major benefactor and an injection of hard cash would work wonders, quickly clearing their long-standing debts. Secretary James West had made considerable inroads into the problem of debt, but there was still much to be done. Davies also realized that success on the pitch would draw large crowds to the Bank Street ground,

providing much-needed gate money to keep the club afloat.

Team affairs became the responsibility of James West and Harry Stafford who together set about improving on Newton Heath's pitiful 15th place in the Second Division at the end of 1901–02. Under their stewardship, Manchester United played their first Football League match on 6 September 1902, at Gainsborough Trinity's Northolme ground. United returned jubilantly to Bank Street, Clayton with both points. Charles Richards's goal secured a 1–0 victory. A week later a crowd of over 20,000 packed into Bank Street to see Manchester United's first home league match, a 1–0 victory over Burton United.

Attendances at Bank Street began to rise, averaging 10,823 in 1902–03 compared with a dismal 4,411 in the final season as Newton Heath. Rising attendances were matched by greater success on the pitch. After finishing two places from bottom in 1901–02, United stormed up to fifth place, but they were still well off the pace, 13 points from promotion.

With this dramatic improvement in the club's fortunes, the fans' level of expectation also increased. From some quarters there was criticism of James West and his abilities, and loud criticism of some of the players he had bought. Davies had given United £3,000 to strengthen the team and some fans expected that this would lead to an immediate return to the First Division.

West and Stafford had used the money to purchase, among others, Tommy Arkesden from Burton United for £150, James Peddie from Newcastle United, Alec Bell from Ayr Parkhouse, Alec Downie from Swindon Town and Tommy Morrison from Burnley. Unfortunately for West and Stafford, an horrendous injury list forced the signing of 22 players during the season,

John Henry Davies, a wealthy brewer, took over Newton Heath and made Manchester United one of England's top teams.

Billy Meredith (right) poses with some of his medals and caps, and some of the trophies won during his long and illustrious career.

yours truly March 20 1911

Billy Meredith

24

and an immediate return to the top division was not forthcoming. Fortunately, United were now on a firm financial and administrative footing and were able to cope with this setback.

For James West, the pressure for success became unbearable and on 28 September 1903, he resigned as secretary of Manchester United. He cited the poor performances of some of the players whom he had been instrumental in signing for the club as the reason for his sudden departure just three weeks into the season. Speculation was rife. Had West jumped or had he been pushed? There is no conclusive answer, but in October 1904 West and Harry Stafford were involved in an FA inquiry into financial irregularities at a number of clubs, including both of those in Manchester. Stafford proclaimed his innocence and declared that everything he had done was purely for the benefit of the club during what had been a very dark hour. Both Stafford and West were found guilty of misconduct and banned from the game until May 1907. In his resignation statement, West declared that he was resigning to avoid embarrassing the board of directors. He may have suspected that the Football Association was beginning to question his activities and resigned before they caught up with him.

Whatever the reason for James West's departure, there was a silver lining to that particular cloud. On 30 September 1903, Manchester United announced that they had appointed the Burnley secretary James Ernest Mangnall as the new secretary of Manchester United. Joining United on the recommendation of J.J. Bentley, president of the Football League and a Manchester United director, Mangnall became the first Manchester United secretary to wield managerial powers.

Mangnall took over total responsibility for team affairs, including scouting, signing and training the players. His aim was

Dick Duckworth, signed from Newton Heath Athletic, gave Manchester United over ten years of service at half-back.

to make United a powerful member of the top division and he used Davies's wealth to that end. He scoured the country, signing, among others, goalkeeper Harry Moger from Southern League Southampton and Charlie Roberts from Grimsby Town, but he discovered Dick Duckworth on his doorstep, playing for Newton Heath Athletic. Despite all this activity, Mangnall found promotion just as difficult as his predecessor had done. In his first season, United were challenging for the runners-up spot until the spring. They eventually finished in third place, a solitary point behind Woolwich Arsenal, the runners-up to champions Preston North End.

At the end of the season, Bank Street hosted an international match for the first time. On 4 April 1904, a Football League XI defeated the Scottish League 2–1, attracting some 40,000 spectators to the rain-soaked ground. However, the use of Bank Street for such matches was a sideshow to the main event – the attempt to gain promotion.

Confidence was high during the 1904 close season. The signing of Charlie Roberts from Grimsby on 22 April for a fee of £600 had strengthened United's defence and a strong challenge for promotion was expected. Roberts slotted into a half-back line that would soon be famous across the country. Dick Duckworth, Charlie Roberts and Alec Bell formed one of the most secure defensive lines in the Football League, ably supported by their full-backs Robert Bonthron and Vince Hayes. United began to gain a reputation for solid defending and for being difficult to beat.

In fact, they remained unbeaten from 24 September 1904 until 21 January 1905. Despite this, they still failed in their bid to return to the First Division. A second consecutive third place was their prize at the end of season. They finished three points behind runners-up

Bolton Wanderers, having won five more points than they had the previous season.

Pressure was beginning to mount on Ernest Mangnall. He had spent considerable sums of Davies's money yet the club was still stuck in the Second Division. It seemed as though it would be third time lucky at the start of the 1905–06 season. Bristol City was an early visitor to Bank Street and some 15,000 spectators saw United demolish the West Country side 5–1. This was Charlie Roberts's first league match as captain of the team, a position he held until 1913.

United had a fantastic season and, ironically, only the outstanding play of Bristol City deprived them of the Second Division championship. A 1–1 draw with third-placed Chelsea before a 60,000 Easter crowd virtually assured United of second place, although it took a victory over Leeds City with three matches remaining to confirm their promotion. Bristol City and United were head and shoulders above the other teams in the division, United finishing a massive nine points ahead of Chelsea. A 6–0 home victory over a totally outclassed Burton United team finished off the season. There were, as the newspapers of the day described it, "remarkable scenes" at Clayton with fireworks and flowers before the match:

During the interval there was another battle of flowers, scores of buttonholes being thrown from the box of the president to the onlookers below. More fireworks were discharged, and a gang of whole-hearted supporters known as the "Rocca Brigade" caused much amusement with their coloured hats and umbrellas.

At the end of the match the ecstatic crowd invaded the pitch and carried each United player shoulder high from the ground.

Now the challenge was to make an impact in the top division. The omens looked good. In the 1906 FA Cup, United had reached the quarter-finals for the first time since 1897, defeating Staple Hill and Norwich City before an amazing 5–1 victory over the Cup holders, Aston Villa, in front of a crowd of 35,000 at Bank Street. According to one local newspaper article:

They smote the proud Cup holders hip and thigh, and made themselves – in one afternoon – the most famous team in England. Even their supporters, who knew very well that in spite of artificial league classification, United were the equals of any side – were surprised by the greatness they showed. They outplayed the crack Birmingham men in all the art and subtlety of attack as well as in dash and endurance.

A 2–3 home defeat by Woolwich Arsenal ended United's best Cup run yet.

Across at Hyde Road, Manchester City was a club in turmoil. Still under investigation by the Football Association over illegal payments to players (at a time of restricted wages) and further player transfer irregularities, in August 1905 their star player, Billy Meredith, was suspended for alleged match-fixing. He was transfer-listed in May 1906. Soon afterwards, the FA imposed bans on the directors and the club secretary, while many of the first team were suspended from playing until 1 January 1907. Clubs from all over the country were delighted and were soon eyeing up the City players as potential recruits to their sides once their suspensions had lapsed. The club organized an auction at the Queen's Hotel and the secretaries of other Football League and Southern League clubs arrived to bid for the City stars – players who only two years before had won the FA Cup.

They were too late. Ernest Mangnall had got there first, quickly negotiating a free transfer for Billy Meredith and soon after that acquiring Sandy Turnbull, Herbert Burgess and Jimmy Bannister. The other clubs were furious that Mangnall had arranged this without their knowledge.

United brought all their new players into action the moment their suspensions expired. On New Year's Day 1907, all four of the former City stars made their debuts in a 1–0 victory over Aston Villa at Bank Street in front of 40,000 spectators. For Sandy Turnbull it was an especially good feeling to be playing again – it was his goal, from a Meredith cross, that won the match. United, renowned for a strong defence, now had a first-rate attacking line and they stormed up the table to finish in eighth place.

After one season in the top division, United were ready for a championship challenge. Three straight wins at the start of 1907–08 showed United's intent and, after a defeat against Middlesbrough, the United bandwagon rolled on with ten more consecutive wins and an impressive 37 goals.

The team was in irresistible championship-winning form, playing an attractive, controlled passing game. Occasional defeats were brushed aside as they dominated the league campaign. Winning 23 of their 38 league matches, United finished the season with 52 points, nine points ahead of runners-up Aston Villa. Sandy Turnbull had been in fantastic form, especially in the first half of the season. His 25 goals in 30 appearances were a club record, and was one that stood until Jack Rowley hit 26 goals in 1946–47. Manchester United were First Division champions just six years after the liquidation of Newton Heath; for John Davies, the taste of success must have been especially sweet.

To celebrate winning the championship, Davies invited the playing staff back to his home, Moseley Hall in Cheadle, for a celebratory dinner, but first United went to play in Europe. The tour was to the Austro-Hungarian empire and the team played matches in Prague, Vienna and Budapest. Generally welcomed, a match against the Budapest league leaders, Ferencvaros, showed the dark underside of touring abroad. United were unbeaten on tour and had sleepwalked through their games. It was soon noticeable that the Ferencvaros side were no match for United's strong defending and quick, agile forwards. A 7–0 victory, with even goalkeeper Harry Moger getting on the scoresheet, was overshadowed by crowd trouble. The players were attacked on leaving the field and later the rioters made further attacks as they left the ground in carriages. The *Manchester Evening News* correspondent reported: "Many arrests were made and the police were compelled to draw their swords." It was an unhappy end to what had generally been a successful tour. Mangnall said that United would never return to Budapest.

Before setting out on their tour, United had been invited to compete in the very first FA Charity Shield match. A 1–1 draw at Stamford Bridge with the champions of the Southern League, Queen's Park Rangers, forced the Football Association to organize a replay. It took place the following season and this time United ran out easy 4–0 victors to become the inaugural winners of the Shield.

In 1908–09, after a seven-match unbeaten start to the season, United's league form deserted them. Still just in contention for a championship challenge in January, they suddenly found it virtually impossible to win their league matches, either home or away. A 4–3 home victory over Notts County on New Year's Day was one of just three wins from then until the end of the season. They did manage to complete a league double over Manchester City, but this was scant consolation as the club plummeted down the table. A 13th-place finish was a huge disappointment, but they did find form in the FA Cup.

Narrow wins over Brighton and Everton were followed by a 6–1 demolition of Blackburn Rovers in the third round. The quarter-finals brought them up against Ernest Mangnall's old club, Burnley. In the middle of a dismal league run, United seemed to be heading out of the Cup as well. Burnley took the lead and held on as the weather conditions deteriorated. A snowstorm descended from the Pennines and, as the pitch became even more of a quagmire and as

Harry Moger endured an unhappy first season at Bank Street before becoming one of the most capable goalkeepers in the game.

Manchester United lines up for the camera at Bank Street at the start of the 1908–09 season with the previous season's haul of trophies. The Charity Shield and the League Championship trophy flank Billy Meredith, while the Manchester Cup is on the extreme right.

the markings became obliterated, the referee abandoned the match. Famously, he was so cold and exhausted he was unable to blow his whistle, passing it to Charlie Roberts to call an end to the proceedings. As the *Manchester Evening News* reported on 13 March:

…the referee was in such a state that prior to calling his linesmen together he found it impossible to hold his whistle.

There were only 18 minutes left on the clock and from then on, perhaps United's name was on the Cup. Replayed four days later, the team at last hit some form and left Turf Moor with both a 3–2 victory and a semi-final place. Then came the stiffest test yet – Newcastle United. While Manchester United's league form had been faltering, Newcastle appeared to be *en route* to becoming the first double-winning team of the twentieth century. Harold Halse spoiled their party by scoring the only goal of the game.

In the final, played at the Crystal Palace, Bristol City fell to a single goal, this time scored by Sandy Turnbull. United's return to

Manchester brought huge crowds on to the streets:

The London train hove into sight, and amid a scene of wild enthusiasm Mr Mangnall emerged carrying the Cup on high, followed by the players, their wives, and other people who had travelled from the Metropolis. The band struck up "See the Conquering Hero Comes" and there was a great scramble by the crowd, which had been permitted to enter the platform, to reach the players. Some were carried shoulder high, and ultimately were comfortably seated in the third waggonette. Sticks were waved and hats were thrown in the air and the enthusiasm was unbounded when Roberts, carrying the trophy, came into view.
Manchester Evening News, 27 April 1909

They lined the streets from Manchester Central station to the Town Hall, and afterwards outside the hotel near the Bank Street ground. A torchlight procession followed the players to their celebratory dinner at the Midland Hotel. With the FA Cup sitting in the Bank

Left Captains Roberts and Wedlock at the coin toss before the 1909 FA Cup final at the Crystal Palace. **Middle** Tense moments for the Bristol City defence as United put pressure on their goal. **Right** Another chance goes begging in front of the Bristol goal as Jimmy Turnbull slips.

Street trophy cabinet, John Davies' bankrolling of Ernest Mangnall's player purchases was vindicated, although the Football Association soon had something to say about the way the club was being run.

Although United was registered as a limited company, and had been since 1907, the FA condemned the club as a private monopoly of John Davies that seldom published accounts and was extravagantly managed. An investigation was organized, possibly in a fit of pique after they discovered that United had had a replica of the FA Cup made and presented it to Mr Davies. Reporting in 1910, the FA Committee recommended that United be "…properly constituted and managed in accordance with the requirements of the Football Association". They also recommended that United issue shares to the general public and make arrangements for much tighter accounting procedures.

During the 1909 close season, United's players become involved in the battle for players' rights. The Players' Union had been set up in 1898, but by 1908 it was a spent force. However, under the influence of Billy Meredith and Charlie Roberts, it found a new lease of life. This provoked a strong reaction from the Football League who, after the union affiliated itself to the Federation of Trades Unions, tried to destroy it. Players were ordered to resign from the union or be suspended by the FA, but United's players stood by the union. On 1 July they were suspended, which shocked the football world. The FA Cup-winning players were banned from Bank Street and forced to train at the Manchester Athletic Club ground in Fallowfield. It was here that the famous "Outcasts" photograph was taken, gaining the

players more publicity and support. It was a desperate time for them. Locked out of Bank Street, they were unable to claim their summer wages. Annoyed at their treatment, Sandy Turnbull and a few other players marched into the Bank Street ground and removed some items that were soon to be found on sale in a local pub. Charlie Roberts had them swiftly returned to the club.

Roberts was a prime target for the football authorities. By enticing his resignation from the union, the FA hoped that he would bring the other players with him. Roberts, however, was made of sterner stuff. He, and the other United players, could have resigned from the Players' Union in July and rejoined in September, once the football season had started. But for Roberts a principle was at stake and despite being due a substantial benefit that season, he and the rest of the players stood firm.

Roberts, the United captain, said they had no grievance with the club, but rather than give way the players were prepared to suffer almost any hardship … they were fighting for what they believed was a just principle, and therefore they intended to retain membership of the Players' Union.
Manchester Evening News, 28 August 1909

United tried to postpone their first league match of the season – all 27 of their players were suspended. Eventually a truce was called and the league programme started, but despite a full settlement being agreed in October 1909, the FA found it difficult to stop United's

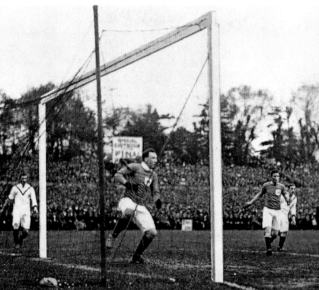

Left All eyes are on the ball as United swing over another corner. **Right** Harold Halse, peering from behind a Bristol defender, sees Sandy Turnbull's shot open the scoring.

players from openly supporting the union.

Never consistent enough to mount a challenge for the title, United finished in fifth place. The real story of the season was United's move away from the noxious fumes and poor playing surface at Bank Street to a brand new, spacious and costly stadium on the other side of Manchester. It is now one of the most famous stadiums in football – Old Trafford.

United started the 1910–11 season in phenomenal form, winning seven of their first eight matches and going top of the First Division table. New signing, Enoch "Knocker" West, who had joined from Nottingham Forest, formed a deadly goalscoring partnership with Sandy Turnbull. West finished top scorer with 19 goals in his 35 appearances. United were in great form, especially at home, with 14 wins and only one defeat. In the FA Cup, they went out to West Ham in the third round, but in the league they battled with Aston Villa for top spot throughout the season. With two matches remaining, United held a single point advantage, but their next match was away to Villa, and they had suffered a record 1–7 defeat at Villa Park the season before.

Villa were too strong for United. Despite two goals from Harold Halse, they returned to Manchester a defeated side,

having conceded four goals. They were one point adrift of the new league leaders. Everything depended on the final match of the season. Third-placed Sunderland were United's opponents at Old Trafford, while Villa travelled to Anfield to face Liverpool.

United had to hope that their old adversaries would defeat the Villa Park men. If they drew, United needed to win by three clear goals to take the title on goal average. At Old Trafford, Sunderland stung United by going into the lead on 22 minutes, but they hit back quickly and powerfully. Goals from Turnbull, West and Halse gave United a 3–1 interval lead as news came through that Liverpool were 2–0 up. At full time, United were 5–1 victors and there followed a tense wait for news from Anfield to filter through. As Charlie Roberts remembered:

At the end of the game our supporters rushed across the ground in front of the stand to wait for the final news from Liverpool. Suddenly a tremendous cheer rent the air, and was renewed again and again, and we then knew we were the champions once again.
The Saturday Post, 3 July 1916

Enoch "Knocker" West was a prolific goalscorer for Nottingham Forest and United until he was banned for life by the FA after the 1915 match-fixing scandal.

Manchester United F.C. 1st League Champions 1910-11.
Team for Season 1911-12.

Manchester United's 1910–11 League Championship winning team line up at their new Old Trafford stadium, ready for the 1911–12 season.

The Charity Shield did not attract a big crowd but at Stamford Bridge, United and Southern League champions Swindon Town served up a 12-goal thriller. Harold Halse was the man of the match, hitting a hat-trick in each half as United won 8–4. The half-time score was 4–3 to United before Swindon collapsed in the second half.

The following season, 1911–12, United barely got into gear, finishing well down the table in 13th place. After 1 January they won just four matches, all at home. There were terrible problems with injuries and illness all season, and it took two wins in the last three matches to drag the club to safety. For long-serving secretary-manager Ernest Mangnall, this was his last season in charge of the club. In August 1912 it was announced to a shocked Manchester public that he would be leaving to join Manchester City. His replacement was the president of the Football League, J.J. Bentley.

United's great side was breaking up – goalkeeper Moger had

retired, Alec Bell had joined Blackburn Rovers, and Dick Duckworth missed many matches through injury. Despite all this, Bentley's team managed a respectable fourth place in the league, reached the third round of the FA Cup and won the Lancashire Cup for only the second time in the club's history.

At the end of the season, a bombshell hit the club – Charlie Roberts was leaving Old Trafford. His move, to up-and-coming Oldham Athletic, caused uproar among the United fans who were amazed that United could even contemplate selling their long-serving captain; but sell him they did, and for a substantial fee of £1,500.

United became one of the also-rans in the First Division. Never strong enough to mount a challenge for the title, they finished 1913–14 in 14th place although they did retain the Lancashire Cup. In 1914–15 – the last season before the hostilities forced the abandonment of national football competitions – they finished in 18th position, a solitary point above relegated Chelsea. In both

Only three years after winning the League Championship, Manchester United had been reduced a mediocre team in the First Division.

seasons, they were ignominiously knocked out of the FA Cup in the first round.

Supporters, increasingly affected by wartime regulations, stayed away. In 1914–15, average attendances more than halved to 11,684 as United managed to win just nine games, all bar one at Old Trafford, and contrived to lose a massive 17 matches. Charlie Roberts, meanwhile, was captaining Oldham to the runners-up position, their highest-ever placing.

There was worse to follow. News leaked out that United's players had been involved in a match-fixing scandal. A flood of bets on a 2–0 scoreline in the home match against Liverpool on 2 April 1915 alerted some bookmakers to a potential fraud. Betting on a specific score was unusual and the sheer number of bets hinted at an attempt to deceive the bookmakers.

Eventually, the Football Association intervened as more and more evidence came to light. As a result of the inquiry, eight players were banned for life – United's Enoch West, Arthur Whalley and Sandy Turnbull, four Liverpool players and a Chester player. The deception was purely about money.

As a result of the escalating hostilities, the players realized that organized league football was coming to an end and they saw this as a last chance to make some money before the war ruined their careers or even cost them their lives.

For the duration of the war, United played in the Lancashire section of the regionally organized league. With 17 of the playing staff having joined up by 1915, the club fielded makeshift teams comprising young prospects and local amateurs. Attendances plummeted and the club, in financial chaos, defaulted on bills, notably those for Old Trafford.

For the players, many found that their careers were cut short by the war and were too old to resume their playing careers when peace eventually broke out in 1918. Others, including Sandy Turnbull, the disgraced goalscorer in United's 1909 FA Cup victory, were killed in action.

1909 FA CUP FINAL

MANCHESTER UNITED (1) 1 BRISTOL CITY (0) 0

24 APRIL 1909, THE CRYSTAL PALACE, LONDON

THE FA CUP was regarded as the country's premier competition, allowing the best team on the day the victors' spoils, and this was the first time in their history that Manchester United had reached the final. The games played on the way had produced some fine victories over some of the top teams in the land, together with one episode of luck against Burnley.

Bristol City were their opponents and for some of the fans, and especially some of the newspaper correspondents, the match was a straight battle between Charlie Roberts and Billy Wedlock. Wedlock was the man preferred by the England selectors and the game was seen as a chance to prove who was the rightful first-choice international.

United had had a difficult 1908–09 season, looking a mere shadow of the team that had won the championship the season before. They finished well off the pace in 13th place, five positions lower than their Cup final opponents. The teams had played each other twice a few weeks before the final, with Bristol winning 1–0, followed by a 0–0 draw.

United began their Cup final preparations by taking up residence in the Royal Forest Hotel, Chingford. From there, on the day of the match, the travelling party took the train into London, had lunch and made their way out to the Crystal Palace by bus.

As United and Bristol City both normally played in red shirts, they both changed colours. Bristol chose blue while United took to the field wearing white shirts with a red V. These shirts had been purchased from Billy Meredith's sports shop in Manchester and were presented to the players by the music-hall star George Robey.

United kicked off and they started well, quickly putting pressure on the Bristol defence in the first ten minutes. They carried on in that vein and when Harold Halse fired a shot against the bar from a cross by Meredith, Clay, the Bristol goalkeeper, was powerless. Sandy Turnbull, reacting quickest to the loose ball, put away the rebound. It was 1–0 to United with 22 minutes on the clock. Turnbull had been a major injury doubt before the match and was nursing a heavily bandaged thigh. Team captain Charlie Roberts felt so confident of Turnbull's striking prowess that he declared he wanted Turnbull in the team, despite the injury, as he could still be a match-winner. Roberts's opinion was vindicated by that goal, but it was United's Welsh Wizard who caused the Bristol defence all sorts of problems.

Meredith, in particular, played beautiful football: his clever forward work, rare control of the ball, sure passes and long shots into goal gave the deadliness to his side's attack.
Fifty Years of FA Cup Finals, 1932

Despite the best efforts of both sets of players, the game became very scrappy with few real goalmouth chances. Tempers frayed towards the end and the referee warned United's players for time wasting. Vince Hayes went off injured with a broken rib, but United reorganized and the ten men managed to hold on to claim a first FA Cup final victory.

For the large number of Mancunians in the crowd, it was time to celebrate. Charlie Roberts walked up the steps to receive the FA Cup from Lord Charles Beresford. Then it was on to a dinner at the Crystal Palace followed by a night out at the Alhambra music hall.

Manchester United (secretary-manager J.E. Mangnall): Moger, Stacey, Hayes, Duckworth, Roberts, Bell, Meredith, Halse, J. Turnbull, A. Turnbull, Wall
Scorer: A. Turnbull (22)

Bristol City (secretary-manager H. Thickett): Clay, Annan, Cottle, Hanlin, Wedlock, Spear, Staniforth, Hardy, Gilligan, Burton, Hilton

Attendance: 71,401

Charlie Roberts leads out the United team followed by George Stacey.

JAMES ERNEST MANGNALL

SECRETARY-MANAGER (MANCHESTER UNITED 1903–12)

J.E. Mangnall was famous around Manchester for his tactical acumen and straw boaters.

ERNEST MANGNALL was the man who put Manchester United on the map. Using John Henry Davies's money, he made the club a success – but that success faded almost as soon as he departed the scene.

Mangnall was not renowned as a player; he made his mark in the field of administration. Joining Manchester United in September 1903 in the wake of the resignation of James West, he came highly recommended by the president of the Football League, J.J. Bentley, who saw in Mangnall the qualities needed by United.

Mangnall played football for Bolton Grammar School before making a name for himself as a prominent member of Bolton Harriers running club. He was also an enthusiastic cyclist, and once cycled from Bolton to John O'Groats in the north of Scotland. By 1897, he was a director of his hometown club, Bolton Wanderers, with special responsibility for team affairs. Two years later he was at Burnley, becoming secretary-manager in December 1899. He guided the club through a major financial crisis. In an effort to keep costs in check, he ended up as the only paid backroom employee – even resorting to mowing the pitch!

In Mangnall, John Davies found a club secretary who was immensely knowledgeable about all aspects of football and football clubs. Not content with the administrative secretarial role, Mangnall took charge of all aspects of team affairs. In effect, he became Manchester United's first modern manager and one whom the *Manchester Evening News* described as "a model official". He was also someone whom Davies trusted to spend his money for the benefit of the team. Mangnall spent thousands of pounds building up a squad of players to challenge for promotion and then for First Division honours.

Mangnall spent the money wisely. His scouting for new players was renowned, and his ability to discover players, such as Charlie Roberts and George Wall, was a rare talent. Mangnall had the foresight to nip in and claim four of Manchester City's stars before the club was able to auction them. Shrewd enough to sell surplus players to other clubs, he often made a profit for United.

A further great strength was his hands-on approach to the game. When things were faltering on the pitch, Mangnall would take the opportunity to change tactics at half-time.

Eager to move United away from the noxious fumes and terrible pitch of the Clayton ground, Mangnall was instrumental in the move to Old Trafford in 1910. He was also the driving force behind the formation of the Central League, a reserve league for many of the biggest clubs in the Midlands and North of England.

In August 1912 United fans were astonished to learn that Mangnall was leaving the club he had built up to be one of the greatest in the land. There was a further surprise in store. He was moving the short distance to Hyde Road, home of Manchester City. At City, Mangnall reorganized the finances of what was an underachieving club and paved the way for a move away from their cramped ground to a new stadium at Maine Road in 1923. After receiving a Football League long-service medal in 1921, he finally left City and retired from football management in 1924.

Back in 1912, after presenting Mangnall with a silver rose bowl as a thank you for his service to United, the board of directors had the difficult task of finding his replacement.

To follow in the footsteps of a gentleman like Mr Mangnall is a very difficult matter indeed, and I can quite understand why the officials do not intend to hurry themselves in the matter.
Evening Chronicle, 19 September 1912

Despite the best efforts of his successors, the success that James Ernest Mangnall had brought to Manchester United would not be emulated until after the Second World War and the arrival of a young man called Matt Busby.

CHARLIE ROBERTS

CENTRE HALF (MANCHESTER UNITED 1904-13)

WHEN CHARLIE ROBERTS joined Manchester United he was a young man with relatively little league experience – just one season – and, at £600, he was regarded as a risky purchase. He soon proved to be an astute investment and became the heartbeat of the side.

Roberts joined United from Grimsby Town after playing locally in Darlington and then for the famous amateur club, Bishop Auckland.

Charlie Roberts was the first of many great Manchester United captains.

He was a supreme athlete with considerable stamina and pace despite his pale appearance, which led to his nickname of "the ghost in boots".

From his central half-back position, Roberts was the hub of United's first great team and, along with Alec Bell and Dick Duckworth, formed a formidable defensive line. His leadership skills were soon noticed and for most of his career he captained the side. Not just a stopper, Charlie Roberts was renowned for his ball distribution and passing skills. Early in his career at United his performances attracted rave reviews as the team strove for promotion from the Second Division. As a newspaper report on United's 2–0 win over Lincoln City in October 1904 mentioned:

One man on the home side stood out by himself both in attack and defence, this being Roberts. He was continually harassing the opposing defence and supplying openings for his forwards and bringing his confreres both at half and back out of difficulties.

His impressive performances attracted the attention of the international selectors and he became the first Second Division player to play in all three Home Internationals in one season. However, he soon found himself out of favour. A prominent founder member of the reformed Players' Union, his outspoken comments and actions supporting the union hindered his international prospects despite the consistent excellence of his play on the pitch. Captaining United to promotion in 1906, followed by league championships in 1908 and 1911 and the FA Cup in 1909, he and United were at the peak of their powers. Internationally, he was ignored despite considerable support from journalists and fellow players. The Football League called on his services nine times for inter-league matches.

Disputes over contracts and benefits forced Roberts to consider moving from Old Trafford and to the surprise of many, United's board of directors were willing to sell their captain, although they turned down offers from Manchester City. In August 1913, Charlie Roberts joined Oldham Athletic for £1,500, a record fee for the Boundary Park club.

Charlie Roberts enjoyed an Indian summer at Boundary Park where he captained the Latics to their highest-ever league placing, runners-up to Everton in 1914–15. A knee injury eventually ended his playing career during the war, leaving him free to build up his tobacconist business. His Ducrobel cigar became famous around Manchester – it was named after the United half-back line of Duckworth, Roberts and Bell.

Enticed back into football as the manager of Oldham in June 1921, he found the stresses of management too much to handle. He resigned in December 1922 to concentrate on his now flourishing wholesale and retail tobacco business based a short distance from United's old ground in Clayton.

BILLY MEREDITH

OUTSIDE RIGHT (MANCHESTER UNITED 1907-21)

BILLY MEREDITH was one of the greatest players of his or any other football era. The Welsh Wizard was famed for his consummate skill, for having a toothpick clamped between his teeth while playing, for a fiery, stubborn temperament and for the controversy that erupted during his long career.

Born in Black Park, near Chirk in North Wales, in July 1874, he started work at the local coal pit at the age of 12. When he was 18, his football talents came to the notice of Northwich Victoria. After playing for Northwich, Wrexham and Chirk, with whom he won the Welsh Cup in 1894, he joined Manchester City in October 1894. It was here that the skinny, bandy legged, but supremely talented, Billy Meredith made his name. To help his concentration while playing, he used to chew tobacco until one of the Hyde Road laundry ladies complained. From then on, he played with a toothpick between his teeth, something that became his trademark. A goalscorer as well as provider, the high point of his City career was scoring the winning goal in the 1904 FA Cup final.

In August 1905 the football world was stunned to read that Meredith was under investigation over match-fixing and bribery allegations. Alec Leake of Aston Villa alleged that Meredith had offered him £10 to throw the last match of the season to give City a chance to win the First Division title. The FA investigation was long and complicated. Meredith first claimed innocence, and then that he had been acting on the orders of the club. Some of his later statements caused yet more anguish. As the FA looked deeper into the financial affairs of Manchester City more and more irregularities became apparent. Meredith and many of his fellow players were suspended from playing, while a shell-shocked Manchester City board were forced to sell almost all their first-team squad.

Suspended until 1 January 1907, Manchester United moved in to sign him in May 1906 on a free transfer. As the *Manchester Evening News* reported on 16 May:

Although Meredith has been playing football for over ten years, he has still few, if any, superiors at outside-right, and he should prove a valuable acquisition to the Clayton club.

His suspension over, Meredith was a catalyst for United. On his

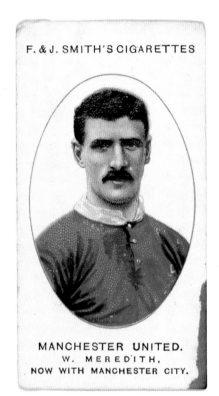

F. & J. SMITH'S CIGARETTES

MANCHESTER UNITED.
W. MEREDITH,
NOW WITH MANCHESTER CITY.

Billy Meredith's long career was spent with Manchester's two big clubs.

debut, against Aston Villa at Bank Street on New Year's Day, it was Meredith's cross that provided Sandy Turnbull with the chance to head the winning goal. He was the star player in United's championship-winning team of 1907–08 and had a great understanding with Dick Duckworth at right half-back. While he found goalscoring harder each season, his extravagant skills and pinpoint crosses laid on many goals for Sandy Turnbull and later for Harold Halse and Enoch West.

By the end of that championship-winning season, his sense of frustration at the iniquities he felt he had suffered and his poor wages came to a head. Along with teammate Charlie Roberts, he helped re-found the Players' Union in the face of considerable opposition from the football authorities.

A second Cup-winner's medal was added to his collection in 1909 followed by a further championship medal in 1911. By this time, Meredith was the grand old man of the team and at the age of 40 the outbreak of war virtually ended his playing career. His rebellious stubbornness prompted disputes with the United directors and during the war years Meredith played, not for United, but for City and Stalybridge Celtic. A final disagreement after the war resulted in him leaving Old Trafford and rejoining City on a permanent basis as player-coach. He finally retired from first-class football at the age of 49 in 1924 and later scouted and coached for United.

Internationally, Meredith was the most capped Welsh player until after the Second World War. He won 48 caps for Wales in a career that lasted from 1895 to 1920, but he missed out on even more caps because of suspension and not being released by his clubs. In his final appearance, Wales defeated England for the first time in his career.

Outside of football, Meredith ran a sports shop in St Peter's Square, Manchester, under the name of Pilling, Briggs & Meredith. It was from here that United purchased their kit for the 1909 FA Cup final. Towards the end of his career, he took up a succession of tenancies at public houses around Manchester. Meredith's death, two months after the Munich air disaster, was generally neglected by the football world as attention concentrated on the rebuilding of the United team. But Meredith's fame lives on and he was recently chosen as a member of the greatest Welsh team ever.

THE BIRTH OF

TODAY OLD TRAFFORD is one of the most famous football stadiums in the world, and one of the largest in Britain. For United, the building of the new stadium was a considerable risk, but one that has certainly paid off.

The cramped nature of United's Bank Street ground, hemmed in by chemical works and other industry, hindered John Henry Davies's ambitions for his club. The limitations of Bank Street were exposed each season as the grass vanished from the pitch, and for big matches hundreds, even thousands, of fans were locked out as the ground struggled to cope.

In August 1907, Manchester United announced that the club was looking for a site for a new stadium and suggested that the most likely choice would be Old Trafford. The land was purchased by the Manchester Brewery Company and rented from the Brewery

by the club. Davies paid for the construction costs, building stands and terracing. But the ground was over eight kilometres from the east of Manchester and United's main fan base. This was a great risk for the club. Would United's fans travel across the city to the new stadium?

Construction began in 1908 under the supervision of the famous football stadium architect, Archibald Leitch. The ground was officially opened on 19 February against Liverpool. United stormed into a two-goal lead, although Liverpool spoiled the party by winning 4–3.

With a capacity of 80,000, somewhat less than the original plan of 100,000, Old Trafford was still one of the largest stadiums in the country. It was all a far cry from the club's original home at North Road with its changing facilities at the local pub.

United's Bank Street ground, in the backgrond, was just not big enough for the crowds they began to attract as the team became successful under J.H. Davies.

OLD TRAFFORD

Thousands of spectators braved the rain to see Sheffield United defeat Chelsea in the 1915 FA Cup final at Old Trafford. It became known as the "Khaki Cup final" because of the large number of servicemen in the crowd.

...when you have had a peep at the new enclosure you will say the new ground has no superior. When complete it will have cost something like £40,000.
Matchday programme, 19 February 1910

There was a grandstand with cover for over 12,000 spectators and 750 plush tip-up chairs in the centre of the stand.

The grandstand with its 60 rows of seats, is considerably larger than any stand on any football ground in the kingdom, and yet the ground is so compact that, unlike the Crystal Palace and other grounds, you always seem reasonably near the playing pitch.
The Umpire, 20 February 1910

Inside the stand, the facilities were equally grand, including spacious modern dressing-rooms with plunge baths, a laundry, games room, gymnasium, masseurs room and offices complete with telephones. With direct access to the trams between the city centre and Altrincham, Old Trafford attracted supporters from all over the southern and western parts of Manchester and nearby Salford.

The stadium was a great success, being chosen as a venue for the 1911 FA Cup final replay and for the 1915 FA Cup final. However, the construction costs, which United were steadily trying to repay, almost bankrupted the club. There was a disastrous decline in gate receipts as success became elusive followed by the disruption of the First World War. United were forced to default on some of their payments and despite the return of league football, continuing lack of success in the 1920s kept the club in a perilous financial position. It was not until the 1930s that a new board of directors felt confident enough to make improvements to their giant stadium.

CHAPTER THREE

UNITED BETWEEN THE WARS

BY SOME DISTANCE, THIS WAS MANCHESTER UNITED'S LEAST
SUCCESSFUL ERA OF THE TWENTIETH CENTURY. NO LEAGUE
CHAMPIONSHIPS, NO FA CUP WINS AND THEY VERY NEARLY
SLIPPED INTO THE THIRD DIVISION!

THE YEARS between the two world wars contributed virtually nothing to Manchester United's emergence as one of the illustrious names in the world of sport. Of all the various eras that comprise the club's remarkable history, this one is without doubt the least auspicious. Not one single top honour found its way to Old Trafford in the 20 seasons that linked the two conflicts.

It isn't just the lack of success that sets this largely depressing spell apart from the rest; it is also the damaging lack of consistency. In a continual switchback ride, the club lurched back and forth between the top two divisions and almost made an unprecedented fall into the third grade. United succeeded in finishing above halfway in the First Division table just once, in the 1925–26 season. The rest of the time was spent languishing in the lower reaches, or in the Second Division.

If United's performances in the league left a great deal to be desired, there was little to console their long-suffering fans when it came to the FA Cup. Twenty appearances in the competition ended in almost blanket disappointment – a lone run to the semi-final in 1926 and another to the sixth round two years later provided the only relief in what must have felt like endless barren years.

At the onset of the First World War, United supporters could have been excused for hoping that the enforced break from fully organized football would help their team to resolve some of the ailments from the immediately preceding years. The glory years of the Roberts-Meredith-Turnbull era had given way to a poor sequence of seasons, which culminated in an 18th-place finish in the 1914–15 season, the last before war broke out in Europe. United, with 30 points from 38 games finished just two places and a couple of points above Tottenham Hotspur, who were relegated and destined to resume, following the cessation of hostilities, in the Second Division.

United therefore approached the return to serious competition without any immediate past glories to emulate. Several players, most notably Billy Meredith, Arthur Whalley (who was severely wounded in Belgium), Wilf Woodcock and Jackie Mew, bridged the four inactive football years and reclaimed their places when the players reconvened to ready themselves for 1919–20. One illustrious name from the pre-war days was missing – Sandy Turnbull, one of the great stars of United's first successful side that won the league championship in 1908 and 1911, and in between lifted the FA Cup, lost his life on active service in France in 1917. Turnbull carved his own indelible place in United history by scoring the only goal in the 1909 Cup final against Bristol City.

John Robson, who had become manager in 1914, retained his position in charge of team affairs. The first side he selected contained several players who were to become the nucleus of United teams for years to come. His teamsheet for the opening Football League Division Two game of the season, against Derby County at the Baseball Ground, included goalkeeper Jackie Mew, fullbacks Charlie Moore and Jack Silcock, and centre-half Clarence 'Lal' Hilditch. All four – Moore, Silcock and Hilditch making their debuts – were destined for lengthy and distinguished Old Trafford careers. They were joined by another young man who was set fair for a remarkable career – Joe Spence, a north-easterner from Northumberland. He pulled on the No. 9 shirt for that opening-day match against the Rams, but would later gain fame for his mercurial wing play.

Wilf Woodcock scored and United gained a point from the 1–1 draw against Derby, the team that had finished the 1914–15 season as Second Division champions.

The season began slowly for United with the opening three games producing just two points. Then came a sequence of three games which all ended in victory, including a double over Preston North End. It was the only time during the season that United won three games in a row.

The erratic pattern of the post-war campaign had already begun to unfold, with the next three matches ending all-square. United fans were given something to cheer in mid October when a Joe Spence goal secured a 1–0 win over Manchester City at Old Trafford, but it was a rare moment to relish in a season that never looked like providing anything more than a mid-table finish. United eventually finished in 12th place. Taking into account the fact that they won just six of the fixtures played following the turn of the year, that was really quite respectable.

The FA Cup campaign provided scant distraction from the mediocrity of the week-to-week league fare. Port Vale were beaten in the first round. They had joined the Second Division part way through the season, taking over the fixtures of Leeds City, who had been expelled for financial irregularities. In the next round, United were eliminated at Old Trafford by Aston Villa, the eventual winners.

If the first season back had provided little in the way of optimism for United's loyal supporters, the following term was hardly any better. The make-up of the team was much the same as the previous season and the success ratio showed only a minute improvement. They completed the season with 40 points, precisely the same number as the previous season, but they were compiled with two extra victories.

The high-point of the season was undoubtedly a streak of four straight wins during December. Bradford Park Avenue were beaten 5–1 at Old Trafford and 4–2 on the other side of the Pennines on successive Saturdays. Then came a 2–0 home win over Newcastle

Manchester United 1922–23 Back row: Frank Barson, Clarence "Lal" Hilditch, John Ballen (Trainer), John Mew, John Silcock, John Grimwood, Neil McBain. Front row: (left to right) Arthur Lochhead, John Wood, Charles Moore, Joseph Spence, Harry Williams, Harry Thomas.

United and another by the odd goal in seven away at Aston Villa.

It appeared that perhaps, just perhaps, the corner was about to be turned and the wonderfully productive days of a decade earlier were about to return. United fans, eager for success, were ready to grasp the moment, but just as their hopes started to grow they were immediately dashed.

The four successive wins and 13 goals were soon consigned to history as the Reds proceeded to lose their next three games. Villa gained ample revenge for the defeat at Villa Park by winning 3–1 at Old Trafford before a record crowd of 70,504. United then tumbled to a 6–3 defeat against Newcastle United at St. James's Park before losing heavily again, 4–1 at home to West Bromwich Albion, the reigning league champions.

Once again, the FA Cup couldn't provide any solace as United slid out at the first hurdle to Liverpool. The teams drew 1–1 at Anfield, but the Mersey Reds won through to the second round after winning the replay 2–1 at Old Trafford.

With aspirations of FA Cup glory extinguished, the prospects for the remainder of the season were just as bleak as they had been 12 months earlier. Amazingly, the second half of the league programme produced six wins, exactly the same as the previous season.

At the end of the season, Billy Meredith left. He was the original Welsh Wizard and one of greatest players ever to wear the famous red shirt. The spindly legged genius had been with United since 1906, playing in more than 300 league and Cup games for the club. He was instrumental in the successes of 1908 and 1911 when the league title was won, and in the FA Cup triumph of 1909. A quite remarkable man, and natural athlete, he was far from finished and later that summer signed for Manchester City where he continued to display wonderful skills for a further three years.

The 1921–22 season dawned with a catastrophic 5–0 defeat against Everton at Goodison Park, which provided a gloomy but ultimately accurate omen for the forthcoming campaign. If the previous couple of seasons had given United supporters little to get excited about, this one was going to be decidedly bereft of favourable results and enjoyable moments.

QUALITY CIGARETTES. SERIES F.A.1/96.

SPENCE, MANCHESTER UNITED C. F.
IN ACTION AGAINST SPURS. F.A.10.

United lost their next match 3–2 at home to West Bromwich Albion, but gained some revenge for the opening-day mauling on Merseyside by defeating Everton 2–1 at Old Trafford. The win briefly blew away the black clouds from Old Trafford, but in the next few weeks they returned to the skies above Warwick Road. Five draws and a defeat in the next six games led to United taking up a lowly place in the First Division table. The unfavourable results also led to John Robson resigning his position as manager to be replaced by former Airdrieonians boss John Chapman.

Successive homes wins over Tottenham Hotspur (2–1) and Manchester City (3–1 with Joe Spence scoring all three goals) eased United's predicament and gave Chapman's tenure an encouraging opening, but it was a short-term reprieve. For the next three months most matches ended with the points being claimed by their opponents. The dismal sequence included a run of seven straight defeats – six in the league and a 4–1 thumping by Cardiff City in the first round of the FA Cup at Old Trafford.

The spectre of relegation had loomed large for most of the season and everyone's worst fears were realized when the season reached its finale with United four points adrift of Bradford City, who were also relegated, and eight points behind Everton, who managed to avoid the trapdoor.

Being sentenced to life in the second grade was, as it always is, a terrible blow for the club and their followers. It was the first time United had suffered the drop since their Newton Heath days back in 1893–94, but the new season opened brightly to give rise to a renewed air of hope and expectancy. Six of the first seven games ended in victory with Joe Spence scoring five goals in the process.

The great start to the season was bolstered by the signing of Frank Barson, a former Barnsley and Aston Villa star and one of most uncompromising defenders of his day. Sheffield-born, he was a member of the Villa side that had beaten Huddersfield Town to lift the FA Cup in 1920, and he had won a full England cap against Wales the same year.

If the acquisition of Barson was designed to stiffen the Reds' defence, as the season unfolded it became clear that the decision to recruit him had been a shrewd piece of thinking. United didn't take the Second Division by storm, but they enjoyed a steady season, finishing in fourth place with 48 points, five behind Notts County, the champions. They lost just 11 games all season – one fewer than County – but failed to accumulate sufficient points because they won 17 games and drew 14 compared with the Meadow Lane club's 23 wins and seven draws.

Ironically, the outstanding performance of the season was a 6–1 trouncing of Notts County in Nottingham. Ernie Goldthorpe scored four goals that day with Joe Myerscough getting the other two. That remarkable win couldn't have arrived at a more fortuitous moment, coming as it did just one week after United had slumped out of the FA Cup in a second-round tie against Tottenham Hotspur at White Hart Lane. Bradford City had been ousted from the first round, following a replay, but Spurs' 4–0 win ended United's FA Cup dreams for another year.

The 1923–24 season began in encouraging style with United winning their first three fixtures. Bristol City were beaten 2–1 at Ashton Gate on the opening day of the season, and back at Old Trafford the Reds defeated Southampton 1–0, and then completed a rapid league double over Bristol City with a 2–1 win.

This early flourish was soon nipped in the bud with none of the following six games ending on a winning note. The last of this less-than-ideal sequence provided one of the rarest statistics in football history when United met Oldham Athletic at Boundary Park on Saturday, 6 October 1923. Oldham defender Sam Wynne scored four goals that day, but it didn't help his side to an emphatic win over the near-neighbours. The trouble was that he bagged two goals for his own side – one of them from the penalty spot – and a couple for United. Fortunately for Wynne, his team-mate Billy Howson found the net to give the Latics a 3–2 win. United got a measure of revenge the following weekend when the teams faced each other at Old Trafford with Jimmy Bain scoring twice in a 2–0 victory.

However, fewer games were won than were lost, and a remarkable number were drawn – exactly a third of the 42 fixtures ended all-square. United finished the season in 14th position, two points behind local rivals Stockport County.

It almost goes without saying that there was no joy on the Cup front either, with United once again being eliminated at the second-round stage. Plymouth Argyle, of the Third Division (South), were beaten 1–0 at Old Trafford in the opening round, but the Reds were then comprehensively defeated 3–0 by Huddersfield Town, one of the great teams of the day and that season's league champions.

After four seasons of largely uninspiring fare, United's success-starved supporters were given something to cheer when in 1924–25 the team won promotion back to the top grade. During the 42-match programme, they lost just eight times, and only one of those defeats, against Oldham Athletic, came at Old Trafford.

Opposite: Joe Spence was arguably Manchester United's greatest player in the years between the two World Wars.

Overleaf: Goalkeeper Alf Steward thwarts a Manchester City attack during the 1926 FA Cup semi-final at Bramall Lane, Sheffield.

United began the season with a 1–0 home win against Leicester City, the only side who were to finish higher in the table. This was a satisfactory start, but then the team went on the road to play Stockport County and Stoke City with a return of just one point. They lost 2–1 to County at Edgeley Park and played out a goalless draw with the Potters. It seemed that United, despite that encouraging start, were set for another dismal winter. But then the team assembled a blistering seven-match winning run which registered them among the serious promotion candidates.

It was easily the best sequence of the season, and it was sufficient to launch United on the road back to the First Division. They ended the season just two points behind champions Leicester, who amassed 59 points. United's defence proved to be their strongest department, conceding only 23 goals, the least by any team in the division.

Sadly, the return to the top grade wasn't combined with a decent run in the FA Cup, United being eliminated in the first round against Sheffield Wednesday at Hillsborough.

Among the players who ended the season in United's first team was centre-forward Albert Pape, who had joined the club in rather unusual circumstances the previous February. Pape, who had played for Rotherham County and Notts County earlier in his career, was in Manchester with his Clapton Orient team-mates making ready for a league fixture at Old Trafford. With the kick-off less than two hours away, a deal was struck and he was transferred to United. He took his place in the side and they beat Clapton 4–2. To crown a remarkable day, Pape scored one of United's goals. His stay at Old Trafford lasted barely nine months before he returned south to play for Fulham.

After three seasons in the Second Division, a return to the top grade came as a breath of fresh air to club and fans alike. John Chapman was still in charge and pinned his faith on the squad that had taken United up a few months before.

The first season after promotion is always looked upon as one of consolidation and that's just what United achieved during 1925–1926. They didn't get carried away with ambitious thoughts of the championship, but they did accumulate 44 points, enough to finish a highly creditable ninth place in the table, 13 behind Huddersfield Town, who became the first club to win the league championship for a third consecutive year. The high-point of the

WILLS'S CIGARETTES

G. MUTCH (MANCHESTER UNITED)

George Mutch
Mid-1930s United star George Mutch illustrated on a contemporary trade-card.

league programme came in late April when Sunderland, who finished third in the table, were beaten 5–1 at Old Trafford. The lowest moment was a 6–1 mauling by City in the Manchester derby at Old Trafford.

The Blues, who in those days generally ruled the roost in Manchester, also put one over their great cross-town rivals in the FA Cup. The teams met in the semi-final at Bramall Lane, Sheffield, and City emerged with a place in the final after winning 3–0. United had beaten Port Vale, Tottenham Hotspur, Sunderland and Fulham in the earlier rounds, but they couldn't make that extra step. City failed to make the most of their triumph over the Reds, losing in the final to Bolton Wanderers, and also being relegated to the Second Division.

Old Trafford, one of the most capacious and well-appointed club grounds in the country, was finally honoured with its first full international on 17 April 1926 when Scotland beat England 1–0, Alex Jackson scoring the goal in front of 49,000 fans.

With City having departed to the Second Division, it was left to United to carry the flag for Manchester, but there was little to celebrate as the 1926–27 season unfolded. Inconsistency was the main feature of the campaign with the Reds taking both points from just 13 of their 42 league fixtures. The team once again relied heavily on the scoring instincts of Joe Spence who bagged 18 goals. Two changes at managerial level did little to promote stability. John Chapman remained in charge until October and was then replaced by Clarence Hilditch who became player-manager before handing over the reins to Herbert Bamlett the following April. Despite the occasional upheavals, the season ended with United in a reasonably comfortable 15th position. Any hopes of making a name for themselves in the FA Cup evaporated when they were knocked out in the third round by Second Division Reading following two replays.

Herbert Bamlett's first full season at the helm brought little respite from the mediocrity that had haunted the club since the end of the First World War. United won three more games than they had the previous season and amassed just one point fewer, but it didn't prevent them from slipping into 18th spot in the First Division table. United avoided relegation by a single point, but there was some consolation to be had in the FA Cup. Brentford were hammered 7–1 at Old Trafford in the third round as United set off on another encouraging Cup run. Bury were beaten, after a replay, in the next round, and Birmingham City came a cropper at Old Trafford in the last 16. Sadly, the Reds' luck ran out in the sixth round when Blackburn Rovers, who eventually lifted the trophy, beat them 2–0 at Ewood Park.

United did, however, finish the league campaign on a high note by trouncing Liverpool 6–1 at Old Trafford, with Joe Spence, almost inevitably, grabbing a hat-trick.

The 1928–29 season threatened to be one of ultimate disappointment. United won just four of 27 fixtures from the opening day, but a remarkable recovery staged during the last third of the term, which included a spell of seven wins in nine games, averted a plunge into the second grade and hoisted the club into a respectable 12th place in the table.

On the Cup front, it was another short-lived interest with the Reds knocking out Port Vale before being eliminated themselves by neighbours, Bury.

"Here we go again" must have been the phrase on United supporters' lips just three days into the 1929–30 season after the Reds had lost the opening couple of fixtures, to Newcastle United and Leicester City, both 4–1 and both away. The rot was halted briefly with a mini-revival of three straight victories, but that renewed hope gave way to further despair as the next six games all ended in defeat. That run of unfavourable results amounted to the worst sequence of the season, but there was still very little to cheer the faithful in the months that followed as United finished below halfway yet again. Defeat at the hands of Swindon Town of the Third Division (South) in the FA Cup helped to keep the club in the doldrums.

United's struggle to retain their place among the country's elite had become increasingly more difficult, but each year they always pulled something out of the bag to preserve their First Division status. That was until the first complete season of the thirties when United's reserves of luck and resolve finally ran dry. Twelve consecutive defeats from the start of the season virtually sealed United's fate as they became racing certainties for the drop. Two home wins, 2–0 against Birmingham City and

2–1 versus Derby County, were all the fans were given to cheer in the first half of the campaign. It was only marginally better after Christmas as the club slid towards the bottom of the table.

United eventually completed the season with a pitiful seven wins to their name – the worst return since the early 1890s. Needless to say, they finished bottom, nine points adrift of Leeds United who were also relegated. Amazingly, they managed to beat Sheffield Wednesday, league champions in the previous two seasons, 4–1, but it was rare bright moment amid the almost constant gloom. Manager Bamlett became a victim of the club's failure and his duties were taken over by secretary Walter Crickmer.

United's involvement in the FA Cup ended in the fourth round with a 1–0 defeat at Grimsby Town. That came after a protracted third-round tie with Stoke City that stretched to a second replay at Anfield, which United won 4–2.

The following couple of seasons produced little to generate any real optimism with modest finishes in the Second Division and early exits from the FA Cup, but at least it went a good way to preparing club and supporters alike for the real scare that lay ahead at the climax of the 1933–34 season.

The club had good reason to thank local businessman James Gibson for his benevolence late in 1931 when he agreed to a cash injection to ease financial problems. He later became club chairman. Second Division Plymouth Argyle dumped United out of the Cup in 1932 while the Reds were shown the door by Middlesbrough 12 months later. United were now managed by Scott Duncan, who had taken the helm before the start of the 1932–33 campaign.

There was an emotional departure for the great Joe Spence during the 1933 close season when he left after a fabulous 14 years at Old Trafford. He moved on to play for Bradford City and later, Chesterfield. Joe was the first player to appear in more than 500 games – 510 to be precise – and he scored a total of 168 league and Cup goals.

Johnny Carey, without question one of United's all-time great players, in action during the early years of his career.

48

United got the 1933–34 season off on the wrong foot with a 4–0 defeat against Plymouth Argyle at Home Park and rarely showed much inclination towards improvement as the winter months progressed. They suffered several heavy defeats – 5–1 at home to Bolton Wanderers, 6–1 at Bradford Park Avenue, 5–1 at Lincoln City and 7–3 at Grimsby Town – as they became engrossed in the relegation dogfight.

These poor results coupled with numerous other less spectacular defeats left United staring at the very real prospect of dropping into the Third Division for the first time. They were in 21st position in the table with 32 points when they travelled to the Den to play Millwall in the final match of the season. The Lions, in 20th place with 33 points, needed just a draw to escape relegation and send United tumbling. It was close call but ultimately United came

through the challenge. Goals from John Cape and Tommy Manley gave them an enormously important 2–0 win. Without question, in playing terms, it was the lowest point in the club's history and from then on the only way was up.

Nevertheless, the remaining five seasons before the dark clouds of war began to gather over Europe once more, were spent commuting between the top two divisions. At least there was enough happening on a regular basis to keep the fans' attention.

United finished fifth in the Second Division 12 months after their close shave at Millwall. George Mutch was leading scorer with 18 goals as the Reds finished 11 points behind Brentford, the champions.

The improvement gave a foretaste of what was in store for the following season when United proceeded to win their first title,

Manchester United 1934–35 playing in unusual cherry and white hoop shirts. Back row: (left to right) Tommy Manley, Henry Topping, Jack Hacking, Tom Jones (T), Jack Griffiths. Front row: Jack Cape, George Mutch, Jack Ball, Billy Mackay, Ernie Hine, Tom J. Jones (JT). Ground: Hugh McLenahan, George Vose.

albeit that of the Second Division, since 1911. The Reds lost just eight games throughout the campaign, one less than Charlton Athletic, who finished runners-up. Mutch was again instrumental in United's success with 21 goals. Harry Rowley wasn't far behind with 19 to his credit.

Sadly, the team couldn't replicate their form in the FA Cup and were eliminated by Stoke City, after a replay, in the fourth round having earlier knocked out Reading.

Happiness quickly turned to despair, once again, when after just one term in the top grade United found themselves heading back to the Second Division at the end of the 1936–37 campaign. Another poor season concluded with just 10 wins on the board and United were consigned to the drop along with Sheffield Wednesday. It was their last relegation for almost 40 years. In the FA Cup, United defeated Reading in the third round for the second successive year before suffering a 5–0 drubbing at Arsenal.

Included in United's defence for most of the latter part of the season was Oldham-born half-back Walter Winterbottom, who was to become England manager after the war.

The club's yo-yo existence continued. They moved in an upwardly mobile direction at the close of the 1937–38 season, claiming runners-up spot and a return to a place among football's elite. Johnny Carey, Stanley Pearson and Jack Rowley, three players who were to make their mark in the great United side of the early post-Second World War era, all made their debut during the season.

Cup glory, however, still eluded them. Brentford knocked them off the road to Wembley in the fifth round.

The return to the top grade proved to be an uneventful season apart from avoiding a swift fall back to the Second Division, which had been their fate two years before. They finished 14th in the league and went out of the Cup in the third round to West Bromwich Albion in what was to be the last completed season before the outbreak of war.

Old Trafford's record attendance figure was set on 25 March 1939, but United weren't involved. The match was an FA Cup semi-final between Wolverhampton Wanderers and Grimsby Town – 76,962 fans crammed into Old Trafford and watched Wolves book their place in the final with a 5–1 win.

Just three games were completed at the onset of the 1939–40 season before the programme was halted following the declaration of war. It was to be seven years before the next peacetime league season commenced.

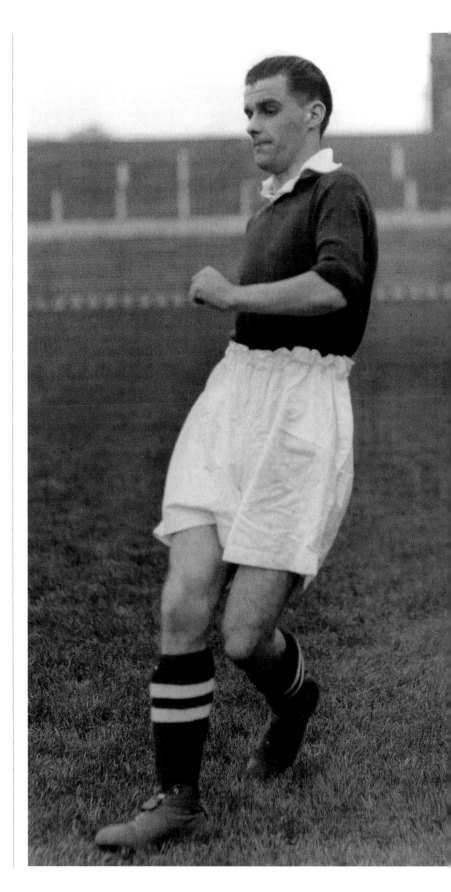

Stan Pearson, one of the hundreds of players who had their playing careers dissected by the Second World War.

JOHN CHAPMAN

JOHN CHAPMAN was Manchester United's manager for a five-year spell in the 1920s but just like his predecessor John Robson and successor Herbert Bamlett, he was unable to restore the glory days of the pre-First World War era.

Formerly manager of Scottish league club Airdrieonians, he joined United in October 1921 after the previous incumbent, John Robson, had resigned. Robson stayed on at Old Trafford in the position of assistant manager and together they tried to steer the club back on to a steady course, but there was little change in United's fortunes. At the end of his first season in charge, they finished at the foot of the table and were relegated to the Second Division. United won just eight games all season, their worst record since the early league days of Newton Heath.

The Reds remained in the Second Division for three seasons before returning to the top grade as runners-up to Leicester City. They made an encouraging return to the First Division, finishing ninth and there were further signs that Chapman was on the right track when he led United to the FA Cup semi-final. Sadly, there was to be no happy ending as United went down 3–0 to Manchester City at Bramall Lane.

In October 1926, the Football Association informed United that Chapman had been suspended from management for the rest of the season. He never returned to Old Trafford and details of his hasty departure were never made public. He died in December 1948.

HERBERT BAMLETT

LIKE JOHN CHAPMAN, Gateshead-born Herbert Bamlett inherited a club in decline and a team in need of revitalization, but in four years at the helm he enjoyed very little tangible success.

Bamlett had made his name as a top-class referee, officiating in the 1914 FA Cup final between Burnley and Liverpool, before going into management with Oldham Athletic. He succeeded in taking the Latics to the runners-up spot behind champions Everton in the 1914–15 season, the highest league position ever achieved

Walter Crickmer, one of United's finest backroom servants.

by the Boundary Park club. After completing military service, he continued to manage Oldham but without further success and he resigned the post at the end of the 1920–21 season.

He was soon back in employment with Wigan Borough who had just gained membership to the Third Division (North). He stayed barely 18 months at Springfield Park before accepting an offer to manage First Division Middlesbrough. His first complete season at Ayresome Park ended with Boro relegated, but he kept his nerve and two years later he led them back into the First Division. He didn't see out that season, resigning in January, and three months later he moved into Old Trafford.

He went on to oversee three uneventful seasons before United were eventually relegated at the end of 1930–31. His time in the job ended in April 1931.

WALTER CRICKMER

WALTER RAYMOND CRICKMER may not be an instantly familiar name to modern Manchester United supporters, but he stands comparison with other great backroom servants of the club such as Louis Rocca and Leslie Olive.

Crickmer joined the club as a junior clerk just after the First World War and gradually rose to the position of secretary, a post he still held at the time of his death in the Munich air disaster in 1958.

He succeeded Herbert Bamlett as secretary-manager in April 1931 and remained in charge until the appointment of Scott Duncan in June 1932. In total, he served under six Manchester United managers – John Robson, John Chapman, Clarence Hilditch, Bamlett, Duncan and Matt Busby.

During the Second World War, Crickmer kept the club ticking over virtually single-handed while at the same time joining the local special constabulary. It was during his service with the police that he had an amazing escape from death while on duty at headquarters. The building was hit by a bomb and he was buried under rubble for several hours. He received injuries to both arms and legs, but was comparatively lucky – a number of his colleagues died in the air-raid.

Walter Crickmer was a marvellous organizer and respected administrator. He missed many a match because he was too busy with the numerous duties he undertook for his beloved Manchester United.

SCOTT DUNCAN

One of the most frequently asked questions regarding Manchester United is, "Who was the manager before Matt Busby?" Strictly speaking, the answer should be Walter Crickmer who twice combined secretarial and managerial duties without ever adopting the title. One of those spells came between Scott Duncan's departure and Matt Busby's arrival.

However, the last to hold the title was Adam Scott Matthewson Duncan, who joined in 1932 after spells in charge of Scottish league clubs Hamilton Academicals and Cowdenbeath. Duncan, a former player with Dumbarton, Newcastle United, Rangers and Cowdenbeath, proceeded to spend a considerable amount of money in acquiring several new players, but initially success continued to be at a premium.

After four seasons in the Second Division, he guided United to promotion as champions. Unfortunately, United were still not ready for life at the top and the following season they slipped back into the Second Division.

Duncan remained at Old Trafford until November 1937 when he left to take up the reins at Ipswich Town, then of the Southern League. He stayed at the Suffolk club for 21 years – earning a Football League long service medal and leading them into the Third Division (South) in 1954. He passed on the Ipswich reins to future England manager Alf Ramsay.

Scott Duncan, the only United boss to claim a championship between the wars.

CHAPTER FOUR
BUSBY'S FIRST GREAT TEAM

FA CUP WINNERS IN 1948 AND LEAGUE CHAMPIONS
FOUR YEARS LATER, MATT BUSBY'S FIRST
GREAT SIDE SET THE STANDARD FOR GENERATIONS
OF FUTURE STARS TO FOLLOW.

54

MANCHESTER CITY, United's fierce rivals from across town, were the area's premier club during the 1920s and 30s. United were the poor relations, constantly struggling to rise above mediocrity. The Blues, on the other hand, were regularly among the game's achievers. League champions and runners-up during those years, City also reached three FA Cup finals, winning the famous trophy in 1934 with a side that included many of the top names of the day. Ernie Toseland, Alec Herd and Eric Brook were just a few of those who helped City to Cup glory over Portsmouth at Wembley.

United fans could be excused for casting envious eyes at their more successful neighbours from Moss Side; and as it turned out, one of the players who helped to bring the FA Cup back to Manchester later moved to Old Trafford to begin the process of transforming them into the most famous club on the planet.

Matt Busby, a Scotsman from Bellshill, Lanarkshire, shared the half-back duties with Sam Cowan and Jackie Bray in that Cup-winning side. He joined City in 1928 and gave the Blues excellent service for eight years as an attacking wing-half, playing in 226 league and Cup games and scoring 14 goals. He also became a full Scottish international when he pulled on the No. 4 shirt against Wales at Ninian Park, Cardiff in October 1933. Wales won 3–2.

Busby's opposite number in that Welsh side was a certain Jimmy Murphy of West Bromwich Albion, who was later to become his trusted friend and lieutenant at Old Trafford. Born in Ton Pentre, South Wales, Murphy spent 11 years at the Hawthorns, during which time he appeared in 223 competitive fixtures for the Baggies – including the 1935 FA Cup final against Sheffield Wednesday – as well as representing his country on 13 occasions.

Matt Busby was just beginning his fifth season with Liverpool when war was declared in September 1939. He had been transferred to Anfield from Manchester City in February 1936. In 1945, with the end of the war in sight, he was offered a job at Liverpool with the backroom staff. Reading, of the Third Division (South), had also approached him to become assistant manager to his good friend Joe Edelston, and Scottish League club Ayr United had offered him employment.

Manchester United, who had been without a manager since Scott Duncan had moved on to Ipswich Town late in 1937, contacted Busby with a view to him taking over the hot seat at Old Trafford. Walter Crickmer had been combining the duties of manager and secretary since Duncan's departure but, with a fresh dawn looming, it was time to find a new man.

Busby evaluated all the employment opportunities and after due consultation with his wife Jean, chose United. He accepted the post of manager at Old Trafford on 22 October 1945. Having agreed to take on the task of returning United to their pre-First World War trophy-winning ways, the Red Devils' new boss quickly set about recruiting a right-hand man.

His opportunity arrived late in 1945 when, still in the forces, he was passing through Bari, in Italy. There he bumped into Jimmy Murphy, whom by then he had faced many times on the soccer field. Murphy had been a redoubtable opponent and a player Busby would have preferred to be playing with than against. So on a warm day in southern Italy, having listened to Murphy talking about football to a gathering of army lads, Busby decided that here was the man he wanted to join him at United. Once Murphy had completed his training session, Busby moved in to make his first recruitment as manager of Manchester United. There and then they shook hands on the partnership that was destined to become one of the greatest double acts football would ever see.

The architects of United's rebuilding programme were now in place and all set to start the hard work of changing the club from perennial underachievers into one capable of challenging regularly for the game's biggest prizes.

Busby was under no illusions about the enormous task that lay ahead. Manchester United was a club on its knees with little financial clout, a bomb-damaged ground and a set-up that had well and truly forgotten how to succeed on the field. On the credit side, he had inherited several players who would eventually form the nucleus of United's first great side in almost 40 years.

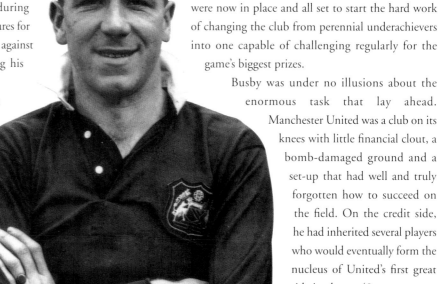

Matt Busby during his days as a classy half-back with neighbours Manchester City.

Busby's first match in charge was a Football War League (North) game against Bolton Wanderers at Maine Road on Saturday, 27 October 1945. His first-ever selection lined up as follows: Jack Crompton, Joe Walton, John Roach, Jack Warner, Bert Whalley, Henry Cockburn, Harry Worrall, Johnny Carey, Jack Smith, Jack Rowley and Billy Wrigglesworth. Goals from Carey and Worrall gave them a 2–1 win. Other players who made appearances in that final war season and who proved to be valuable assets in future years included Allenby Chilton, Stanley Pearson, John Aston, Charlie Mitten and Jimmy Delaney.

The FA Cup returned to the calendar during the 1945–46 campaign. Just for that season it was decided to play the rounds over two legs. United were drawn against Accrington Stanley in the third round, playing away at Peel Park in the first match. They held Stanley to a 2–2 draw in Accrington and completed the job in the return with a 5–1 win. In the fourth round United were pitched in against Preston North End, and after winning the home leg 1–0, they were eliminated after losing 3–1 at Deepdale.

So, with the country slowly getting back to some form of normality after six years under the leaden skies of war, football also resumed normal service with a complete 42-match league programme prepared for the start of the 1946–47 season. United were still unable to play home games at Old Trafford, which remained in a state of disrepair after being damaged by enemy action during the war. They had been playing their war league games at Maine Road, and that arrangement was set to continue as serious football got under way again.

United's opening fixture was against Grimsby Town (as it had been at the start of the ill-fated 1939–40 season) at Maine Road. They lined-up: Jack Crompton, Johnny Carey, Billy McGlen, Jack Warner, Allenby Chilton, Henry Cockburn, Jimmy Delaney, Stanley Pearson, Jimmy Hanlon, Jack Rowley and Charlie Mitten. Warner, Carey and Pearson were the only ones who had played in the side that had defeated the Mariners 4–0 at Old Trafford those seven years before. This time the Red Devils won again, but by 2–1 with Mitten and Rowley scoring the goals.

Jimmy Murphy pictured during his playing days with West Bromwich Albion and Wales.

It was an encouraging start to the season and there was plenty more to raise supporters' spirits as their favourites went on to claim maximum points from the subsequent four matches. Chelsea, Charlton Athletic, Liverpool (the eventual champions, who were beaten 5–0 at Maine Road) and Middlesbrough were all despatched as United recorded their best opening to a First Division season in decades. It was a good omen as they went on to challenge for the league title.

The gathering of points slowed somewhat in the weeks that followed, with United winning just one and drawing four of the next eight fixtures. During this sequence, another of the club's great names from the early post-Second World War period was given his league debut. Johnny Morris, a local lad born in Radcliffe, had been learning his trade with the MUJAC (Manchester United Junior Athletic Club) before the outbreak of war and after service in the forces he returned to pick up the pieces of his career with the club. His first game, against Sunderland at Maine Road late in October, ended with the Wearsiders leaving for home with the points as reward for their exertions. It wasn't an ideal first appearance for the talented inside-forward, but it provided the first steps in a career that later included spells with Derby County and Leicester City. Morris also won three full caps for England.

Sunderland's 3–0 win at Maine Road was the only time United lost at their temporary headquarters. They ended the season just one point behind Liverpool. The teams met at Anfield during the closing weeks of the campaign and a single first-half goal from Albert Stubbins was enough to give Liverpool the points. United finished the season with two home wins against Portsmouth (3–0) and Sheffield United (6–2), but it wasn't enough to snatch the title.

However, that close shave in the title race wasn't mirrored in the FA Cup. After they had put out Bradford Park Avenue in the third round, United were eliminated by Nottingham Forest in the fourth at Old Trafford.

Football was enjoying a post-war boom with interest sky-high and attendances running at enormous levels. United had pleased their fans with a good first season and that vast

Johnny Morris gets in a header during United's 2–0 FA Cup fifth round victory over Charlton Athletic at Huddersfield Town's Leeds Road ground.

improvement on what had been served up during the pre-war days was continued the following year.

Matt Busby refrained from taking a plunge into the transfer market during the close season, opting to pin his faith on the line-up that had done so well in taking the club to the runners-up spot. Jack Crompton remained the number one goalkeeper while the two Johns, Carey and Aston, continued to provide the full-back pairing. Allenby Chilton was at centre-half with Jack Warner and Billy McGlen completing the middle line. The five men who comprised the forward line – Jimmy Delaney, Johnny Morris, Jack Rowley, Stanley Pearson and Charlie Mitten – pretty well chose themselves. It was a combination that was as good as any front five operating in the era.

United opened the 1947–48 First Division fixture programme with a trip to the north east to face Middlesbrough at Ayresome Park. Jack Rowley grabbed both goals in a 2–2 draw as Busby's team got off to a satisfactory start. In those days of two points for a win and one for draw, sharing the spoils while on excursion was looked on as equally acceptable as winning on home territory.

United returned to Maine Road to entertain Liverpool in midweek and Charlton Athletic the following Saturday. Both games provided good victories with the Mersey Reds being beaten 2–0 and the Londoners losing 6–2. Rowley claimed four of the goals against the Addicks.

It was an extremely encouraging start to the season, but that three-match, five-point opening was followed by a less than ideal sequence of nine games without a win.

A 2–0 home win over Aston Villa in late October brought the poor run to an end and the very next Saturday United recorded one of their best wins of the campaign when they slammed Wolverhampton Wanderers 6–2 at Molineux. Surprisingly, Rowley,

who finished the season as top scorer with 23 league goals, failed to find the net. The half-dozen goals were shared among his co-attackers – Morris and Pearson netted two each, Delaney and Mitten contributed one each.

The FA Cup challenge began in the second week of January with an away tie against Aston Villa – and what a tie it turned out to be! The huge crowd of 58,683 packed into Villa Park was enthralled by an astonishing match that many claim to be one of the greatest ever played in the competition. United eventually won 6–4, but the outcome remained in the balance right up until the final minutes.

United were drawn at home to Liverpool, but with Old Trafford still out of action and Maine Road unavailable (with City having drawn a home tie against Chelsea), the match was switched to Everton's Goodison Park. Another vast crowd, this time numbering 74,721, witnessed a terrific encounter which ended with United 3–0 winners.

The same scenario applied in the following round when both United and City drew home games, so the fifth-round tie against Charlton Athletic went ahead at Leeds Road, the home ground of Huddersfield Town. The Yorkshire air obviously agreed with United, as they reached the last eight courtesy of a 2–0 win.

In the quarter-final, United were again drawn at home this time against Preston North End, who had ousted Manchester City at Maine Road in the previous round. North End, with great players including Bill Shankly and Tom Finney in their line-up, were one of the country's top sides in those days, but they couldn't repeat their fifth-round success and United ran out 4–1 winners.

Busby had guided United to their first FA Cup semi-final in 22 years and the Red half of Manchester was gripped with Cup fever. Derby County stood between United and their first Wembley final. Hillsborough staged the game and United completed their run to the final, with Stanley Pearson scoring a hat-trick in the 3–1 win. They made no mistake at Wembley, serving up an exciting 4–2 win over Blackpool. Jack Rowley scored twice with Stanley Pearson and Johnny Anderson getting the others.

United also made a fine showing in the league after that early poor run. Arsenal took the title, but United finished as runners-up for the second successive season. The Red Devils really were back in business.

There were high hopes that it would be third time lucky as the 1948–49 season opened towards the end of August. United started with a home game against Derby County, but the eager anticipation of the huge crowd gathered inside Maine Road was stifled as United went down 2–1. It wasn't the ideal launch to a campaign which many people hoped and believed could bring them the league championship for the first time since before the First World War. Early disillusionment was quickly nipped in the bud when United proceeded to win their next two fixtures. A 3–0 win over Blackpool at Bloomfield Road was followed by an even more impressive triumph as Busby and his team returned from Highbury having defeated Arsenal, the reigning champions, 1–0 in front of almost 65,000 fans.

Buoyed by their team's spectacular away wins, United's supporters looked forward to the next match with some relish. It was the return fixture with Blackpool at Maine Road and, having enjoyed a day by the seaside the previous week, an early double over the Tangerines was predicted. Unfortunately, Blackpool were reading from a different script and took their revenge with a 4–3 win.

Unpredictability was to be a feature of the early part of the season as the team sought to find some consistency. Only three of the next nine matches ended with the points in United's possession and it wasn't until the middle segment of the campaign that they finally clicked into serious point-gathering form. During the run-up to Christmas, they put together a sequence of results that included a half-dozen wins and an equal number of draws. As a result of that improved stability, they were installed among the title contenders as the New Year dawned.

On the second weekend of January, United began the journey along the road they hoped would end in a second successive visit to Wembley. Bournemouth and Boscombe Athletic travelled north to provide the opposition in the third round, but were sent tumbling out of the competition after losing 6–0 at Maine Road.

Bradford Park Avenue were next and United eventually overcame them, but it took three matches. The original fourth-round tie, played at Maine Road, ended 1–1 as did the replay at Park Avenue. United finally stepped forward to the fifth round after they had trounced the Yorkshire club 5–0 in the third match back at Moss Side.

Charlie Mitten clashes with Blackpool's Eddie Shimwell during the classic 1948 FA Cup final at Wembley.

That season's fourth round provided one of the biggest upsets in the history of the competition. Yeovil Town, of the Southern League, sent shock waves through the country when they defeated First Division Sunderland 2–1 on their famous sloping pitch at Huish. It was an astonishing win, which sent the green-and-white shirted heroes forward for a tilt against the Cup holders at Maine Road. An enormous crowd in excess of 81,000 packed the ground for the match. It had all the romance that makes the FA Cup so special.

Most of the country was rooting for underdogs Yeovil, but Busby's team of all-stars won the game comfortably, 8–0, with Jack Rowley claiming a handful of goals. A 1–0 sixth-round win against Hull City at Boothferry Park moved United into the last four for the second year running, where they came up against Wolverhampton Wanderers. Leicester City and Portsmouth were the other two semi-finalists.

The game was allocated to Sheffield Wednesday's well-appointed headquarters at Hillsborough. Charlie Mitten scored for United; Sammy Smyth netted for Wolves. The tie went to extra-time, but there were no more goals. The 1–1 draw meant that the teams had to meet again, this time on Merseyside at Goodison Park. Another huge crowd gathered and they saw the Black Country club win through to the final with a single goal from Ulsterman Smyth.

Meanwhile, on the league front, United continued to put in a serious challenge for the title. In a strong finish, they won seven of their final ten games. Portsmouth, who lost out to Leicester in the FA Cup semi-final, found huge consolation in winning the league championship. United, for the third successive season, finished in second place. Appropriately, the teams met on the final day of the season at Maine Road. Pompey had already clinched the title, but United, with goals from Jack Rowley (2) and Charlie Mitten, enjoyed a small slice of compensation with a 3–2 win.

In March 1949, the first of United's great post-war stars took his departure from the club. Johnny Morris, a richly gifted inside-forward, had played an important part in the re-building process, but a difference of views with Matt Busby led to him being transferred and he moved on to join Derby County.

United were proving to be the most consistent side of the early post-war period, but after three highly successful seasons they were still looking for a top-place finish. During the summer of 1949, the club bade farewell to their temporary home at Maine Road and made their long-awaited return to Old Trafford.

Supporters were hoping that a return to their own patch on Warwick Road would prove to be the missing element in converting their team from runners-up to champions. They had done well at Maine Road, losing just seven league matches in three seasons, but

there is nowhere like home so it was with more than the usual feverish excitement that the first home game was anticipated.

The season began with a 1–0 win over Derby County at the Baseball Ground and then it was on to Old Trafford and a meeting with neighbours Bolton Wanderers. The game was played on a Wednesday afternoon, but it still attracted a crowd of more than 40,000, the majority of whom were delighted to see United run out 3–0 winners.

Two matches, two wins was a good start and the encouraging opening continued with United remaining unbeaten in the opening eight games. In the main, the same line-up had served the club with distinction since the end of the war. Sammy Lynn, who had made three league appearances a couple of seasons earlier, had began the campaign at centre-half, but it wasn't long before the ultra-reliable Allenby Chilton was restored to the side. Up front, the tried and tested pairing of Jack Rowley and Stanley Pearson continued to form one of the most potent spearheads of the era. They were ably assisted in the goalscoring department by classy winger Charlie Mitten.

By and large, form was maintained and as a result United were installed as one of the front-runners in the championship race. Wolverhampton Wanderers led the field early on with Liverpool taking over the top spot as the season headed towards Christmas. Busby's team were hot on the heels of Liverpool at the turn of the year and it appeared that the title would end up at either Old Trafford or Anfield.

United continued to pick up points on a regular basis and in early March they took over from Liverpool at the head of the table. In one remarkable fixture at Old Trafford, United beat Aston Villa 7–0 with Charlie Mitten scoring four of the goals, three of his haul being claimed from the penalty spot.

United and Liverpool met at Old Trafford in mid-March with Busby's team heading the table by two points. The game ended goalless, leaving United still in pole position with ten games left to play. Portsmouth, the eventual champions, were trailing United by six points. The Fratton Park club appeared to be one of the outsiders, but by the time they travelled to Old Trafford in mid-April, they had closed to within two points of United who by this time had slipped into second place, a point behind leaders Sunderland.

Pompey, the reigning champions, were not about to give up their title without a fight and goals from Jack Froggatt and Douglas Reid gave them a vital 2–0 win in front of almost 45,000 fans. The match against Portsmouth was a special occasion for Jeff Whitefoot, who was called up to make his league debut at the tender age of 16 years 105 days, which made him the youngest player to make a league appearance for the club. Hopes of landing the championship had

Charlie Mitten lobs the ball over Wolverhampton Wanderers goalkeeper Bert Williams to score United's goal in the 1949 FA Cup semi-final at Hillsborough.

begun to evaporate. Portsmouth had made a late charge in defence of their title and in the final outcome they finished top with 53 points, just above Wolves on goal average, one point ahead of Sunderland in third place and three points better off than United in fourth.

It was also a less than ideal season in the FA Cup. Having won the trophy and reached the semi-final in the previous two seasons, United had begun to earn a reputation as Cup specialists. Southern League side Weymouth were beaten 3–0 at Old Trafford in the third round with Watford, then a Division Three (South) club, ousted 1–0 at Vicarage Road. A 3–3 home draw with Portsmouth in the fifth round meant that United had to travel to Fratton Park for a replay, which they won 3–1. They were drawn away to Chelsea in the quarter-final and it was at Stamford Bridge that the Cup dream came to an end following a single goal defeat.

At the season's close, United embarked on a month long tour of the United States and Canada, playing 11 matches in far-flung places including New York, Los Angeles and Toronto.

United began the 1950–51 season with a couple of new faces in their starting line-up. Reg Allen, signed from Queen's Park Rangers, donned the goalkeeper's shirt for the opening game of the campaign, and at No. 4 was Eddie McIlvenny. A few months earlier he had skippered the United States of America side to a famous 1–0 victory over England in a World Cup match in Belo Horizonte, Brazil. McIlvenny retained his place in the side for the next match, but despite staying at Old Trafford for three seasons, he didn't make another competitive appearance. Allen, by contrast, became the club's first-choice keeper for the next couple of seasons. Missing from the line-up was winger Charlie Mitten, who had left to join Colombian club Santa Fe of Bogota.

The club once again got off to a reasonable start, losing just three of the first dozen matches. During that spell they remained unbeaten at Old Trafford, a record which did much to ensure that United were once more installed among the contenders for the league championship.

As the season wore on, United stayed, for the best part, in touch with the leaders, but it wasn't until the closing stages that their real credentials began to surface. Tottenham Hotspur had emerged as the front runners during the second half of the season and they eventually claimed the title with a four-point advantage over United. Busby's team were forced to settle for second best yet again and there wasn't any consolation where the FA Cup was concerned.

Drawn at home in the opening three rounds, United defeated Oldham Atheltic (4–1), Leeds United (4–0) and Arsenal (1–0), but were eliminated 1–0 at the quarter-final stage by Birmingham City at St Andrew's.

The 1951–52 season dawned with many United supporters beginning to wonder if their team was ever going to claim the league championship. They were becoming accustomed to seeing other teams lift the trophy while United were the perennial runners-up. Four times in five seasons they had appeared to be in with an excellent chance of collecting the silverware, but each time they missed out.

The FA Cup triumph in 1948 was a marvellous achievement that everyone cherished and wouldn't have been missed for the world, but however happy they were to wallow in the glitz and glamour of the Cup and revel in its unparalleled excitement, the holy grail for them and every other club remained the league title. United had proved beyond all doubt that they were up to the job with a remarkable level of consistency, but they still needed to go that extra mile to claim their first championship in more than 40 years.

The team was packed with top-bracket players – United were one of the top sides of the day and each season opened with optimism brimming over. On Wednesday, 22 August 1951, the faithful gathered for the first home game of the season, and this time they were embarking on a voyage that would end with all their hopes and dreams fulfilled. Middlesbrough provided the opposition that afternoon and they were sent on their way back to Teesside having lost 4–2. Jack Rowley grabbed a hat-trick, his second in four days. He scored a trio against West Bromwich Albion at the Hawthorns on the season's opening day.

It was a great start for Rowley and an equally satisfactory launch to the campaign for the club. They were, as so often in recent years, instantly looked upon as one of the teams likely to succeed. A series of favourable early results put them at the top of the table on a couple of occasions, but it wasn't all plain sailing. Successive defeats at Tottenham and at home to Preston at the end of September caused them to slip from grace, but overall there were many opportunities to celebrate the collection of two points. As Christmas loomed United found themselves in a good position among the front-runners.

The basis of the team remained much the same as it had for the previous five seasons, but several new players were introduced as the season unfolded. Johnny Berry, an import from Birmingham City, made the right-wing berth his own; Roger Byrne, a future captain, and Jackie Blanchflower both made their debuts in a goalless draw against Liverpool at Anfield.

Any fears that a protracted run in the FA Cup could derail United's championship ambitions were quickly removed when Hull City, of the Second Division, produced a shock 2–0 third-round win at Old Trafford. It was a disappointing early exit, but at least it left the way clear for Busby and his boys to press on with the season's more important work – the task of trying to land the league championship.

Arsenal, Portsmouth and Tottenham Hotspur emerged as the biggest threats to United's ambitions, but as the final day of the season arrived only the Gunners – who, by an amazing quirk of the fixture list, were in Manchester to play United – still had an outside chance of snatching the title from Busby's grasp. They would have to beat United by seven clear goals to take the honour on goal average.

More than 53,000 gathered at Old Trafford to see if United could brush aside Arsenal's challenge and end the long wait for the ultimate in domestic football glory. They had no need to worry. Jack Rowley proceeded to end the season in the same style in which he had opened it by claiming a hat-trick as United stormed to a spectacular 6–1 victory.

The league championship flag was back at Old Trafford for the first time in 41 years and the tag of "champion runners-up" had finally been shed. There was no added prize of European qualification in those days, just the glory of becoming champions of England, but after five seasons of near misses, both United and their supporters were ecstatic.

After another extensive tour of North America, United prepared to defend their hard-won title. Busby pinned his faith on the men who had brought glory to the club the previous season, but it was soon evident that the make-up of the side would need a major overall.

The campaign opened poorly with United slipping into the lower reaches of the First Division table after winning just three of the opening 11 fixtures. Concerns were aired in various quarters, but they were alerting Matt Busby to nothing he hadn't already identified.

The team was beginning to age, but he was already making his plans for the future and was quick to declare that there was a deep pool of talent in the club's junior and reserve sides and that there was no cause to worry. His assessment of the situation was to prove uncannily prophetic.

The talented players to whom he referred were youngsters such as Duncan Edwards, David Pegg, Eddie Colman, Wilf McGuinness and Bill Foulkes. Their day was to come and in a steady transition they took over from the old-guard.

The first of Busby's great sides was starting to suffer the ravages of time, but they had helped to lay the foundations of a modern Manchester United that would eventually be accepted as one of football's greatest clubs. It was another three seasons before the league title returned to Old Trafford and by then the likes of Allenby Chilton, Jack Rowley, Stanley Pearson and Johnny Carey had moved on. Their part in the United story was completed and their place in the club's history assured.

Opposite: Reds' goalkeeper Jack Crompton collects the ball as an Aston Villa forward closes in during United's 4–0 win at Villa Park in March 1950.

1948 FA CUP FINAL

MANCHESTER UNITED (1) 4 BLACKPOOL (2) 2

24 APRIL 1948, WEMBLEY

UNITED AND THEIR staunchly loyal supporters were hungry for success after more than 30 years without a senior trophy to celebrate. Only the more senior of the club's legion of fans could remember the glory days before the First World War and the only FA Cup victory to date, against Bristol City in 1909. So when United reached the FA Cup final in 1948, the achievement was greeted with predictable excitement and relief!

Busby's team, who were still in enforced exile and playing their home games at Manchester City's Maine Road, endured a tortuous route to the final. Three times they were drawn at home, but on two of those occasions, with City also coming out of the bag first, they were forced to make alternative arrangements. Having already overcome Aston Villa (away) 6–4 in the third round, they played Liverpool in the fourth round at Goodison Park winning 3–0, and Charlton in the fifth at Huddersfield Town's Leeds Road, winning 2–0. Preston North End were comfortably dealt with 4–1 at Maine Road and then it was on to Hillsborough where the final hurdle, in the form of Derby County, was negotiated – a 3–1 victory.

So for the first time in 39 years, United supporters became engaged in the annual scramble for Cup final tickets. Blackpool, of Stanley Matthews and Stanley Mortensen fame, were the opponents and those fans lucky enough to obtain a precious ticket were treated to a terrific match. United, playing in a changed strip of royal blue shirts, twice fell behind, but eventually prevailed to take both the game and the FA Cup with a 4–2 win. Jack Rowley (2), Stanley Pearson and Johnny Anderson scored the goals which United supporters cheered to the echo.

It was a match of rare quality that many observers believed to be among the finest ever to grace the twin towers. Blackpool were twice in front and held the lead at half-time after Rowley's 30th minute goal had been sandwiched between Eddie Shimwell's 14th minute penalty and Mortensen's strike ten minutes before the interval.

The Seasiders, it seemed, were destined to spoil United's day for with 20 minutes remaining it was white-shirted Blackpool who were still in charge. But then there was a remarkable transformation, and three goals – from Rowley, Pearson and Anderson – in the next 15 minutes swung the tie in United's favour.

It was a great moment for United, for Manchester and for Matt Busby who had restored the club to trophy-winning status in only his second full season. Manchester went wild with jubilation when the gleaming trophy was paraded through the streets of the city and shown to a vast throng waiting in Albert Square. The club's supporters had waited a long time to see their team emerge from the shadows and they were determined to enjoy this momentous event to the full.

Manchester United (manager Matt Busby): Crompton, Carey, Aston, Anderson, Chilton, Cockburn, Delaney, Morris, Rowley, Pearson, Mitten
Scorers: Rowley 2, Pearson, Anderson

Blackpool (manager Joe Smith): Robinson, Shimwell, Crossland, Johnston, Hayward, Kelly, Matthews, Munro, Mortensen, Dick, Rickett
Scorers: Shimwell (pen), Mortensen

Attendance: 100,000

Jack Rowley rises above the Blackpool defence to send in a powerful header as United battled to win their first major trophy since 1911.

THE RETURN TO OLD TRAFFORD

Enemy action by the Luftwaffe's bombers left Old Trafford's main stand almost totally destroyed.

MANY YOUNGER Manchester United supporters find it hard to accept that their team once spent three entire seasons at Maine Road, the home of arch-rivals Manchester City. It wasn't by choice that the Red half of Manchester trekked to Moss Side on the days when the Blues were either out of action or playing away, but they were mightily grateful that City's huge stadium had been generously made available while their own headquarters was out of commission.

Matt Busby and his team were forced into exile after Luftwaffe bombs had inflicted severe damage on Old Trafford during air raids in the early 1940s. It wasn't that the German air crews were deliberately trying to demolish the famous football stadium on Warwick Road North, or put United on the street. It was just that a few bombs had strayed from the intended target of nearby Trafford Park, at the time one of the biggest industrial estates in the world. Several heavy engineering factories were based in Trafford Park along with countless other manufacturing facilities. The Park was also in close proximity to Manchester Docks, which at the height of their powers were the third busiest in the United Kingdom. Hitler's air force was making sorties in that area to try to debilitate the vast industrial complex and cut off its supply lines, but in doing so, struck Old Trafford Football Ground on more than one occasion.

The most serious was on the night of 11 March 1941 when the ground's 10,000 seat main stand was destroyed along with parts of the standing terraces, the dressing-rooms and club offices. The scene was one of massive destruction with the main stand taking the brunt of the Luftwaffe's poor marksmanship.

When Old Trafford opened in 1910 with an 80,000 capacity, it was envisaged that it would eventually be developed to hold 100,000. For various reasons, chiefly the club's lack of success and subsequent shortage of funds, those plans were never implemented. Nevertheless, it remained one of the largest and best-equipped stadiums in England at the outbreak of the Second World War, a status that was left in ruins following the air strikes. United were not then the hugely wealthy club they became in later decades, so the enormous damage to their home patch was a grievous blow. There was no possible chance, particularly with the country in the grip of war, of funding what would amount to huge repair bills. The club filed a claim for war damage, but that was a long drawn-out procedure. It eventually provided some financial assistance; in the fullness of time, money was made available for demolition and essential construction work.

Some matches were staged at Old Trafford in the early years after the end of the conflict, but the ground wasn't considered ready for the first team until the onset of the 1949–50 season. Over the next 40 years, United's famous home ground was transformed into one of the world's greatest football arenas, but to the club and supporters of the 1940s, it was enough just to be back on familiar territory.

JOHNNY CAREY

DEFENDER (MANCHESTER UNITED 1936–53)

DOZENS OF GREAT PLAYERS have pulled on the famous red shirt over the years, but few enjoyed the universal admiration that was bestowed on Johnny Carey during his distinguished career. A gentleman footballer, he gave United loyal and unswerving service in two spells separated by the Second World War. Captain of the excellent post-war side, he was Matt Busby's voice on the field as football returned to normality.

Having played for Home Farm and St James' Gate, two famed clubs in his native Dublin, Carey broadened his horizons in November 1936 and moved to England to sign for United. Within 12 months he had made not only his league debut for United but also his first appearance in the full Republic of Ireland side.

His league bow came in a Second Division game against Southampton at Old Trafford on 25 September 1937. Carey played at inside-left and United lost 2–1. His debut on the international stage six weeks later was a slightly happier occasion, the Republic drawing 3–3 with Norway at Dalymount Park, Dublin.

Over the next two seasons, Carey steadily established himself in United's first team and became a regular choice for his country. His progress was interrupted when war was declared against Germany and he joined the army. He returned to Manchester at the end of the conflict to pick up the pieces of his career.

Carey resumed at inside-forward during the 1945–46 wartime league season, but before the end of that campaign he made the transition to right full-back via a spell at half-back (midfield). That was the position he occupied with distinction for the next seven seasons. Matt Busby made Carey the team captain, which turned out to be a masterstroke. The Irishman was a dedicated, fanatically loyal professional who would do anything for the good of the team, and did on many occasions.

It is as a right-back in United's first great post-war side that he will always be remembered. In fact, he pulled on every other shirt, except No. 11 outside-left, at some point during his days at Old Trafford. He even started one match, against Sunderland in February 1953, in the goalkeeper's jersey, after the club's recognized custodians had been ruled out.

Carey skippered United to victory in the 1948 FA Cup final and the league championship four years later, and was captain of the Rest of Europe side against Great Britain in 1947 at Hampden Park. He was voted Footballer of the Year by the professional football writers in 1949.

When his playing days came to an end in 1953, he moved into management with Blackburn Rovers, and later filled the same post with Everton, Leyton Orient, and Nottingham Forest before returning for a second spell at Ewood Park.

Johnny Carey with the FA Cup following United's 4–2 win in the 1948 FA Cup final over Blackpool at Wembley.

ALLENBY CHILTON

DEFENDER (MANCHESTER UNITED 1938–55)

UNITED HAVE HAD their fair share of top-quality centre-halves over the years; Charlie Roberts, Frank Barson, Bill Foulkes, Gordon McQueen, Gary Pallister and Jaap Stam immediately spring to mind. There's no doubt that Allenby Chilton belongs, on merit, in the midst of that esteemed company. He was the rock on which Matt Busby built his first great side in the years following the end of the Second World War. United had great players in every department including the heart of the defence. Chilton was a mighty tower of strength for almost nine seasons.

He was born in South Hylton, County Durham, in September 1918 and played local football before joining Liverpool as an amateur in 1938. He didn't make the first team and moved on to sign for United in November that year. It was the start of a career that spanned almost two decades although it was disrupted by the ravages of the war.

He made his league debut for United against Charlton Athletic at The Valley on 2 September 1939. That was the last peacetime fixture the club undertook before organized football was suspended. Having survived active service, but not without being wounded, he returned to take his place in the side being assembled by Matt Busby and Jimmy Murphy. He was in the team that opened the 1946–47 First Division programme, making his second league appearance almost seven years after he had made his debut.

Chilton, a strapping six-footer, became a fixture in United's defence until he handed over the position to Mark Jones in 1955. In fact, his last league outing, against Wolverhampton Wanderers at Old Trafford on 23 February 1955, came at the end of a four-year stint without missing a single league match – a run of 166 games – a marvellous testimony to his determination, fitness and consistency.

Chilton collected an FA Cup winner's medal in 1948 and was an ever-present in the team that lifted the league championship four years later. He won two full caps for England, playing against Northern Ireland in 1950 and France the following year.

Within a month of his final league appearance for United, he had left Old Trafford to take the job of player-manager at Grimsby Town. He inherited a club in trouble and despite playing in their last 13 games of the season, they still finished bottom of the Third Division (North) and were forced to seek re-election. Having retained their status, Grimsby, under Chilton's leadership, won their section the following season. He retired as a player in October 1956, but continued as their manager until April 1959 when he moved to Wigan Athletic and, later, Hartlepool United. However, it's as a no-nonsense, dominating centre-half that he will always be remembered.

Allenby Chilton, a centre-half who became one of the stalwarts of United's great post-Second World War side.

JIMMY DELANEY

FORWARD (MANCHESTER UNITED 1946–50)

Jimmy Delaney delivers a cross in the 1948 FA Cup sixth round tie against Preston North End at Maine Road.

SCOTTISH INTERNATIONAL Jimmy Delaney joined United from Celtic for £4,000 in February 1946. He had been out of the game for close on a year with a shoulder injury and his acquisition was looked upon as something of a gamble, which Matt Busby was obviously prepared to take. Busby's judgement proved to be spot on; Delaney gave United wonderful service for more than four seasons before he moved back north of the border to play for Aberdeen.

Delaney was, in fact, the first player to be signed by Matt Busby in exchange for a fee. Another forward, Ted Buckle, had put pen to paper some months earlier, but he had arrived direct from serving in the Royal Navy.

Born in Cleland, Lanarkshire, in September 1914, Delaney started his senior career with Celtic 19 years later after spending time with several junior clubs. He made his Scottish League debut away to Heart of Midlothian in August 1934 and was an immediate hit with Celtic's fanatical following. He went on to end the season scoring 15 goals in 30 league appearances.

The following season – 1935–1936 – he collected the first of his two Scottish League championship medals. The other came two seasons later, and in between, Celtic defeated Aberdeen 2–1 at Hampden Park to win the 1937 Scottish Cup and provide Delaney with another medal.

It was the signing of Tommy Bogan from Hibernian in February 1946 that hastened Delaney's departure from Celtic Park to Old Trafford; a few years later Bogan also joined Manchester United.

Delaney's earlier injury problems seemed to have disappeared when he began his career with United; he was rarely missing from the United side during almost five years at the club. He collected an FA Cup winner's medal in 1948 and in total he scored 28 goals in 183 league and Cup appearances. His goalscoring ratio had slowed somewhat from his Celtic days, but the return was nevertheless creditable for a player who was predominantly a winger.

Delaney, a fast, skilful flank player, moved back to Scotland in November 1950 to join Aberdeen and a year later he signed for Falkirk. Three years later he crossed the Irish Sea to join Derry City, with whom he won an Irish FA Cup winner's medal in 1954. It made him the first player to win FA Cup winner's medals in Scotland, England and Northern Ireland. Remarkably, he almost added to his collection in the Irish Republic, but Shamrock Rovers beat his side, Cork Athletic, in the 1956 final.

He eventually concluded his career in football, which included 13 full caps, back in his native Scotland as manager of Highland League club Elgin City. Delaney passed away in September 1989, but he left behind a wealth of memories for those lucky enough to have seen him in action.

JACK ROWLEY

FORWARD (MANCHESTER UNITED 1937–55)

THE MAIN OBJECT of the game of football is to deposit the ball in your opponents' net and there have been few better exponents of that vital art than Jack Rowley, a powerful forward with United either side of the Second World War.

A Midlands lad who first saw the light of day in Wolverhampton in October 1920, he launched his football career with the famous local club. His stay at Molineux failed to bring him first-team football and early in 1937 he moved south to Bournemouth and Boscombe Athletic. Rowley's luck changed soon after arriving at Dean Court and he started to find the net on a regular basis, a fact that soon caught the eye of clubs around the country. Nine months after joining Bournemouth, he was on the move again to join United.

He made his league debut for the Red Devils in a Second Division match against Sheffield Wednesday at Old Trafford on 23 October 1937. He failed to score in that match, but it was a different story when he made his second appearance six weeks later. Swansea Town (now City) were the visitors and United romped to a 5–1 win. Rowley, playing on the left wing scored four of the goals. Rowley's pursuit of goals on Manchester United's behalf had started in dramatic fashion and he was barely two months beyond his 17th birthday.

Rowley quickly made himself at home in the team alongside established Old Trafford favourites such as George Vose, Billy McKay and Billy Bryant. He became a virtual fixture in the side as United won promotion to the First Division. The following season was the last before war broke out and Rowley's highly promising career was put on hold.

Like many of his fellow professionals, Rowley joined the army and saw active service during the war. When the hostilities came to an end, he made his way back to Manchester in order to continue his career under the stewardship of Matt Busby.

He proceeded to develop into a centre-forward of the highest calibre as part of one of the finest front lines ever to represent Manchester United. His ferocious shooting quickly got him dubbed "The Gunner", although it wasn't only on the ground that Rowley plundered his goals for he was also highly proficient with his head.

He scored twice as United beat Blackpool to lift the FA Cup in 1948, and four years later, he scored 30 goals for the side that won the club's first league championship since before the First World War.

Rowley won six full caps for England, a total that would have been considerably more but for the remarkable number of top-class centre-forwards at the national side's disposal, including Tommy Lawton, Stanley Mortensen, Jackie Milburn and Roy Bentley.

When Rowley's United career ended in February 1955, he had scored 208 goals in 422 league and Cup matches. On leaving Old Trafford, he joined Plymouth Argyle as player-manager and after retiring from playing in 1957 he continued to act as their manager until 1960 when he took on the same post at Oldham Athletic. He later managed Wrexham and Bradford Park Avenue as well as coaching top Dutch club Ajax.

Jack Rowley, a prolific goalscorer in Matt Busby's first great side.

CHAPTER FIVE

THE
BUSBY
BABES

DESPITE UNITED'S LEAGUE CHAMPIONSHIP SUCCESS IN
1951–52, MATT BUSBY KNEW HE MUST REJUVENATE HIS
AGEING SIDE. OVER THE NEXT FEW YEARS, HIS BOLD
INVESTMENT IN YOUTH HELPED TO CREATE ONE OF THE MOST
EXCITING TEAMS IN ENGLISH FOOTBALL HISTORY.

Hit it with your instep! Manager Matt Busby advises his babes on the finer points of football technique.

IT SAYS SOMETHING about the impact of the Busby Babes that nearly half a century later the nickname still evokes all the best traditions of Manchester United – youth, attacking football and, of course, success.

The policy of finding young players and nurturing them into the first team was one that Matt Busby had always had in mind. He wanted to create a team made up of youngsters whom he had taken from school and brought up in what he believed to be the right way. To help him achieve that goal, he gathered around him a carefully chosen team of assistants and advisers led by assistant manager Jimmy Murphy whom Busby had met towards the end of the war. A former player, Murphy had made up for any technical deficiencies in his game with guts, spirit and intelligence. In some ways, he was Busby's complete opposite; where Busby was calm, Murphy was fiery, but they made a perfect team. As Harry Gregg once observed, "Jimmy and Matt together could have climbed Everest. Matt made Jimmy and Jimmy made Matt. They needed each other." Eventually, Busby brought into the first team all of Jimmy's "Golden Apples" as he called them. He never liked the term Babes.

But it wasn't just Busby and Murphy who ran what was to prove to be a spectacularly successful youth policy. Bert Whalley looked after the first team and also acted as chief scout. Tom Curry was the first-team trainer and Bill Inglis looked after the second team. Busby ensured that he had the right people looking for youngsters to pour into these ranks. Joe Armstrong kept a steady influx of schoolboy

talent coming in, particularly from Ireland and Northern Ireland where Billy Behan (Dublin) and Bob Bishop and Bob Harper (Belfast) made sure no potential was overlooked.

The quality of the people appointed by Busby can be seen in United's dominance of the FA Youth Cup, which they won on five successive occasions from its inception in the 1952–53 season. It can also be seen in the promotion to the first team of so many young players. During the 1952–53 season, Jackie Blanchflower, Bill Foulkes, Dennis Viollet, Jeff Whitefoot, David Pegg, John Doherty and Duncan Edwards were all drafted in on occasion, together with new signing Tommy Taylor.

However, the groundwork for the emergence of the Babes began some years before. From the summer of 1949, Busby intensified the scouting operation and put into place a "nursery" system to help young players develop. Landladies were interviewed and appointed so as to ensure that the boys who came to United would have something of a home away from home and therefore feel less homesick.

The club acted quickly when they spotted talent. The signings of David Pegg and Duncan Edwards are good examples. Both were playing for England Schoolboys when United become aware of them.

Pegg's father, a miner, was determined that his son would not be exploited cheaply. He met every manager who expressed an interest and always asked what they thought of his prospects. Busby, never one to employ hyperbole, merely said, "With reasonable luck, your son will be successful as a professional footballer." The matter-of-fact approach won over Pegg senior and David signed.

Duncan Edwards needed little persuasion. Although the pride of Dudley, the Midlands and England Schoolboy was snatched from under the nose of rivals Wolves.

"I didn't need to 'sell' United to big Duncan," recalled Matt. "As soon as I introduced myself, he said, 'I think Manchester United is the greatest team in the world. I'd give anything to play for you.'"

Edwards, Pegg and the other youngsters, including Roger Byrne, Albert Scanlon and Blanchflower, gave Busby a faith in the future of his team that few on the peripheries of the club could understand. They only saw an ageing first team and were astonished when the manager declared, "There is nothing to panic about. Before long you will see Manchester United back on top, beating the best."

When the team finished eighth in 1953, it was not the end of an era but the beginning, as Busby's second great team began to take shape. At the time, however, few saw it in that way. In fact, there wasn't a lot of optimism in English football in general. The humiliating defeat of the international team in 1950 by the football novices of the United States was compounded in 1953 and 1954 by 6–3 and 7–1 embarrassments at the hands of the Hungarians.

Typically though, Busby took inspiration from the quality of attacking play displayed by the Eastern Europeans. On a golf course in Scotland during the close season of 1953, he decided that the time had come to bring in some of the youngsters he had nurtured. Jackie Blanchflower, Duncan Edwards, Bill Foulkes and Dennis Viollet were drafted in for the league games against Huddersfield and Arsenal – two games many now declare to be the birth of the Babes, although Roger Byrne, Tommy Taylor and Johnny Berry had already established themselves as first-team players by this stage. Nonetheless, the team was undoubtedly now a predominantly young one, very different from the ageing first XI who had won the title in 1952.

Success did not come overnight. It took a couple of campaigns before the true potential of the players became apparent. The 1953-54 season ended with United fourth. The next season they were fifth. More youngsters had been introduced, notably Albert Scanlon, Mark Jones and Billy (Liam) Whelan.

The manager's faith was rewarded in the following campaign as his team stormed to championship glory, beating runners-up Blackpool by a margin of 11 points. The average age of the United players that season was 22. The line-up usually read: Wood, Foulkes, Byrne, Whitefoot (to begin with, then Eddie Colman), Jones, Edwards, Berry, Blanchflower (or Doherty or Whelan), Taylor, Viollet and

David Pegg vied with Albert Scanlon for the left–wing spot in the 1950s.

Pegg. The only players still in the team from the title-winning side of four years earlier were Johnny Berry and Roger Byrne.

Byrne, a full-back, had become the cornerstone of the team. He was the first of the Babes to break through and he established himself as a great leader in the process. A superb reader of the game with excellent positional sense, he was always making telling passes that rarely missed their target. Busby once said he never saw Tom Finney or Stanley Matthews have a good game when Byrne was playing opposite them. He was also pretty useful going forward as an attacking overlapping full-back, at a time when the phrase had yet to be coined.

Berry was a right winger of no little skill who could also poach goals. He quickly secured his place in the team after signing from Birmingham City in 1951. Despite being only 5ft 5ins tall, he possessed a powerful shot, and with his pace and sharp footwork, he

72

was very difficult to tackle.

A number of big names had made way for their younger counterparts. John Aston was one of those replaced, his reaction showing the esteem in which the manager was held by all at the club.

"Matt Busby had established himself as a far-seeing and shrewd manager," he said. "He had won the respect of all of us which meant that it was easier for him to put over these new ideas. It was very disappointing for the players who had to give way to new men but we were not blind to the fact that the Boss had created a tremendously successful youth team. We accepted the changes because when he said it was for the good of the club, we knew that it was. He treats everyone with respect and in turn is greatly respected. It's this quality which enabled him to move from one successful era to another with a team that became the great Busby Babes."

The team that won the championship in 1956 was indeed made up of great players; young or not, they had all earned their place in the starting line-up.

In goal, Ray Wood made the position his own after initially vying with Jack Crompton and Reg Allen. United had paid Darlington £5,000 for him, aged 18, in 1949. He had previously made just a dozen league appearances. When he didn't get into the first team to begin with, he could sometimes be found playing in the A team as a centre-forward. Later in his career, he moved to Huddersfield Town and subsequently Bradford City and Barnsley before a series of coaching appointments took him to Canada, Zambia and America.

In front of Wood was Byrne at left-back and Foulkes at right-back. Foulkes, a defensive rock from a mining background, had come to United after being spotted as an amateur with Whiston Boys Club. By 1953, he had established himself in the first team and he went on to become one of the club's longest servers, having a spell as captain.

During the 1955–56 season, there was a battle for the right-half position. Jeff Whitefoot started the season there and played enough games to earn a championship medal. A schoolboy international who made his league debut aged 16, he came to United as an office boy and established himself in the first team during the 1953–54 season. A good

passer and tackler, it was an indication of the competition for places at United that he couldn't hold on to his first-team place, which was eventually occupied by Eddie "Snake Hips" Colman.

Some said Eddie could send the stand the wrong way with his shimmy, such was the quality of his deceptive body swerve. This, together with his dazzling dribbles, ball-winning skills and creative ability, made him a favourite of the crowd. Off the pitch, he took a fancy to the Teddy Boy outfits of the day and was a bit of a jiver in his drainpipe trousers and crepe-soled suede shoes. On the pitch, he struck up an astonishing understanding with Duncan Edwards. Together, these two contributed greatly to the attacking force of the young United team.

The name Duncan Edwards still evokes misty-eyed nostalgia from anyone lucky enough to have seen him play. "The only player who ever made me feel inferior" is how Bobby Charlton described him. Edwards had every attribute needed to become the complete footballer. Speed, power, control, courage – you name it, Edwards had it. Jimmy Murphy had no doubts about just how good the half-back from Dudley was.

"When I used to hear Muhammad Ali proclaim to the world that he was the greatest, I used to smile," said Murphy. "You see, the greatest of them all was an English footballer named Duncan Edwards."

Probably to balance the attacking instincts of Colman and Edwards, Busby put Mark Jones between them at centre-half. A sturdy, dependable stopper, Jones was a bricklayer's apprentice before he joined United. He came through the ranks and made his first league appearance at the age of 17. Having to wait in line for a first-team place behind club captain Allenby Chilton required some patience – Chilton once had a run of 166 consecutive appearances – but Jones got his chance in the 1954–55 season and quickly established himself as a regular.

Tommy Taylor was by now the regular centre-forward. The "smiling assassin", as he was called by one reporter, always looked as though he was enjoying his football, a perpetual smile beneath his mop of black

Mark Jones was just 17 when he made his first team debut in 1950.

Overleaf: Ray Wood won two league championships with Manchester United.

hair. Busby signed him from Barnsley in March 1953 for the odd fee of £29,999. Legend has it that Matt gave the spare pound to the tea lady so as not to burden Taylor with a £30,000 tag. The grandson of a Barnsley player, Taylor had been taken on to the groundstaff at the club straight from school. Later, during his army national service, he sustained a serious knee injury and was discharged. Fortunately, he made a full recovery and as an inside-forward was the target for a number of clubs before Busby's customary charm persuaded him to leave Barnsley. He became an instant success at United at centre-forward with his fierce shot and powerful heading. His apparently endless stamina also enabled him to make countless unselfish runs, creating spaces for his team-mates to exploit.

At inside-left, Dennis Viollet was settled in the first team. A graduate of United's nursery system, he had joined the club at 14 and become a professional at 17. Captain of Manchester Schoolboys and capped five times by England Schoolboys, he made his debut at inside-right during the 1952–53 season, but switched flanks to become one of the club's finest ever players in a No. 10 shirt.

The inside-right position alternated between Jackie Blanchflower and John Doherty to begin with and then Billy Whelan staked a claim. Jackie Blanchflower's older brother, Danny, was the captain of the Tottenham Hotspur team that won the double in 1961. Jackie, an Irish Schoolboy international, made his league debut at right half-back before moving into the inside-right role. Despite a lack of pace, he was an adaptable and stylish player. Doherty was skilful and thoughtful but plagued by a succession of knee operations that didn't help his chances in what was becoming a very competitive squad.

David Pegg occupied the left wing for the majority of the campaign. His stream of highly accurate crosses was gratefully pounced on by Taylor and Viollet.

Although the Babes won the 1955–56 championship by 11 points, it wasn't until the turn of the year that their superiority really became apparent. Having gone top of the table in early December, the team moved into top gear, losing just twice in the second half of the season and establishing a winning margin equalled only by Preston, Sunderland and Aston Villa in the previous century. Taylor got the lion's share of the goals, with 25; Viollet and Pegg contributed 20 and nine respectively. Perhaps most remarkable was Bobby Charlton's contribution, hitting the target 10 times in 14 league appearances. Clearly one for the future, Charlton came in whenever Taylor or Viollet were injured. A miner's son and the nephew of Newcastle great Jackie Milburn, Charlton was to become one of the most popular players in Manchester United's history. He began as an inside-forward but later spent a considerable spell at outside-left where his surging runs and awesome shooting were always a powerful combination. He eventually played at centre-forward for both club and country and was renowned not only for his sublime skills but also for his consummate professionalism and sportsmanship. The 1955–56 season proved to be just a taste of what was to come from Charlton.

Matt Busby's nursery system had come good. All but three of the title-winning team were home-grown players and it came as little surprise when United went on to repeat their championship success the following season. This time it was Tottenham who finished a distant second, eight points behind the leaders.

The team had altered little over those 12 months, the noticeable changes being Whelan's securing of the inside-right position and the continuing emergence of Bobby Charlton. Whelan's tally of 26 goals was remarkable for an inside-forward whose primary role was to create for others. Billy was a product of the famous Dublin nursery, Home Farm FC, that had served United well over the years. A superb dribbler with tremendous close control, Whelan seemed to glide effortlessly past players as well as having the rather handy attribute of being a clinical finisher.

It was a high-scoring season all round with Taylor striking 22 times and Viollet on 16 occasions. The championship was taken care of by Easter, and United's final points total of 64 was the highest for 26 years.

As well as winning two successive titles, United were making progress in both the European Cup and the FA Cup. The European run was of particular interest as United were the first English team to take part in the competition.

Back in April 1955, the French sports paper *L'Equipe* had arranged a meeting between 16 European clubs, including the English champions Chelsea, to discuss a champions cup. The Football League were not enthusiastic about what they saw as a competition that would intrude on domestic fixtures, and dissuaded Chelsea from taking part. But when United became champions the following season, there was no stopping Matt Busby. Allegedly, he went to see Stanley Rous of the FA and asked if there was anything in the small print that actually prevented United from entering. Satisfied there wasn't, Busby persuaded the United board to accept the invitation, citing the extra revenue that would be generated for buying floodlights and covering an expanding wage bill. An extra competition also meant more opportunities to utilize all his players. Most of all, though, it was a challenge that the manager just couldn't resist, a chance to prove that United were not only the finest team in the country, but also in Europe. So began his quest for the holy grail, European glory.

Fans invade the Old Trafford pitch to celebrate the 1955–56 league championship triumph.

Anderlecht were the first opponents in United's inaugural European Cup run of 1956–57. Two legs later, Busby's youngsters had scored a dozen goals and the Anderlecht captain Jeff Mermans admitted, "It was an education. They should pick this whole team for England."

Borussia Dortmund were next. A 3–2 victory took United to the quarter-finals and a meeting with Athletic Bilbao. The first leg was away, and United were in trouble before they even arrived. Bad weather meant the plane had to circle for 20 minutes in gale-force winds, causing Duncan Edwards to be airsick. The rain hadn't stopped for two days and United ended the first half 3–0 down. They staged a recovery of sorts after the interval and the final score was 5–3 to Bilbao.

There was certainly plenty for United to do in the second leg but, not for the first time under Busby, the team responded to the challenge. Berry, Taylor and Viollet got the goals in a match one newspaper described as "the greatest victory in soccer history".

The scene was set for an encounter with Real Madrid, winners of the inaugural European Cup the previous year. United's run in the competition at their first attempt had already captured the imagination of the public and cemented the reputation of the Busby Babes as the most exciting English football team in living memory.

The first leg in Madrid was a passionate affair with Real running out 3–1 winners. The return match – the first floodlit European night at Old Trafford – was, if anything, even more heated than the first. A 2–2 draw wasn't enough to keep United in the competition but the fans' appetite had been whetted. The European obsession was growing.

On the domestic front, there was further excitement when United put together an FA Cup run that took them all the way to the final. With the league already won, an historic double was up for grabs. Aston Villa stood in the way.

Busby later admitted that on the morning of the match, he had never been more sure of victory in his footballing career, but he hadn't foreseen the controversy that was to follow.

Six minutes into the match at Wembley, Ray Wood collected a header from Villa's Peter McParland and was about to kick it clear. But McParland continued his run and charged into the keeper, shattering Wood's cheekbone. Even in the days of little protection for goalkeepers, it was an outrageous challenge and Wood had to be carried off the field.

Overleaf: Ray Wood is carried off at Wembley in the 1957 FA Cup final. Bill Foulkes believed that Peter McParland deliberately head-butted Wood.

Eddie Colman shoots for goal against Red Star Belgrade on the eve of the fateful crash. The picture is a colourised still from a TV documentary broadcast in 1998.

"Looking back, I believe that Ray was targetted, deliberately put out of the game," insisted Bill Foulkes. "It was the way it was done. I watched McParland, he went right for him, he head-butted him. It was too obvious because Ray had the ball in his hands for seconds before McParland came in. His head went straight into his face and he was out of the game."

United struggled on, holding Villa to a scoreless first half. No substitutions were allowed and Jackie Blanchflower took over in goal, Wood bravely playing on in the wing position to make up the numbers although he was little more than a passenger. The team had lost their balance and Villa exploited their advantage in the second half, McParland scoring twice to add insult to injury. Taylor pulled one back and, in the final few minutes, Wood went back in goal but it was not United's day.

Nonetheless, it had been an exciting season and Busby's team was clearly on the up. The squad he had assembled was years away from peaking and already challenging for honours on three fronts. It all boded well for the 1957–58 season.

Things began brightly with three straight wins, over Leicester, Everton and Manchester City, and 10 goals scored, only one conceded. After six games, the goals tally had risen to 22 scored. Around Christmas, United went on a seven-match unbeaten run including a 4–0 thrashing of Leicester City. The game marked the debut of new signing Harry Gregg for whom Busby paid Doncaster Rovers £23,500. It was a record fee for a goalkeeper and showed once again that Busby was not afraid to spend money when he felt it was necessary.

"It was an honour," said Gregg. "Of the 40-odd players who had come through the club, the manager had only bought four, and I was one of them. The very fact they were interested was unbelievable. The team were already becoming known worldwide and I was joining the illustrious Busby Babes."

It became clear to the new keeper just what a strong squad he was

joining when he noted that the reserve team had 10 current international players in it! Others also noticed the strength of the Babes. Europe's leading sportswriters voted both Duncan Edwards and Tommy Taylor into the top five players in Europe.

Matt Busby planned to make full use of the players at his disposal with a triple assault on the League, FA Cup and Europe. By the turn of the year, everything was going to plan. United were in good shape in the League, had reached the fifth round of the Cup and were, again, creating excitement in Europe.

Shamrock Rovers were beaten 6–0 and 3–2, Dukla Prague 3–1 on aggregate and the quarter-final first leg against Red Star Belgrade ended in a 2–1 home win. Before the return leg, two league encounters took place. The first was a 7–2 win over Bolton that included a Bobby Charlton hat-trick. The second was a trip to Highbury that turned out to be the Babes' last match on English soil. It lives in the memory of all lucky enough to have witnessed it.

The team that lined up to face Arsenal were the same XI who were later selected for the second leg against Belgrade. Harry Gregg was in goal, Bill Foulkes and Roger Byrne were the full-backs, with Eddie Colman, Mark Jones and Duncan Edwards supporting the front line of Ken Morgans, Bobby Charlton, Tommy Taylor, Dennis Viollet and Albert Scanlon.

Within 10 minutes, United had taken the lead. Viollet's pass was met by a thunderous shot from Edwards. Charlton made it 2–0 with a trademark blast that left the Arsenal keeper Jack Kelsey with no chance. Tommy Taylor added a third before half-time and victory seemed assured. But in the second half the home team staged a tremendous recovery. David Herd (later to join United) pulled a goal back, and then a brace from Jimmy Bloomfield levelled the scores.

Any thoughts that the visitors would settle for a draw were quickly dispersed. Matt Busby had built a team founded on entertainment and attacking football. As Bobby Charlton recalled, "For men who work on the shop floor, the one highlight of their week is to go and watch football. Matt used to say you should give that man something he can't do himself, something exciting. That's why Manchester United always play attacking football."

The team certainly stuck to their principles that afternoon in North London. The visitors pushed forward looking for a winner. Scanlon and Charlton combined to provide Viollet with United's fourth and then Taylor grabbed his second and United's fifth. But the drama wasn't over yet. Derek Tapscott slipped through United's tired defence to ensure the game finished on a knife-edge. United held on for an epic 5–4 victory. When the referee blew for time, the players collapsed in each other's arms. Supporters knew they had witnessed a magnificent game that had confirmed the Babes as the most exhilarating team of their generation. It was a fitting testament.

After that footballing exhibition, United prepared to make the trip to Belgrade and attention turned to the task ahead. Could United defend their slim one-goal advantage?

An answer seemed to be provided 90 seconds into the match when Viollet gave United a 1–0 lead. Charlton added two more and victory seemed assured. Of course, this being United there had to be more drama. Two minutes after half-time, Kostic pulled one back for Red Star. Then a mix-up between Foulkes and Tasic, Red Star's centre-forward ended with both players falling over each other and the referee pointing to the penalty spot. Tasic duly converted and the crowd were driven into a frenzy. Still United continued to attack, and several times came close, but Red Star were the next to score. A precise free-kick from Kostic eluded Gregg's fingertips and the game was level at 3–3. Despite further incidents at both ends, that was the way it finished and United were through, 5–4 aggregate winners.

After the match there was a formal ceremony and banquet before the night dissipated into rather less formal drinks and card games. The next morning everyone was in good spirits as they prepared for the flight home, via a refuelling stop in Munich, and what could be a title-deciding clash with Wolves.

But the team didn't get home, not that day, and some of them not at all. In the February snow and ice of Munich, the second great team built by Matt Busby came to a premature end. The footballing world was deprived of seeing the Babes grow up and many families had loved ones stolen from them. A glorious adventure ended in tragedy.

Busby and his babes in 1957: Back row (left to right): Colin Webster, Wilf McGuinness, Jackie Blanchflower, John Doherty, Eddie Colman. Middle row: Tom Curry (trainer), Bill Foulkes, Bobby Charlton, Fred Goodwin, Ray Wood, Bill Whelan, Mark Jones, Duncan Edwards, W. Inglis (assistant manager). Front row: Dennis Viollet, John Berry, Matt Busby (manager) Roger Byrne (captain), Jimmy Murphy (assistant manager), Tommy Taylor, David Pegg.

THE MUNICH

6 February 1958, the day a team died.

THE PLANE CRASH at Munich on 6 February 1958, which claimed the lives of 21 people including eight United players and three staff, left an indelible mark on the history of Manchester United Football Club. The tragedy tore apart a team seemingly destined for greatness. "We felt we were good enough to win the European Cup, we really felt it," said Munich survivor Bill Foulkes later reflecting on the impact of the tragedy.

Duncan Edwards, Roger Byrne, Eddie Colman, Mark Jones, David Pegg, Tommy Taylor, Billy Whelan and Geoff Bent (average age 24) all perished. The dead also included United coach Bert Whalley, trainer Tom Curry, club secretary Walter Crickmer and eight British journalists. It was both a football and human tragedy of immense proportions.

The team's ill-fated visit to Munich was a scheduled refuelling stop on the way back from Belgrade. The previous night, they had drawn 3–3 with Yugoslavian champions Red Star Belgrade to reach the European Cup semi-finals; 2–1 up from the home leg, United scored three in the first half, including a 30-yard thunderbolt shot by Bobby Charlton, but Red Star came back strongly and United only just hung on for an aggregate win.

After the match, the United team attended an official banquet in Belgrade and then they could relax. Matt Busby found a quiet room to have a couple of drinks with journalists and friends. The players meanwhile either went on to the British Embassy with the

pilots and stewardesses or played poker into the early hours. No one went too mad because there was a match the following Saturday against Wolves to consider, but there were still a few mild hangovers when the players assembled for the journey home the next morning.

From the beginning, nothing went to plan. On arrival at Belgrade airport, Johnny Berry couldn't find his passport and the flight was delayed. Eventually an immigration officer decided to unload the luggage from the plane's hold and they found Berry's passport in his suitcase.

The weather was murky and visibility was poor when the players finally boarded Flight 609 in mid-morning. However, Captain James Thain at the controls of the Elizabethan Class G–ALZU AS 57 Lord Burghley, with his co-pilot and friend Captain Kenneth Rayment alongside, made a smooth take-off and everything seemed to be going to plan. Following a short fuel stop, they expected to arrive back in Manchester by teatime.

But as they landed in Munich, snow was already falling. Refuelling took less than 20 minutes and by 2pm the pilots were ready to take off again and continue their way to Manchester. Captain Rayment took over the controls and at 2.31 pm clearance was given for take-off, but he abandoned the attempt when the engines sounded an uneven note. He wasn't unduly worried because this 'boost surging' was not unusual for Elizabethan

DISASTER, 1958

aeroplanes. Rayment tried again at 2.34, but encountered the same problem. The pilots agreed to taxi the plane back to the airport terminus for further investigation.

The players disembarked and passed the time waiting for the departure call buying presents and cigarettes. Although there were a few jitters about the situation, the lads were in good spirits. Some of them joked that they might have to go home overland via the Hook of Holland, reckoning it would be a good chance to relax and have a few beers. With the weather deteriorating, Duncan Edwards sent a telegram to his landlady in Manchester which read: ALL FLIGHTS CANCELLED – STOP – FLYING TOMORROW – STOP – DUNCAN.

Soon though, they were called back on the plane. It started off down the runway, but then someone shouted that Alf Clarke, a journalist for the *Manchester Evening Chronicle*, was missing. The plane rumbled back to the terminus yet again and Clarke (who would be fatally injured minutes later) got a lot of light-hearted stick from fellow hacks when he belatedly appeared.

As the snow continued to fall outside, nerves frayed. Team captain Roger Byrne didn't like air travel at the best of times and his face was as white as a sheet as the plane prepared to take off. Johnny Berry, another reluctant flier, voiced his fears more graphically saying, "We're all going to get ****ing killed here."

"Well, if anything happens, I'm ready to die," replied devout Catholic Billy Whelan.

Seconds later, the pilots made their third attempt to take off and it went horribly wrong. The Lord Burghley careered off the runway and skidded across a road towards a residential area. The left wing and part of the tail were wrenched off on impact with a house, the cockpit ploughed into a tree and the fuselage crashed into a wooden hut containing a fuel-loaded truck which exploded into a fireball.

Goalkeeper Harry Gregg vividly remembers the screeching and banging as the plane spun out of control and then the eerie silence when it finally came to a halt. "There was no screaming or shouting. It was pitch black and I thought, 'I'm dead, I'm in hell.'"

Gregg realized he was alive only when he felt blood trickling down his forehead and saw daylight and flames above him. As he kicked his way out of the wreckage, one of the pilots James Thain (Kenneth Rayment died later in hospital) came past and urged him to run away. But Gregg heard a baby crying and went back into the wreckage ignoring the explosions all around him.

His heroism saved the life of the baby, the child's mother and numerous colleagues. Even

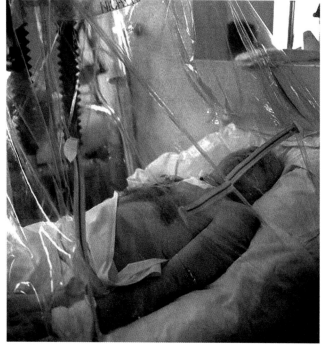

Matt Busby lies gravely ill in hospital following the plane crash.

though Gregg thought Bobby Charlton and Dennis Viollet were dead he dragged their bodies clear and both survived. He also went to the assistance of Matt Busby, who'd suffered punctured lungs and broken leg bones, and Jackie Blanchflower who was lying badly injured with Roger Byrne's dead body on top of him.

Eventually, vehicles arrived at the desolate scene and the injured and dead were rushed to Munich's Rechts Der Isar hospital. Three of United's party – Matt Busby, Johnny Berry and Duncan Edwards – were fighting for their lives. The last rites were twice administered to Matt Busby, but he pulled through and returned to Manchester 71 days later. Berry survived although the injuries he sustained ended his football career. Edwards fought bravely for 15 days, but finally died of kidney failure.

On the night of the disaster, Harry Gregg asked James Thain why the take-off had failed. "He told me about Velocity One, when you have to lift the undercarriage off the ground. He said that point of no return had been reached."

There was no going back for United either. The club would never be the same again.

The headlines the day after Munich reflected the shock of football fans around the world.

BILL FOULKES

DEFENDER (MANCHESTER UNITED 1952–70)

IN HIS PRIME, Bill Foulkes looked as though he had been chiselled from stone and he was the rock of United's defence for the best part of two decades. A resilient man and a consistent footballer, Foulkes survived the Munich air disaster and won four league championship medals, more than any other United player of his era. He also picked up an FA Cup winner's medal in 1963 and crowned his distinguished career by helping United to European Cup success in 1968 at the ripe old age of 36.

Foulkes grew up in St. Helens, Lancashire, where he was spotted by United scouts. Although 18-year-old Foulkes jumped at the chance to join United, he decided to continue the job he'd taken at the Lea Green Colliery immediately after leaving school. It seems incredible now, but Foulkes was still working part-time in the mines when he won his first, and only, England cap four years later.

After a couple of years learning the ropes playing for United reserves in the Manchester League, Foulkes was given his first taste of first-team action in the 1952–53 season. He made his league debut against Liverpool in December 1952 as a right full-back. Within a season he was manager Matt Busby's first choice in that position and he remained an immovable fixture in the United team until the end of the decade. He was only dropped from the team during the last couple of months of United's 1955–56 league championship-winning campaign. Foulkes could justifiably have claimed that national service commitments were a distraction, but typically he didn't complain, trained harder than ever and by the start of the following season he'd won his place back.

In the immediate aftermath of the Munich air crash, it was Foulkes who took over the club captaincy. Having lost so many friends in the crash, it was a credit to Foulkes's strength of character that he led a savagely depleted United team to the FA Cup final that year, losing 2–0 to Bolton Wanderers.

Although Foulkes was a competent enough full-back, it wasn't until Matt Busby moved him into central defence during the 1959–60 season that he truly fulfilled his potential. At full-back, Foulkes's lack of mobility was occasionally exposed, but his bull-like strength and aerial power made him a formidable centre-half throughout the 1960s.

Foulkes knew his ball-playing limitations and concentrated on keeping things tight at the back, allowing United's extravagantly gifted attackers to provide the frills and goals. Indeed, in 18 years and nearly 700 games, Foulkes netted just nine strikes for United, but he did score one of the most important goals in the club's history. With the score poised at 3–3 on aggregate in the 1968 European Cup semi-final second leg against Real Madrid at the Bernabeu, it was Foulkes who pounced on George Best's cross to sidefoot home the winner. Two weeks later at Wembley, Foulkes received his just reward for a lifetime of dedication to the Red cause – a European Cup winner's medal.

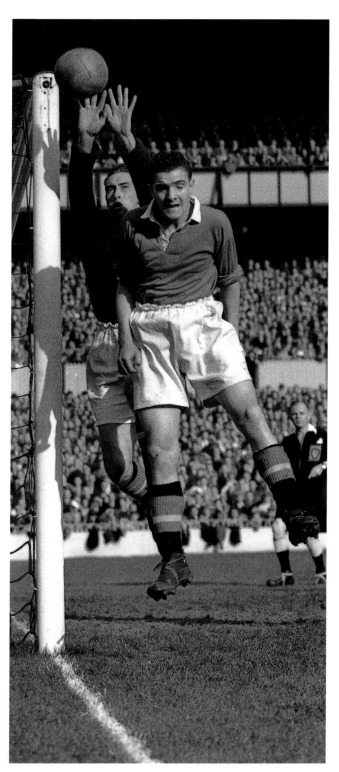

Bill Foulkes was blessed with bull-like strength.

DUNCAN EDWARDS

HALF-BACK (MANCHESTER UNITED 1952–58)

"THE BEST PLAYER I'VE EVER SEEN, the best footballer I've ever played with for United or England, the only player who ever made me feel inferior" – so says United and England legend Sir Bobby Charlton about Duncan Edwards. It is an amazing tribute considering Edwards was just 21 years and 143 days old when he died following the Munich air crash.

Born in 1936 and raised in the West Midlands, Edwards started out playing for Dudley Boys – average age 15 – when he was 11 years old. Freakishly big for his age and blessed with extraordinary skills and a perfect temperament, Edwards was already a giant on the football pitch. Word spread rapidly about the young prodigy and by 1952, all the top English clubs were scrambling to sign him. Although United manager Matt Busby and coach Jimmy Murphy pulled out all the stops to get him, in truth Edwards didn't need much persuading – he was a lifelong fan.

Within a year of signing amateur forms for United, Edwards was thrown into first-team action making his debut against Cardiff City in April 1953. At 16 years and 185 days old, Edwards became the youngest ever footballer to play in the First Division, but with his 5foot 11in, 13stone frame of solid muscle, he didn't look at all out of place. In the same month, Edwards also helped United's junior side to the first of three consecutive Youth Cup wins. Six months later, he signed professional forms for United.

Although his usual position was half-back, Edwards was the complete footballer as fellow Busby Babe Wilf McGuinness recalls: "He could play as an attacker, midfielder or defender and be the best player on the pitch." Edwards' all-round ability was simply irresistible and earned him his full international debut in April 1955. By playing in England's 7–2 demolition of Scotland, aged 18 years and 183 days, Edwards became the youngest England international of the 20th century, a record not beaten until Michael Owen made his England debut 33 years later.

Edwards had previously represented his country at Schoolboy, Youth, B team and under-23 level, and he went on to win 15 full caps. He also played a massive role in two league championship-winning campaigns for United and represented the Football League on six occasions.

Even on his deathbed at the Rechts Der Isar hospital in Munich, Edwards demonstrated his superhuman strength and indomitable spirit. The multiple injuries he sustained in the air crash – a shattered right thigh, broken ribs, a collapsed lung, a broken pelvis and chronic liver damage – would have killed most people instantly, but Edwards joked with Jimmy Murphy that he'd be fit for the next game. He fought against the odds for 15 days before finally succumbing to the inevitable at 12.16 am on 21 February 1958.

Forty years on, Manchester United players and staff gathered at Manchester Cathedral to pay tribute to those who died at Munich. "I was particularly moved when Duncan Edwards' mum, with tears in her eyes, lit a candle for her son," commented Gary Neville afterwards. Even though Duncan Edwards died so young, his contribution to Manchester United FC will never be forgotten.

Duncan Edwards could lay in defence, midfield or attack and be the best player on the pitch.

ROGER BYRNE

FULL-BACK (MANCHESTER UNITED 1951–58)

THE BRIEF BUT BRILLIANT football career of Roger William Byrne was a mass of contradictions. How could a lad not considered good enough to play for his RAF team become one of the most outstanding defenders in the history of the game? How could a right-footed player become the first name on Matt Busby's teamsheet at left-back? How could someone who looked so ordinary in training transform himself into a true leader of men on matchday, one of United's greatest-ever captains? There are no logical explanations. Stylish and charismatic, Byrne was a one-off.

Roger Byrne was born in the Gorton district of Manchester in 1929, but while many of the other Busby Babes joined United in their teens, he had to wait a bit longer for his chance. He spent most of his formative years playing football for a local Manchester side called Ryder Brow and it wasn't until after his 20th birthday that United signed him. Still his prospects of making it looked rather bleak. During his two years in the RAF, he couldn't get a place in his station's football team so he played rugby union instead, and back at Old Trafford, no one was sure of his best position. A practice game by chance revealed his potential as a left-back.

Aged 22, Byrne made his league debut in that position against Liverpool in November 1951. United drew 0–0 and Byrne looked utterly assured. He made 23 more appearances that season and played a key role in United winning the league championship. With a few games remaining and United's challenge seemingly fading, Busby pushed Byrne forward to the left-wing position. Byrne responded by scoring seven times in the last six games as United clinched their first title win for 41 years.

Naturally, Busby decided to keep playing Byrne on the left wing at the start of the following season, but Byrne's non-conformist streak came to the surface – he didn't like playing there and handed in a transfer request. Busby backed down and moved him back to his preferred left-back role. Furthermore, in February 1954, Busby gave Byrne the captaincy. Even though Byrne's fiery temper meant they sometimes clashed, Busby never regretted his decision and there was enormous mutual respect between them.

When he became United skipper, 25-year-old Byrne was charged with the responsibility of leading a hugely talented but youthful team (average age 22) and he thrived on the pressure. He lead them to two consecutive league titles in 1956 and 1957, only just missing out on a momentous double in 1957 when United were beaten 2-1 by Aston Villa in the FA Cup final.

His own game flourished, too. Even though he wasn't the best tackler, Byrne's innate football intelligence allowed him to snuff out danger without diving in. He was an innovator, making overlapping runs before any other full-back of his era had even entertained such an idea.

Byrne made his debut for England in 1954 and won 33 consecutive international caps. He was widely expected to captain England in the 1958 World Cup finals. But Byrne was killed in the Munich air crash and football lost an extraordinary character – he truly was a class act.

Roger Byrne was one of Manchester United's greatest captains, a true leader of men.

TOMMY TAYLOR

FORWARD (MANCHESTER UNITED 1953–58)

FOR SOMEONE WHO WENT ON to become arguably the most lethal finisher in United's history, it is ironic that at school Tommy Taylor, normally a left-back, only played striker when the first-choice forwards were unavailable.

Taylor left school at 14 and immediately started work in a South Yorkshire pit. He didn't play football again until, two years later, he was drafted in to his local pub team to deputise for his uncle, a centre-forward. Young Taylor made an instant impression, scoring in his first match, and it wasn't long before his hometown club, Barnsley, offered him an amateur contract.

Taylor turned professional a year later and made his league debut for the Tykes on 2 May 1950. However, while doing his national service Taylor sustained an horrific knee injury during a regiment game. He was discharged after just eight months in the army and it looked as though his football career was over. Happily, two operations mended the torn ligaments, cracked bone and cartilage damage and 11 months later Taylor was back in the Barnsley team. Remarkably, he looked better than ever and went on to score 26 goals in 44 appearances for the club.

Manchester United manager Matt Busby followed Taylor's progress closely for seven months before splashing out £29,999 to buy him in March 1953. Taylor made an immediate impact, scoring twice on his debut against Preston at Old Trafford. He went on to score seven goals in eight matches before the end of the season, becoming a firm favourite with United fans and establishing himself as a worthy successor to the great Jack Rowley.

Taylor's main attributes were searing speed, a thunderbolt shot and an extraordinary gift for heading the ball. In addition, he passed the ball tidily and constantly made unselfish runs to drag defenders out of position and create space for team-mates.

These striking qualities earned Taylor an international call-up just 10 weeks after signing for United. In summer 1953, he jetted off on a South American tour with England, scoring on his debut against Chile. Although there was a wealth of talented English strikers around in the mid-1950s, Taylor cemented his place in the side and went on to score 16 goals in 19 games for his country.

Taylor was just as potent at club level, helping United to consecutive league championship successes in 1956 and 1957. His extraordinary tally of 128 goals in 189 games still stands as the best goals-per-game record of any striker who has played more than 50 games for United.

Taylor's tragic, untimely death at Munich eight days after his 26th birthday robbed United and English football of one of the greatest striking talents of all time. The great Alfredo di Stefano's simple description of the Yorkshire hotshot stands as a fitting epitaph: 'Magnifico'.

Tommy Taylor could head the ball harder than most players could kick it.

CHAPTER SIX
AFTER THE CRASH

MATT BUSBY AND MANCHESTER UNITED RECUPERATED SLOWLY
AFTER MUNICH. SOON THERE WERE SIGNS OF PROMISE FOR
THE FUTURE, BUT THERE WERE ALSO MANY TESTING MOMENTS
FOR BUSBY AND HIS TEAM.

88

MATT BUSBY'S slow and painful recuperation continued during the summer of 1958, depriving him of the chance to add an intriguing new dimension to his managerial career.

In January, with Scotland having qualified for that summer's World Cup in Sweden, he had accepted his country's invitation to be their team manager for the tournament. Busby's ambition and confidence had led him to declare at the time of his appointment, "I aim not to have a team content merely to put up a respectable show, but one that will take the field with the aim of winning the global trophy." It was not to be. Post-Munich, Busby was not fit enough for the stresses of such a job and he had to watch on television as his country exited at the group stage.

The tournament still had a considerable influence on Busby. As he watched the black and white images at his home in Kings Road, Chorlton, during those June weeks, he enthused about the attacking play of Didi and Garrincha of Brazil, Lennart Skoglund of Sweden and Just Fontaine of France, the man who set the all-time World Cup scoring record of 13 goals at the tournament. Watching those players in the first World Cup to be televised was, as he put it, "more education!" It also helped to rekindle his fascination with the game as it was played outside the British Isles. Busby's belief in European competition had been shaken by the Munich disaster but watching that World Cup helped cement his desire to build a new United team capable of competing in Europe.

He almost had the chance to take United into the European Cup straightaway, despite the club having finished ninth in the First Division at the end of the 1957–58 season. In the aftermath of the Munich disaster, which had won sympathy around Europe, the club received a generous invitation from the European Cup's ruling body to enter the 1958–59 tournament. The Football Association gave their consent but the Football League did not. United went to the Football League's board of appeal who upheld United's right to accept the invitation but the League then went to the joint FA and League

United's first match after Munich was an FA Cup tie against Sheffield Wednesday and a goal by Brennan, direct from a corner, set them up for a heart-warming win.

Consultative Committee who denied United entry to the European Cup on the grounds that, as it was a tournament for champion clubs, they were not qualified to enter. Leaving aside the fact that some of the clubs who entered the competition in those early days were not actually champions of their countries, the League's determination to thwart United looked like revenge for Busby's hurdling of that body's opposition two years earlier.

United began the 1958–59 league season in style, with Bobby Charlton collecting a hat-trick in a 5–2 opening day thrashing of Chelsea at Old Trafford. Albert Scanlon was back on the left wing for that match, having made a successful recovery from the head and leg injuries he had sustained in the crash. He was to be an ever-present over the season, scoring 16 goals. Half-back Fred Goodwin was the only other United player to appear in every one of the club's matches that season. Wilf McGuinness, only 20 years old but a first-team regular since Munich, played in all but three of United's matches. His appetite for hard work in midfield was of enormous benefit. He held together the reshaped team and helped it to gel.

Centre-forward Dennis Viollet shared 50 league goals with Charlton, who became fully established as a first-team regular. Still only 20, the youngster was suddenly the focal point of the United side. "The Munich air disaster came at a time when I was trying to establish myself in a regular first-team position with Manchester United," he commented in 1961. "I seemed to become a sort of symbol, particularly with youngsters, of the new United. Simultaneously, it was urged I should be given an England place. I am naturally shy and all this confused me; too many people were making too much fuss."

Charlton and Viollet were joined in the forward line by Albert Quixall, whom Busby made a British record signing when he paid Sheffield Wednesday £45,000 for him – £10,000 more than the previous British record – in September 1958. Quixall was a skilful, creative inside-forward but something of a luxury player. He was at his best when United were well on top in a game but less effective in adversity. He managed just four goals in his debut season.

There was no European competition to distract the players from the League and a surprise 3–0 third-round FA Cup defeat at Third Division Norwich City ensured that the First Division remained central to everyone's thoughts. The club played the absolute minimum of matches necessary – 43 in all. That lack of fixture congestion was a major boon and progress was such that a 2–1 win over Wolverhampton Wanderers in February 1959 brought United level with the Midlands club at the top of the table. However, United lost three of their last 12 games and finished second to Wolves, six points behind the champions. Amidst the

disappointment at missing out on the title there was satisfaction and surprise that the first full season after Munich had gone so well.

The Stretford End was covered in the summer of 1959, increasing the comfort of the thousands who stood there, and at the start of the season optimism ran high that there would also be progress on the pitch. The opening game delivered a clue as to how United would fare. Dennis Viollet scored twice in the match at West Bromwich Albion but United ended it 3–2 losers. Between then and the final fixture of the season, Viollet scored another 30 times, giving him a total of 32 league goals for the 1959–60 season. It remains the league scoring record for a United player. Viollet missed six matches so his tally averaged out at almost a goal a game. A deft player with a delicate touch, and another whose injuries at Munich had threatened to curtail his career, Viollet was popular and his achievement was well-received.

Although Viollet and Charlton once again shared a total of 50 goals, as they had the previous season, the team proved less consistent overall. Convincing wins would be followed by hefty defeats and vice versa. This inconsistency continued right up until the closing fixtures, with United beating West Ham 5–3, then losing 5–2 to Arsenal before defeating Everton 5–0 in the final league match of the season. Despite such volatile fluctuations in their results, United still managed to finish in seventh place in the First Division. They had scored 102 goals over the season, just one short of the tally of the 1956–57 championship-winning team. They had, however, conceded the not so grand total of 80.

Matt Busby had made it clear that it would take a full five years for United to recover from the crash and, as so often, his words were ringing true, despite the optimism that had been generated by United's stirring finale the previous season. Thoughts of the crash were still never far away even two years on and on a rainy day in late February 1960 Matt Busby unveiled the Munich memorial plaque in honour of all those who had lost their lives in the crash. A fifth-round draw against Sheffield Wednesday in that month brought memories flooding back of the emotional fifth-round tie two years previously. This time it was to end in defeat for United. A penalty conceded by half-back Maurice Setters resulted in the only goal of the game for Wednesday. Setters had been bought from West Bromwich Albion for £30,000 in January 1960 to add some grit to the midfield after the unfortunate, premature retirement of Wilf McGuinness following a severe leg break in December 1959.

Shay Brennan, who had made his debut in that FA Cup tie against Wednesday two years earlier, partnered Setters in the middle

Overleaf: Bobby Charlton darts in from the wing at Tottenham to shoot.

David Herd played against United for Arsenal the weekend before Munich but moved to Old Trafford in 1961. The Scottish international was a prolific goalscorer.

of the field during the 1959–60 season, with Ronnie Cope, another who had received speedy promotion to the first team after Munich, enjoying a steady second season at centre-half.

Warren Bradley, who had joined United as an amateur from Bishop Auckland after the crash and who had signed professional terms later that year, was the regular selection on the right wing. Scanlon remained on the opposite flank, with Charlton, Viollet and Quixall again the first-choice attacking trio. Quixall, now settled at the club, managed a respectable 13 goals in 33 games. Alex Dawson, who was occasionally brought into the front line, still managed more goals – 15 – in only 22 appearances. Harry Gregg remained in goal, with Bill Foulkes and Joe Carolan the full-backs. It was an entertaining team but it still lacked the solidity Busby would have liked. The defence in particular was too fragile, too prone to unforced errors.

In a poor start to the 1960–61 season, United haemorrhaged goals, leaving them third from bottom of the First Division at the beginning of October. Busby quickly took steps to remedy the situation. Brennan was pulled back from midfield to right-back. A player who combined a highly disciplined approach to his duties to the team with fine ball-playing skills, he was the ideal full-back for Busby. Bill Foulkes switched to centre-half, a position in which the rugged ex-miner appeared born to play. They were joined in November 1960 by Irishman Noel Cantwell for whom Busby paid

West Ham United £29,500, making him Britain's most expensive full-back.

Johnny Giles, an 18-year-old Irishman, became a regular in midfield over the season. He was joined there by two other well-loved youngsters – 18-year-old Nobby Stiles and Jimmy Nicholson, a well-built, skilled 17 year old from Belfast whom the crowd immediately took to their hearts. Both were fortunate enough to be part of the United side that played host to Real Madrid in a friendly match that October of 1960. While United struggled in the League, this glamorous fixture was a pleasant reminder to the Old Trafford faithful of the joys of European football. The president of Real, Santiago Bernabeu, had met Matt Busby in Madrid and had told him that, in sympathy with United for the Munich crash, he would waive his club's usual substantial fee for friendlies whenever Busby wished him to bring the five-times European champions to Old Trafford. A crowd of 51,000 watched enthralled that autumn night as Real, led by the magnificent Alfredo Di Stefano, won 3–2. United's goals were scored by inside-left Mark Pearson and Nicholson. It was a reminder to all of the glamour involved in floodlit European games, those nights when the green rectangle of the footballing stage, the focus of so many lives, was lit up by the colour and charisma of cosmopolitan talents.

That inspirational night helped spur United on in the League for the remainder of the year and by the time they faced

Manchester City at Old Trafford on New Year's Eve they had moved into the top half of the table. It proved to be a fond farewell to 1960 – in the 5–1 win Alex Dawson netted the first hat-trick in a Manchester derby since October 1921 when the great Joe Spence had scored all three goals for United in their 3–1 win.

Busby was aware that United were still far from the finished article but that year he mused, "I should like to see the honours in England won by a pure footballing side, the sort of team that concentrates on ball skills above all else. Such a team could inspire the other ninety-one clubs. But for the air disaster, I like to feel that others would now be copying United to the benefit of the whole League."

United suffered a serious blow when goalkeeper Harry Gregg badly damaged his shoulder against Spurs in January 1961. With substitutes still not yet allowed under Football Association rules, Dawson replaced him in goal. Gregg, with his shoulder strapped up, took Dawson's place at centre-forward and it was Gregg, bizarrely, who played a decisive role in United's winning goal. His natty backheel set up Pearson to make the final score 2–0.

The combination of firm defensive football and clever attacking evident in that game had been encouraging but the optimism was short-lived. United immediately suffered their most severe defeat of the season, going down 6–0 away to Leicester City. Ronnie Briggs, a 17 year-old from Belfast, made his debut in goal in that game and his confidence was shattered further when United took on Sheffield Wednesday in the fourth round of the FA Cup the following week. After a 1–1 draw at Hillsborough, the two sides met in the replay at Old Trafford four days later. Goalkeeping errors by Briggs allowed Wednesday to take a 4–1 lead by half-time and they eventually ran out 7–2 victors.

Briggs returned to the reserves and Mike Pinner, a 26-year-old amateur and law graduate from Cambridge University, was signed from QPR in February 1961 as Busby reacted to his goalkeeping emergency. Pinner and 20-year-old David Gaskell shared goalkeeping duties in the absence of the incapacitated Gregg.

United participated in the Football League Cup, then in its first year. A second-round defeat at Bradford City in October 1960 ended their interest in the tournament, then treated very much as a minor affair by the bigger clubs and their supporters. It would be six years before United played in that competition again.

The 1960–61 season ended with United in seventh place for the second successive year, a commendable effort after their sluggish start. Bobby Charlton was United's top scorer, despite having been moved from inside-left to the left wing. The player preferred the inside-forward position but his pace and precision made him an excellent winger. "I would still eventually find more satisfaction in a return to an inside-forward position, should the Boss come to think me sufficiently mature," said Charlton. "Inside, you're more in the game for longer spells. It gives more satisfaction. You are less likely to let your mind wander and lose that all-important concentration."

Charlton was joined in the forward line for the 1961–62 season by David Herd, a 28-year-old Scottish international centre-forward who was purchased from Arsenal for a fee of £35,000. Busby had played alongside Herd's father Alec, an inside-forward, at Manchester City in the 1930s. David too had played alongside his father for Stockport County before moving to Highbury. Herd had been Arsenal's top scorer for four successive seasons yet, puzzlingly, the Arsenal manager, George Swindin, had tried to sell the player on numerous occasions. A few months earlier, Swindin had attempted to arrange a move to Huddersfield Town for Herd in part-exchange for Huddersfield forward Denis Law. Herd had scored 30 league and FA Cup goals for Arsenal in the 1960–61 season. A fearsome right foot combined with a hearty appetite for the game made him an exciting capture.

With a surplus of forwards at the club, Dennis Viollet was subsequently sold to Stoke City in January 1962 for £22,000. There he joined up with Stanley Matthews who decades later compared Viollet to Teddy Sheringham for his deft touches and underrated contributions to the team.

United were among the favourites for the 1961–62 championship but despite a good start, a disastrous run of results in the autumn torpedoed their championship

Bobby Charlton was United's top scorer in 1960–61 despite playing on the left wing.

94

chances. From a place in the leading pack of clubs, United tumbled towards the relegation zone. By Christmas they were second to bottom but the now usual rally in the second half of the season took them clear of the drop and into a final position of 15th. It was the club's lowest finish since Busby had become manager.

The Cup produced better cheer. A win over Bolton Wanderers in the third round was followed by a stylish victory over Arsenal. Freakishly, the fifth round produced yet another FA Cup tie with Sheffield Wednesday, but this time after replays in that match and in a quarter-final with Preston North End, United found themselves in the semi-finals. There their luck ran out and they were outclassed by opponents Tottenham Hotspur, the holders of the trophy. The match at neutral Hillsborough finished 3–1 in the Londoners' favour.

Busby now seemed generally happy with his defence and midfield. One of the few changes to those sections of his team was the introduction of Tony Dunne as a regular in the left-back position, which he shared with fellow Irishman Noel Cantwell during that 1961–62 season. The manager was less happy with his side's attacking qualities, constantly chopping and changing his front players to little avail. Herd scored 17 times but, overall, goals were scarce – Quixall and Charlton only just made it into double figures.

The guiding hand of Matt Busby is on Denis Law's shoulder as he signs for United, watched by Law's agent Gigi Peronace (left) and Jimmy Murphy.

Drastic measures were required if United were to become a consistently strong force in English football once again. Busby's attempts at bringing through youngsters had been partially successful and it was always his preference to mould a player into the right type for Manchester United. Despite that, if the right player was available to buy, the United manager was not averse to purchasing talent and in the summer of 1962, when Scottish international forward Denis Law became available, Busby did not hesitate to dip deep into the Old Trafford coffers to find the necessary transfer fee.

Busby had been keeping an eye on Law ever since the mid 1950s when the player had joined Huddersfield Town as an amateur. "When we were losing 2–0 at half-time in a youth match at Heckmondwike, I wondered who was taking us apart," Busby recalled. "Then I realized it was a little will-o'-the-wisp called Law, who had scored both goals. I knew then that Huddersfield had found someone more than a bit special." By the early 1960s, Law had become a fully fledged goalscorer of the highest calibre with Manchester City and in 1961 his talents had taken him to Torino in Italy. A new British record fee of £115,000 secured his return to Manchester a year later. It also put United in debt for the first time in the Busby era.

The United attack had a more settled look in the 1962–63 season. Law took his place at inside-left with Charlton outside him on the wing. On the other flank, Johnny Giles was on the right wing, with Quixall inside him. Herd was at centre-forward. Law's debut for United, a home league match with West Bromwich Albion in August 1962, began with a flourish. After 90 seconds, Stiles slipped a pass into the path of Herd whose shot went darting into the net. Five minutes later, Johnny Giles took a pass from Brennan and curved a cross into the heart of the penalty area. Law, under pressure in the air, got in front of his defender to glance the ball into the far corner of the net. That was as good as it got for United on the day. Unable to add to their 2–0 lead, West Brom pegged back two late goals for a draw and the United players found themselves being slow-handclapped by their own supporters in the latter stages of the match.

Throughout the season, rich entertainment alternated with lapses of on-field discipline that undid the team's constructive work. A series of patchy performances caused United to plummet to the foot of the table and by mid May they were in grave danger of relegation. Their third-last fixture took them to Maine Road to face a City side that was in a similar predicament. This game would decide which Manchester outfit would join Leyton Orient in demotion to the Second Division.

United had three matches remaining while City had just two. United also had one point more than their rivals. It looked ominous for United when Alex Harley's strike put City ahead after eight minutes and City were still 1–0 up as the match entered its final stages. Then David Wagstaffe, City's outside-left, was short with a long-range passback to his goalkeeper Harry Dowd. Law was on to it in a flash and as he reached the penalty area, Dowd appeared to grab his ankles. The two opponents tumbled to the ground in a ball of confusion. The referee decided it was a penalty, Albert Quixall netted and United emerged with a somewhat fortunate draw. United's 3–1 defeat of Leyton Orient at Old Trafford three days later sent City down.

Despite the team's troubles, Busby had kept his nerve, kept confidence in his players and had maintained a largely settled side. The only notable addition to the team during the season had been Pat Crerand, a midfielder signed from Celtic in February for a fee of £56,000. As with Law, when the player had become available for transfer, Busby had not hesitated to swoop. Crerand added real finesse to the midfield.

One of the most severe winters in history had frozen Britain in early 1963, leading to a two-month mid-season hiatus. United went from late December 1962 to late February 1963 without a match. It meant that the FA Cup did not begin until March and United compressed four FA Cup ties into that month, defeating Huddersfield Town in the third round, then knocking out Aston Villa and Chelsea, before ending March with a quarter-final victory over Coventry City. The semi-final with Second Division Southampton was a dour affair that was settled when Denis Law scraped the ball over the Southampton line midway through the first half. It was enough to take United into their fourth FA Cup final under Busby.

At Wembley, Busby's side secured a vibrant 3–1 victory over Leicester City and on their return to Manchester more than 300,000 people lined the streets to welcome their heroes home. The United players were astonished at the crowds. Busby had stood by his men throughout a testing season and his loyalty had been rewarded by his players' performances at Wembley. The manager had stated that it would take five years for the club to recover from Munich and, as in so many matters, he had been proved prescient.

"Our supporters have helped considerably in our success," Busby commented in the minutes after the Cup final. "I want them to share in it and to reassure them about our future. I believe that it will be a bright one. The pattern and the tempo for the future was, without question, set at Wembley."

Manchester United's rehabilitation was complete. The club could now look to the future with confidence.

1963 FA CUP FINAL

MANCHESTER UNITED (1) 3 LEICESTER CITY (0) 1

25 MAY 1963, WEMBLEY

MANCHESTER UNITED were the most unlikely of FA Cup final underdogs – they were by far the most expensively assembled side ever to have reached that stage of the competition. That was counterbalanced by the fact that they had only just escaped relegation days before. Their opponents Leicester City, in contrast, had finished the season in fourth place.

It was the Football Association's centenary year and the 1963 Cup final was a fitting celebration of that sporting body's great tournament. Freed of the drudgery of keeping the club free of relegation, United's players revelled in the occasion and controlled the match from the start. Giles went closest to scoring, sending a shot narrowly past the Leicester post. After half an hour, a Bobby Charlton effort was held by Gordon Banks, the Leicester goalkeeper. He attempted to distribute the ball to a team-mate but Pat Crerand anticipated his throw and cut past two defenders on the United left before centring the ball. It looked easy for Denis Law, close to the penalty spot, to take it quickly on his left foot. Instead, he tamed the ball with his left then cleverly shielded it as he turned with his back to goal, putting two defenders on the wrong side of him as he did so. That calculated movement opened up the whole target for him and allowed him to hit a swift but highly controlled right-foot shot on the turn past Banks.

Law almost got a second shortly afterwards but his on-target effort was cleared off the Leicester line and the score remained 1–0 at half-time. Leicester had been overwhelmed in the first half by United's sharp, cohesive passing and United maintained their momentum after the break. With 57 minutes gone, Giles picked out Charlton on the left. The forward's strong shot was parried by Banks

David Herd (right), watched by Denis Law, hits United's third.

but it fell at the feet of David Herd, who planted it in the net.

Leicester, stung into retaliation, went looking for a goal to get them back in the game. They got one in the 80th minute through centre-forward Ken Keyworth's fine diving header. Law, with a clever flying header of his own, almost scored immediately after that. With five minutes of the match remaining, Banks spilled a cross from Giles and once again Herd was waiting to take advantage by battering the ball home.

"It went just as we had planned it," said Matt Busby afterwards. "We displayed exemplary teamwork. It is difficult for a manager to single out one player above another for individual praise but I was, on this occasion, especially pleased by the performances of Denis Law and Pat Crerand. They were the men of the match. They helped us find the rhythm that was missing during our league campaign."

Manchester United (manager Matt Busby): Gaskell, Dunne, Cantwell, Crerand, Foulkes, Setters, Giles, Quixall, Herd, Law, Charlton
Scorers: Law 30, Herd 58, 85

Leicester City (manager Matt Gillies): Banks, Sjoberg, Norman, McLintock, King, Appletonm Riley, Cross, Keyworth, Gibson, Stringfellow
Scorers: Keyworth 80

Attendance: 100,000

United players clown with the FA Cup after beating Leicester.

BOBBY CHARLTON

FORWARD (MANCHESTER UNITED 1956–73)

BOBBY CHARLTON epitomized all that England expects of a footballer. A player of brilliance, an exemplary sportsman and a man who was modest about his talents, he became, in 1994, the first footballer to be knighted since Stanley Matthews three decades earlier.

Equally effective as an attacking midfielder, a winger or as a centre-forward thanks to his beautiful balance and sleek speed, Charlton provided numerous goals for team-mates and when he went for goal himself, the results would often be awe-inspiring. He possessed the precious ability to hit a dead or moving ball first time from long range with unerring accuracy and was equally powerful on either foot. It was close to impossible for goalkeepers to guess where his shots would go. George Best saw Charlton's skills at close range and said, "Just to be on the same pitch as Bobby was a great pleasure. I've never seen anyone go past players as easily as he did. He glided past."

Born in Ashington, Northumberland, Bobby Charlton was a nephew of Jackie Milburn, the great Cup-winning Newcastle United centre-forward of the 1950s. Although infused with the Geordie's passion for football, it was Manchester United Charlton supported as a boy and he watched them on every visit to the north-east. His favourite player was Johnny Carey.

Charlton joined United in January 1953 as an amateur, turning professional on his 17th birthday in October 1954. His debut came two years later at centre-forward when he scored twice in a 4–2 win over Charlton Athletic at Old Trafford. He went on to score 12 goals in 17 appearances in that 1956–57 season, also scoring on his European Cup debut, against Real Madrid in the semi-final. As a young player, Charlton was stubbornly independent and wilful, always determined to do things his own way. As he matured, he was to become the perfect team player.

His upward progress continued during the 1957–58 season and he scored twice in Belgrade against Red Star in the match that preceded the Munich crash. A shy individual as a youngster, Charlton channeled all his self-expression into each 90 minutes. "Even in the peak of that strange post-Munich period," he said in 1961, "when the pressure from all sides was at its greatest, I never once felt I did not want to play football for a living. The game was always there for me, the best company a fellow could have."

Successes with United were more than matched by his performances for England. He scored on his England debut against Scotland in October 1958 and in a 12 year international career won 106 caps, then a record, and set the England goalscoring record, which he still holds, with 49 goals.

His greatest moment in an England shirt was lifting the World Cup in 1966, with his brother Jack alongside him at centre-half. Bobby Charlton was the midfield driving force in that team and scored both goals in the 2–1 semi-final win over Portugal. He was named European Footballer of the Year and Footballer of the Year in 1966.

After two decades of service to United as a player, Bobby Charlton had scored 247 goals in a record 754 appearances, making him the highest scorer in the club's history. After retiring as a player in 1973, he became manager of Preston North End but resigned on a matter of principle after a disagreement with the directors in 1975. After a spell as a director of Wigan Athletic in the early 1980s, he became a director of Manchester United in 1984.

Shortly after becoming established at United, Charlton said, "I crave the experience that will enable me to make the most of what I've got. So that one day I, too, can create something, consistently and well. Something that might be remembered." He was to fulfil that ambition a hundred times over as he became one of the greatest players ever to grace the game of football.

Bobby Charlton was consistently classy for United.

DENIS LAW

FORWARD (MANCHESTER UNITED 1962–73)

DENIS LAW wanted to be an architect when he was a boy but as a footballer he rarely had time for carefully drawn-up plans. He freely admitted that Matt Busby's Friday team-talk would have gone out of his head by Saturday afternoon. That approach suited both player and manager because Busby loved to see Law play it off-the-cuff, scoring and creating goals with exceptional verve and vigour.

Law was embarrassed by a squint as a boy and was still afflicted by it when he left home in Aberdeen to join Huddersfield Town in 1955. Shortly after moving to Huddersfield, he returned to Aberdeen for an operation to correct the squint and after the removal of that blight the youngster's confidence soared.

Bill Shankly, the Huddersfield manager, built up the undernourished, slightly built Law by frequently sending him off to a local café for steak and milk. When Shankly took over as manager of Liverpool in December 1959, Law decided it was time for him to move as well. Matt Busby wanted to bring Law to Old Trafford but he had a proliferation of forwards and had to resist making an offer for the 19 year old. Manchester City instead paid £53,000 for him in March 1960 and Law was soon scoring freely for the Maine Road club.

Law moved on to Torino in 1961 for a fee of £100,000 but found the Italian game stiflingly defensive. "It was rubbish – it really was," he said. A British record fee of £115,000 finally brought him to Old Trafford where he was top scorer in his debut season of 1962–63, topping it off with an outstanding goal in that year's FA Cup final. He was again top scorer in 1963–64, with his best season's haul of 46 goals, and was named 1964 European Footballer of the Year.

The leading scorer in five seasons for United, including the two championship-winning seasons of 1964–65 and 1966–67, Law scored 236 goals in 399 appearances for the club. That total leaves him second in the list of all-time United goalscorers, just 11 behind Bobby Charlton. "I think the word 'electric' sums up Denis Law," said Charlton. "Sparks seemed to fly everywhere whenever he was around." Law scored no fewer than 18 hat-tricks in his time at Old Trafford and on five of those occasions scored four goals. One hat-trick, against Spurs on 9 November 1963, came less than 48 hours after he had scored four for Scotland against Norway.

A great showman, Law would beat the ground or stare heavenwards in disbelief after a missed goalscoring chance. In a match against Aston Villa in May 1967, he became so frustrated at perceived refereeing injustices that five minutes from time he untied his boots, put them under his arm and spent the rest of the game in his stockinged feet.

A reserved man off the pitch, his intense involvement in a match led to him receiving several lengthy suspensions during his time at Old Trafford. He later commented, "I never liked watching myself playing on television. I found it embarrassing. The character who was supposed to be me on the screen was not really me at all.

He couldn't be, throwing a punch at someone, glaring at the linesman, arguing with the referee and making rude signs. I didn't behave like that in real life."

Law had played for Tommy Docherty with Scotland but they failed to see eye to eye after Docherty's appointment as United manager in December 1972. The following summer, Law returned to Manchester City. After just a year at Maine Road, however, he retired from football at the age of 34.

A passionate patriot, Law famously went for a round of golf on the afternoon England won the World Cup. He became the youngest 20th-century player to represent his country in a full international when he made his Scotland debut at 18 and he won his 55th and final cap against Zaire in the 1974 World Cup – his final match as a professional footballer. He remains Scotland's record goalscorer on 30 goals, holding the honour jointly with Kenny Dalglish. United's supporters nicknamed Law "The King" and his regal progress in the blue of Scotland and in the red of United made him truly worthy of that soubriquet.

Denis Law was a master at unlocking defences.

PAT CRERAND

MIDFIELDER (MANCHESTER UNITED 1963–71)

"I WANT TO BE A BUSBY BABE," declared Pat Crerand on asking for a transfer from Celtic at the end of January 1963. Within days he had arrived at Old Trafford after an emotional departure from the Glasgow club. Poignantly, Crerand, then 23 years old, signed for United on 6 February 1963, the fifth anniversary of the Munich disaster, and he was the ideal midfield playmaker whom Busby had desperately needed in the five years since the crash.

George Best was to say that Crerand's name was the first he always looked for on the United teamsheet. Although not blessed with pace, Crerand had the quickness of mind to provide perfect service for those who did have helium in their heels. His precision passing and quick eye for an opening gave his forwards time and space whenever they received one of his through-balls. Crerand also occasionally joined the attack and although he didn't score too many goals, when he did so they were usually spectacular, long-range efforts. He tended to save his goals for crucial times in crucial games.

A product of Glasgow's tough Gorbals district, Crerand was a fiery competitor who knew how to look after himself, and he came to Manchester with a less than perfect disciplinary reputation. He had suffered lengthy suspensions after sendings off in Scotland and had finally quit Celtic after a stand-up row with assistant coach Sean Fallon at half-time in the 1963 New Year's Day Old Firm derby. In his first Manchester derby, in May 1963, he reportedly punched City's David Wagstaffe to the ground outside the dressing-rooms at half-time.

His commitment and intense involvement in a game, combined with his tough tackling, meant that he was often the flash in a flashpoint, as when he was sent off in Hungary for violent conduct in the second leg of United's 1965 Fairs Cup semi-final against Ferencvaros. More often, though, Crerand's gritty approach to football was channelled productively and his combination of sophisticated skill and a desperate will to win drove his team-mates on.

Crerand played a major role in helping United win the FA Cup in 1963. He was in superb form on the day, patiently dismantling Leicester City's defence with his probing passes. He was a key member of both of United's championship-winning sides of the 1960s and had another outstanding game in the victorious 1968 European Cup final against Benfica. At national level, he won 16 caps, all by the age of 27.

He remained a regular in the United midfield until the end of the 1970–71 season, at which point he joined the United coaching staff. Crerand was appointed assistant manager to Tommy Docherty the following year but the two Gorbals boys rarely saw eye to eye. "As an enemy, Doc was vicious, vindictive and callous," Crerand commented on his relationship with the then United manager. The subsequent acrimonious parting of the ways was a sad way for one of the club's most consistently excellent stars of the 1960s to leave the Old Trafford staff.

Pat Crerand lines up for the 1963 FA Cup final against Leicester City at Wembley.

CHAPTER SEVEN

LAW, BEST AND CHARLTON

THREE OUTSTANDING FORWARDS BLENDED TOGETHER IN THE 1960s TO LEAD THE WAY ON CREATING A DECADE OF DELIGHT AT OLD TRAFFORD. THEIR NAMES WERE DENIS LAW, GEORGE BEST AND BOBBY CHARLTON.

George Best (far left), during one of his early starts for United against Tottenham, helped to illuminate the Reds' attack.

F AST, FLOWING, ATTACKING FOOTBALL was always the central concern of Manchester United's three most famous players of the 1960s – Denis Law, George Best and Bobby Charlton. All three were obsessed with driving play forward, getting goals and overwhelming opponents through their sheer desire to win matches in the most stylish manner possible. That consistent commitment to entertaining football won the club thousands of new fans as the 1960s progressed because more and more teams were adopting a defensive guise as a means of sneaking off with results. That was never United's way. They had to play to the strengths of their key performers and that meant the entire team was oriented towards attack.

Law, Best and Charlton were world-class talents, each of whose attacking skills on their own would have lit up any club. That all three came together at Old Trafford was fortunate for the club's followers, but it was no accident – they were the type of players that Matt Busby had devoted his life to encouraging and nurturing for

Manchester United. At the outset of the 1960s he had made clear his commitment to entertaining football in the face of the increasing functionalism that was disfiguring the face of the English game. "We are breeding a number of teams whose outlook seems to be that pace, punch and fitness are all that is required to win all the honours in the game," he commented. "They forget that without pure skills these virtues count for precisely nothing."

As the 1963–64 season began, Law and Charlton were firm fixtures in United's array of starts, especially after their contribution to the FA Cup win the previous May, the club's first trophy in six years. That spring had also been a momentous time in the life of George Best. He had been on the United groundstaff since August 1961 but on 22 May 1963, three days before United's Wembley win, he turned 17 and was offered professional terms by Busby.

Best was soon ready for first-team football and was given his debut in a 1–0 home win over West Bromwich Albion on 14 September 1963. Law was missing through injury that day and afterwards Best returned to the youth team. It was more than three months before Busby judged the time was right to have Best back in the first team, for a match with Burnley on 28 December. Law was missing from the line-up again. The Football Association had suspended him for 28 days on 5 December after he had been sent off against Aston Villa in mid-November. By the time Law was ready to return, for a home match against Birmingham City on 11 January, Charlton was missing through injury.

It meant that the trio's initial first-team appearance together was in an away match against West Brom on 18 January 1964. United lined up with Charlton at centre-forward – this was the season in which Bobby Charlton finally got his wish and moved from the left wing to a more central role – Law at inside-left and Best on the left wing. From the start, they were a success, blending together beautifully. They scored all four of the goals in United's 4–1 win that day, Law hitting the net twice and Best and Charlton once each. Best's goal was his second for United, but while his first for the club had been a straightforward strike this one was of the type that would establish his reputation as master of the unexpected. Taking a clever pass from Law, Best went skating across the slippery surface, flitting wide of the West Brom defenders, shaking them off but simultaneously reducing the angle at which he could shoot at goal. With his opponents baffled, Best swiftly swiped the ball into the tiniest space inside the post to score United's second goal of the game.

United were now proving the benefits of a positive approach to football. They were among the challengers for the league title, they were defending the FA Cup and they were managing that rare trick of blending instinctive individualism with intricate teamwork. They were also back in Europe after a five-season absence, much to Matt Busby's joy. "Once again we will be able to bring inter-continental football to Manchester," the United manager had said in the immediate aftermath of the 1963 FA Cup win over Leicester, "and this is something I am personally delighted about. Over the years this has always been a major objective for United. I fervently believe that only by meeting the great sides of Europe can we hope to improve our game in this country. This is something we must aim at, for British football needs the impetus, at club and international level, which competitive football against other European sides will provide."

While Busby remained a man who could be entranced by the romance of football, he also had the necessary core of steel required by any manager. At the beginning of that 1963–64 season, Johnny

Giles, a good prospect for the future, had been transferred to Leeds United for £37,500 after one disagreement too many with Busby. It hardly seemed to matter at the time because the club had young talent aplenty; Ian Moir took over from Giles at outside-right while David Sadler, a 17 year-old whose signature had been sought by almost every First Division club, made his debut as a centre-forward in August, and the club soon topped the First Division.

It was as league leaders that they travelled to Holland for their opening European Cup-Winners' Cup tie with Willem II Tilburg in late September. Harry Gregg and Bill Foulkes were the only players in the side who had also been involved in United's last European tie, with Milan in 1958, although Munich survivor Bobby Charlton was also in the line-up. The match had been moved from Tilburg to Rotterdam in expectation of a sizeable crowd, but the Feyenoord stadium was two-thirds empty. It was an unhappy night for United. They went 1–0 behind to the part-timers although David Herd, back in the side at the expense of Moir, quickly equalized. Near the end, Herd was dismissed for foul play. The return at Old Trafford three weeks later was much more encouraging, United streaking to a 6–1 win that included a spectacular hat-trick from Denis Law.

David Sadler was one of the most versatile talents in the United squad during the 1960s. He was equally at ease in defence, midfield and attack.

The next round promised to be much more testing. United were drawn against the holders, Tottenham Hotspur, who in May 1963 had become the first British club to win a European trophy. This tie was given an additional edge since Spurs and United had both taken turns at leading the First Division. United warmed up nicely for the European meeting with a 4–1 league win over Spurs at Old Trafford, a match in which Graham Moore, a £35,000 signing from Chelsea, made a sparkling debut at inside-right.

Harry Gregg was still United's first-choice goalkeeper, but in late November 1963 he suffered a broken collarbone in a clash with Liverpool's Ron Yeats. So for the Fairs Cup first leg, at White Hart Lane on 3 December 1963, David Gaskell was in goal and in superb form. He was unfortunate in conceding two second-half goals after the right side of the United defence had been left exposed. Six days later in the return at Old Trafford, United were in storming form, quickly wiping out the 2–0 deficit through a double from Herd. Jimmy Greaves put Spurs ahead again on aggregate and within minutes the match became 10-a-side when Maurice Setters had to leave the field with blood pouring from a head wound; Spurs midfielder Dave Mackay had been carried off the pitch with a broken leg in the first half.

United now drew on all their resources. Charlton sent a shot whistling over the crossbar, but when Crerand sent a pass into his path with 10 minutes remaining, he found the target. With seconds to go and Tottenham on the back foot, Crerand and Charlton produced a replica of that goal, Crerand slipping the ball down the inside-right channel and Charlton making no mistake from close range. Even though it had been a tie between two English clubs, the match had produced the type of drama and excitement Busby always anticipated from European competition.

The quarter-finals threw up a tie with Sporting Lisbon and 60,000 United fans went home from Old Trafford delighted with a 4–1 win in the first leg. A goal from Charlton and a hat-trick from Law, which included two penalties, had done the trick. The Portuguese had keenly disputed both of United's spot-kicks, but Sporting got one of their own after two minutes of the second leg. Tony Dunne had a penalty awarded against him for handball and Osvaldo scored from the spot. Ten minutes later the same player poked the ball into the United net from close range.

With Sporting moving the ball around at whirlwind speed and incessantly running off the ball swiftly and surely, United were in trouble. Portuguese pressure told once again shortly after half-time when Geo levelled the aggregate score. That inspired his side to make a final push for the winner in the second half. Morais made it 4–0 on the night, then Osvaldo finished it off with a 35-yard free-kick that streaked past Gaskell. Not only were United out of Europe, the 5–0 reverse was the club's heaviest defeat in European competition. Unusually, Busby laid into his players afterwards, which was out of character for the manager, who was expert at keeping his emotions in check. He had, however, been infuriated by the poverty of United's performance.

Either side of that match in Lisbon on 18 March 1964, the club's chances of winning a domestic trophy had disappeared. An FA Cup semi-final with West Ham United had resulted in a 3–1 defeat and when they lost 3–0 at Liverpool, United were out of that year's championship race. Sporting won the Cup-Winners' Cup, West Ham the FA Cup and United finished the league season in second position, four points behind Liverpool.

It was a massive improvement in the side's fortunes to have gone so far in all three competitions. Having put together a young, settled side, Busby now made only the finest of adjustments to his team, tinkering with its components when necessary. He made two such signings in the spring of 1964. Goalkeeper Pat Dunne was bought from Shamrock Rovers for a fee of £10,500 and English international outside-right, John Connelly, came to Old Trafford from Burnley for a fee of £60,000. Albert Quixall, who had struggled with injuries throughout the 1963-64 season, and who was gradually fading from the picture, was transferred to Oldham Athletic for £8,500 in the autumn of 1964.

There would be no further major signings for the next two-and-a-half years because the club was diverting its financial resources into the erection of a new cantilevered north stand. The United directors had been informed in 1963 that Old Trafford had been chosen as one of the venues for the 1966 World Cup and they were improving the ground's facilities for the tournament. The new construction would seat 10,500 spectators with a standing enclosure holding 10,000 more. It would also contain 34 heated executive boxes, an innovation for the UK, something that Busby had first seen on a visit to the USA. At a projected cost of £250,000 (it eventually cost £320,000) it sent United heavily into debt. Consequently, there was no money available to spend on strengthening the playing squad, but Busby had told his directors that in his opinion he would have little need of such funds in the near future.

It was easy to see where his confidence sprang from. United were now a seriously dynamic attacking force, with the flashing feet of Connelly on one wing and Best on the other. Law and Herd were rapier-sharp goalscorers while Crerand and Charlton complemented

Opposite: Few defenders managed to hold Denis Law down. During a match he would constantly be on the move, twisting and turning to seek out the main chance.

each other beautifully in the midfield. Brennan and Tony Dunne were established as the team's full-back partnership, Foulkes remained rock-solid at centre-half and Nobby Stiles would gradually become the first-choice half-back alongside him as the 1964–65 season progressed.

Two defeats, three draws and one win in the opening six matches made for a less-than-impressive start to the season. Then five successive victories pushed off a run that eased United in among the championship contenders. The fifth, at the end of September 1964, came against Chelsea, one of their key rivals in the league and then managed by Tommy Docherty. United won 2–0 and played with such aplomb that they were sportingly cheered off the field at the end by the London crowd. "George scored a goal that night that I just stood and applauded," said Pat Crerand. "He changed feet so quickly and hit a screamer into the top corner. His performance was as good as Alfredo Di Stefano's for Real Madrid against Eintracht Frankfurt in the 1960 European Cup final, which was one of the great individual performances of all time."

Chelsea remained on top after that match, but United picked up nine points out of the 10 available to them in October 1964, culminating in a 7–0 victory over Aston Villa and a 2–0 win over champions Liverpool at Anfield that took the Old Trafford side a point clear of Docherty's team at the top of the table. It was a nice situation from which to launch another European expedition.

United's second place in the league at the end of the 1963–64 season provided the club with entry into the Fairs Cup, the precursor

Nobby Stiles established himself as Bill Foulkes' half-back partner during the 1964–65 season.

of the UEFA Cup. Their opening tie found them in a similar situation to that of the previous year, when they had met Willem II. This time they met the part-timers of IF Djurgardens in Stockholm in front of just 6,537 people. Again United stuttered to a 1–1 draw and again they trounced their part-time opponents in the Old Trafford return by 6–1, with Law once again getting a hat-trick.

The second round provided much tougher opposition; Borussia Dortmund of West Germany, who had been European Cup semi-finalists in the spring of 1964 and who were challenging for the Bundesliga title. United got off to a wonderful start at the Rote Erde Stadium when Herd and Charlton gave them a two-goal half-time lead. After the interval, Best went on one of his special runs, which ended with the ball in the back of the Dortmund net. The Germans pulled a goal back with a penalty and at that stage United were sitting on a superb away result. Nevertheless, in true United style, they went looking for more goals and a header from Law and a double from Charlton brought them an exceptional 6–1 victory.

Having remained top of the table throughout November 1964, a stylish 3–2 win at Arsenal at the end of the month moved United three points clear thanks to Chelsea losing on the same afternoon. The following midweek, four more United goals in the return with Dortmund at Old Trafford gave them a 10–2 aggregate in the tie. Things went less smoothly in the league during December and January; an unlucky 1–0 home defeat by Leeds United and a series of drawn games pulled United back level with their chief pursuers, Chelsea and Leeds.

Everton were also going well in the league, but United's main business with them was in the Fairs Cup. Yet again, United had been drawn against an English side in Europe, and in the first leg at Old Trafford United switched the power on full, with every part of the team playing a full role in overwhelming their opponents. Only a series of acrobatic saves by Everton goalkeeper Gordon West stopped United taking a sizeable lead, but a mistake by Foulkes allowed Everton's Fred Pickering to dart towards goal and send the ball past a stock-still Pat Dunne. Late in the first half, United got a well-deserved equalizer when Jimmy Gabriel was short with a backpass to West and Connelly stole in between the two to slip the ball home. It ended 1–1.

The return at Goodison Park, watched by a crowd of 55,000, was equally tight. John Connelly opened the scoring after six minutes, zipping away from the Everton defence to curve a shot past West. Pickering equalized for Everton, with a shot that took a deflection on its way into the net. As in the first leg, it was an attractive, open game and Connelly was revelling in the unrelenting pace of the action. His bursts from deep were a constant threat to Everton and

it was one such burst that looked sure to bring a goal but for another fine save from West. The goalkeeper could only parry Connelly's shot, though, and David Herd, on the chase, followed up to prod the ball into the net. That ended the scoring and United's 2–1 win sent them through to a quarter-final with Racing Strasbourg of France.

That return leg with Everton had been preceded by disappointing 1–0 defeats at Tottenham and Sunderland in the league, leaving United three points behind joint leaders Chelsea and Leeds as February ended. All three had 12 games left to play. It meant that Chelsea's visit to Old Trafford in mid-March 1965 would be crucial – United could not afford to lose if they were to maintain a serious title challenge.

The game began with one of the most extraordinary goals ever seen at the stadium. As Chelsea right-back Eddie McCreadie went to clear, Best raced at him, charging the ball down with his right leg after it had bounced between the two players. Best got his toe to it and sent it spinning towards the outside edge of the penalty area. Best's efforts left him off-balance and McCreadie got to the ball first but, under pressure from Best's constant movement at his back, unnerved by Best's audacity and persistence, and unsure where to turn, the Chelsea defender slipped and lost control of the ball. Best pounced on it and without pause, dug under the ball with his right foot, scooping it high over the head of Chelsea goalkeeper Peter Bonetti, who had come to his near post, and into the far side of the goal. The tenacity, the speed of execution, the precision in this goal encapsulated Best's strengths. He was still only 18.

That goal knocked the stuffing out of Chelsea, who were overwhelmed by United's ceaseless attacking. With a double from Herd and one from Charlton, the match ended 4–0, putting United just one point behind Chelsea and Leeds. A fine, left-footed half-volley by Connelly gave United a 1–0 victory at Elland Road in mid-April, and two days later, on Easter Monday 1965, Manchester United were once more top of the First Division, with a 4–2 win at Birmingham City.

A 3–0 win over Liverpool followed and when United won their second-last match of the season, beating Arsenal 3–1 at Old Trafford, they were once again champions. As an attacking force, United were close to perfection. With both wingers extraordinarily sharp and quick, the ball was delivered into the box quickly, the midfielders were always pressing forward and Law's and Herd's swift reactions made goals more likely than not.

"We had a mixture of everything – guile, class, goalscorers and people who could mix it when required," said Denis Law of that team. "To have a championship side you really have got to have a mixture of all of those things." United finished on the same points total as Leeds but took the title through having a better goal average. That year, Louis Edwards succeeded Harold Hardman as chairman on the latter's death. Edwards was friendly with Matt Busby and offered him strong support on the board of directors.

There was still much for United to play for over the remainder of the 1964-65 season. Although they had lost an FA Cup semi-final replay to Leeds in late March, they remained in the Fairs Cup. Bad weather had caused postponements and, together with FA Cup replays, had resulted in severe fixture congestion for United. As a result, the FA gave the club permission to extend their season. United therefore played their Fairs Cup tie with Strasbourg two weeks after their final league match. There were no hard and fast dates for European ties in those days, and it was up to the clubs to arrange dates for the fixtures.

A straightforward 5–0 win in the first leg in France on 12 May 1965 made the return a week later a formality. It was distinguished only by United receiving the league championship trophy and Law being presented with his trophy for European Footballer of the Year. A 0–0 draw put United into a semi-final with Hungarians Ferencvaros. With the rest of the First Division's footballers relaxing on the beach, United found themselves a goal down in the first leg at Old Trafford when Novak's long-distance free-kick streaked past Dunne. A penalty from Law evened it up and two goals from Herd put United into a 3–1 lead. A late goal from Rakosi made it 3–2.

The return, at the Nep Stadium in Budapest on 6 June, proved to be a physical battle, with Crerand and Orosz of Ferencvaros dismissed after they had squared up to each other in the middle of the park. The only goal came from a penalty after the referee adjudged Stiles to have handled inside the penalty area. Novak netted from the spot. The away goals rule had yet to be introduced in European competition so the tie had to be decided by a replay. United lost the toss for the choice of venue so they had to return to Budapest 10 days later to try to win a place in the final with Juventus.

This time, the Hungarian crowd saw the qualities of the two teams in a match filled with exhilarating football. Karaba's long-range free-kick, something at which the Hungarians were expert, went whistling past Dunne to give the Budapest side a 1–0 half-time lead. After the break, Karaba was again at the heart of the action, speeding away with the ball to spearhead an extraordinarily swift counter-attack. When he reached the goalline he diverted the ball back and into the path of Kenyvesi, who swept a volley into the United net. A late goal from Herd brought United back into things, but they couldn't get the second that would have prolonged the tie

even further. Ferencvaros went on to beat Juventus 1–0 in the final.

Prior to the play-off with Ferencvaros, Busby had described the Fairs Cup as "not only a test of reputation and ability but also of temperament. It is an especially good test for us in view of our European Cup commitments next season." It was significant that the manager was thinking about the European Cup even before the final of another European tournament. Busby had been rebuilding his side for another crack at the European Cup ever since the dark days that had followed Munich. Now, in the 1965–66 season, he would have his chance.

United were untroubled by their first set of opponents, HJK Helsinki, winning 9–2 on aggregate. That was followed by home and away wins over ASK Vorwaerts Berlin, champions of East Germany, giving United another comfortable aggregate win – 5–1 this time. It took them into the quarter-finals, where they faced serious opposition in the shape of Lisbon side Benfica, the Portuguese champions.

One of the more notable aspects of the HJK Helsinki game was that George Best was dropped for the away leg. United had been out of sorts in the early stages of the season and Best had lost his place after Busby became concerned that the youngster's liking for nightlife was hindering his game. Another young winger, 18-year-old John Aston, had taken Best's place. The team's indifferent start to the season left them with a lot of ground to make up in the league. One of those disappointing matches was notable for United's first-ever use of a substitute, John Fitzpatrick replacing Denis Law in a 5–1 defeat at Tottenham on 16 October 1965.

By the time the first leg of the Benfica tie came round in February 1966, Best had been restored to the side but United's title hopes had been fading ever since a 2–1 defeat by Liverpool at Anfield on New Year's Day. There had been too much individuality and not enough teamwork on display at times, but everyone would have to pull together if Benfica, twice winners of the European Cup, in 1961 and 1962, and finalists in 1963 and 1965, were to be defeated.

United were in attacking mode from the start of the first leg at Old Trafford and a Herd header pitched off the post after just five minutes. Benfica were a quick-thinking, pacy side and were always dangerous, as they proved on the half hour. A corner from Eusebio, the European Footballer of the Year for 1965, flew to the head of José Augusto, who sent Benfica ahead. United's response was quick and effective, with goals from Law and Herd putting the home side 2–1 ahead at half-time. A rare goal from Foulkes, a diving header at

Right: A dip of the shoulder or an instantaneous change of direction from the supremely skilled George Best could quickly sway a game United's way.

110

that, made it 3–1 to United, but near the end Eusebio provided the ball for Torres to score, so it finished 3–2 to United on the night.

It teed up a potentially tense return five weeks later at Benfica's Stadium of Light, where the Portuguese side had played 19 previous European Cup ties, winning 18 and drawing one. Busby, for one, would not be intimidated by that record or by Benfica's 80,000 home support. "It would be foolish to let Benfica get the initiative, especially here," he said. "We shall defend when necessary, and attack when we can, for to play defensively would be foolish for us. We shall play to the usual policy which won us the championship last year and we shall have four forwards just when we want them."

One of those forwards, Best, was just where United wanted him after six minutes when Tony Dunne angled a free-kick into the Benfica penalty area. A deft flick of the head from the United winger produced the opening goal. Best excelled further when he took a Herd knockdown in his stride and went whirring past three

defenders at speed before clipping the ball past goalkeeper Costa Pereira to make it 2–0. When Connelly made it 3–0 to United there were only 15 minutes on the clock. An own goal from Shay Brennan in the second half gave Benfica a glimmer of hope, but strikes from Crerand and Charlton meant the game ended 5–1 in United's favour. It was one of the greatest of all European Cup performances and it delighted Matt Busby. He stated afterwards that he thought it had been United's finest hour.

"As to whether we play it off the cuff, well we always hold tactical talks every week and before every match," he said. "But we do encourage individualism, especially that of Best, Charlton and Law. Unless you encourage that sort of individualism, you really have nothing."

The semi-final brought back memories for several of the United party – it took place at the Yugoslav People's Army Stadium, Belgrade, where the Busby Babes had played their last match before

Matt Busby leads the celebrations in the dressing room at Upton Park after United's 6–1 victory had given them their second league title of the 1960s.

the Munich crash. This time United's opponents were not Red Star but Belgrade's other major club, Partizan. The Yugoslavs made it clear beforehand that they felt they needed a clear two-goal lead to take to Old Trafford for the second leg. They got the first of those goals shortly after half-time when Hasanagic headed past Gregg and they got the second when Becejac controlled the ball in style before spinning to shoot past the United goalkeeper.

Law had hit the crossbar during the first half but that piece of misfortune was overshadowed by Best seriously aggravating a knee injury he had been carrying. His season was over and he would need a cartilage operation before eventually returning to the side after several months of recuperation.

Busby remained confident for the second leg, but Partizan defended in depth and United badly missed Best's ingenuity in their attempts at breaking down the Yugoslavs' defence. The first leg had been fiercely competitive, with the tackles flying in hard and fast. That theme was continued at Old Trafford and when Crerand and Partizan left-winger Pirmajer took things too far they were sent off by Swiss referee Gottfried Dienst. With just over quarter of an hour remaining, Nobby Stiles finally found a weak spot in the Partizan resistance and threaded a shot past goalkeeper Milutin Soskic, but it was too late. Partizan held on for a place in the final with Real Madrid in Brussels.

United ended the season fourth in the First Division, 10 points behind champions Liverpool. Once again they crashed out of the FA Cup at the semi-final stage, losing 1–0 to Everton just three days after the second leg with Partizan. Losing the European Cup semi was the most bitter blow, though, and several of United's senior players wondered whether they would ever again get such a good opportunity to lift the trophy.

The only way back into Europe's premier competition was by winning the League and in 1966–67 United directed almost all of their efforts to that end. A surprise fourth-round exit from the FA Cup at home to Second Division Norwich City, and defeat by Blackpool in their only League Cup tie that season would allow plenty of recovery time in between league fixtures. The line-up remained settled and for the opening match with West Brom at Old Trafford on 20 August 1966. Best returned to the right wing, with Connelly switching to the left.

In the opening minute of that game, Charlton, a World Cup winner with England three weeks previously, passed the ball into the path of Best, who opened United's goals account for the season. By the 20th minute, the score was 5–1 to United and the points were in the bag. United had started as they meant to continue, slackening off to allow West Brom a couple of goals for a final score of 5–3. In

George Best is presented with a new set of wheels in the summer of 1968. His increasingly fast off-field life had led to a driving ban.

the early weeks of that 1966–67 season, Best and Law were in fine individual form and United played some stunning football, but there were also some careless defeats and the defence looked shaky at times.

Busby realized some adjustments were needed. In September 1966, he made what turned out to be a far-reaching change, signing Alex Stepney from Chelsea for £55,000, a record fee for a goalkeeper. Stepney immediately made the goalkeeping position his own. Connelly, 28, was replaced by the younger Aston and moved on to Blackburn Rovers for £40,000. David Sadler, still only 23, became a regular over the season, sometimes at centre-half, sometimes in midfield, sometimes at centre-forward.

Shay Brennan and Bill Foulkes were both dropped after a particularly poor performance led to defeat at Blackpool in October. Foulkes had made more than 500 appearances for the club – only the second player to do so after Joe Spence – and was 34 years-old, but he was soon restored to the team. Tony Dunne was switched to right-back in place of Brennan with Bobby Noble, a 20 year-old, coming in to the side in the other full-back position.

Chelsea, still under the management of Tommy Docherty, were once again setting the pace at the top of the league. United went to Stamford Bridge at the start of November and, with Best in inspirational form, came away 3–1 winners. By the end of that month United were top of the First Division. They lost just one more league game – away to Sheffield United on Boxing Day – between then and the end of the season. United and Liverpool took turns at topping the table in the opening three months of 1967, but by April United were two points clear although the slightest slip would spell disaster as they were being pursued by no fewer than five clubs.

As their rivals stumbled, United coped with the pressure and on 6 May 1967 they travelled to Upton Park to face West Ham United in their penultimate fixture of the season, knowing a point would give them the title. With a post-war record crowd of 38,424 inside the ground, United settled the issue in style. Goals from Charlton, Crerand and Foulkes put them 3–0 ahead after just 10 minutes. Best and Law added to the tally after the interval, and with 10 minutes remaining Law hit a sixth to give United a 6–1 victory.

United finished as champions once again, four points clear of nearest challengers Nottingham Forest. There was champagne in the dressing-room and the following day Matt Busby gave his thoughts on the triumph.

"I don't think we would have won the championship without Stepney. The cup defeat at Norwich, although a bitter disappointment at the time, proved to be a good thing. With only the League to worry about we have been better equipped both physically and mentally. Ability is no longer enough – although there is no substitute for it. You have to have a combination of ability plus work rate.

"We would obviously like to win the championship again. But we all feel that we must have a real go at winning the European Cup. I believe the present team is good enough but obviously if the right player comes on the market we shall buy."

As it turned out, there were only two prominent new faces for the 1967–68 season, both of whom had come through the reserves. Francis Burns, a left-back, and Brian Kidd, a striker, were both 18 years-old. They blended in easily with the established first-team players. David Herd, who had suffered a leg break the previous season, had played his last game for the club. Shay Brennan featured in fewer and fewer games for the first team as Tony Dunne was often switched to right-back to accommodate Burns.

A straightforward 4–0 aggregate win over minnows, Hibernians of Malta in the first round of the European Cup gave United a second-round tie against FC Sarajevo of Yugoslavia. The first leg was scheduled for mid-November and United travelled to Eastern Europe as league leaders after a 2–1 victory over Liverpool the previous Saturday. Sarajevo proved tough as teak, dishing out severe physical punishment to United forwards Best, Kidd and Charlton, but at the end of the 90 minutes United had a 0–0 draw to show for their pains.

There was more of the same to come from Sarajevo in Manchester, but they were finally brought to heel when Fahrudin Prijaca was sent off for an ugly, slicing tackle on Best. By then, United were a goal up through John Aston and they capitalized on their one-man advantage when Best made it 2–0 midway through the second half. Two goals down, the Yugoslavs started to play some neat football and got a goal back, but United, backed by a 62,000 crowd, hung on for the winner.

The quarter-finals, where they met Polish champions Gornik Zabrze, proved equally tough. Best was again subjected to a series of fouls in the first leg, at Old Trafford, but he maintained his discipline and in the second half his low, hard centre forced Gornik centre-half Florenski to stretch awkwardly for the ball and put through his own goal. A last-minute, close-range effort from Kidd made the scoreline much more comfortable for United. On a snow-covered pitch in sub-zero Katowice for the return, in a game watched by 100,000 Poles, United looked surefooted in the tricky conditions. Snow fell steadily during the game and soon it was impossible to make out the pitch markings, but Italian referee Concetto Lo Bello insisted the match should continue. A second-half strike from Wlodek Lubanski had United living on their nerves, but they held out for the aggregate 2–1 win. "It was too much of a gamble," said Busby afterwards. "It would have been a sad way to have gone out. This is a prize we have been fighting for for years and it would have been terrible if a two-goal lead had been lost under conditions such as they were."

Opposite: The eyes of supporters young and old are glued to the great Bobby Charlton as he comes within touching distance to take a corner.

114

Brian Kidd closes in but he has nothing because Real's Zoco turns the ball past his own goalkeeper to make it 2–1 to Madrid on the night. Having won the first leg 1–0, United knew that a draw would be enough to send them into the Final and goals from David Sadler and Bill Foulkes ensured the second leg ended in a 3–3 draw.

United were three points clear of Liverpool at the top of the league on Boxing Day 1967 and they retained that three-point lead for the succeeding two months. Three calamitous defeats in March – by Chelsea, Coventry City and Manchester City – pulled them back within reach of the chasing pack but by late April they were top once again as they prepared for their European Cup semi-final against Real Madrid. The Spanish champions and six-times European Cup winners held no fears for Busby. "I feel this is our year," he said. "I think things are running for us this time and I feel happier than on previous occasions when we have got so far. We were the first English club to enter the European Cup because we felt it was a world game. It is the one thing the club wants to win and the one thing I want to win."

The first leg was played at Old Trafford and although Crerand hit the post in the early stages, United stuttered and struggled to find fluency throughout the match. Shortly before half-time, though,

Aston picked his way past Real defenders on the left wing before zipping a diagonal pass back towards Best. He swivelled swiftly and sent a left-footed shot racing high into the Real net. It was the only goal of the game.

Three days later, away to West Bromwich Albion in the league, United went down 6–3, leaving their title hopes hanging by a thread. That defeat allowed Manchester City to go top of the First Division for the first time that season. United won their next match, against Newcastle United 6–0, but in their final league outing of the season they trooped off the pitch after a 2–1 home defeat by Sunderland. It handed the title to City. United were second on 56 points, two behind their local rivals.

It didn't seem like the best send-off for the trip to Madrid but it stiffened the resolve of the United players, making them more determined than ever to land the European Cup. Real's multi-tiered Bernabeu Stadium was packed to capacity for the return, with

125,000 pairs of eyes glued to every move from the moment the players strode out side by side.

Amancio, Real's most dynamic forward, had been suspended for the first leg and Real's hopes of making the final rested heavily on him. He carried the burden lightly. After 10 minutes he met the ball powerfully with his head, sending it speeding towards the net, but Stepney pushed it on to the crossbar. Real continued to probe at United's defence, with Amancio floating around searching for openings. Eventually, he was successful when he crossed for Perez to head the ball past Stepney.

Three minutes before half-time, Real went two up through Paco Gento, but within a minute Zoco turned the ball into his own net to make it 2–1. Another minute passed, and half-time was fast approaching, when Amancio bent a superb shot past several United defenders and Stepney to put Real 3–1 ahead at the interval. There was silence in the United dressing-room at half-time, with the players traumatized at having been pulled apart by Real. Just as they were about to take the field for the start of the second half, Busby quietly reminded them that they were only a goal behind on aggregate and that one goal would get them back on level terms.

The United players gradually grew in confidence. With 15 minutes to go, Best's header found Sadler, in for the injured Law, and he clipped the ball past Betancourt in the Real goal. Five minutes on, Bill Foulkes pounded forward, gathered a pass from Best and planted the ball in the Real net to make the final aggregate score 4–3 to United. It was a suitably glorious way for United to make history, paving the way for Matt Busby to crown his career by lifting the greatest trophy in club football.

Below: The United squad and staff bask in the glow of greatness after Matt Busby's players had made United the first English club to win the European Cup.
Overleaf: George Best receives his trophy after being named European Footballer of the Year for 1968.

1968 EUROPEAN CUP FINAL

MANCHESTER UNITED (1) 4 BENFICA (1) 1 AET

29 MAY 1968, WEMBLEY

BOBBY CHARLTON thought that it was fated that United would win the 1968 European Cup after the dramatic semi-final with Real Madrid. United had a more tangible advantage for the final in that the match was to be played at Wembley, but they were without Denis Law, who watched from his hospital bed after a cartilage operation. The sides' first-choice strips were identical so United wore all-blue, Benfica all-white.

David Sadler came closest to scoring in the early stages. He got on the end of Pat Crerand's free-kick but his shot rolled harmlessly into goalkeeper Henrique's hands. Eusebio, Europe's top scorer in 1967–68, was being tightly marked by Nobby Stiles but he veered away to send a sweet, swirling, 20-yard shot past Stepney only to see it strike the underside of the crossbar.

United's next good chance came after a clever one-two involving Brian Kidd and Sadler but, free in the box and with only the goalkeeper to beat, Sadler's shot rolled wide. It was a fractious match, with tight marking and tackling, and it boiled over into a brawl just before the interval. The teams left the field at half-time to the booing of the crowd after a tense first half.

Eight minutes after the break, Sadler curved a clever cross into the penalty area, where Charlton glanced a neat header past Henrique. Best nearly made it 2–0 when he swerved past three men and thumped in a right-foot shot that Henrique saved well. The rebound fell to David Sadler whose shot was saved.

A relieved Benfica struck back. With nine minutes remaining, José Torres headed the ball down, Jaime Graca's run was not picked up, he got to the ball on the edge of the six-yard box and struck a superb, low, angled shot past Stepney.

Eusebio had three chances to wrap it up for Benfica in the final five minutes. His low shot was saved by Alex Stepney; Antonio Simoes's through ball found Eusebio bang in front of goal but his powerful left-footed shot was saved excellently by Stepney; then a Eusebio header drifted just wide of the right-hand post as referee Concetto Lo Bello whistled for the end of the 90 minutes.

United kicked off extra-time. After three minutes, Stepney's long kick was flicked on by Kidd to Best who whisked the ball away from his marker, deftly sent Henrique the wrong way, sidestepped him in style and sidefooted the ball into the unguarded goal.

The crowd barely had time to get used to United being in the lead again when Sadler headed Charlton's corner goalwards, Kidd headed it on, Henrique saved and Kidd rose to the rebound, sending a second header arcing over Henrique's outstretched fingers and into the net.

Minutes later, Kidd raced up the right wing and crossed low and hard for Charlton to send a magnificent scooped shot spinning over Henrique and into the net. Eusebio had two good, hard shots saved well by Stepney in the second half of extra-time, but United stayed in control, finishing 4–1 winners.

"That was my greatest moment," said Matt Busby. "I had lived for it for a long time. This was the combination of all my ideas, my ambitions – winning the European Cup."

Manchester United (manager Matt Busby): Stepney, Brennan, Dunne, Crerand, Foulkes, Stiles, Best, Kidd, Charlton, Sadler, Aston
Scorers: Charlton 53, 98; Best 93; Kidd 95

Benfica (manager Olto Gloria): Henrique, Adolfo, Humberto, Jacinto, Cruz, Garcia, Coluna, Jose Agusto, Eusebio, Torrel, Simoes
Scorer: Graca 81

Attendance: 100,000

Matt Busby revives United's spirits before extra-time begins.

NOBBY STILES

MIDFIELDER (MANCHESTER UNITED 1960–71)

FEW MANCHESTER UNITED PLAYERS have been more dearly loved by the club's supporters than Nobby Stiles. He played every game as if it was his last, giving his all to the team, just as any supporter would if given the chance. His gait and running style were slightly awkward – here was no clean-limbed super-athlete – which helped to reinforce his identification with those who watched from the sidelines. The man on the Stretford End could see himself in Nobby and this was no wishful illusion – Stiles had stood on the terraces with his fellow Mancunians until the club had come calling for him in 1957 when he was a 15-year-old schoolboy.

"I used to walk over the bridge at Old Trafford when I was a kid," he later recalled, "with my Uncle Peter, and also with my brother when he got older, and imagine that the tannoy was going to announce that there was a player short and would Norbert Stiles come and get changed. So to become a player at Manchester United was unbelievable."

Stiles's value to the team was evident from his debut against Bolton Wanderers when his through-ball set up Johnny Giles for United's goal in a 1–1 draw. His best work, however, could easily be overlooked. His ability to read a game enabled him to take up positions where he could intercept and snuff out opposition attacks. He would then play a simple ball forward to start the glittering whirl of the team's attacks. For this he was valued greatly by his team-mates. As United goalkeeper Harry Gregg commented, "There were times when Nobby should have drawn the wages of some of the people he played with. He not only did his job, he made sure everyone else did theirs."

Bespectacled off the park, Stiles was one of the first footballers to wear contact lenses. He had been knocked down by a bus when a child and suffered from defective vision. During evening fixtures, he would tell referees that a mistimed challenge was due to the floodlights shining in his contact lenses. His enthusiastic tackling intimidated many an opponent – quite a feat for a man who only stood at 5ft 6ins in his stockinged feet. For all his fearsome reputation, however, Nobby was sent off just twice for United – in a 1966 pre-season friendly with FK Austria Vienna and in the violent 1968 World Club Cup clash with Estudiantes.

Although it took Stiles until the 1963–64 season to become fully established in the United side, he remained a fixture in it for the remainder of the 1960s. He was a vital component of the teams that won two league championships and the European Cup, making almost 400 appearances overall. He was equally effective for England, helping his country to defeat West Germany at Wembley in 1966 to win the World Cup and winning 28 caps from Alf Ramsey. Nicknamed "Happy" by his United team-mates, the Collyhurst boy was a popular presence both on and off the pitch.

Two years after moving on to Middlesbrough for a £22,500 fee

Nobby Stiles always kept things ticking over for United.

in the spring of 1971, Stiles retired as a player, going on to manage Preston North End and West Bromwich Albion. He returned to Old Trafford as youth team coach in 1989 at Alex Ferguson's behest and was later appointed Youth Development Officer by the manager. However, the job was unsuited to Stiles and Ferguson later admitted deep regret at having to dispense with the services of one of United's great servants in 1993.

GEORGE BEST

FORWARD (MANCHESTER UNITED 1963-74)

GEORGE BEST claimed that on his Manchester United debut at 17 in September 1963 he found top-level football "easy". His football was equally easy on the eye for those who saw him play. He could make top defenders look as mobile as table footballers.

Best's abilities resulted from years of concentrated practice. As a boy in his native Belfast, he honed his control by using a tennis ball, often kicking it off doorknobs. "A ball comes off a doorknob in all sorts of directions so you have to strike it so that it hits the centre of the doorknob and comes back to you," he recalled. Having built up an extensive repertoire of superb street skills, the 15-year-old Best was introduced to Manchester United by Northern Ireland scout Bob Bishop in 1961.

He was at home with his family for Christmas 1963 when Matt Busby decided it was time to put him into the first team for a second time, against Burnley. The club contacted Best in Belfast to tell him he was required for the match. He demanded that they fly him back home immediately afterwards – a brazen request from a 17-year-old getting a chance to establish himself at Manchester United. His request was granted and he rewarded the club with a goal and an excellent performance in a 5–1 victory.

Best had outstanding pace, was an accomplished header of the ball and could launch himself into tackles with precision and power. Matt Busby once told him he was the finest tackler at Manchester United. He put in extra training work in the afternoons when other players had gone home, improving his heading, shooting and perfecting two-footedness. Nominally a winger, Best was soon told by Matt Busby that he could rove anywhere he liked on the park.

"I did have this quality of being able to sway around players like a matador," said Best, looking back on his playing days. "That was due to my great sense of balance. It is the most important quality if you want to be able to ride challenges. If that bull is rushing at you at a hundred miles an hour and you've got to get out of the way, you need balance. I had perfect balance from an early age. I never

had to think about the angle at which a player was coming in at me; I simply used to adjust myself. It takes a sort of bravery as well, to take on people when you know they will try and clobber you."

Best saw himself as different, as a man in the pop-star mould. By the mid-1960s, he was receiving 1,000 fan letters a week, mainly from teenaged girls attracted by his gleaming good health and dark good looks. He was dubbed "the fifth Beatle" by the press, he opened a string of boutiques and he could be seen darting around Manchester with a variety of females in a variety of sportscars.

Named European Footballer of the Year and Footballer of the Year in 1968, Best was the top Manchester United league goalscorer from season 1967–68 to season 1971–72. Then, in May 1972, at the age of 25, he announced from Marbella, Spain, that he had retired as a footballer. The pop-star lifestyle that he had embraced so fully had extracted its price. Excessive drinking meant that the boy who had once come back for extra training was now missing it altogether in exchange for sleeping off hangovers.

Within days of that announcement, Best withdrew his words, but he couldn't stop the momentum of his own decline. He quit United in January 1974 after a clash with Tommy Docherty and during the next decade played football on an irregular basis for an eccentric collection of clubs – Dunstable Town, Stockport County, Fulham and Hibernian in the UK; San Jose Earthquakes, Fort Lauderdale Strikers and Los Angeles Aztecs in the US. Directors would shell out good money in return for Best's drawing power. He won the last of 37 Northern Ireland caps in 1977. In the

George Best was voted European Footballer of the Year in 1968.

early 1980s, United considered bringing Best, then 35, back to Old Trafford, but it didn't develop beyond initial talks. Instead, he finished his playing days at Bournemouth, aged 37, in 1983.

"I gave everything to Manchester United for 11 great years," was Best's response when accused of finishing with the club too early. United fans are forgiving of his excesses, caring to remember Best only for the very best of times he gave them.

BRIAN KIDD

FORWARD (MANCHESTER UNITED 1967–74)

MANCHESTER UNITED have always been prepared to give youth a chance, but Brian Kidd's debut year in the first team took that maxim to extraordinary lengths. He achieved his boyhood dream while still a boy when selected for the first-team squad at 17. They were about to embark on one of the longest tours the club had ever undertaken – an exotic, six-week, 12-game expedition to the USA, New Zealand and Australia in summer 1967 – and Kidd was lucky enough to be taken along for the ride. He made his Old Trafford debut in the Charity Shield match with Tottenham Hotspur in August and his league debut at Everton the following Saturday.

Over that 1967–68 season, Kidd established himself at inside-forward, making 45 appearances and scoring 17 goals, a total bettered only by Bobby Charlton and George Best. An ever-present in the run to the European Cup final with Benfica at Wembley, his goal in that game was, literally, the icing on the cake for Kidd. The day of the final, 29 May 1968, was his 19th birthday and a giant birthday cake for the teenager was a central part of the celebrations when the team returned to the Russell Hotel in central London for the post-match celebrations. Earlier, at Wembley, the crowd had sung "Happy Birthday" to him after his goal had put their side 3–1 ahead.

It was easy to see why Matt Busby had thrown the teenager into the top team. He was quick and skilful and had a confident approach to the game. He would show defenders the ball and then let them flail in his wake as he swept past them, he was good in the air and an often spectacular finisher. Diving headers were a particular speciality.

Kidd had been with United since he was a 14-year-old schoolboy and joined the staff as a professional on his 17th birthday in May 1966. After the exceptional progress of his first year, Kidd lost his scoring touch, managing just two goals over the 1968–69 season. He was in among the goals again the following season, but Kidd found the early 1970s as tough as everyone else at United and in 1974 he was transferred to Arsenal for £110,000.

After further moves, to Manchester City, Everton and Bolton Wanderers, Kidd tried football in the United States before being appointed manager of Barrow in 1984. He moved on to Swindon Town as assistant manager the following year before joining Preston North End in 1986, where he was assistant manager and manager.

Two years later, United came calling and in the spring of 1988 Kidd rejoined the club as Youth Development Officer, in which role he revamped United's scouting network. Kidd replaced Archie Knox as Alex Ferguson's assistant in 1991 and proved himself to be a fine coach and excellent organizer of the players' training. After seven years in that post, he was desperate to test himself as a manager and quit United in December 1998 for the manager's post at Blackburn Rovers. He took over a relegation-bound team and within a year Kidd had been sacked. In 2000, he joined Leeds as Youth Development Officer and became head coach in 2001. In January 2003, he took on a part-time coaching role with England. This became his only job in May 2003 when he parted company with Leeds.

Brian Kidd's early years at United were the stuff of fantasy.

SIR MATT

MATT BUSBY was more than just one of the finest of all football managers – he was the man who invented Manchester United as the great institution that it is now. On taking over as manager he went about constructing a club where the game would be played in the way he saw best, with verve, vigour and style. Never one for lapping up personal glory, Busby always suggested that the best reward for his efforts was for people to enjoy the club he had created in his own image. Modern Manchester United remains his living legacy.

Born the son of a coalminer in Orbiston, a village near Bellshill, Lanarkshire, on 26 May 1909, Matt Busby joined Manchester City as a 19 year-old in 1928. It was a fruitless struggle for Busby to get into the first team and after two disappointing years at Maine Road he was the subject of an enquiry from Louis Rocca, a Manchester United scout. When Rocca was told that Busby's transfer fee would be £150, cash-strapped United lost interest. City persevered with the young player and were rewarded when he finally broke through to the first team as a highly intelligent, playmaking half-back. What he lacked in pace he made up for in skill and vision.

Busby reached the 1933 FA Cup final with City, but they lost 3–0 to Everton. The followng year he was back at Wembley with City, collecting a winner's medal after the 2–1 defeat of Portsmouth. In between those matches, he won his only peacetime cap for Scotland in a 3–2 defeat by Wales in Cardiff. He won another seven Scotland caps during the Second World War and also captained his country. Busby moved from City to Liverpool in 1936 for a fee of £8,000 and after wartime service in the army retired as a player in 1945.

League football had been suspended during the war and Busby, like many professional sportsmen, had joined the Army and RAF Physical Training Staffs. Late in the war, as Sergeant Major Busby, he had taken charge of the army team that played exhibition games to entertain the tommies in Italy. Busby had international players such as Tommy Lawton and Joe Mercer in his charge and this experience brought to the fore his gift for team management. So when Louis Rocca wrote to Busby in December 1944, suggesting that there was "a great job" for him at Old Trafford, Busby was most interested.

Matt Busby was one of the first tracksuited managers. The key to his success lay in the sheer strength of his imposing personality.

BUSBY

The "great job" was that of manager of Manchester United and when Busby signed on at Old Trafford in February 1945 he was wearing his khaki army uniform. Trees grew on the ground's bombed terraces and resources were scarce, but Busby's Manchester United would soon become a shining example of post-war reconstruction. With his assistant, Jimmy Murphy, whom he had recruited in Italy near the war's end, Busby set to work to build something special.

Using his innate knowledge of football and its practitioners, he created three great teams – one in the 1940s, one in the 1950s and one in the 1960s. Each one was distinctive in character but they had in common an ability to win championships and cups with thrilling football. Since the 1930s, United had followed a policy of bringing through their own young players, and that was a huge advantage to Busby, who always preferred to mould a young player the way he wanted rather than buying one. He would tell his scouts to look for players with natural talent and ability and not to worry about which position they might play in – he decided on that after he had made them Manchester United players.

In those postwar days, few managers would don a tracksuit and join their players for training as Busby did. Few would care solicitously for their welfare as individuals, as was his way. Equally importantly, Busby, a dapper individual, carried himself with understated dignity – no one ever heard him swear. A pointed remark or an expressive glance was all Busby needed whenever it was necessary to bring an individual into line. He was strongly opposed to bullying, believing in subtle persuasion as a means of getting results from his men. This style of management made his players want to do really well for him. As Bobby Charlton said, "If I was playing particularly badly, I couldn't get him out of my mind. I'd be thinking, 'He's not going to be happy with this.'"

A thoughtful, sensitive individual with a gift for understanding and getting along with people, the loss of eight of his Babes at Munich shook Busby badly and made him doubt whether he wanted to continue in football. It troubled him that a trip to Europe for a football match had extracted such a heavy toll. His wife Jean persuaded him to continue with his life's work and he started to build his third great team. He had seen the European Cup as "the future of the game" and pursuit of that trophy re-energized him for the challenges of the 1960s.

The European Cup semi-final defeat against Partizan Belgrade in 1966, however, again almost persuaded Busby to quit as manager. He descibed it as "the lowest ebb since the Munich air crash" and was convinced that United had lost their chance of winning the European Cup. However, the players remained solidly behind Busby and after discussions with the board of directors he was persuaded to remain in charge. Although liked by his players, Busby was very much the Boss, as he was habitually called by all

Matt Busby shows off the European Cup at Old Trafford.

of them. "He doesn't hand out toffees when he calls you into his office," Nobby Stiles once commented.

Five league titles, the European Cup and two FA Cups arrived at Old Trafford during Busby's time and he came agonizingly close to capturing a dozen more trophies. He was knighted after the 1968 European Cup victory and on his 60th birthday a year later retired as United manager. As general manager, Sir Matt oversaw the appointment of Wilf McGuinness, taking charge again briefly after McGuinness was sacked. In the early 1970s, Busby took up a position on United's board of directors, later becoming club president. He remained in that position until his death in January 1994.

"Many, many times when they tried something that didn't come off, I was happy," said Busby of his 1960s team. "I was always very happy that they were a creative side, building up rather than destroying. I was quite happy because that's the right thing to do." As an epitaph for the positive, benevolent influence Matt Busby had on football and Manchester United, it could hardly be bettered.

McGUINNESS AND O'FARRELL

MATT BUSBY'S SUCCESSOR WAS ALWAYS GOING TO HAVE A
DIFFICULT TASK. WILF McGUINNESS AND FRANK O'FARRELL
BOTH TRIED TO FILL HIS SHOES,
BUT UNITED WERE SOON ON A DOWNWARD SPIRAL.

THE SUCCESSOR TO MATT BUSBY was always going to be presented with a difficult task. Wilf McGuinness and Frank O' Farrell tried their best to fill his shoes but both had limited success. The post-Busby years soon found United on a dangerous downward spiral.

Matt Busby's passionate desire to win the European Cup had been driven by his belief that increased international club competition would improve the British game. Sadly, that belief was strained to the limit early in the following season. By beating Benfica, United gained entry to the World Club Cup, a two-legged prestige match between the European and South American champions. United's opponents in the autumn of 1968 were Estudiantes de La Plata of Argentina.

There were serious overtones even before the match began. Nobby Stiles and Bobby Charlton had been members of the England team that had beaten Argentina in the World Cup quarter-final two years previously, after which England manager Alf Ramsey implied that the Argentinians had acted like "animals". Then, in 1967, six players had been sent off in a violent World Club Cup play-off between Celtic and Racing Club of Argentina.

"It is so difficult for any manager to ensure there is no hot-headedness and that players do not retaliate," said Busby before the first leg in Buenos Aires on 25 September 1968. "You can do all the talking in the world and advise in every way, but somebody on the field will be provoked and do something they really do not want to do. But this is a world game and we must try to break down barriers."

There were 2,000 police keeping an eye on the 85,000 crowd. That ensured there were no problems off the field but on it the Argentinians ceaselessly punched and spat on the United players, goading them with numerous on and off-the-ball fouls. The two World Cup men were particularly badly treated – Stiles required stitches in an eye injury and Charlton's leg was sliced open. Late in the match, Stiles was dismissed for disputing a dubious decision by the Uruguayan linesman. Estudiantes' Conigliaro had headed the only goal of the game in the 29th minute. "It was disgraceful," said Busby afterwards. "If you held the ball you were in danger of your life. Is it all worth it? I think we must keep on trying to educate these people to our way of thinking."

In the return leg at Old Trafford three weeks later, Denis Law left the field after Estudiantes goalkeeper Poletti's studs had become embedded in the United forward's leg. That was after Veron had headed Estudiantes 1–0 ahead. Late in the match, George Best was sent off with Estudiantes centre-back Hugo Medina after a punch-up. Medina had to be held back by a linesman as the Argentinian attempted to thump Best on their way to the dressing-rooms. Willie Morgan, a winger whom Busby had signed from Burnley for

Estudiantes' José Mendina is led away after his sending off in the heated World Club Cup match with United.

George Best's inspired second goal against Rapid Vienna helped United to ease through to the semi-finals in defence of the European Cup.

£100,000 in the summer, equalized but Estudiantes took the World Club Cup, now a tarnished trophy, with a 2–1 aggregate.

United's defence of the European Cup was more enjoyable. After a 10–2 aggregate victory over Irish champions Waterford, they faced Anderlecht. A 3–0 win at Old Trafford set them up nicely for the return in Brussels, where newly introduced midfielder Carlo Sartori gave United a 1–0 lead. Anderlecht threw everything into attack and fought back to lead 3–1. They were just unable to get a fourth. The United players applauded a distinguished set of opponents off the pitch. That aggregate win put United into a quarter-final with Rapid Vienna.

On 14 January 1969, Matt Busby announced that he would be resigning at the end of the season. He was almost 60 and had been manager for nearly quarter of a century. "It is only right that my successor should be ready to start at the beginning of a new season," said Busby.

Rapid Vienna were overwhelmed by United in the first leg at Old Trafford in March. Two goals from Best and one from Morgan produced a superb 3–0 victory. For his second, Best exchanged passes with Stiles before dancing across the face of the Rapid defence, evading a series of barbed tackles. Then, while falling backwards and with four men still between him and the goal, he spiked the ball into the roof of the Rapid net. A goalless draw in Austria a week later sent United into the semis.

Winter postponements meant that United had a backlog of fixtures and they were given special dispensation by the Football Association to extend their season into mid-May for their European Cup semi-final with AC Milan. The first leg, in the San Siro, was watched by 85,000 people inside the stadium and by 200 million on television across Europe. The match was beamed back to Old Trafford, where nearly 25,000 fans watched it on big screens at the ground.

Milan dominated from the start. In the 34th minute, Foulkes failed to head clear convincingly and Crerand mistimed his attempt at booting the ball away. It rebounded off his back and Angelo Sormani swooped to plant it past Jimmy Rimmer in the United goal. Sormani missed an open goal shortly after the break but with 50 minutes gone, Kurt Hamrin ended an excellent Milan move by steering home the Italians' second. The night became even more bleak when John Fitzpatrick was dismissed for kicking Hamrin in an off-the-ball incident. "We are not beaten yet," said Busby after the 2–0 defeat. "We never give up when we have a chance. If we can score one at Old Trafford that will worry them and a second will earn us a replay."

On the night of the second leg, the Italians were forced to defend in depth as United swarmed towards their goal, but intensive defending was something Italian sides delighted in. Rimmer did make a crucial save from midfielder Gianni Rivera but Milan goalkeeper Fabio Cudicini made many more. It took until the 70th minute for United to open the scoring. Best steered clear of three of the Italian defenders who had shackled him all evening and found Charlton, who swiftly hit the target with a fine, angled shot. United now redoubled their efforts in search of an equalizer. Ten minutes on, Crerand sent a low ball into the Milan six-yard box and Law appeared to have shepherded it over the line before it was hacked

128

away. United players who were on the spot were convinced it was a goal but French referee Machin waved play on.

"My team were magnificent and gave everything they had to pull the game around," commented Busby afterwards. "Perhaps we had one or two chances we did not take and you have to accept those when playing against a team that has such a capable defence as Milan." United had succumbed showing the spirit that had always marked Matt Busby's teams. Two days later, the Boss drew down the curtain on his managerial career, waving farewell to the fans at the final league game of the season, a 3–2 win over Leicester City.

A new structure at Old Trafford was designed to ease the burden of living up to Busby's reputation. On 1 June 1969, Wilf McGuinness stepped up from the position of reserve team coach to become chief coach. Busby, as general manager, was to work with McGuinness to relieve some of the pressure on him. McGuinness was responsible for team selection, tactics, training and the coaching of the senior side. Busby would oversee all the other aspects of the manager's job, such as dealing with press enquiries, players' wages and transfer business. It freed McGuinness, still only 31 years-old, to work purely as a coach.

"We'll just see how it works out," said Busby. "We've been watching Wilf closely as he has gone about his duties and we're satisfied he can do the job. Perhaps he lacks experience but he knows our ways and he has plenty to bite on for the moment. In a year or so, perhaps he could have full command."

McGuinness did indeed have much to chew over as he prepared for pre-season training. United had raised their game for the 1968–69 European Cup, but had finished 11th in the First Division, their lowest position for six years, and had been knocked out in the FA Cup quarter-finals. His first game was away to Crystal Palace, where United treated the biggest crowd of the day – 48,000 – to a fine show of clever, passing football on a sweltering August afternoon. With Best, Morgan, Kidd and Law up front, prompted by Crerand and Charlton in midfield, United attacked from all directions. Only John Jackson in the Palace goal prevented United from hitting the Londoners for six and the match ended 2–2.

Disappointingly, this was followed by a 2–0 home defeat by Everton and things got worse the following Saturday when United were beaten 4–1 at home by Southampton. Bill Foulkes had struggled to cope with probing crosses and Southampton's Ron Davies took full advantage to notch all four of his side's goals. "Uneasiness at the back," was Busby's terse explanation of how United had lost the game. He suggested to McGuinness that Arsenal centre-half Ian Ure would make a good replacement for Foulkes and within hours Ure was at Old Trafford, purchased for £80,000.

Ure, a Scottish international, was best known to the United support as the man who had fought a running battle with Denis Law in a league game two years previously, as a result of which both men were given six-week suspensions. A strong stopper, Ure brought stability to the team through his central defensive partnership with David Sadler. His arrival ended Foulkes's playing career. United's results gradually began to improve. They finished the 1969–70 league season in eighth position.

The two domestic Cup competitions yielded fair results. A lengthy League Cup run produced a semi-final with Manchester City. In the first leg, at Maine Road on 3 December 1969, the score was 1–1 when, two minutes from time, City's Francis Lee tumbled over Ure's leg and City were given a penalty, much to the chagrin of the United players. City scored but even then it took an outstanding save from goalkeeper Joe Corrigan and a goalline clearance from Tony Book to preserve their lead. At the end of the match, Best was seen to jostle the referee, knocking the ball out of the official's hands. He was later fined £100 and suspended for four weeks for that incident.

A crisp atmosphere surrounded the Old Trafford return a fortnight later when goals from young defender Paul Edwards and Law put United 2–1 up and level on aggregate. With seven minutes remaining, Lee hit an indirect free-kick at goal. Stepney had no need to make any attempt to save but he parried the ball instinctively and Mike Summerbee pounced, putting the ball in the net and City in the final.

A month later, United exacted revenge with a 3–0 home win over City in the FA Cup, part of a run that took them to the semi-finals. There they met Leeds United and after two 0–0 draws, lost the second replay 1–0. On the afternoon of the first replay, McGuinness had found Best ignoring team orders by absenting himself in a girl's bedroom. Late in the match, the Irishman had a fine scoring opportunity that could have decided the tie but he stumbled over the ball. Leeds went on to lose the final, beaten by Chelsea in a replay at Old Trafford.

A run of bad results at the start of the 1970–71 season left United sixth from bottom at the end of August. The team looked spiritless. They picked up very slightly during the autumn and by the time of a 2–2 draw at Tottenham in early December, McGuinness was enthusing about his team's "brilliant and breathtaking football". A hard-fought, sometimes vicious, local derby with City at Old Trafford the following week resulted in a 4–1 defeat. Arsenal, second in the table, were next at Old Trafford in the league and United were played off the park, beaten 3–1 in front of the lowest home crowd of the season – 33,182. On the two Wednesdays either side of that game, United played their two-legged League Cup semi-final against

Ian Ure brought stability to the United defence following his £80,000 move from Arsenal in 1969.

Aston Villa of the Third Division. Villa were the best team in each leg, completing a 3–2 aggregate victory in front of their fans that had the Birmingham crowd chanting "Easy Easy" at the end.

Now in serious danger of relegation, United's 4–4 draw at Derby County on Boxing Day proved to be the last throw of the dice for McGuinness. On 29 December 1970, Busby stated, "The directors called a special meeting last night to discuss the performance of the team and decided to relieve Mr McGuinness of his duties as team manager. As he did not want to leave the club and as the club felt he still had a part to play, he has been offered his former position as trainer-coach to the Central League team, which he has accepted. I am sorry it has not worked out because Wilf McGuinness was my choice."

Busby reluctantly took over as caretaker manager. "I thought I had left all this behind me," he said. Stability was injected into the

United side and they had manoeuvred themselves into eighth position by the end of the season. Busby bowed out in style at Maine Road on 5 May. City enlisted *This Is Your Life* presenter Eamonn Andrews to make a special presentation to him and his team presented him with 90 minutes of graceful, flowing football as they defeated their old rivals 4–3 with Law, Best and Charlton, appropriately, scoring all the United goals.

On 8 June 1971, Busby's second successor was announced – Frank O'Farrell. He was appointed team manager while Busby was to join the board of directors. Busby had met O'Farrell three days earlier and had guaranteed that considerable funds would be available to buy new players. O'Farrell said, "I shall have full control at Old Trafford. I have been given that assurance. Sir Matt Busby will be on the board, but I shall be the manager in every sense of the word."

As well as a new manager, there would be a new backdrop to the

action at Old Trafford. Building work, which would last a year, began in 1971 to extend the cantilever stand round behind the goal at the traditional Scoreboard End. The scoreboard itself was to be replaced by an electronic screen which would give scores, news and announcements.

Thunder and lightning heralded the start of United's league season, which began at Derby County, the scene of McGuinness's final outing as United manager. A 2–0 half-time lead was surrendered early in the second half and only a string of superb saves by Alex Stepney stopped Derby snatching a winner. There were more dramatics the following Wednesday at Stamford Bridge when George Best sat down on the pitch after being dismissed by referee Norman Burtenshaw. United recorded a useful 3–2 victory.

Hooliganism had plagued United for several years. The Fairs Cup semi-final with Ferencvaros back in 1965 had been held up after missiles were thrown on to the pitch from the Stretford End. The same thing had happened during the 1969 European Cup semi-final when Milan goalkeeper Cudicini was felled by an object thrown from the crowd. In the spring of 1971, during a 2–0 home defeat by Newcastle, a knife was thrown on to the pitch, prompting an FA Disciplinary Committee to punish United by ordering the club to play their opening two home fixtures of the 1971–72 season at least 25 miles from Old Trafford. That first "home" match, at Anfield, drew a crowd of just 27,649 for the meeting with champions Arsenal. Best was in effervescent form and Kidd was thriving under O'Farrell and they helped United to come from a goal down to win 3–1. For the final goal, Kidd swerved round three defenders before sending a shot flashing past Bob Wilson.

Only 23,000 were at United's next "home" match, this time at the Victoria Ground, Stoke. Best sashayed and swayed past opponents in brilliant fashion time and again throughout the 90 minutes. He scored twice and inspired United to a 3–1 win over West Bromwich Albion that put them briefly on top of the First Division. After his sending off against Chelsea, Best, who was already sitting on a six-week suspension, seemed in real danger of a three-month ban but this did not seem to faze him one bit. As it turned out, his explanation of the Chelsea incident – that he had been swearing at team-mate Willie Morgan and not the referee – was accepted and he incurred no further punishment for the incident.

A golden autumn yielded an exceptional run of results and as Christmas approached, United were top of the First Division and five points clear of nearest challengers Derby and Manchester City.

Ian Storey-Moore arrived from Nottingham Forest in March 1972 and added fizz to the United attack, helping them to finish eighth in the table.

That lead was whittled away game by game as United faltered to a series of disappointing draws over the Christmas period. The new year began with Best missing training for the week before United lost 3–1 at home to Wolverhampton Wanderers. He was fined two weeks' wages and ordered to move out of his high-tech, futuristic new home in Bramhall and back into digs with his original landlady, Mrs Fullaway, in Chorlton.

It did little to help United deal with their alarming decline. Best was off-form on his return and they tumbled from the top in late January, dropping down to third after a 1–0 home defeat by Chelsea. With the defence looking flimsy and the attack lacking fizz, United were soon in freefall. After a 5–1 hammering at Leeds they were in seventh position. By mid-March, they had gone 11 league games without a win and the impetus provided by O'Farrell's appointment had worn off.

It prompted O'Farrell to start spending on new signings. The first was Martin Buchan, a stylish centre-back who cost £125,000 from Aberdeen. Ian Storey-Moore, a graceful goalscoring winger, cost £200,000 from Nottingham Forest. Buchan strengthened the defence and Storey-Moore pepped up the attack. United were steadied and finished the 1971–72 season in eighth place.

It proved to be a temporary reprieve. By December 1972, United, table-toppers at exactly the same stage the previous year, were sixth from last, just two points above bottom club Crystal Palace. Ted MacDougall had been bought from Bournemouth for £200,000 and Ron Davies from Manchester City for £25,000 in the autumn, but both strikers failed to spark the United attack.

George Best was the rock on which O'Farrell finally foundered. While the team struggled on the pitch, Best was struggling to turn up for training. Matters came to a head at the start of December 1972 when he was dropped after having failed to appear three times in a week. At a board meeting on 5 December, he was placed on the transfer list and suspended for 14 days. But on 14 December, without O'Farrell's knowledge, Busby and Louis Edwards privately agreed with Best to lift his punishment. Despite his authority having been so blatantly undermined, O'Farrell refused to resign. If Busby and Edwards no longer had any confidence in him, they would have to sack him.

Minus Best, United travelled to London to face Crystal Palace on 16 December 1972 and in the opening minute, Jackson saved superbly from Storey-Moore. Then the walls caved in as Palace strolled to an easy 5–0 win. By the end of the afternoon, United were second from bottom and staring relegation in the face. Three days later, O'Farrell was gone from Old Trafford. After more than three years, United were still searching for Busby's successor.

WILF McGUINNESS

"MANCHESTER UNITED is my life," said Wilf McGuinness on his dismissal as team manager in 1970, but the club that had nurtured his career extracted a heavy price in return for his devotion. All McGuinness's hair suddenly fell out after his final departure from Old Trafford in 1971 – a shocking outward sign of delayed reaction to the huge nervous strain he had been under as United manager.

McGuinness had captained Manchester, Lancaster and England Schoolboys, had been a coach to the 1966 England World Cup squad, and England youth team coach. At Old Trafford he had coached the reserve team. Despite those credentials, senior players bridled at being instructed and disciplined by a man half Matt Busby's age when McGuinness was appointed chief coach in 1969. When some began complaining to Busby about McGuinness and were given a hearing, his days were numbered.

Alex Stepney commented: "Wilf wasn't very good at handling players at training. It wasn't all his fault perhaps, but he lacked experience."

That inexperience had shown itself in his very first signing. Busby, on a hunch, had insisted on signing Ian Ure as a central defender. McGuinness was sceptical about the signing but deferred to Busby – Ure turned out to be only a partial success.

"In the end, being 31 was a handicap," said McGuinness, looking back. "It would have been better, from my point of view, if Matt Busby had stayed on as manager initially and taken me on as his number two. That way I would have possibly learned and developed more."

At the time of his sacking McGuinness said, "Obviously it is disappointing to me but managers are judged by results. I have had the full support of the board and Sir Matt and all at the club. With a bit of luck, we might have been in three Cup finals."

McGuinness's subsequent managerial career took him to Greece for three years, with Aris Salonica and Panachaiki Patras, before it ground to a halt at York City in 1977, just as he turned 40.

Wilf McGuinness suffered as a result of his time at the United helm.

FRANK O'FARRELL

MATT BUSBY WAS SO IMPRESSED by Frank O'Farrell that he said on O'Farrell's appointment as Manchester United manager, "I look upon Frank O'Farrell as my last great signing, possibly the greatest of the lot."

As a half-back, Cork-born O'Farrell represented West Ham United and Preston North End, where he had played alongside Tommy Docherty in the 1950s. He went on to manage Weymouth with whom he won the Southern League championship twice in five years. In 1968, after three years at Torquay United during which they were promoted, he joined Leicester City, reaching the 1969 FA Cup final but failing to prevent relegation. City had just won promotion back to the First Division when O'Farrell, then in his early 40s, joined United.

Alex Stepney said of him, "We thought at first it was a great appointment and we went like a bomb for a time. But he didn't buy new players at the beginning and you need new players sometimes to give you that extra boost. Otherwise there's not enough competition for places and some players tend to get complacent."

O'Farrell received little respect or loyalty from United players. Some still addressed Busby as "Boss" in O'Farrell's presence and O'Farrell, like McGuinness, was frustrated by what he saw as Busby's interference during his time as manager. Busby maintained, "I have always given full cooperation and since Frank O'Farrell came here he has had a completely free hand."

A disillusioned O'Farrell commented, "I had never admired a man as much as Matt Busby. But when I left Old Trafford I had never been let down by any man as much as by him."

O'Farrell went on to manage Cardiff City and the Iranian national team. At Old Trafford he had been on a lucrative five-year deal worth £12,000 a year. His £78,000 compensation claim against United was settled shortly before its scheduled court hearing in late 1973.

Later in the 1970s, he rejoined Torquay as a consultant. It was during his time in this post that he was offered the job of Newcastle United manager. O'Farrell, who had at times been stung by the intense press coverage of affairs at Old Trafford, opted not to uproot his family from their settled surroundings on the south coast.

Frank O'Farrell found it hard both to emerge from the shadows of Matt Busby and to gain the respect of the United players.

CHAPTER NINE

TOMMY DOCHERTY

DECISIVE ACTION WAS REQUIRED AT OLD TRAFFORD TO BRING
BACK PRIDE TO MANCHESTER UNITED. TOMMY DOCHERTY WAS
THE POLAR OPPOSITE OF MATT BUSBY BUT, AS MANAGER,
HE RESTORED THE CLUB'S STANDING.

136

Tommy Docherty had been a spectator at Selhurst Park for the first half of United's catastrophic defeat by Crystal Palace in December 1972. He watched the second half as manager-elect of the Old Trafford club. In the boardroom at half-time, he had been asked if he would like to take over at United. Docherty, then the manager of the Scottish national team, immediately said 'yes'.

"Managers don't mind moving to a club at the bottom because they know it can't get any worse," said Matt Busby as United hovered between the official sacking of Frank O'Farrell, which took place the following Tuesday, and the official appointment of Docherty the following Friday, 22 December 1972. "I have always thought this was the greatest club in the world," said Docherty.

Docherty immediately imposed his own identity on the club. George Graham had conveniently been placed on the Arsenal transfer list on the day O'Farrell was sacked, and five days after Docherty's appointment he splashed out £120,000 for the Scottish international midfielder. The following day, another of Docherty's Scottish internationals, under-23 full-back Alex Forsyth, arrived at Old Trafford. He cost £100,000 from Partick Thistle.

Pat Crerand was promoted from youth coach to assistant manager. "He is a man I can trust and that's important," said Docherty. As 1973 began, Docherty purchased Jim Holton, another Scot and a hugely aggressive centre-half, from Shrewsbury Town for £80,000. Lou Macari, a striker, arrived from Celtic for £200,000 in mid-January.

Docherty had spent the awe-inspiring sum of £450,000 in less than a month. He was as much clan chief as manager. There were eight Scots in the side that drew with West Ham United at Old Trafford in late January 1973 – Forsyth, Denis Law, Holton, Martin Buchan, Willie Morgan, Ted MacDougall, Macari and Graham. That game produced United's first league point of the year. United were 2–0 down but a Bobby Charlton penalty and a prodded shot from close range by debutant Macari levelled the score.

Docherty had introduced fighting spirit into the team and they were uncompromising and aggressive in their pursuit of points. Graham was used as a holding player in a pragmatic 4-4-2 formation that was more defensively oriented than anything United fans had seen before. Tight man-marking tactics were a key feature of this team. At Highfield Road, 40,000 Midlanders booed United off the field after a 1–1 draw with Coventry City that had been riddled with fouls and gamesmanship.

Docherty would frequently use the long-ball game, skipping the midfield to seek out his strikers. It wasn't pretty and pretty often it was ineffective – it took nearly two months for him to record his first victory as United manager. Eventually, though, United scrambled out of the relegation mire. Macari and Brian Kidd were Docherty's preferred strikeforce so Ted MacDougall had been offloaded to West Ham in February 1973 for £150,000.

Holton was sent off against Newcastle United in mid-March after butting Malcolm Macdonald on the back of the head. Bobby Charlton, in contrast, was never booked in his entire career and he reached a notable landmark when he made his 600th league appearance, against Stoke City in April 1973. Two days after that game, Charlton, flanked by Louis Edwards and Sir Matt Busby, announced that he would be retiring at the end of the season. "I would have hated to leave under worse circumstances but things are rosier now," he said. "I am delighted to see Tommy Docherty doing so well. It will be a clean break for me at the end of this season. I'll always remember how lucky I've been at Old Trafford."

A 45,000 crowd at United's next match, against Leeds United at Elland Road, gave Charlton a

Lou Macari was one of many, busy, hungry players bought by Tommy Docherty as he transformed Old Trafford.

Bobby Charlton, who had been United captain for six years, prepares to kick off his final 90 minutes for the club, against Chelsea in April 1973.

standing ovation and he bade farewell to 58,000 Old Trafford fans on Easter Monday against Sheffield United. The chant "Sir Bobby Charlton" bounced around Stamford Bridge the following Saturday as he made his final appearance, against Chelsea, and then one of the greatest of all United players was gone.

As one legend left, another returned. George Best, who had been absent from Old Trafford for five months, was given training facilities at the club. Denis Law, the other member of United's great 1960s treble act, was given a free transfer by Docherty two days after Charlton's swansong against Chelsea. Law had played in the first team just three times since Docherty's arrival. Another long-time United servant, David Sadler, went to Preston North End on a free transfer that summer.

Off the field, a consortium of businessmen mounted a takeover bid. They wanted the United board to resign and wished to reinstate Frank O'Farrell in place of Docherty. The board responded with an Extraordinary General Meeting in mid-April 1973 at which it was agreed that first option on any sale of shares should be given to the existing directors. This further tightened Louis Edwards' grip on the reins of power at Old Trafford.

The new season promised a fresh start, but Docherty's team looked stale at Highbury on the opening day, producing a flat performance as they lost 3–0. Wins over Stoke City and Queen's

Park Rangers followed, although after the latter Docherty admitted, "We were terrible." Subsequent defeats at Leicester City and Ipswich Town left United seventh from bottom.

The team lacked inspiration but Best was back again, looking for a chance to regain his place in the team. Docherty expressed himself "delighted" at Best's return. Best, so overweight that his shirt buttons looked ready to pop at any moment, said, "I've missed the game more than I thought I would. I would like to think that the drinking problems I had, and the depressions they caused, are behind me."

United had a solid defence but were punchless in attack, leading the Old Trafford crowd to chant for Best's return as United fell to a second defeat by Leicester City that autumn of 1973. Joe Lancaster, a specialist fitness coach, was brought in to help Best, who tipped the scales at 12st 4lb. He had Best making daily five-mile runs and put him on a special diet that cut out bread, potatoes, sugar and milk. With his fitness improved, the Irishman made his first appearance of the year in early October when Ajax Amsterdam visited Old Trafford for Denis Law's testimonial. A 45,000 crowd saw Best produce some neat touches although he clearly still lacked fitness.

Tommy Docherty had promised to rejuvenate United, but his decision to gamble on Best hinted that the manager was close to desperation in his attempts to inject some life into his team. At the

138

annual meeting of shareholders at Old Trafford on 9 October 1973, the directors announced a loss of £390,000 on the previous year. On the night before, in front of just 23,000 home fans, Docherty's expensively assembled side had gone out of the League Cup to Second Division Middlesbrough. "This is my first meeting," Docherty told United shareholders, "and I hope it's not my last. I appreciate we are going through a dodgy time and we have a long road ahead. But the youth policy has been put on a better footing and the second team is top of the Central League. We are getting geared up for success and we feel things are improving."

Things soon got worse. Lou Macari, who had been performing poorly, was fined £400 and transfer-listed by Docherty after refusing to turn out in a reserve match at Mossley. Macari had scored just five goals since joining United and had yet to hit the net in the current season. Ian Storey-Moore, who had been battling an ankle ligament injury for a year, was forced to quit professional football in late 1973 at the age of 28.

Docherty still had the chance to play his wild card – George Best – and regardless of Best's fitness, he could still draw the crowds, something that attracted the attention of the shareholders. A match with Shamrock Rovers in Dublin had to be abandoned with ten minutes to go when a large number of the 30,000 present raced on to the field to mob Best in his second comeback game. He had done enough to be recalled to the colours for a league game against Birmingham City the following Saturday, 20 October, for which Macari was also brought back. A bearded Best had obviously lost pace while gaining weight. Still, his touches and his passing were in a healthy condition as United achieved their first league victory in five games. Alex Stepney, now United's penalty taker, scored from the spot for the only goal of the game.

Docherty stated that consolidation and not adventure was to be United's objective, but even that modest ambition appeared beyond them as their form, and the crowds, continued to dip. After a dispiriting sequence of results, a 2–1 defeat by Sheffield United two days after Christmas plunged them into the third from bottom position. That season, for the first time, three clubs were to be relegated from the First Division.

A 3–0 defeat at Queen's Park Rangers on New Year's Day 1974 heralded Best's first absence from training since his return. For several days, neither Docherty nor Crerand heard from the player. The following Saturday he was dropped for the Cup tie against Plymouth Argyle. Docherty complained afterwards of Best's poor form – at Loftus Road his lack of sharpness had been exposed as he was caught in possession embarrassingly often. He was no longer worth the trouble he generated and when Best again failed to turn

up for training in the week following the Cup tie, his time at Old Trafford had finally expired. "I have more important things on my mind than George Best," said Docherty. "My concern is in looking after the first team and running club affairs. I am too busy with this to be making statements on Best every five minutes and I certainly shall not be running about after him."

Best was put on the transfer list and suspended by the club for a fortnight. He emerged to say, "I will never play in a league match in this country again. I know that I have lost for ever that certain spark that set me apart from other players and I also know that I can never get it back." There was a further sign of strife when Bill Foulkes, the reserve team coach, was sent home from Old Trafford by Docherty in late January 1974.

Docherty continually chopped and changed his team but to no avail. A 2–0 defeat by Leeds United in February 1974 deposited United at the bottom of the league table and the previously unthinkable prospect of relegation was now at the forefront of everybody's minds. Alex Stepney put his thoughts into words.

"If Manchester United go down – and there's a fair chance that we will – well, that's life," he said. "We might go down and there will be a few who won't be sorry, but it's not the end of the world. It might take a couple of years to build again and get back into the First Division but we can do it. Others have and they weren't Manchester United.

"Manchester United aren't just a club, they are an institution, which means they are something special. It doesn't mean they can't have some bad times, but they'd still be Manchester United, no matter what division they're in. No matter what people think and say or what they write about us in the papers, the spirit at Old Trafford is as good as it was when we were doing well. We've got a good boss, a good staff, some promising youngsters and the directors are behind us."

By late March 1974, United were seven points adrift of safety, but a Willie Morgan-inspired 3–1 win over Chelsea at Stamford Bridge offered hope. A 3–3 draw with Burnley moved them into the second from bottom spot, above Norwich City, whom they faced next at Carrow Road. An inspired afternoon on Stepney's part kept the Norwich forwards out and goals from Macari and Brian Greenhoff gave United a 2–0 win, continuing the revival. Greenhoff, a midfielder, had joined United as 15-year-old in 1968 and had been given his first-team debut by Docherty in the autumn of 1973. Docherty sent his players back out from the dressing-room to salute

Opposite: Alex Stepney made more appearances for United than any other goalkeeper – 539. Only Bobby Charlton and Bill Foulkes have played more games for the club.

United supporters take to the field as the club are relegated on the final day of the 1973–74 season.

the fans and on the train home the manager mingled freely with United supporters throughout the journey. He promised them that if United did go down they would be back in the First Division the following season.

Stewart Houston, a £55,000 full-back signed from Brentford in December 1973, was working well with fellow Scottish defenders Forsyth, Buchan and Holton. Jim McCalliog, a Scottish international signed for £60,000 in March 1974, had teamed up with Greenhoff to form a useful midfield pairing. Morgan and Gerry Daly, a 19 year-old who had cost £12,000 from Bohemians a year previously, were making things happen on the wings. With Macari and 19-year-old youth product Sammy McIlroy a sharp-witted front two, there was now a very nice balance about the United team. Despite the club's predicament, Docherty had abandoned his previous stifling tactics, which had included the occasional use of a lone striker.

Busby had suggested to Docherty that if United were to go down, they should do so in some style. It now looked possible that an expansive approach might even be rewarded with salvation from relegation. Spirited victories over Newcastle United and Everton took United to within three points of fourth-bottom Southampton so United travelled to the Dell in late April 1974 knowing that a win would take them out of the relegation zone. Docherty had instilled real belief in the side and they were playing a neat, crisp, passing game orchestrated by Greenhoff and McCalliog.

At Southampton, a patient display yielded results when McCalliog put United 1–0 up with a 20th minute penalty, but a Mick Channon equalizer made the final score 1–1. With three games to play, United still had games in hand on Birmingham City and Southampton, the two sides immediately above them, but a midweek defeat at Everton – United's first in seven matches – cloaked Old Trafford in gloom.

United's penultimate match of the season was an encounter with Manchester City at Old Trafford and Denis Law, now captain at City, was given a tremendous welcome back by the United support. United pressed into attack from the start and had two goalbound efforts cleared off the City line but the game remained goalless until nine minutes from time. Then Law stuck out a heel to divert the ball past Stepney. "I didn't particularly want to go there and win the game," said Law. "Equally, I didn't want to go there and get beaten. It was 0–0 and then Frannie Lee crossed the ball. I hadn't a clue where the goal was. I backheeled it and it was a complete fluke. It was an awful moment. I was very sad. In fact, that turned out to be my last kick of a ball in league football."

The goal signalled a mass pitch invasion and it took the police seven minutes to clear the playing area of hundreds of young United fans who were hoping their actions would bring about an abandonment and a replay. Missiles rained down on the pitch when the players reappeared and then, despite Sir Matt Busby's tannoyed appeals for calm, a second pitch invasion sent the players to the dressing-rooms once more. Four minutes of the 90 had still to be played but when referee David Smith heard that Birmingham City had beaten Norwich 2–1, he knew that the outcome of the Old Trafford match was irrelevant and he kept the players inside. In the intervening years a myth has developed that Law's goal sent United down but it was Birmingham's victory that sealed United's fate. Even if United had beaten City convincingly, they would still have been facing up to the prospect of Second Division football for the first time in 37 years.

"We have the best supporters in the world," said Busby in the aftermath of the pitch invasion, "but a small number of them have done our name so much harm. How does one cope with this sort of thing? I don't know." Even in the Second Division, the hooligans stalked United. In their opening game at Orient, there was another pitch invasion, and a linesman had to be replaced after being cut on the leg by a missile thrown from the terraces. Morgan made a more positive contribution to United's relaunch, chipping Orient goalkeeper John Jackson after half an hour. Houston's header from McIlroy's free-kick made for a steady 2–0 start.

Stuart Pearson, a £200,000 signing from Hull City in May 1974, was the only significant addition to the team. Two-footed, useful in the air and the possessor of superb reflexes, Pearson was a fine striker and the focal point of United's attacks. He would go on to finish the season with 18 goals. As had been suggested by their form in the latter stages of the 1973–74 season, United looked too good for the Second Division. Four wins out of four put them top of the table at the end of August 1974. Docherty's brisk, lively team were unbeaten until a 2–0 defeat at Norwich City in late September, but that still left them three points clear at the top. The team's strong-running, one-touch football was a cut above anything else on offer in the division. Macari had moved back into midfield, making way for Pearson and displacing McCalliog.

By November 1974, Sunderland were United's closest challengers for promotion and when the Wearsiders visited Old Trafford that month, 5,000 fans were locked out of the ground. The 60,585 who did get in saw a tremendous game end in a 3–2 win for United, stretching their lead at the top to six points. Some of the rough edges had been knocked off Holton as part of United's reformed, refined

Jim Holton, a muscular, ball-winning centre-half, brought stability to the United back four during the early 1970s.

style but, sadly, he suffered a broken leg in a 4–4 draw at Sheffield Wednesday on 7 December that was to end his United career.

Spiked fences 9ft high had been installed at the front of the terraces at Old Trafford after the pitch invasion against Manchester City, but the club was still plagued by trouble. At Hillsborough, pitch invasions led to 105 arrests. "What can we do?" said Docherty. "We have a minority of supporters who are a disgrace. Every club has one or two troublemakers among their supporters but because of the size of our following the problem is bigger for us than for any other club." It led to a new policy whereby United's away games were made all-ticket with the only point of sale for their fans being Old Trafford. That way, United supporters could be segregated.

United had made little impact in Cup competition since the days of Wilf McGuinness, but a fine League Cup run took them to the 1975 semi-finals. Pearson was missing with a hamstring injury for the first leg of the semi with Norwich in January 1975, when 58,000 Old Trafford fans saw two dinky goals from Macari – one a sweet overhead kick – match two from Norwich's Ted MacDougall in a 2–2 draw. Pearson also missed the second leg in which United fell to a 1–0 defeat.

In the early weeks of 1975, United faltered slightly, as might have been expected of a side with an average age of 22. At times this team of quick, light players tended to look fragile and they were being tested to the limits by highly motivated, physical opponents. As Docherty said, "All the teams in this division have played as well as they possibly can against us, simply to try to beat Manchester United." His team had the character to remain on top throughout, though, and they ended the season as Second Division champions, three points clear of

Martin Buchan holds aloft the Second Division championship trophy at the end of United's successful promotion season.

second-placed Aston Villa.

There was little change in policy or personnel for United's return to the First Division. The emphasis remained on attack. Wingers Daly and Steve Coppell, a signing from Tranmere Rovers during the 1974–75 season, together with attacking midfielder Macari, formed the three-pronged pitchfork that spurred on the Red Devils' attacks. McIlroy and Pearson were the devilish duo up front. In defence, Jimmy Nicholl took over from Forsyth as the regular right-back early in the 1975–76 season while Greenhoff moved back to partner Buchan in central defence.

Docherty was modest in his ambitions for the 1975–76 season, stating that he would be happy merely to finish outside of the bottom three, but his side's sumptuous attacking football propelled them to the top of the table. United were a slick, cohesive unit, thoroughly familiar with each other's play. Docherty now raised his sights, stating that a mid-table position at season's end was a realistic proposition. Throughout the autumn of 1975, United and QPR took turns at leading the First Division. Competition at the top was tight and when United lost 3–1 to Liverpool at Anfield in November, despite having played with wonderful flair, they slipped to fifth.

Docherty remained confident enough to raise his sights once again, stating that he hoped his team would finish high enough in the league to win a place in European competition. He further strengthened his team in late 1975 by signing outside-left Gordon Hill from Millwall for £70,000. Daly made way for him by switching from the left wing to central midfield.

Two days before Christmas, United went top again. A stunning overhead kick from Macari just inside the penalty area earned them a 1–1 draw at Everton in a match that was held up for

Sammy McIlroy steps over the ball as Stuart Pearson scores in the 4–0 win over Blackpool with which United bade farewell to the Second Division in April 1975.

15 minutes when the Goodison Park floodlights failed. On Boxing Day, Liverpool resumed their leadership of the First Division, but United were back on top in January 1976. That month, Pat Crerand left the Old Trafford staff; Tommy Cavanagh was now Docherty's assistant. After a 1–1 draw at Coventry City in February, United were overtaken at the top by Liverpool once again. Defeat at Aston Villa later that month meant they slipped to third.

However, United still remained in contention for the title and a thrilling FA Cup run took them to the final, putting them in with the chance of the double. Not since the 1956–57 season had United been faced with such a pleasant prospect. Docherty had fielded an unchanged team for 18 successive matches from December 1975 to March 1976 and there was a smooth understanding between his players. He said, "We've got this terrible affliction – we can play. Our players have this bad habit – they keep passing the ball to members of their own side."

A crowd of 61,879 – United's biggest for six years – saw a 2–1 win over Everton keep United in the title hunt but four days later, Stoke City crept away from Old Trafford with a 1–0 win thanks to a breakaway goal three minutes from time. United's attacking style

always left them vulnerable to the counter-attack and that defeat ended the Old Trafford side's brave challenge for the 1975-76 title. They finished third, four points behind champions Liverpool.

"I have never been with a team that is so calm," said Docherty as he turned his thoughts to the Wembley Cup final. United didn't train in the week before the final – the manager believed that after a full season's games they were as fit as they would ever be. By now, Docherty's players were well aware of what was required of them. Said Steve Coppell, "He has always been conscious that he wanted a certain type of football. Short, low crosses to the near post are something he has worked on for two seasons. Even now, when someone hits a long cross in training he stops the game and gives us a mouthful. We are told to get our hair cut when it gets too long and you cannot play with your shirt outside your shorts. Tommy Cavanagh says if you look smart you play smart."

One of Docherty's characteristics was to criticize other clubs and players publicly. Prior to United's FA Cup semi-final with Derby County, he had said, "This is the first time a Cup final will be played at Hillsborough. The other semi-final is a bit of a joke really." That match, between Second Division Southampton and Third

United supporters reflect on the strike-ridden 1970s with humour as they await the start of the 1977 FA Cup final with Liverpool.

Division Crystal Palace had ended in a 2–0 win for the south coast club who had doubtless taken note of Docherty's words.

United had stuttered and stalled in the weeks before the final and Southampton's coaching staff had carefully scrutinized all of their matches. At Wembley, the experienced Saints defenders shackled United's sparky forwards with maximum efficiency. Southampton created the greater number of chances and only a point-blank save by Stepney prevented Mick Channon giving Southampton a first-half lead. After an hour, in a rare United attack, McIlroy leapt to head Hill's corner off the crossbar. With just five minutes remaining, McCalliog, discarded by Docherty a year earlier, slipped a super pass through the middle of the United defence. Bobby Stokes glided on to the ball and from 20 yards placed a first-time, left-footed shot on the run past Stepney for the only goal of the game. Docherty could only look on wistfully as Southampton celebrated with the Cup.

It was a disappointing end to a distinguished season, but United had plenty to look forward to as the 1976–77 fixtures began, in particular a return to European competition after eight-seasons' absence. Their UEFA Cup place, as reward for third position in the league, produced a first-round tie with Ajax. The first leg was played at the Olympic Stadium, Amsterdam. United's supporters were quarantined by empty terraces all around them in their section of the ground. A goal by sweeper Ruud Krol, when he eased past four United defenders, gave Ajax the only goal of the game.

In the return, watched by 59,000, United had to play a more watchful game than usual, as they guarded against opponents expert in the counter-attack. A Macari goal levelled the tie shortly before half-time and midway through the second half McIlroy's strike put United into the second round. An even more difficult task presented itself when they were drawn against Juventus. By coincidence, Manchester City had faced the Italians in the first round, winning 1–0 at Maine Road but losing 2–0 in the return. Tony Book, City's manager, offered to assist United by providing his observations on Juventus but Docherty responded, "We do our own thing at Old Trafford and we always have. I will not seek advice from anyone outside my own staff."

At the time of the draw United were once again top of the First Division, but by 20 October 1976, when they met Juventus, they had dropped to eighth, although still only two points behind leaders Liverpool. At Old Trafford, Juventus's calculating, high-grade football brought them several good scoring opportunities early in the match but it remained goalless for the first half hour. Then a cross from Nicholl was headed on by Coppell and dropped for Hill, leaning back, to steer a sharp volley past goalkeeper Dino Zoff. There was no further scoring although the rest of the match was littered with vicious fouls and off-the-ball incidents.

Buchan was injured for both legs and his composure was badly missed in the Stadio Comunale, Turin, where 65,000 Juventus fans roared on their team as the Italians flew in to attack. It was United who made the best early chance when Hill's diving header from Coppell's cross went narrowly wide of Zoff's post. At the back, United kept Juventus out for the opening half hour. Then a swift four-man move ended with Roberto Boninsegna sweeping the ball into the United net. Midway through the second half, Boninsegna met Marco Tardelli's cross with a neat flick to put Juventus ahead in the tie. The Italians made sure of their progress when, in the final minutes, Romeo Benetti crashed a crushing shot past Stepney.

By November, United were rooted in mid-table in the league and young wingers Coppell and Hill were starting to look jaded. United played 4-2-4 when attacking, with the full-backs pushed up in support of the wingers, but they reverted to 4-4-2 when the opposition had the ball, with the wingers carrying out defensive duties. It was a heavy burden for such young players and Docherty rested Hill, switching Coppell to the left wing.

A series of indifferent results meant that the league title was already out of reach by Christmas. United diverted all their energies towards the FA Cup and extracted a measure of revenge on Southampton by defeating the holders on their way to the 1977 final. At Wembley, they beat a powerful Liverpool side 2–1.

On 4 July 1977, six weeks after victory in the Cup final, Docherty was sacked by United after his affair with Mary Brown, wife of club physiotherapist Laurie Brown, was made public. "A meeting of the directors has decided unanimously that Mr Docherty is in breach of the terms of his contract and his engagement is terminated forthwith," was the official statement from the club. Applications were invited for the post.

In a rare contemplative moment, Docherty had once said, "A manager of any football club is a lonely individual. He has many associates but few genuine friends. At least we know where we stand." He had counted Matt Busby among those friends and had hoped that Busby and the United board would stand by him after his affair with Mary Brown was revealed. They didn't and it seemed strange that Docherty, this tough, streetwise Glaswegian, should be brought low as a result of a love affair. "I have been punished for falling in love," he said. "What I have done has nothing at all to do with my track record as a manager." Docherty had exchanged his love affair with United for personal happiness. An entirely different chapter in United's history was about to begin.

Kevin Keegan of Liverpool feels the pressure as his man-marker Martin Buchan gets tight on him during the 1977 FA Cup final.

1977 FA CUP FINAL

MANCHESTER UNITED (0) 2 LIVERPOOL (0) 1

21 MAY 1977, WEMBLEY

MANCHESTER UNITED had won many friends with their flowing football but Liverpool were not in a friendly mood when the two sides came face to face on a balmy day at Wembley to fight for the 1977 FA Cup. It was one of the most stirring finals of all. Liverpool were chasing an unprecedented treble of European Cup, League and FA Cup, but United were also desperate for an FA Cup victory.

During the opening five minutes, Liverpool frequently played the ball in to Kevin Keegan, but each time a serious tackle from Martin Buchan stopped the striker in his tracks. Buchan's mastery of Keegan in the air and on the ground continued for the remainder of the afternoon, nullifying Liverpool's most dangerous threat. On the one occasion when Keegan did manage to escape Buchan's guard, midway through the first half, a superbly precise tackle by 19-year-old left-back Arthur Albiston robbed him of the ball.

United managed one first-half shot on goal but Stuart Pearson's powerless effort was saved easily by Ray Clemence. Soon after, a 20-yard shot by David Johnson flew narrowly over the United bar. Ray Kennedy's header, shortly before half-time, was booted round his near post by Stepney and from the corner Joey Jones's shot went inches over the bar. Liverpool had had the better of the first half and both United wingers, Steve Coppell and Gordon Hill, had been subdued.

Out of the blue, United took an early second-half lead with their first serious attempt on target. Sammy McIlroy's centre-circle header deceived Liverpool captain Emlyn Hughes and Jimmy Greenhoff, a recent signing from Stoke City, headed the ball on past Hughes's central defensive partner Tommy Smith. It fell neatly into Stuart Pearson's path. Despite Jones breathing Welsh fire at his back, Pearson coolly nodded the ball on and teed himself up nicely to pelt a right-foot volley past Clemence. Pearson celebrated in now familiar fashion, slowing his run to a stiff walk towards the United fans with his right fist raised in triumph.

The lead lasted two minutes. Jimmy Case, with his back to Buchan on the edge of the United area, controlled Jones's pass on his thigh, took another touch, then turned quickly to hit a fine spinning shot towards goal. Stepney got a hand to it but couldn't prevent the ball racing into the net. He lay face down in the turf as Liverpool celebrated.

Typically, United responded with another goal. Jimmy Nicholl's long, high ball forward was nodded on by Lou Macari, who beat Hughes in the air. Jimmy Greenhoff tussled with Smith for the ball and when it bounced clear to Macari, his stabbed shot looked as though it was going wide until it took a deflection off Jimmy Greenhoff's midriff and the ball veered crazily past Clemence.

United defended with desire but there were worrying moments. A Brian Greenhoff back-header a couple of yards from goal forced Stepney into a flying leap to prevent an equalizer. Two low shots on the turn from Case were saved low down by Stepney and a Kennedy shot nicked the outside of the post.

Tommy Docherty, flanked by physiotherapist Laurie Brown and assistant Tommy Cavanagh, sat anxiously chewing gum on the bench, nervously glancing at his watch before it was finally over and United had won the Cup for the first time since 1963.

Manchester United (manager Tommy Docherty): Stepney, Nicholl, Albiston, McIlroy, B. Greenhoff, Buchan, Coppell, J. Greenhoff, Pearson, Macari, Hill (substituted by McCreery, 82 minutes)
Scorers: Pearson 50, J. Greenhoff 55

Liverpool (manager Bob Paisley): Clemence, Neal, Jones, Smith, Kennedy, Hughes, Keegan, Case, Heighway, Johnson (substituted by Callaghan, 64 minutes), McDermott
Scorer: Case 52

Attendance: 100,000

Stuart Pearson and Gordon Hill show the FA Cup to the United fans.

TOMMY DOCHERTY

MANCHESTER UNITED reflected Tommy Docherty's personality during his time as team manager – fast, fiery and endlessly energetic. The supporters loved the resultant spectacle as United once again became Britain's most exciting team.

Tommy Docherty began his five decades in football at Celtic in 1948, aged 20. He had previously served for two years with the Highland Light Infantry, during which time he was stationed in Palestine. A fine player, nevertheless he couldn't break into Celtic's first team and was disappointed to be transferred to Preston North End a year later.

In nine years at Deepdale, he helped Preston reach the 1954 FA Cup final, alongside winger Tom Finney, the player whose style he admired above all others. Finney said of the mid-1950s Docherty, "He is a great footballer and he could be a great manager one day. Mind you, he takes some understanding, but wherever he goes and whatever he does, they will certainly know he has been there."

Docherty won 25 caps for Scotland and played in the 1958 World Cup. After a dispute with Preston that summer, Arsenal paid £27,000 to take him to Highbury where he spent three successful years before joining Chelsea as coach, being promoted to manager in 1962.

His ambition was to be the world's greatest manager, but he soon became one of its most travelled. After five years at Chelsea, where he won the League Cup, he bossed Rotherham United, Queen's Park Rangers, Aston Villa, Porto and Scotland before arriving at Old Trafford. He had been a potential choice for United in December 1970 after returning from Portugal. Some fine work with Scotland finally convinced United he was the man for the job.

"I look for success," said Docherty while he was at Chelsea, "for my club and my players. If that success comes, obviously I must benefit and my reputation as a manager must be enhanced. When I can look back on a career like that of Matt Busby, then maybe I can say I am a good manager."

Docherty's admiration for Finney and wingplay helped shape the style of his United team, which brought genuine wingers – as opposed to wide players – back into fashion during the 1970s, when they had appeared almost obsolete. Docherty's United became popular for their attacking style at a time when negative tactics were rife.

He entertained press and public alike with a non-stop stream of caustic, quickfire one-liners, often aimed at opposing teams and players. As United prepared to welcome a muscular, somewhat negative Middlesbrough side to Old Trafford in the mid-1970s he said, "When you see them come out in that strip of theirs they look like Wakefield Trinity – and that's no disrespect to Wakefield Trinity. If they bought Johan Cruyff, they'd play him in the back four. Still, Middlesbrough aren't my problem – thank God!"

He was even more candid when outlining his philosophy at a Football Writers' Association dinner. "Lots of managers have to be cheats and conmen," he said. "People say we tell lies. Of course we tell lies. We are the biggest hypocrites. We cheat. In our business the morals are different. The only way to survive is by cheating. That's the law of our life."

After United, Docherty managed Derby County, QPR again, Sydney Olympic, Preston, Wolverhampton Wanderers and Altrincham before successfully moving on to the after-dinner speaking circuit.

Tommy Docherty crowned his career as manager of Manchester United with the 1977 FA Cup victory.

ALEX STEPNEY

GOALKEEPER (MANCHESTER UNITED 1966–78)

Alex Stepney punches the ball clear during the 1977 FA Cup final.

ALEX STEPNEY'S SUPERLATIVE SAVE from Eusebio in the 1968 European Cup final is engraved on the hearts of United's followers, but that was just one of a number of magic moments from the long-serving goalkeeper.

"I had come out too far and I was trying to get back when he shot. Fortunately, he hit the ball straight at me." That was how Stepney, typically modest, described his save from Eusebio. He forgot to mention the concentration that enabled him not only to stop the striker's shot but to hold the ball as well. Then, as Eusebio immediately tried to congratulate him, Stepney insisted on remaining focused on play, waving away the Benfica man so that he could get on with the game without any fuss.

A less celebrated aspect of Stepney's performance that evening is the part he played in United's all-important second goal, his kick-out almost directly leading to George Best's strike. It was equally significant and underlines the quiet but effective contribution Stepney consistently made to the United team.

Nicknamed "Steptoe" after the Cockney TV character, Alex Stepney was born in Carshalton and joined local Isthmian League club Tooting and Mitcham as a 16 year-old in 1958. He moved on to Millwall in 1963 before being signed by Tommy Docherty for Chelsea three years later. After just four months and one game at Stamford Bridge, Stepney switched to Old Trafford, helping United win the league title in his debut season at the club.

Stepney was occasionally involved in scoring as well as saving goals. He was elected penalty-taker after scoring from the spot in a friendly against Penarol during a penalty shoot-out at the end of a 1973 pre-season game in Spain. He scored his first competitive goal for United in September that year, sending Peter Shilton the wrong way from the spot in a 2–1 defeat by Leicester City. There had been murmurs of astonishment around Old Trafford as the goalkeeper sauntered forward to take the kick. Stepney scored once more that season but missed his third penalty, at Wolverhampton Wanderers, and had to race back to goal.

During his 12 years at United, he saw off various challengers for his position. After going off injured at Arsenal in August 1970, he found himself replaced in succeeding games by Jimmy Rimmer. Stepney sought a transfer, but when Wilf McGuinness was sacked at the end of that year, one of Sir Matt Busby's first moves as caretaker-manager was to restore Stepney to the team.

Stepney's steadiness did much to help United win an immediate return to the First Division in the 1974–75 season, but he found himself dropped again in November 1975, leaving him despondent. Paddy Roche took over for five games but Stepney's experience and agility brought him back into the team. His show-stopping performance at Leicester City in February 1976 kept United in the Cup and afterwards Tommy Docherty admitted it had been a mistake to replace Stepney with Roche earlier in the season. At the end of the Leicester match, Docherty ran on to the pitch and made straight for Stepney to congratulate him on his performance.

"You've got to take the bad things along with the good. If you've done well, be grateful; if you haven't, then try to do better. Otherwise you might as well pack the whole thing in," Stepney once said. That gritty attitude, allied to his meanness in giving away goals, made Stepney one of United's greatest goalkeepers.

LOU MACARI

FORWARD (MANCHESTER UNITED 1973–84)

THE SHARP, SCORING SKILLS of Lou Macari were synonymous with the buccaneering Manchester United side of the mid-1970s and his talents shone equally brightly when he moved back to become prompter-in-chief in midfield.

The ball always seemed to be drawn to Lou Macari rather than him having to exert energy in pursuit of goalscoring opportunities. This was deceptive. His excellent eye for a scoring opportunity meant that all the hard work had been done in advance of the chance. Freed of defenders and having made sure he was in the right place at the right time, Macari would swiftly swing a boot to despatch yet another ball into the back of yet another net.

His £200,000 fee was a record for a player moving from Scotland to England when he joined United as a 23 year-old from Celtic in early 1973. At Celtic Park, Macari, a Scot of Italian descent, scored 57 goals in 102 games and at the time of his transfer had already won two Scottish League titles and two Scottish Cup medals. He had also begun a Scottish international career that would yield 24 caps and an appearance at the 1978 World Cup.

Macari's early days at United were troubled and three months after his move south, he crashed his car, writing it off.

On the field, things were equally problematical. Macari performed poorly in his early days at United and in autumn 1973 he was fined £400 and transfer-listed by Docherty after refusing to turn out in a reserve match at Mossley.

The player claimed there had been a misunderstanding but Docherty responded, "There has been no misunderstanding. He knew the score. Earlier in the day he told me that he would not go to Mossley although he had been selected. He refused to come to the ground."

In a tempestuous Manchester derby in March 1974, Macari and Mike Doyle were sent off after half an hour. When both players refused to leave the field, referee Clive Thomas took the teams into the dressing-room for five minutes before resuming the game without the offending pair.

Macari's career at United soon began to go more smoothly. He was one of the main movers and shakers in the team that won promotion in 1974–75, tucking away 16 goals in the process despite having been moved back into the midfield role in which he played out much of the rest of his United career.

The goals continued to flow during the remainder of the 1970s and Macari remained a key player in the side after Docherty's replacement by Dave Sexton. The dawning of the Ron Atkinson era brought an end to Macari's United career and he joined Swindon Town as player-manager in the summer of 1984. Allegations of illegal payments and a controversial betting incident when he was at Swindon followed him after he had moved on to become manager of West Ham United in 1989. He resigned from the manager's job at Upton Park after just seven months.

Macari, a non-drinker and non-smoker but an inveterate gambler, moved on to manage Birmingham City, Stoke City twice, and Celtic during the 1990s. In October 2000 he succeeded Steve Bruce as manager of Huddersfield Town and kept the job until June 2002.

Lou Macari shows off his impeccable close control.

MARTIN BUCHAN

DEFENDER (MANCHESTER UNITED 1974–82)

MARTIN BUCHAN brought an assured sense of stability and style to United's central defence for more than a decade. His composure and awareness were exemplary and his footballing intelligence reflected his cleverness off the field.

Buchan became United's record signing when he arrived from Aberdeen in exchange for a £125,000 fee in March 1972. The move also made the 22 year-old the most expensive export from the Scottish League.

His maturity and bearing were such that he had been made captain of Aberdeen in 1969, aged 20, and he had led the Dons to a 3–1 Scottish Cup final victory over Celtic in 1970.

He had been given his Scotland debut by Tommy Docherty the following year and went on to win 34 caps for his country, appearing in the 1974 and 1978 World Cup finals.

Simultaneously an under-23 international, Buchan's move to United was finally clinched by his expert defending in a 2–2 draw with England under-23s at the Baseball Ground, Derby, on a pitch that Scotland manager Tommy Docherty described as one on which "you wouldn't ask horses to perform".

On signing Buchan, Frank O'Farrell commented, "He is a skilful, enthusiastic and determined player and one possessed of exceptional talent. He will be a tremendous asset to United."

Buchan said, "I didn't need any second thoughts. I am very pleased indeed to be joining Manchester United where good football is encouraged." He was instrumental in providing a platform on which such football could be played.

At the time, United were struggling to live up to the reputation that had attracted Buchan to Old Trafford, and he did much to strengthen a porous defence. He began his United career in his favourite No. 6 shirt, unusually combining the marking and tackling qualities of a centre-back with the vision and awareness of a

sweeper. He was able to bring the ball out of defence and pass it accurately to prompt attacks.

Buchan got on well with the thoughtful O'Farrell but when Docherty descended on Old Trafford, he used Buchan as an overlapping right-back.

That brought the player into conflict with the manager. For several months Buchan's request to be restored to the centre-back position was refused. In December 1973, Docherty declared, "Buchan will continue to play at right-back for the club," but he moved Buchan back to his favourite position after Christmas. In the promotion season of 1974–75, Buchan grew greatly in composure and he was made captain in 1975.

"I believe that a captain must lead by example," he said. "I'm not the most experienced player in the United side by any means and that's why it's important to take notice of what other players do and say.

"If players spot weaknesses or faults, it's their duty to point them out and we can thrash them out together."

After a decade of solid service, Buchan departed for Oldham Athletic in 1983. Injury forced him to retire and he went on to manage Burnley, but resigned after four months.

His thoughtful approach to his football was reflected in his off-field hobbies – he enjoyed learning foreign languages and playing Spanish classical guitar. Although he had played rugby at school, he was from a strong footballing family background.

His father had played professionally in Scotland while his younger brother George joined United from Aberdeen in 1973 and made four appearances in the 1973–74 season.

His son Jamie defended for Dundee United, Partick and Aberdeen.

A young Martin Buchan proves a picture of concentration.

SAMMY McILROY

MIDFIELDER (MANCHESTER UNITED 1971-82)

SAMMY McILROY WAS DISCOVERED by Bob Bishop, Manchester United's Northern Irish scout and the man who had also introduced George Best to the club. Those who expected another Irishman with sparkling feet were not disappointed.

Frank O'Farrell gave Sammy McIlroy his competitive debut against Manchester City at Maine Road in November 1971. Taking over the No. 10 shirt from no less a man than Denis Law, the youngster helped make this one of the most outstanding of all Manchester derbies. It was also one of the most memorable debuts by any United player. A fast, stylish United attack reached its climax with George Best laying the ball off to his fellow Irishman and McIlroy reacting swiftly to sweep the ball into the net for the opening goal. It was the first of six goals in a roisterous 3–3 draw.

McIlroy made sporadic appearances in the first team for the next six months, but injuries sustained in a car accident midway through the 1972–73 season put him out of action just as he was becoming an established member of the first-team squad. It was nearly a year before he reappeared in the first-team.

Best, shortly before quitting Old Trafford in early 1974, said that he was unwilling to wait around for the four or five years that he considered it would take Sammy McIlroy to become a great player. It was a wild prediction and McIlroy proved it wrong by becoming fully established in the side just as Best was finally leaving the club.

A graceful but hardworking player, McIlroy was always fully alert on the field. He was light and quick both in stealing into good positions and in carrying the ball. It was unsurprising that he found himself very much in favour with Tommy Docherty when the manager decided to alter United's style of play from a negative to a highly exciting, positive one. An expert crosser of the ball, McIlroy also scored numerous goals from the edge of the area, flighting in shots that seemed to dip just inside the angle between post and crossbar.

Dave Sexton valued McIlroy's talents highly, but when Ron Atkinson began to build his own team McIlroy, still only 27, left for Stoke City, who paid £350,000 for his services in 1982. He later joined Manchester City, playing against United in one derby, and Bury. After a seven-month spell at FC Modling in Austria, McIlroy moved to Preston North End as player-coach in 1990.

He began his managerial career in 1991 on the non-league scene, initially with Vauxhall Conference side Northwich Victoria. He briefly moved on to Ashton United before taking charge at Macclesfield Town in 1993. During his seven-year spell at the Cheshire club, he led them to the Vauxhall Conference title twice and brought them into the Football League in 1997, winning promotion to the Second Division the following season.

As a 17 year old, McIlroy had become one of Northern Ireland's youngest internationals when, alongside Best, he made his debut against Spain in February 1972. Having appeared in the 1982 and 1986 World Cup finals, his 88th and final cap came against England at Wembley in 1986. Sammy managed Northern Ireland from February 2000 to October 2003, before joining Stockport County.

Sammy McIlroy was an exciting new talent for the 1970s.

CHAPTER TEN

DAVE SEXTON

DAVE SEXTON GUIDED MANCHESTER UNITED IN A NEW
DIRECTION, MAKING THE TEAM MORE DEFENSIVELY AWARE
AND EMPHASIZING TECHNIQUE
AND TACTICS OVER PURE INSPIRATION.

Jimmy Greenhoff looks to ease the ball away from Liverpool's Phil Thompson during the 1977 Charity Shield match at Wembley.

Manchester United had to move quickly once the decision had been made to dismiss Tommy Docherty as manager. The first fixtures of the 1977–78 season were fast approaching and as the players returned from holiday to begin pre-season training in July 1977, moves were afoot to land Docherty's successor.

United were looking for a manager "with experience and a proven ability" and within days one of the prominent candidates for the job, Dave Sexton, had negotiated his release from his contract as manager of Queen's Park Rangers. Sexton had been expected to leave Loftus Road over the summer to join Arsenal as a coach, but when United invited him to become manager at Old Trafford he eagerly accepted. Eight days after Docherty's dismissal, Sexton was in place as the new Manchester United manager.

On a three-game tour of Norway with Sexton in charge, United scored 21 goals; and they played their part in an absorbing 0–0 draw with Liverpool in the Charity Shield match in August. Sexton had immediately earned the affection of the players, to some extent because he had not done anything to disturb Docherty's successful

side. The unusual and unexpected nature of Docherty's resignation, allied to the short space of time between the new appointment and the start of the season, meant that games were upon them before Sexton had a chance to make changes.

"How could anyone not like him?" said Lou Macari after United had won 4–1 at Birmingham City on the opening day of the season. The team that day was almost the same as the Cup-winning one; the only change was that David McCreery was in the side in place of Jimmy Greenhoff, who had been injured at Wembley in the Charity Shield match. The team's explosive style remained intact. Macari scored a natty hat-trick against Birmingham and he said afterwards, "People say that we're apt to go flat during a game but at the pace we play we need a quiet period to get our second wind."

United went on to garner a series of mixed results that meant they were in the top half of the First Division table as they prepared to meet St Etienne in the European Cup-winners' Cup first round on 14 September 1977. The French team had been practising defending the type of high balls they associated with the English game, despite United's style being a ground-based, passing one. As a result, six St

Etienne players had suffered broken noses in the days prior to the match. Among the casualties was star striker Dominique Rocheteau, who thus would not start the game.

There were further casualties on the night of the match. Thirty-seven United supporters ended up in hospital after becoming involved in violent confrontations with St Etienne fans on the terraces shortly before the match was due to begin. The bulk of the 1,000 or so United supporters inside the Stade Geoffroy Guichard had found that their tickets admitted them to the terracing behind a goal where they were surrounded by French fans. Pushing and jostling developed into a full-scale battle that led to French riot police, who had anticipated trouble, wading in with batons drawn.

All of this happened before kick-off, with some fans being chased out of the ground and others harried on to the playing surface. It led to the abandonment of a youth match that was taking place on the field, and for a while there were doubts about whether the tie would even begin as a succession of casualties were led around the side of the pitch.

Chairman Louis Edwards commented, "I saw innocent people beaten down by police. When our supporters misbehave I am the first to condemn them, but this was not one of those occasions. They were the victims of the reputation with which our club is associated." Les Olive, the United secretary, added that the club had written to St Etienne in advance of the match to ask for the supporters of both clubs to be segregated. St Etienne, however, had responded by saying that this would not be possible as their ground was municipally owned.

The United players behaved impeccably on the night. They put on a smooth show of attacking football, Gordon Hill scoring their goal in a 1–1 draw. Christian Synaeghel equalized for St Etienne in the final minutes. Before the second leg could take place, however, United faced an anxious wait as UEFA considered the report of their match observer.

Five days later, Manchester United were expelled from the European Cup-Winners' Cup by UEFA. It was only the second time UEFA had ejected a club from an ongoing competition. As United immediately prepared to appeal, St Etienne manager Robert Herbin commented, "The excesses of supporters certainly have to be stopped, but I never imagined a punishment like this. I would have preferred to obtain our qualifi-

cation in another way – on the pitch, not over a table."

A week later, on Monday, 26 September, Louis Edwards, Sir Matt Busby, Les Olive and Denzil Haroun, a United director, represented the club when they made their appeal to UEFA's disci-

Dave Sexton strikes a typically thoughtful pose as he watches his United players. A keen student of the game, Sexton was excellent at preparation for matches.

plinary committee in Zurich, Switzerland. They put the case to UEFA that St Etienne's lack of supporter segregation had sparked the violence. UEFA responded by emphasizing that "a serious lack of discipline by some United supporters" had inflamed the trouble, but they also decided that their earlier decision to ban the club had been "too harsh". United's punishment was altered to a £7,500 fine and a ruling from UEFA that they should play their second leg a minimum of 125 miles from Manchester. The second leg would now take place on 5 October, a week later than scheduled.

The United board wanted to play the tie as far away as possible, while remaining on the British mainland. Aberdeen was their preferred choice, but when Aberdeen FC stipulated that the tie should take place on the Tuesday and not the Wednesday, the game was switched to Plymouth, 280 miles from Manchester.

Ticket distribution ensured that the bulk of the crowd would be neutral. On Sunday, 2 October, Plymouth Argyle FC sold 20,000 tickets to their own supporters – everyone who had been at the Third Division match with Gillingham the day before was entitled to two tickets each. A 31,634 crowd at Home Park saw United, nonplussed by the fuss surrounding the tie, overwhelm the French side. After half an hour, Steve Coppell's low cross caused a flutter in the St Etienne defence and Stuart Pearson sent the ball into the net. A neat second-half goal by Coppell settled the tie, United winning 3–1 on aggregate. On the terraces, the Devon evening passed off peacefully.

A fortnight after St Etienne had been despatched from Plymouth, United were in another port, Oporto, facing Portuguese Cup-winners Porto. This first leg of their second-round tie took place in front of 70,000 of Porto's fervent followers in the Estadio Das Antas. United's following was restricted to 160, each of whom had been stringently vetted by the club.

After eight minutes, one of Porto's Brazilians, Duda, hit a 25-yard shot high past Alex Stepney to open the scoring. Two further Porto efforts were cleared off the line as the Portuguese side seized the initiative. After 25 minutes, Duda volleyed Porto into a 2–0 lead. Buchan inspired his team-mates to dig in as Porto played the ball slickly and at speed. United steadied and early in the second half even began to look good for an away goal. They couldn't find a way through the Portuguese defence with their counter-attacks, though, and a third goal from Duda and a strike from Oliveira left United 4–0 down with an hour played. There was no further scoring. United's Cup-winners' Cup hopes seemed to have been dashed

*Oppostie: **Steve Coppell** could hit a good shot from distance as well as crossing accurately and effectively and he often burst inside to score goals.*

before a ball had been kicked in the second leg.

A second 4–0 defeat in three days, at West Bromwich Albion the following Saturday, once again exposed United's lack of a dominant centre-half. In addition, Stepney was clearly reaching the end of his career. When United lost 2–1 at Aston Villa a week later, it left the club 13th in the First Division and already out of contention for the title. "We're a Cup side," commented Macari. "We're not consistent enough over 42 league games."

United were without both Macari and Brian Greenhoff, both of who were injured, for the return with FC Porto, but they had the support of 53,000 Old Trafford fans as they began their uphill task. With seven minutes gone, Coppell turned swiftly on the edge of the penalty area to shoot and score the opener. United rode into attack after attack, spurred on by their raucous support, but they were stung by a Porto counter-attack from which Seninho equalized on the half hour.

The match quickly took on a new dimension when Murca put through his own goal five minutes before half-time and Jimmy Nicholl cracked a shot into the Porto net shortly before the break to make it 3–1 for United. If United could score another three in the second 45 minutes, without conceding any, they would be through. Midway through the second period Coppell, from close-range, made it 4–1, but United were undone when Seninho again rounded off another breakaway five minutes from time with his and Porto's second goal. A second own goal by Murca ended the scoring, making it 5–2 to United on the night but 6–5 to Porto on aggregate. United were cheered off the pitch by their supporters after their valiant but ultimately vain victory.

The credit gained by that performance soon evaporated. United suffered their fourth league defeat in five games – 2–1 to Arsenal – the following Saturday, leaving them eighth from bottom of the First Division, two points above the relegation places. Another defeat, 2–1 at Nottingham Forest a week later, emphasized their plight.

Sexton said, "Recent results have been very cruel to us. We crushed FC Porto yet went out of the Cup-winners' Cup. Then we pounded Arsenal and lost 2–1. Our performance at Forest on Saturday was good enough to have earned at least a point, but we lost a fine game. Nothing is wrong that a couple of wins will not put right. We have been without players of the calibre of Lou Macari, James Greenhoff and Brian Greenhoff, to name three. My family has settled down quickly in the north and I am very happy at United."

A Stuart Pearson goal in a 1–0 win over Norwich City in late November 1977 brought Sexton some relief and United slowly but steadily made their way up the table from then onwards. The modest revival in their fortunes was not strong enough to prevent the FA Cup-holders exiting the tournament in the fourth round after a replay against West Bromwich Albion. They ended the 1977–78 season in tenth position, 22 points behind champions Nottingham Forest. By then, Sexton had started to ring the changes. Alex Stepney had been replaced in goal by Paddy Roche, while a combined total of £800,000 had been spent on striker Joe Jordan and centre-half Gordon McQueen, both Scottish internationals.

Steve Coppell was pleased with a major change that Sexton had made to United's style, thanks to the arrival of the 6ft tall Jordan. "He gives us the let-out of a high ball into the middle, which we never had before," said Coppell. "It has been drilled into us that we must play football right into the penalty area and get to the line, keeping our crosses low. Now we have more options."

Old Trafford crowds thinned considerably in the spring of 1978 as United ambled slowly and unspectacularly towards the end of the season. By then, Sexton had made the significant decision to sell Gordon Hill to Derby County for £250,000. From now on, United would play with just one winger. Hill's move prompted an exchange of insults. He claimed there was a serious lack of team spirit at Old Trafford. He also attacked Sexton's methods, stating, "You need an O-level or a degree to understand the tactics at Old Trafford." Sexton responded, "Hill is a very selfish player. The other lads have had to do a lot of work to accommodate him."

Sexton's other winger, Steve Coppell, was more supportive of his manager. "It sounds corny I know," he said, "but injuries made us struggle. With Martin Buchan, Lou Macari, Stuart Pearson and Jimmy Greenhoff out at various times, we were unable to consolidate the work that Dave Sexton was putting in. We never had tactical talks with Tommy Docherty. We had a set way of playing and we improvised around that. We never discussed other teams before we played them. The changes have not been too extensive, but what has been done has tended to involve the players more. It is appreciated and that will soon begin to show through our results."

The centenary of United's founding under the name Newton Heath was marked at the beginning of the 1978–79 season when Real Madrid provided the opposition for a match at Old Trafford. Goalkeeper Alex Stepney was given a guard of honour by the directors and players as he took the turf before the game – it would be his last major appearance as a United player. Bobby Charlton, Johnny Carey, Jimmy Delaney and other prominent figures from the past also took a bow before kick-off. Stepney saved a Pirri penalty, and Sammy McIlroy and Jimmy Greenhoff each scored twice as United won 4–0 in front of 50,000 fans. It was a heartening overture to the season.

Stuart Pearson had undergone a cartilage operation so Jimmy Greenhoff partnered Jordan in attack. United were now using a more measured, deliberate style under Sexton and goals proved hard to come by as the players adjusted. In the autumn of 1978, four successive 1–1 draws reflected their unspectacular progress. That, in combination with a 2–1 home defeat by Watford in the League Cup in early October, meant Old Trafford crowds continued to tumble. United used a 4-4-2 system, with Coppell still wide on the right but he was now being deployed more in midfield rather than as an attacking winger. It was a stuffy style and it had knocked much of the excitement out of United's style of play.

After another 1–1 draw, with Southampton in November 1978, Sexton's team were booed from the pitch at Old Trafford. Sexton's popularity plummeted even further after a 5–1 defeat at Birmingham City later that month. It had been six years since United had conceded five goals in one match.

Louis Edwards responded by promising Sexton £1 million for players – the money would be raised by a share issue that Edwards proposed for later in the year. Sexton wasted little time in entering the transfer market. Within hours he had made a £440,000 offer for Jim Blyth of Coventry City, but a failed medical thwarted his bid to bring Blyth to United. It would have been a record fee for a goalkeeper but the move was slightly puzzling as Blyth had been in Coventry's reserves for several weeks, attempting to recover from the serious back injury that had vetoed the transfer.

The following Saturday Paddy Roche, who had been between the sticks for the 5–1 defeat at Birmingham, found himself replaced by Gary Bailey, a 20-year-old, Ipswich-born South African making his United debut.

"I went straight to the Boss," said the deposed Roche, "and he explained that I was not being made a scapegoat for our performances. It was more a question of consideration for my feelings after what has happened this week. He did say he thought I had been looking a bit shaky in recent games, but we went through all the goals and he agreed that I couldn't be blamed for any of them. He assured me that I am still the first-team goalkeeper."

As it turned out, Bailey's form was so impressive that his confident debut, in a 2–0 home win over Ipswich Town, proved to be the first of 85 consecutive first-team appearances. For the following eight seasons, he was the first-choice goalkeeper for United. Instead of purchasing a goalkeeper, Sexton signed Mickey Thomas, a left-sided midfielder, from Wrexham for £300,000.

Louis Edwards's son Martin, 33 in 1978, now had 1,904 United shares, nearly twice as many as the total held by the rest of the United board. Members of the Edwards family held 75 per cent of

Joe Jordan played to win. Here he turns away after scoring one of his two goals against Nottingham Forest in December 1979.

United's 3,678 shares. Under the proposed share issue, one million new shares were to be issued at an Extraordinary General Meeting to be held on 18 December 1978. Louis Edwards and Martin Edwards would take up the full number of new shares to which they were entitled – at a cost of around £750,000 – doubling their number of shares in the club.

The new share issue was something that Sir Matt Busby had initially opposed when it was originally discussed. He and others feared that it might leave United vulnerable to a takeover from external speculators at some point in the future. Sir Matt eventually relented, saying, "In the interests of this great club of ours I have gone along with the scheme."

Some dissenters did remain, however, and on 15 December 1978 John Fletcher, a 61-year-old businessman, went to the High Court in London to try to prevent the rights issue. He wanted the new shares to be offered to the public rather than to existing shareholders. Fletcher believed that at £1 each, the shares were vastly undervalued but Mr Justice Golding ruled that the board had the right to value shares to be issued at whatever price they wished.

While new funds were being created for Sexton off the field, on it United entered the New Year once again well out of contention for the title and out of the League Cup. The fans were losing patience with Sexton. Results were mediocre and United's style was stultifyingly dull. In March 1979, there were 36,085 at Old Trafford for a match with Leeds United, the club's smallest attendance for a league match since they had returned to the First Division in 1975.

"We're a young team in transition and we're still learning," insisted Sexton. "We always play with a lot of spirit. We've got a good, fighting squad and there's also a lot of skill there. If we play badly, I take the responsibility and I am my own hardest critic. Once I have given myself stick, anything I may read in a newspaper will inevitably seem that much milder. I have the same aspirations as the crowd, although I have had it brought home to me this season that winning is not enough if we don't win well."

In the second half of the season, United concentrated all their energies on the FA Cup and reached the semi-finals, where they faced a Liverpool side already certain of the title. The Anfield club would eventually finish the 1978–79 season 23 points ahead of ninth-placed United in the First Division. The game was played at Maine Road. Liverpool were unbeaten in 16 matches and had conceded only three goals in those games. United had conceded seven goals in their previous three matches – a win, a defeat and a draw – but they ignored the form, taking a 2–1 lead through goals by Brian Greenhoff amd Joe Jordan. Alan Hansen scored a rare goal to equalize five minutes from time and the result brought a feeling of deflation.

"It was as though we had lost," said Martin Buchan. "We had had the feeling that this was going to be our day. We'd gone behind, drawn level immediately, they'd hit the post with a penalty and then we had gone ahead. It was very disappointing not to win. Now, an hour after the match, the spirit in the dressing-room is reviving."

In the replay at Goodison Park four days later, a high-spirited United sped into attack, pressing Liverpool back with some superb attacking play. A host of chances resulted, culminating in a Joe Jordan header that smacked off the crossbar before being scrambled clear. When a goal failed to follow, Liverpool came into the game and Ray Kennedy hit Bailey's bar with a headed effort. Twelve minutes from time, Jimmy Greenhoff stylishly stole on to Thomas's cross to head the ball, on the bounce, past Ray Clemence. That took United into their third final in four years.

Their opponents at Wembley were to be Arsenal and tickets were changing hands for £300 – 30 times their face value – in the hours before the match. Those United supporters who had not been struck dumb by those prices were speechless after 11 minutes of the game when Brian Talbot put Arsenal ahead. Although United recovered sufficiently well to play some eye-catching football, on half-time Frank Stapleton rose to head Arsenal into a 2–0 lead.

United toiled hard to get back into the game but no tangible reward arrived until the 87th minute when Jordan's low centre was met by McQueen, sticking out a long left leg, heron-like, to jab the ball into the net. Two minutes later, McIlroy pursued a difficult ball with unquenchable determination, twisted past three opponents and stretched to nick an equalizer just as the ball appeared to have

finally eluded his control. Arsenal attacked from the restart and Liam Brady burst down United's right flank, passing to Graham Rix. His cross found Alan Sunderland who nicked Arsenal's winner at the back post. Less than a minute had passed since McIlroy's goal. The cruelty of such a climax left Sir Matt Busby in tears at the final whistle. Four days later, at Old Trafford, a 40,000 crowd warmly applauded the team who had given their all in the final as they took the field before a 1–1 draw with Chelsea.

Sexton maintained that United could challenge for the title in the 1979–80 season. "These are super lads," he said of his players. "They know they're at the number-one club and no one likes to rock the boat. They have respect. You look around the walls at Old Trafford and see photographs of the great sides and you might say we can never live up to that tradition, but it's impossible to improve on memories. My job is to get this side up on the walls and then nobody would remember our struggles. Believe it or not, this is the enjoyable part for me. Any success is preceded by a struggle and the struggle is the fun."

The manager added £750,000 midfielder Ray Wilkins to his squad shortly before the season began. Offsetting that purchase, Brian Greenhoff went to Leeds United for £350,000, Stuart Pearson to West Ham United for £220,000 and David McCreery to QPR

for £200,000. Three days after Wilkins's arrival, United travelled to Southampton for their opening league fixture. United were "poor and lost cohesion", according to Sexton after the 1–1 draw.

Wilkins, McIlroy and Thomas now made up the midfield, with Coppell as a deep-lying winger. Macari had returned to the attack, alongside Jordan. Nicholl and Arthur Albiston were the regular full-backs, with McQueen and Buchan the central defenders who protected goalkeeper Bailey. By mid-September this settled line-up had started to work well as a unit and, with Wilkins at his playmaking best, United were top of the First Division. They swapped the top spot with Nottingham Forest throughout the autumn until, in November, Liverpool seized the lead.

United responded to that challenge with a fast, flowing 5–0 win over Norwich City that repositioned them at the top. Sexton described it as "football as it should be played; the best display of my time at Old Trafford". By Christmas, Liverpool and United were equal on points and six points clear of the rest of the First Division. They met at Anfield on Boxing Day, but United were well beaten in a 2–0 defeat. "We just didn't play," said Jordan.

Sexton's first signing of the 1980s was a most significant one –

Sammy McIlroy glides away from Steve Walford, evades Pat Jennings and shoots past Willie Young for his 1979 Cup final goal against Arsenal.

Nikola Jovanovic, the first of many foreign signings.

Nikola Jovanovic, United's first foreign player. The 27-year-old Yugoslavian international cost £300,000 from Red Star Belgrade and it had taken United three months to sort out the details of the centre-back's transfer. "It is marvellous for us to have such a player in his prime," said Sexton, "but he won't go into the first team straightaway. He'll have to settle down domestically first."

One of the most familiar figures on the Old Trafford scene, chairman Louis Edwards, passed away in February 1980 at the age of 65 after suffering a heart attack in the bath at his home in Cheshire. Matt Busby described the death as a tragedy for Manchester. Louis Edwards's son Martin succeeded him.

Although ushered out of the FA Cup in the third round by Tottenham Hotspur, United continued to chase Liverpool valiantly, but at the beginning of March they hit a low when they were thumped 6–0 at Ipswich, the club's heaviest defeat for more than 19 years. "We haven't got where we are by not being resilient," said Sexton afterwards.

The gap between Liverpool and United soon widened ominously to six points. In April, Sexton instructed his team to go all out for victories and they obliged, winning six games in succession to bring them, once again, level on points with Liverpool. The Merseysiders, however, had a considerably better goal difference and a game in hand and when United lost their final match, at Leeds, while Liverpool were beating Aston Villa 4–1, the title went to Anfield. United ended the season two points behind Liverpool.

Before that dramatic denouement, Martin Edwards had awarded Sexton and his assistant Tommy Cavanagh new three-year contracts on the basis that the team had improved in every season in which it had been under Sexton's charge. "I am already looking forward to next season," said the delighted manager.

Unfortunately, the 1980–81 season produced only stunted development on all fronts. United fell at the first hurdle in the League Cup when they were knocked out by Coventry City. A month later they went out of the UEFA Cup in the first round on away goals after drawing 1–1 on aggregate with Polish side Widzew Lodz. A fourth-round FA Cup defeat at Nottingham Forest was embarrassing, since United had whisked away Forest's star striker Garry Birtles for a United record £1.25 million fee just three months earlier. Despite being United's first £1 million-plus player, Birtles scored just once in 28 appearances during the season. United finished eighth in the First Division, a dozen points behind champions Aston Villa.

In his four years at the club, Sexton had made radical changes to the Manchester United style. They were now by and large perceived as being a stuffy side, packing the midfield and as concerned about stopping the opposition playing as in playing themselves. It had been difficult for the Manchester United support to suffer this approach to the game even when the team were challenging for trophies. It was indefensible when it took the club nowhere. Sexton was dismissed in the spring of 1981. By then, the Old Trafford fans had begun voting with their feet and were staying away in considerable numbers. They knew, if Sexton did not, that United demanded a much more expansive style than the one that he had been able to provide for them.

Opposite: Joe Jordan, the attacking spearhead of Sexton's United, chases the ball in typically single-minded fashion, watched by winger Steve Coppell.

DAVE SEXTON

DAVE SEXTON WAS THE FIRST ultra-modern coach to become manager at Old Trafford. His studious preparation for matches and respect for players made for a new and vastly different approach to Manchester United management.

Dave Sexton's father Archie had fought Jock McAvoy in Manchester for the British boxing middleweight title in 1933, but London-born Sexton opted for football as a career. He played for Chelmsford City, Luton Town, West Ham United, Orient, Brighton & Hove Albion and Crystal Palace before a cartilage injury ended his playing career in 1962.

At West Ham he had been one of a group of players who had gone on coaching courses during their summer holidays and on his retirement as a player he became assistant coach at Chelsea under Tommy Docherty. Moving on, in 1965 he became manager of Orient, coach at Fulham in 1966, and at Arsenal later that year. When Docherty quit Chelsea in 1967, the Chelsea players, on being asked by the board whom they wished to have as manager, nominated Sexton.

During Sexton's seven years as manager at Stamford Bridge, Chelsea won the 1970 FA Cup and the 1971 European Cup-winners' Cup, but Sexton was dismissed in October 1974. He immediately joined QPR and, using a carefully controlled passing game, took them agonisingly close to winning the First Division title in the 1975–76 season. At QPR he was more coach than manager, happy to let the board deal with financial matters such as players' wages.

"The whole business of being a manager is to put things together," said Sexton as he outlined his philosophy in the mid-1970s. "My entire thinking is based on that principle, building not destroying. You also have to act the way you feel is right, regardless of whether or not it is popular. Managing and coaching are all about unison."

Dave Sexton's theories sometimes struggled to communicate with players on more basic aspects of football management

On his arrival at Old Trafford in July 1977, Sexton was 47. He had unusual interests for a football manager and relaxed by reading the work of esoteric American poet Robert Frost and philosopher Ludwig Wittgenstein. In the field of football Hennes Weisweiler, the studious coach of Borussia Monchengladbach, was a man he particularly admired. A devoted student of football, Sexton spliced together his own coaching videos for his players and frequently travelled to Holland and Germany to learn from matches.

"Some people only respond to the whip," he said shortly before joining United. "I would much prefer to get co-operation. Football's a joint thing; if you get co-operation, there isn't anything you can't do. I would only use the whip reluctantly because I don't think it's the way to get someone to a peak and to make it last for a long time. I go for the constructive thing that will pay off in the long run. That's why I do a lot of reading – to find the answers without having recourse to the whip."

At Chelsea, he had disliked dealing with the outspoken, opinionated players of the 1970s and at United he built a team imbued with the work ethic. Sexton distrusted "luxury" players because others had to do more work to compensate for them. He got United's players on his side – Lou Macari described Sexton as "the nicest man in football" – but his United team often seemed blinded by their own sweat when it came to seeking inspiration.

Sexton coached the England under-21s during his time at Old Trafford and continued to do so after his departure, lifting the European Championship twice with them in the early 1980s. He also managed Coventry City between 1981 and 1983. Dave Sexton's qualities as a coach was recognized by the Football Association who retained his services throughout the two decades after his departure from Old Trafford.

GORDON McQUEEN

DEFENDER (MANCHESTER UNITED 1978–85)

GORDON McQUEEN'S GUNG-HO GAME made him the perfect centre-half for Manchester United. He had the ability to make the art of defending seem truly exciting.

Gordon McQueen had toyed with the idea joining the police as a teenager, but it was an act of violence on his part that led to his arrival at Old Trafford in early 1978. The centre-back was fined a substantial sum by Leeds United for "ungentlemanly conduct" in January 1978 after he had apparently struck his own goalkeeper, David Harvey, during an FA Cup tie with Manchester City. McQueen accepted full responsibility for the Harvey incident but, openly discontented at Leeds, asked to be put on the transfer list.

Joe Jordan moved from Elland Road to Old Trafford that same month and McQueen, a close friend of his fellow Scot, commented, "I feel that my game will not improve further if I stay at Leeds. The departure of Joe Jordan to Manchester United brought the matter to mind although it did not result in my decision to seek a transfer."

United soon entered negotiations for McQueen but they were protracted, leading Tommy Docherty, then manager at Derby County, to step in with a bid. McQueen turned it down, saying he wished to join "a bigger club". Tottenham also came in with an offer but McQueen said his wife did not want to move to London. Tottenham had offered £450,000 and Leeds quickly insisted that Manchester United should match that.

After five weeks of extensive talks, United made a third offer for McQueen, matching Spurs' bid. McQueen finally signed for Manchester United on 9 February 1978 for a British record transfer fee of £450,000. "Quite honestly, I didn't think they would go so high for me," he said.

McQueen had joined Leeds from St Mirren for £30,000 in September 1972 – St. Mirren had asked for £100,000 but Leeds had refused to pay it – and after making his debut six months later had remained a first choice team member at Elland Road, winning a championship medal in the 1973–74 season.

United had lacked a dominant centre-half since the days of Jim Holton and there were few superior sights at Old Trafford in the late 1970s than the gargantuan McQueen, with his distinctive mane of blond hair, rising majestically to head the ball clear out of central defence. McQueen's form in a Cup tie with Fulham even led Dave Sexton to attempt a joke – "Gordon was getting up so high tonight that Brian Greenhoff asked him if he could see his car parked outside."

McQueen also frequently went roving forward to score and set up goals and was expert at directing long-range passes out of defence. His close control was quite exceptional for a man who stood 6ft 4ins tall and weighed 13½ stone. He had played on the left wing in Scottish junior football and never lost his speedy turn of pace.

McQueen's tally of 30 caps for Scotland was ridiculously low for a man with the credentials of a world-class centre-back. He was also cruelly denied the opportunity of appearing in a World Cup finals when he suffered ligament damage colliding with a Hampden goalpost in a match with Wales days before the 1978 tournament.

After a seven-year career at United, McQueen moved into management with Airdrieonians in 1987, later joining the coaching staff at St. Mirren. In the mid-1990s he teamed up with Bryan Robson at Middlesbrough as reserve team coach. He remained at the Riverside Stadium until June 2001 when Robson resigned.

Gordon McQueen was a fine ball-playing centre-half.

JOE JORDAN

FORWARD (MANCHESTER UNITED 1978-81)

JOE JORDAN'S SUBTLE SKILLS were often overlooked because of his aggressive, combative approach to football. That single-minded desire to win led many critics in press boxes and on the terraces to label him as little more than an unsophisticated battering ram. He was always much more than that.

Ajax Amsterdam, Anderlecht and Liverpool were interested in Joe Jordan when he became available for transfer from Leeds United in late 1977. He was on the verge of joining Ajax until he discovered the details of their terms. "The true fact is that no

signing-on fee was mentioned and when I heard what they paid their players I could not believe it," he said. Leeds were reluctant to let him go but Manchester United offered to pay £350,000 for him with wages to match the sizeable transfer fee. Jordan, who always knew his own worth, gladly moved to Old Trafford.

Jordan failed to score in his first two months at United and fans chanted for the return of the dropped Stuart Pearson during a 0–0 draw with Middlesbrough at Old Trafford. Even when he began scoring regularly, the press and some sections of the United support remained unimpressed. Jordan commented, "They say I just collide with people and knock balls down for others in the box. Well, nothing I say is going to change their minds but for what it's worth, I don't think that image reveals the whole truth."

His critics failed to notice his excellent positional sense, his skilful touches on the ground, his neat, precise short passes, his exceptional courage and his clever, driving runs that distracted defenders, allowing team-mates to flourish. After a 5–0 victory over Norwich City in 1979, in which Jordan had scored twice, Dave Sexton said, "Joe is so unselfish that he would be a great asset even if he never scored another goal in his life."

Leeds United, whom he had joined from Morton in 1970, had used him as a target man for high balls into the box and it had been effective – Leeds won the league title in 1974. Jordan credited Manchester United with smoothing off some of his rough edges and allowing him to develop his skills as a good all-round player. "I am more experienced, more involved in the build-up and general pattern of the game," he said as he looked back on his first two years at Old Trafford. "I get more touches of the ball than at Leeds. Lou Macari and I are as involved as anyone, linking up and bringing other players into the game. I only head the ball a few times in a match – just from kick-outs and set-pieces mainly."

Jordan was capped 52 times for his country and was always hugely popular with the Scotland support due to his ferocious commitment. He scored vital goals that helped take them to the World Cups of 1974, 1978 and 1982 and he remains the only Scot to have scored in the finals of three World Cup tournaments.

On quitting Old Trafford in 1981, Jordan moved to AC Milan where again his commitment made him a crowd favourite. He was nicknamed 'The Shark'. He switched to Verona before returning to the UK with Southampton and Bristol City, where he became manager in 1988 after having joined the playing staff a year earlier. His subsequent managerial career took him to Heart of Midlothian as manager and to Celtic as assistant manager. He later managed Stoke City and Bristol City again before joining Northern Ireland as assistant to Lawrie McMenemy. In 2000, he went to Huddersfield Town as assistant to Lou Macari.

Joe Jordan always had a direct, uncompromising attitude to the game.

JIMMY GREENHOFF

FORWARD (MANCHESTER UNITED 1976-80)

JIMMY GREENHOFF was an underrated talent before joining Manchester United, despite being one of the most complete footballers in the English game during the 1970s. He was in the latter stages of his career on arriving at United but he always showed a youthful enthusiasm for playing football.

He first came to the attention of many United supporters in the autumn of 1975 when he missed half a dozen chances for Stoke City in a 1–0 United victory. He joined United a year later at the age of 30 and went on to prove that his performance that afternoon had been a mere aberration.

By then a highly experienced player, Greenhoff had joined Leeds United in the early 1960s and played in two Fairs Cup finals in the latter part of that decade. Leeds lost to Dinamo Zagreb in the first and defeated Ferencvaros in the second. Late in 1968, Greenhoff was transferred to Birmingham City for £75,000.

After a year at St. Andrews, Jimmy moved on to Stoke City for a fee of £85,000, making him Stoke's record signing. He enjoyed his time with Stoke so much that it was a wrench to leave the Victoria Ground for Old Trafford in a £125,000 transfer. Equally painfully, his move from the Potteries cost him a pay cut!

He was excellent at shielding the ball and laying off superb passes to team-mates. He also finished goals in style. In situations where some players might need two touches, he would need only one, bringing him numerous goals that might otherwise have been lost.

Greenhoff seemed to thrive on close marking, the better to confound his harassers with his sleight of foot. He could then work the ball quickly into the space that he had created for team-mates by having drawn markers tight on to him. He was excellent at anticipating situations and a quick reader of how play was about to develop. More than once he capitalized on an underhit backpass that he had anticipated before the goalkeeper. He could also be relied on to make a run in anticipation of a team-mate's intentions well before the pass or header had been made. Jimmy would also unselfishly help younger players through games.

He had many excellent United displays, such as that of October 1977 when, after two months out with a muscular injury, he returned to the team and orchestrated a stunning 2–1 victory over champions Liverpool. His productive partnership with Stuart Pearson brought United many goals in the mid 1970s and whenever the side was without Greenhoff, United usually toiled in attack.

In February 1978, however, Greenhoff was displaced by the arrival of Joe Jordan. Tommy Docherty offered Manchester United £100,000 to take him to Derby County, but Greenhoff opted to stay and try to get back into the United team. He became unsettled again the following summer when United stalled on his request for a pay increase. United agreed terms with Chelsea on a £75,000 transfer, but Greenhoff again decided to remain at Old Trafford

Jimmy Greenhoff finds himself marked by brother Brian against Leeds.

and was finally awarded his increase just before the start of the season.

He soon formed a partnership with Jordan, thriving on the big Scot's headed knockdowns and runs into space and became top scorer for the 1978–79 season. A pelvic injury plagued him the following season and in January 1980 he was reported to have given up the game on medical advice. Instead he appeared as a substitute against Everton in March and then, on his first start of the season, scored in a 2–1 win over Liverpool with an impudent back-flicked header.

It proved to be his farewell goal for United. He moved on to Crewe Alexandra later in the year, but Jimmy Greenhoff had gone out in the style to which he had made the United fans accustomed.

RAY WILKINS

MIDFIELDER (MANCHESTER UNITED 1979–84)

Ray Wilkins acknowledges the support of the United fans.

RAY WILKINS had an almost aristocratic bearing on a football field – there was never anything hurried or harried about him as he smoothed his way through a game. His delightful skills made him a player for the football connoisseur.

His father had played for Leeds United and his brothers Graham and Dean also enjoyed professional careers. At the age of 18, Ray Wilkins became the youngest-ever captain of Chelsea. "The kid takes these things in his stride," said his manager, Eddie McCreadie. "He has all the qualities of leadership." Five years later, on Chelsea's relegation from the First Division, Old Trafford seemed the inevitable destination for one of England's most outstandingly talented midfielders.

The signing saga of Ray Wilkins continued for three months during the summer of 1979. United began proceedings with an offer of £600,000, but rival bids by Everton and Ipswich Town forced the price up to £750,000. Eventually, just before the season began, United agreed to pay it. On 15 August 1979 he became United's new record signing.

Wilkins had stated all along that he wanted to go to Old Trafford. "It is not really a question of money," he said. "United are a great attraction and I'm sure Dave Sexton can make me a better player. United play the kind of football I like. With no disrespect to Everton, I don't think they have United's potential. I hope coming to United will bring out the best in me."

Sexton, who had known Wilkins since the player's days as a teenager at Chelsea, commented, "It's such a relief to see this deal completed. It's like having a toothache for three months and finding it's gone away. I'll have to find something else to worry about now. Ray will be our link between attack and defence and I'm sure he'll help our strikers, like Joe Jordan, because he has the ability to pinpoint his passes. He's a midfield general."

Wilkins added real finesse to United, his subtle touches making the team's attacks much more unpredictable. With "Butch" directing operations from the middle of the park, a team-mate needed only the slightest opening and Wilkins would pick him out with a tip-top through ball. "Ray helps to open up the game," said Sexton. "He has the ability to end a series of short passes with one long, accurate ball and, what is more, he can do this with either foot."

A captain of both Manchester United and England, Wilkins' 84-cap international career took in the finals of the World Cups of 1982 and 1986 and the European Championship finals of 1980 in Italy. His typically clever curving lob over the Belgium defence for a goal was one of his favourite moments. A similarly sweet strike for United against Brighton & Hove Albion in the 1983 FA Cup final was one of the most memorable moments in a United shirt for Ray.

On leaving United, he moved to AC Milan in a £1.5 million transfer – a then record sale for United. He was well loved at the San Siro, not only for his playing abilities but for conducting himself like a typical English gentleman. After three years in Italy, he moved, briefly, to Paris St. Germain before joining Glasgow Rangers and then Queens Park Rangers. He became player-manager at Loftus Road in 1994, leaving in 1996, before becoming manager of Fulham for a year in 1997. He later worked as a coach at Chelsea, Watford and Millwall, United's opponents in the 2004 FA Cup Final.

STEVE COPPELL

FORWARD (MANCHESTER UNITED 1975-83)

STEVE COPPELL had the traditional talents of a winger thanks to his pace and ability to cross the ball with sharp accuracy. Unusually for a wide man, he also had the all-round abilities of a total footballer.

Stories about life at Liverpool Football Club almost prevented Steve Coppell becoming a Manchester United player. Coppell, while playing for Tranmere Rovers, heard tales from ex-Liverpool men Tommy Lawrence and Ron Yeats about how Bill Shankly would walk past them and ignore them when they were injured, and of how managers and crowds could destroy a player's career. Coppell, an intelligent individual studying for a degree in economic history at Liverpool University, was therefore wary of joining United and placing all his hopes in football. So the club offered him the chance to continue with his degree and during term time the young student would train on his own, only taking part in one United session per week. As a student of economics, Coppell also believed that the footballers of the 1970s were badly paid in comparison to the rock stars of the same era.

The 19-year-old Coppell cost United £40,000 from Tranmere, where he had played as a striker. He had only just become a regular in the 1974–75 season when United pounced. He came on as a substitute for Willie Morgan against Cardiff City on his debut appearance for United and laid on goals for Stuart Pearson and Lou Macari in a 4–0 win.

Two-footed and versatile, Coppell appeared as a striker for United on numerous occasions. Early in the 1979–80 season, Coppell – 5ft 7ins – formed a diminutive, but useful, striking partnership with Lou Macari. He could perform equally effectively on either wing and even played in the back four on one occasion after Brian Greenhoff had been sent off.

Even after becoming established at United, Coppell remained suspicious of the vagaries of the professional game. When United signed Gordon Hill in November 1975 those insecurities emerged again.

"Most footballers are very jealous of their positions," said Coppell. "I didn't think there was room for two wingers in the team, so for a week I concentrated entirely on my studies. I thought I had a lot to make up since it seemed football was not to be my chosen career."

He wrote his thesis on "The Economic Development of British and American Railways" and took his finals in June 1976. He had plans to become a teacher if football didn't work out for him, but the United support and successive United managers Docherty, Dave Sexton and Ron Atkinson were all fully appreciative of his talents.

Coppell won his first cap for England against Italy at Wembley in November 1977 and went on to win a total of 42 for his country. It was his quick, accurate throw-in in England's opening game of the 1982 World Cup, against France, that enabled Bryan Robson to open the scoring after just 27 seconds.

After a two-year battle against a severe knee injury, Steve retired as a player in 1983 and the following year, aged 28, became the Football League's youngest manager when he joined Crystal Palace. He led Palace to promotion to the First Division and to the FA Cup final, losing to United, during nine years at Selhurst Park.

Coppell had three further spells as Palace boss in the 1990s. He has also managed Manchester City (for a month), Brentford, Brighton and Reading. Other roles on his CV include Chief Executive of the League Managers' Association and PFA Chairman.

A consistent footballer, Steve Coppell holds the record for the longest run of consecutive league games for United, 206, which he set between January 1977 and November 1981.

Steve Coppell's football career was cruelly cut short by injury.

CHAPTER ELEVEN
THE ATKINSON ERA

THE EARLY EIGHTIES WERE EXCITING YEARS FOR MANCHESTER
UNITED SUPPORTERS. TRIPS TO WEMBLEY, FAST-FLOWING
FOOTBALL AND BIG-MONEY TRANSFERS WERE JUST SOME OF
THE HALLMARKS ON RON ATKINSON'S MANAGERIAL REIGN.

THE MANCHESTER UNITED that Ron Atkinson inherited at the outset of 1981–82 seemed set for a serious title challenge. They had ended the previous season by winning their last seven league matches but while such sprints to the finishing line are all well and good, Ron recognized that his team would need greater stamina and strength of character to perform throughout the course of a season.

Turning his attention to the midfield, Atkinson broke the British transfer record to buy Bryan Robson for £1.5 million. For good measure, he also signed Remi Moses. Both had played under Ron at his previous club, West Bromwich Albion.

New players always create a buzz around a ground, but some of the established players also produced the goods for Atkinson. Sammy McIlroy scored a hat-trick against Wolves, ironically on the day that his eventual replacement, Bryan Robson, signed for United. Even Garry Birtles silenced his critics, not to mention a few comedians, when he brought his miserable goal drought to an overdue end. Previously the club's record signing, Birtles benefited from playing alongside Atkinson's first acquisition, Frank Stapleton.

"Frank was one of the best headers of the ball I'd ever seen," says Arthur Albiston, one of the United defenders retained by Ron Atkinson. "He would direct the ball into the net with his head like some people kick a ball. He was a great target man, great for us at the back because he'd make our passes look perfect."

While the new arrivals were exciting, no one expected miracles from what was essentially a season of transition. United did well to finish third, but in the FA and League Cups they fell at the first hurdle.

Atkinson sold Sammy McIlroy to Stoke City, and in the summer of 1982 made one more change to his midfield, signing Arnold Muhren from Ipswich Town. Slotting in alongside three England internationals, the creative Dutchman completed one of the finest midfield quartets in the country.

"Arnold wasn't the quickest of players, but he had a fantastic brain and it was great for me to play with him on the left," recalls Arthur Albiston. "In the middle of the park, we had Robson and Ray Wilkins and on the right side we had Steve Coppell. He was a flying machine but he could also tuck in and help out. We had great balance in midfield."

The midfield still needed a forward who could put the finishing touches to their artistry. Atkinson took the advice of his "best-ever signing", youth coach Eric Harrison, and called up Norman Whiteside from the team that played in the 1982 FA Youth Cup final (losing to Watford 7–6 on aggregate).

While Stapleton scored in the first win of the 1982–83 season against Birmingham City, Norman netted in the second, third and fourth victories over Nottingham Forest, Everton and Ipswich Town. The two strikers, brought together from different sides of the Irish border, seemed to have formed the perfect partnership. But just as Atkinson became accustomed to the idea of things going well, his dream team was broken up by an injury to Ray Wilkins. The United and England captain fractured a cheekbone in a League Cup game at Bournemouth and missed almost three months of action.

Although Remi Moses filled in well in terms of tenacity, the team missed the guile of Wilkins. This was best illustrated by a run of three games over Christmas 1982 when United were unable to unlock the defences of Swansea City, Sunderland or Coventry City.

League points were thrown away, and United eventually finished third for the second year running. Injuries had certainly thrown a spanner in the works, or as Arthur Albiston put it, "If we had played with a settled midfield for the whole season, I think things could have been different."

If the league was again a source of disappointment, the fans had plenty to cheer about in the cups. In the FA Cup, United knocked out West Ham, Luton Town, Derby County and Everton in the early rounds. Meanwhile in the League Cup, which was now sponsored by the Milk Marketing Board, the Reds beat Bournemouth and Bradford City over two legs, then Southampton and Nottingham Forest in single ties.

So the twin towers of Wembley beckoned Atkinson's team on two fronts in the spring of 1983, but one obstacle remained, the same one in both competitions – Arsenal. The Gunners were almost the national stadium's resident club side, having played there in the FA Cup finals of 1978, 1979 and 1980. In 1979, they defeated United 3–2 in the final, with Stapleton among the Arsenal scorers. It seemed inevitable that he would eventually strike against his old club, and he did just that in the first leg of the League Cup semi-final on 15 February 1983. United won the match 4–2 at Highbury, thanks to Frank and the other scorers, Coppell (2) and Whiteside. After seeing out the second leg at Old Trafford (2–1, scorers Moran and Coppell), the Reds were ready for Wembley, where they would meet the holders Liverpool.

Fans of the two biggest clubs in the north west, if not the entire country, descended on north London on 26 March 1983 for what would prove to be a classic League (Milk) Cup final. Playing in their white and black away strip, United took the lead after only 12 minutes.

Opposite: Frank Stapleton (white shirt) evades the challenge of West Ham defender Alvin Martin. The Republic of Ireland striker was Ron Atkinson's first signing for Manchester United.

174

"Norman Whiteside scored a great goal," reports Arthur Albiston. "He turned Alan Hansen inside out and hit it in with his weaker foot, his right foot, and for long periods we were well on top. Then we allowed Alan Kennedy, the Liverpool left-back, to score from about 25 yards out."

Kennedy's equalizer was a cruel blow for United, and extra-time looked ominous for a side that had sustained two injuries in the heart of its defence.

"We ended up with Lou Macari and Frank Stapleton playing across the back four with myself and Mike Duxbury," remembers Albiston. "Big Gordon McQueen was injured and had to play on the right wing."

It was a makeshift defence but Liverpool still needed a special goal to beat United. After his attempted pass was blocked, Ronnie Whelan decided to shoot for himself and curled the ball perfectly around Gary Bailey.

"Even then, Liverpool were hanging on. They knew we'd given them a game and I remember their striker, Kenny Dalglish, taking a ball into the corner and just booting it into the crowd. For a player of his ability to do that, they must have been worried. We had them on the rack for a while, considering we'd suffered some serious injuries."

If losing the League Cup to Liverpool dismayed Atkinson's men, it failed to destroy them. The manager would not allow it, not with another semi-final against Arsenal on the horizon. This time, in the FA Cup, it was a one-off tie to be played on neutral ground. The teams met at Villa Park, Birmingham on 16 April 1983.

A crowd of 46,535 witnessed Tony Woodcock give Arsenal the lead before half-time. United's season of promise was on a precipice. They had fallen too far behind Liverpool in the league; the FA Cup was their last chance of silverware. They needed strong men to turn it around, and they found them in Robson, who levelled the scores, and Whiteside, who netted a wonderful winner on the volley.

So eight weeks after losing to Liverpool, Ron Atkinson led his team out at Wembley again, this time against Brighton and Hove Albion in the biggest domestic match of them all – the FA Cup final. The game ended in a 2–2 draw after extra-time and five days later United won the replay, also played at Wembley, 4–0.

By winning a major trophy in his second season, Atkinson had whetted the fans' appetite for his third. But the start of the campaign was hampered by another major injury problem. England winger Steve Coppell, a favourite player of the United faithful, had

Ray Wilkins in action during the 1983 FA Cup final, in which he scored United's second goal. The midfielder made almost 200 appearances between 1979 and 1984.

Action from the 1983 Milk Cup final. From left to right: Arnold Muhren, Ian Rush (Liverpool), Gordon McQueen, Graeme Souness (Liverpool), Steve Coppell. Liverpool won 2–1 after extra-time.

sustained a serious knee injury while on international duty. The damage proved irreparable and Coppell's playing career came to a premature end at the age of 28.

Needing a new No. 11, Atkinson overlooked Alan Davies – who had replaced Coppell for the FA Cup final and replay – in favour of Arthur Graham, signed for £45,000 from Leeds United. Graham was a first-team regular for one season only. The campaign produced some high-scoring victories, but also some of the lowest points of the Atkinson era.

Just before Christmas, Atkinson's old club Oxford embarrassed him in the League Cup, knocking United out over two legs. But Ron's face turned an even deeper shade of red in the New Year, when his FA Cup holders slipped up on the south coast. United's third-round opponents, AFC Bournemouth, were the envy of their lower league rivals when they were drawn at home against the kings of the competition, but instead of rolling over and merely raking in the much-needed gate receipts, the Cherries beat their illustrious opponents 2–0.

"I came off at half-time with a back problem and had to sit in the dug-out in the second half," says Arthur Albiston. "It wasn't a nice experience when we were 2–0 down, with all the cameras and flashbulbs focused on us, ready to get the manager's reaction. I really felt for Ron that day.

"It was unfortunate, but our cup results that season summed us up. We could lose to a Third Division team and yet still get to the semi-finals of the Cup-winners' Cup."

As the nation laughed, the United players licked their wounds. After being humbled by Bournemouth, it seemed they would be on a hiding to nothing against Barcelona, their quarter-final opponents in the Cup-winners' Cup.

The Barcelona squad boasted two international strikers in Diego Maradona and Bernd Schuster, while Atkinson's United were still novices on the Continent, at least by comparison. They had been knocked out of the UEFA Cup in 1982–83 by Valencia, and slender victories over Dukla Prague and Spartak Varna in the early rounds of 1983–84 had barely enhanced their European status.

The first leg, away at the Nou Camp, followed the form guide. The home team won 2–0 and flew to England a fortnight later, confident they would finish off United in Manchester.

Man for man, 11 against 11, Ron Atkinson's Reds were clearly the underdogs. But backed by some incredible support inside Old Trafford, United found the courage and quality of finishing not only to draw level, but to win the tie 3–2 on aggregate with two goals from Robson and one from Stapleton.

"The atmosphere that night was the best I ever experienced at Old Trafford," says Albiston. "It wasn't just the Stretford End or United Road or the Scoreboard End, all the stands were bouncing. They gave us such a lift, it was like having two extra men in the team."

If that momentous cup match showed the feats which Ron Atkinson's United could achieve, the very next fixture demonstrated their major flaw, a lack of consistency. Ten days after beating Barcelona, the Reds lost to West Bromwich Albion, Atkinson's former team. In a nutshell, inconsistency and injuries wrecked their challenge for the title. The final ten matches, starting with the Albion result, produced two wins, four draws and four defeats.

The European adventure ended in something of an anti-climax in the semi-final against Juventus. The damage was done in the first leg at Old Trafford. Juventus frustrated the injury-hit Reds, who were missing Muhren, Robson and Wilkins, and held them 1–1.

"We still could have won," maintains Albiston. "There was a massive scramble at the Stretford End and I was holding on to their goalkeeper, which shows you just how desperate we were to get a result. I stopped him getting up and it should have been a free-kick. The referee didn't give it and the ball fell to Frank, but his shot was blocked on the line. It was one of those games."

Finishing fourth in the league, United had to be content with a place in the UEFA Cup the following season. Access to the Continent's premier tournament, the European Cup, was then exclusively for the winners of the previous year's competition and the champions of each country. United's bitter rivals Liverpool accomplished both criteria in 1984. They won the league and the European Cup and also, just for good measure, the League Cup.

United had been pioneers of the European Cup, the first English team to enter it in 1956, and the first English side to win it in 1968. But now the Reds of Manchester were trailing 4–1 to the Reds of Merseyside in terms of European titles, and there was an even greater deficit in league championships – Liverpool 15, Manchester United 7.

Atkinson sensed he needed some big signings to close the gap, hence his triple plunge into the transfer market during the summer of 1984.

Danish winger Jesper Olsen was imported from Amsterdam, where he'd been one of the stars of another great Ajax team. Scotland striker Alan Brazil was bought from Tottenham. He had previously been one of Ipswich Town's heroes in the period when they won the FA Cup, UEFA Cup and twice finished second in the league. The third and final acquisition was Gordon Strachan from Aberdeen. He replaced Ray Wilkins who had joined AC Milan in June.

Exciting times were ahead, it seemed, for all three of the new boys were old hands at winning trophies. Both Strachan and Olsen had experienced winning a league championship, in Scotland and Holland respectively. No one else in the United dressing-room could speak of such an experience.

The new trio were all in the starting line-up as the 1984–85 season kicked off, but although Strachan scored on his debut against Watford, United could not muster a victory in their first four league matches. Old Trafford witnessed 1–1 draws with Watford and Chelsea, while the same scoreline was recorded away from home at Ipswich Town. Even less inspiring was the 0–0 stalemate at Southampton.

Three goals was a poor return from the first four games, and United fans couldn't help but look enviously at Liverpool, who had the prolific Ian Rush in their armoury. All the Reds could hope for was a revival of the club's long-standing tradition of goal-sharing, and it duly came during a fruitful September. In the space of seven days, six different players scored for United against Newcastle United (5–0) and Coventry City (3–0). Opposing defenders just didn't know who to mark as the shots rained in from Moses, Olsen, Hughes, Robson, Strachan (twice) and Whiteside (twice).

Speak of the devil, United faced Rush in their very next fixture at Old Trafford. Not for the first or last time during Atkinson's reign, Arthur Albiston and his fellow defenders prevented the Liverpool striker from scoring and matched the champions. The final score was 1–1, with Strachan on the scoresheet for United.

"Liverpool were obviously the dominant team of that period," says Albiston. "They had a fantastic squad and great managerial staff, but we knew we could beat them on the day.

"Just before the Big Ron era, Joe Jordan used to cause them all sorts of problems. He'd put his head in where some people wouldn't even dream of kicking the ball and that seemed to disrupt Liverpool. Mark Hughes and Norman Whiteside were in that same physical mould. They really gave the best of defences a hard time and that's why we got results against them."

It was against some of the smaller teams that United failed to get the results expected of them. During the 1984–85 league season, they lost to Stoke City, Sheffield Wednesday, Coventry City and Luton Town. Finishing fourth, they were again forced to mine the cup competitions for silverware.

In the UEFA Cup, for example, they knocked out Raba Gyor Eto from Hungary, the Dutch side PSV Eindhoven and, from north of the border, Dundee United. But just when United seemed on course for their first European final in 17 years, they were bounced out with two rounds to go.

Jesper Olsen was one of three players signed during the summer of 1984. The Danish midfielder made more than 150 appearances before leaving the club in 1988.

Norman Whiteside takes on Liverpool's Mark Lawrenson in the 1983 Milk Cup final. His goal made him the youngest player to score in a Wembley final.

Videoton, their curiously named quarter-final opponents from Budapest, had restricted the Reds to just one goal, scored by Stapleton, at Old Trafford. The Hungarians then won 1–0 on their home soil to send the tie into extra-time and finally a penalty shoot-out. Goalkeeper Peter Disztl crucially saved the sudden-death kick by Hughes. United kicked themselves; it was a tie they should have won comfortably.

"That was a hard result to take," admits Albiston. "You don't mind going out to a team that's head and shoulders above you, but they were a poor side really. It was a quagmire of a pitch. I don't know whether they'd watered it to make it that way, but no excuses, we should have beaten teams like that."

At least United were compensated by their FA Cup run in 1985, despite a third-round draw which reminded them of their premature exit in the previous season. This time, with Bournemouth coming to Old Trafford, there was no repeat of the nightmare episode at Dean Court. Instead, goals by McQueen, Strachan and Stapleton buried the Cherries 3–0.

Next out of the FA Cup hat were Coventry City, fresh from winning 1–0 on United's turf in the league. That surprise result gave the Sky Blues plenty of confidence and made the fourth-round tie a tough one to call – that is until Mark Hughes and Paul McGrath scored for the Reds in their 2–1 triumph.

Reaching the fifth round of the FA Cup was just what the doctor ordered for Ron Atkinson, especially after medical reports had ruled out Bryan Robson for a few months with a dislocated shoulder. United fans knew the loss of the captain would be detrimental to the team's chances of success in the weekly rigours of league football, but round by round in the Cup, a solution could be found.

McGrath seemed to be the answer, especially when he scored again in the 2–0 victory at Blackburn in the fifth round. In fact, the versatile Irishman could play in a number of positions. In the quarter-final against West Ham, he resumed his customary role at the heart of defence, following an injury to Kevin Moran.

Further forward, Atkinson shuffled his pack and proceeded to play Whiteside, Stapleton and Hughes in the same attacking side.

The tactic worked a treat, as the Reds turned West Ham over 4–2 at Old Trafford with a second goal in the FA Cup run for Hughes adding to Whiteside's tremendous hat-trick.

For the people of Merseyside, the semi-final draw kept alive their dream of the perfect final – Liverpool versus Everton at Wembley Stadium. For United, drawn against Liverpool, it was the opportunity to spoil that dream and remind a few people that Manchester was still a football city to be reckoned with. Everton's Goodison Park was selected as the neutral venue. The landlords had hammered the Reds 5–0 earlier in the season, but United had just beaten Liverpool 1–0 in the league at Anfield, thanks to a strike by Stapleton.

Big Frank struck again in the semi-final in extra-time, after Ronnie Whelan had cancelled out the opening goal by Hughes. United were leading 2–1 in the 120th minute of the match when Paul Walsh, seemingly from an offside position, levelled again for Liverpool to make the final score 2–2.

Everton, in the meantime, had won through to the final where they hoped to clinch the first league and FA Cup double in their history. They waited patiently as United and Liverpool squared up again in the replay, this time on a ground much closer to Old Trafford, Manchester City's Maine Road.

After twice being behind in the first match, Liverpool took the lead in the second game when Paul McGrath inadvertently headed the ball past his own goalkeeper, Gary Bailey.

The all-Merseyside final looked odds-on at half-time in the replay, but Bryan Robson, back from injury, had other ideas. The Manchester United midfielder equalized with one of the greatest goals of his career, a long-range drive into the top corner of Bruce Grobbelaar's net. Then as captain, he cajoled his colleagues into completing their comeback with another marvellous finish by Mark Hughes. The final score was United 2 Liverpool 1.

United had reached their fifth FA Cup final in ten seasons, and the third Wembley final of Ron Atkinson's reign. So far, he'd won one against Brighton and lost one to Liverpool. How would his team fare against Everton, the Cup holders and newly crowned league champions? Very well, as it turned out. They won 1–0.

Arthur Albiston (left) says Mark Hughes could terrorize the best of defences. Liverpool's Mark Lawrenson could vouch for that after the 1985 FA Cup semi-final.

United also fared very well at the start of the following league season, 1985–86, winning their first ten matches in a row. It was a remarkable run, not least because the team scored so many goals, 27, and conceded so few, three. Even the full-backs joined in at the attacking end – Duxbury and Albiston both scored in the Manchester derby at Maine Road, the eighth win of the sequence.

"Everything we did just seemed to turn into gold," remembers Albiston fondly. "It was a fantastic period to play in."

With maximum league points gained from the first 10 games, it seemed that United would never be in a better position to go on and win the league championship. After all, none of the great sides at Liverpool had ever made such a perfect start to a season. But Ron Atkinson believes his team were closer to the title in 1983–84, when they were ahead of Liverpool with only 10 games left to play. Then an injury to Robson had ruined United's chances and he was absent again in 1985 when the team's 10-point lead disappeared. United won just four of the next 10 games and lost at Sheffield Wednesday and Leicester City in the process. By the end of the calendar year, they had suffered two more defeats, back-to-back against Arsenal at Old Trafford and away to the league champions Everton on Boxing Day. They had also been knocked out of the League Cup, at Anfield of all places. Unlucky for Atkinson, it was the 13th time his United side had faced Liverpool, and yet it was only their third defeat.

Arthur Albiston remembers the Reds were still in contention for the title until March. "Then we just seemed to crack up, with the same old mix of injuries to key players and poor performances," he says.

The poor form in March ended United's run in the FA Cup. After drawing 1–1 at West Ham in the fifth round, they lost the replay 2–0 at Old Trafford. By May, the Reds were in no position to prevent their great rivals Liverpool from achieving their greatest feat so far – the league and FA Cup double.

After all they had promised with their opening run of ten wins in a row, United again finished fourth in the First Division, with exactly the same record of results as the previous year – played 42, won 22, drawn ten, lost ten.

The captain and star player, Bryan Robson, had played half of those fixtures but it wasn't just his No. 7 shirt that had been passed around the squad. Goalkeeper Gary Bailey lost his No. 1 jersey through injury and was replaced by Chris Turner from February onwards. The central defensive pairing went through several per-mutations, from Graeme Hogg and McGrath to Moran and Billy

Left: **Arthur Albiston** hardly missed a match during Ron Atkinson's reign as manager. The Scot served the club for 14 years, making 482 appearances.

Garton. Even Arthur Albiston missed a few games in December, when Colin Gibson played at left-back.

"We didn't have the same strength in depth that the United teams in the late nineties had," laments Albiston. "If we had two or three influential players out, we couldn't cope."

The televised 1986 World Cup finals provided more moments of anxiety in Ron Atkinson's living room. Several of his players were representing their countries in Mexico, and several of them returned home with injuries that would delay their starts to the new season. Bryan Robson, inevitably, was among the walking wounded. After dislocating his shoulder again on England duty, he missed United's first four games of 1986–87 – three straight defeats and a score-draw against Leicester City.

When Robson returned to the team, United returned to winning ways, but for one match only. Impressive though it was to beat Southampton 5–1, the euphoria was soon forgotten when the Reds lost their next three in a row, to Watford, Everton and Chelsea.

"We made an horrendous start," says Albiston, reflecting on the run of six defeats in eight games. "Teams that we would normally wipe the floor with could sense that we were not quite firing on all cylinders. I remember we lost at home to Charlton when they had only just been promoted, and that's not right. Again, you can harp on about certain players being injured, but even so, results like that shouldn't happen to a club of Manchester United's stature."

Atkinson was sinking. He had already given some thought to resigning in the summer but had been persuaded to stay for at least one more season by his chairman, Martin Edwards. By the end of September, both parties must have been regretting that stay of execution. United were languishing in the lower half of the table, and although their league form in October showed some improvement, their next meeting with Southampton indicated otherwise.

Drawn out of the hat together in the League Cup, the sides drew 0–0 at Old Trafford and headed for a replay at the Dell. Future England star Matt Le Tissier destroyed United, who were again without their own national hero, Bryan Robson.

"They gave us a real hammering," says Albiston. "We were all over the place that night."

On the following morning, Wednesday, 5 November, Atkinson finally became the fall guy. Later that day, while people across England celebrated Bonfire Night with firework displays, the sacked United manager reminisced about his five-year reign in the company of friends and a few of his now former players. Gordon Strachan, Bryan Robson and Norman Whiteside, all present at the farewell party, would now have to live up to their big reputations for a new man at the helm of Manchester United.

1983 FA CUP FINAL

21 MAY 1983, WEMBLEY **MANCHESTER UNITED (0) 2 BRIGHTON AND HOVE ALBION (1) 2 AET**

REPLAY, 26 MAY 1983, WEMBLEY **MANCHESTER UNITED (3) 4 BRIGHTON AND HOVE ALBION (0) 0**

182

BRIGHTON AND HOVE ALBION were the biggest Cup final underdogs since 1976. The last team who'd been expected to turn up, roll over and die were Southampton, and Manchester United knew all about them, having been their unsuspecting victims in that particular year.

The Reds recovered from that shock defeat soon enough to win the 1977 final, but when they lost to Arsenal two years later and then the League Cup final in 1983, it seemed that Wembley could still expose the weaknesses in United's game. Complacency was one and it reared its head 14 minutes into the game when Gordon Smith headed in the first goal. The unlikely score was Brighton 1 United 0, and if you could have told the scorer then that he'd be forever associated with that match, he'd probably have danced a jig of joy across the rain-soaked turf.

It seemed inevitable that United, enjoying more of the possession, would eventually equalize, even though this was clearly not one of their better afternoons. After 41 minutes of staring embarrassment in the face, United drew level when Mike Duxbury's cross reached the far post and Frank Stapleton lashed the ball high into the net.

The game seemed won when, in the 74th minute, Ray Wilkins scored one of Wembley's all-time classic goals by curling the ball in from 30 yards with his left foot. The overwhelming favourites at last had their noses in front and few could see a way back for brave Brighton. But then, just as the red and white ribbons were about to be wrapped around the handles of the Cup, Gary Stevens stepped into the path of a team-mate's shot and finished it himself to make the score 2–2 at the end of 90 minutes.

That late equalizer must have revived nightmare memories for Gary Bailey, who had conceded a late winner to Arsenal in 1979. But on this occasion, the United goalkeeper enjoyed the last laugh.

"We were all caught attacking and they had a chance in the last minute of extra-time," remembers Albiston. "Everybody remembers it as Gordon Smith missing an easy chance to score the winner for Brighton, especially the commentator's line, 'And Smith must score.' But in fact, Gary Bailey saved it, almost with his legs and his backside. The ball just seemed to get stuck under his body. That save probably won the Cup for us because if Smith's shot had gone in, I don't think there would have been enough time to kick off. Instead, we won the replay quite easily, destroying them in the first 45 minutes."

The Thursday night replay was wrapped up with two Bryan Robson goals and one from Norman Whiteside in the first half, then Arnold Muhren's penalty in the second. Ron Atkinson had won his first trophy as United manager, but only after an almighty fright.

Manchester United (manager Ron Atkinson): Bailey, Duxbury, Moran, McQueen, Albiston, Davies, Robson, Wilkins, Muhren, Stapleton, Whiteside. **Scorers:** Stapleton 55, Wilkins 74

Brighton and Hove Albion (manager Jimmy Melia): Moseley, Ramsey (substituted by Ryan, 45 minutes), Pearce, Grealish, Gatting, Stevens, Case, Howlett, Robinson, Smith, Smillie.
Scorers: Smith 14, Stevens 87
Attendance: 100,000

REPLAY:
United team changes: none.
Scorers: Robson 25, 43, Whiteside 29, Muhren (pen) 62
Brighton team changes: Foster replaced Gatting
Neither team used substitutes
Attendance: 92,000

Arnold Muhren scored United's fourth goal in the replay.

1985 FA CUP FINAL

MANCHESTER UNITED (0) 1 EVERTON (0) 0 AET

18 MAY 1985, WEMBLEY

EIGHT YEARS AFTER wrecking Liverpool's tilt at the treble, Manchester United were ready to ruin the dream season of Everton, who had already won the 1985 league championship and European Cup-winners' Cup.

Arthur Albiston, an FA Cup-winner in 1977 and 1983, knew it wouldn't be an easy match. After all, Everton had already thrashed United 5–0 during the season and had knocked them out of the League Cup. They had also won two trophies and boasted a perfectly balanced midfield.

"They had two wide men, Trevor Steven on the right and Kevin Sheedy on the left, with two hard-working players in the middle, Paul Bracewell and Peter Reid," remembers Albiston, as if he were reading from the Wembley teamsheet once again. "They weren't the tallest of players, but they were very determined and they did a lot of defensive work in front of the defence itself."

In a bid to break down what effectively was an eight-man defence, Ron Atkinson selected an attack-minded team, including a former striker in midfield, Norman Whiteside. Between them, the two teams had enough talent to thrill Wembley's capacity crowd of 100,000, not to mention the millions watching on television. Yet the sides managed to cancel each other out and produce more than 90 minutes of stalemate.

"Everton had won the Cup-Winners' Cup three days earlier, so they were bound to be tired," explains Albiston. "And we had played in a lot of cup matches ourselves, on top of the forty-two league games. By the end of the season, everyone was shattered and that's why you would often see players in Wembley finals strolling around with their socks rolled down."

Socks were already low down shattered legs when the crowd was stirred from its slumbers by the first major incident. Kevin Moran's controversial sending off, the first in an FA Cup final, brought the game to life and forced United to reshuffle for the last 12 minutes of normal time, then extra time.

"Although Kevin was hard as nails, he wasn't malicious," says Albiston. "I think he just mistimed his tackle on Peter Reid, who was back on his feet quite quickly. But the referee had to make a decision on the spot and he decided that Kevin had to go."

With Frank Stapleton replacing Moran as an emergency centre-half, United played on with ten men, and finally made the breakthrough in the 110th minute of the match.

"Gordon Strachan deserves a pat on the back," says Albiston, "because he ran 40 or 50 yards, overlapped Norman and distracted Van den Hauwe and Ratcliffe. Norman then cut inside and scored a wonderful goal.

"I had been substituted by then, so I was sat on the bench, directly behind Norman and as soon as he took it inside on his left foot, I could see the goal coming. He hit the exact spot where Neville Southall had put his spare gloves, right in the corner of the

Norman Whiteside lifts the FA Cup after scoring the winning goal.

net. I'd injured my ankle, kicking Peter Reid, but somehow I managed to leap in the air and jump on top of Ron. Daft, I know, but it was an incredible goal."

It was an extraordinary goal to win a very ordinary match. Yet another contradiction in the life of Manchester United in the eighties.

Manchester United (manager Ron Atkinson): Bailey, Gidman, Moran, McGrath, Albiston, Strachan, Robson, Whiteside, Olsen, Stapleton, Hughes
Scorer: Norman Whiteside 110

Everton (Howard Kendall): Southall, Stevens, Van Den Hauwe, Ratcliffe, Mountfield, Reid, Steven, Gray, Sharp, Bracewell, Sheedy

Attendance: 100,000

RON ATKINSON

Ron Atkinson felt at home at United's training ground.

IT WAS IRONIC that two clubs from Ron Atkinson's native city overshadowed his reign as Manchester United manager. After picking up the baton in the summer of 1981, he played second fiddle to Liverpool and Everton during his five-year pursuit of the elusive league championship.

Born in Liverpool, but educated as a footballer in the Midlands, Ron Atkinson was never very far away from Manchester United in his formative years. When he arrived at the club in July 1981, his steps were not those of a stranger in town, tentative and testing the water. Instead, the new manager marched into Old Trafford and declared to the world that he and the club were "made for each other".

It was a bold statement, but Atkinson instinctively knew how to back it up, serving the supporters with a devil-may-care style of football they could fully appreciate, and feeding the hungry newshounds who had survived on mere scraps of stories during Dave Sexton's spell in charge.

The popular press certainly warmed to Ron's open-door policy, and when he conducted one of his early press conferences from the comfort of his sunbed, they knew the ice around "Cold Trafford" had melted forever. For five whole seasons and one third of a sixth, Atkinson's name was splashed across the back pages. He won trophies, he lost titles, he signed a few stars and missed out on others. Ron's reign was a sporting soap opera, entertaining for the public, the press and the players.

"It was the most enjoyable period of my career," admits Albiston, a stalwart of Ron's side. "We had some superstars, some great players and some good players. I was probably in that Denis Irwin mould, consistent, reliable, not a superstar, but then Ron's confidence in my ability made me feel ten feet tall. When I ran out at Old Trafford, I felt I was on a par with Bryan Robson and Ray Wilkins."

Atkinson's empathetic style of man-management seemed to bring out the best in his players. The stars of Dave Sexton's team who were asked to leave, including Jimmy Nicholl and Sammy McIlroy, might tell a different tale, but most of those who remained with or later joined Ron's revolution revelled in his keen sense of dressing-room humour and his infectious enthusiasm for the game.

If the sharply dressed Atkinson now seems perfectly suited to his media career, he was then more comfortable in a red, black and white tracksuit, and far happier meeting a cross with his head on the training ground than meeting with football's administrators and businessmen. Ron's office of choice did not contain a desk of mahogany, paintings by Monet or magnums of Moet; it was green, rectangular and in the open air.

"Ron was a frustrated player," remembers Albiston. "In training, he thought he was the world's best uncapped centre-half, and he was actually a good passer of the ball...with both feet! Even now he'll tell you he should have played 400 games for United or Liverpool, instead of Oxford and Kettering."

Training like a 20 year-old would be something that players at his other clubs – Cambridge United, West Bromwich Albion, Atletico Madrid, Aston Villa, Coventry City, Sheffield Wednesday and Nottingham Forest – would identify as Big Ron behaviour.

BRYAN ROBSON

MIDFIELD (MANCHESTER UNITED 1981–94)

BRYAN ROBSON was one of Manchester United's greatest ever captains, a born leader who was prepared to stretch every sinew and break every bone in his body for the cause. It was just a pity that he managed to injure himself too often at critical times in the mid-1980s.

Born on 11 January 1957 in Chester-le-Street, County Durham, Bryan Robson OBE was nurtured in a hotbed of footballing talent; but unlike Peter Beardsley, Chris Waddle, Paul Gascoigne and Alan Shearer, Robson did not pull on the black and white stripes of the nearest big club, Newcastle. Instead, he made his name as a player in the red and white strip of Manchester United. The north-east's loss was certainly the north-west's gain, until he moved back to his native area as Middlesbrough manager in 1994.

In the intervening years, he became a legend for club and country, leading both by example when his injury-prone frame permitted. Signed for a British record fee of £1.5 million from West Bromwich Albion in October 1981, he served United admirably for almost 13 years. Had he not been so unlucky with bone and muscle problems, he almost certainly would have won more honours, earned more than his 90 caps and scored more than 26 goals for England.

By the time Sir Alex Ferguson had turned Manchester United into title-winners in 1993, Robson was no longer a regular member of the team. But as captain of the side for more than a decade of near misses, Bryan knew better than anyone else in the dressing-room the true emotional value of Fergie's first championship.

Perhaps Bryan's biggest disappointment was the 1985–86 season when United won their first ten matches only to fade and finish fourth, stricken by injuries to himself and other key players. The explanation of United's gallant failures in the 1980s was that simple. When the captain was injured, the Reds were rudderless and destined for the rocks of mediocrity; when Robson was in the team, they could beat anybody, even Liverpool.

That wasn't only because he had the knack for scoring crucial goals in the biggest games, such as the 1983 and 1985 FA Cup semi-finals, the 1983 Cup final replay and the epic European Cup-winners' Cup quarter-final against Barcelona in March 1984. Arthur Albiston, his team-mate for seven years, remembers Robson's other qualities.

"Bryan wouldn't think twice about rollicking you if you made a mistake or if you weren't pulling your weight," admits Arthur, clearly speaking from experience. "He always knew how to get a little bit more effort from each of us, he kept everybody on their toes. I think he did the job perfectly. Robbo was head and shoulders above everyone."

It was a shame that Bryan's own shoulders caused him so much grief. One of the enduring images of his England career was of him leaving the field during the 1986 World Cup finals in Mexico, grimacing with the pain of a dislocated shoulder. In the previous World Cup, he'd scored the second fastest goal in the tournament's history, after just 27 seconds of the match against France. If only England and United had seen more of the latter image, and less of the former, football history could have been so different.

Bryan Robson led by example for nearly 13 years.

MARK HUGHES

FORWARD (MANCHESTER UNITED 1983–86; 1988–95)

LESLIE HUGHES certainly made his mark on English and European football in the 1980s and 1990s. More commonly known by his middle name, the powerful Welsh forward struck fear into even the most accomplished defenders during his two successful spells with Manchester United. Twice voted the PFA Player of the Year by his peers, he was without question one of the greatest players of his generation.

United's supporters knew as much, even the older connoisseurs of attacking quality who'd witnessed Best, Law and Charlton in their pomp. The fans lauded Mark's debut in November 1983, applauded his PFA Young Player of the Year award in 1985, and loathed his first departure from the club in the summer of 1986.

When Hughes was allowed to leave again in July 1995, the fans had fewer complaints. This time they were satisfied with his legacy of heroic performances, which had helped United to win three FA Cups, one League Cup, one Cup-Winners' Cup and finally, at long last, two league championships in 1993 and 1994.

'Sparky' went on to play some useful football for Southampton, Everton, Blackburn and Chelsea, with whom he won the FA Cup for a record fourth time in 1997 and the Cup-winners' Cup in 1998. But by 1995, he had completed his work for United, and was ready to hand over the hero's role to the younger men in the squad – David Beckham, Andrew Cole, Ryan Giggs and Paul Scholes.

As a young man, Mark's career had led him away from Old Trafford, a move which might seem unthinkable now to a player such as Giggs, who was a boyhood fan of the club and of Hughes. But Manchester United was not then the wealthy empire it has since become, so Barcelona's bid of around £2 million for the 22-year-old striker represented good business for the men balancing the books.

The move might have benefited the bank account, but it was of little use to the team, the player or the manager who was forced to sell him, Ron Atkinson. Although the transfer forms were signed in secrecy in January 1986, with Hughes retained by United until the end of the season, the news eventually filtered through to the Old Trafford faithful. With that, it all became clear – one of the main reasons why the form of the team, previously ten points clear in the title race, and in particular the form of Hughes, had faltered.

It was to the relief of Reds fans everywhere that Hughes did not become a hit in Barcelona. By his own admission, he was a lonely Welsh boy lost in the intimidating arena of Spanish football, and when a loan spell with Bayern Munich only marginally improved his morale, there seemed just one way he could go – back to Old Trafford.

Once Sir Alex Ferguson had re-signed him for United in July 1988, there was no looking back for Mark – except that is when he was performing trademark manoeuvres on the field, turning towards his own goalkeeper to receive and hold on to possession while his colleagues took up threatening positions around him. This tactic worked time and time again for the trophy-winning teams of the early nineties, but Hughes was more than just a ball magnet and distributor. He could score goals too, and he was especially lethal from long range, as Barcelona in 1991 and Oldham in 1994, among many, many others, found to their cost.

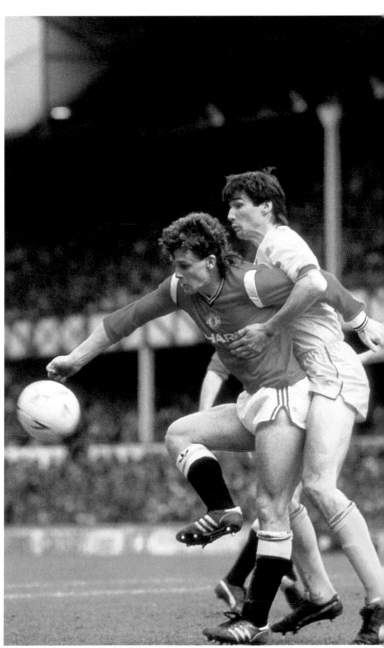

Mark Hughes scores one of his trademark goals against Liverpool.

NORMAN WHITESIDE

FORWARD/MIDFIELD (MANCHESTER UNITED 1982–89)

JUST WHEN UNITED NEEDED a new spark, the city of Belfast in Northern Ireland again came up with the goods. Bob Bishop, the talent scout who had found George Best there in the early sixties, discovered Norman Whiteside in the late seventies and sent him to Manchester for closer inspection.

Whiteside wasn't typical of the teenagers who attended trials with Manchester United. While talented but lightweight hopefuls were sometimes turned away, the big lad from Belfast had the average weight and height of a much older man. His mature build and unquestionable ability impressed not only the coaches but also the senior players, including Arthur Albiston.

"We watched him in the youth team, playing alongside Mark Hughes in attack," recalls Albiston. "They were a handful for anybody, but Norman in particular looked five or six years ahead of his time. He was built like a 19 or 20 year-old when he was 14 or 15."

Norman was 16, and still an apprentice, when he made his first-team debut as a substitute against Brighton in April 1982. Just 13 months later, the same opponents witnessed him becoming the youngest player to score in the FA Cup final, aged 18 years and 18 days.

Earlier in the same season, he'd set a similar record in the League Cup final with his opening goal against Liverpool. Even though United eventually lost the match, Whiteside – then aged 17 years and 323 days – merely shrugged off the disappointment in the same carefree way he shrugged off defenders.

For several seasons, Norman took everything in his imposing stride. His first cap for Northern Ireland made World Cup history in 1982, when he replaced Pele as the tournament's youngest ever player, a distinction he held until Michael Owen represented England in the 1998 World Cup finals.

Yet for all Norman's international achievements, nowhere in the world could rival his romance with Wembley Stadium in north London. After scoring there in two finals during 1983, he returned to the twin towers in 1985 to save an over-hyped FA Cup final from the threat of anti-climax. Norman had by then been converted from a bustling centre-forward into a battling midfield player, but as opponents Everton discovered in extra-time, he could still win matches with a shot that any striker would be proud of.

However, there was one major feat that repeatedly foiled Whiteside and his United colleagues – winning the league championship. In his later campaigns with the club, he appeared to embody the frustration felt by all at this failure. Sometimes he would lash out at opponents, his behaviour bringing fines and suspensions his side could ill-afford, and earning him the undesirable nickname of "Nasty Norman" in the critical press.

The new manager, Alex Ferguson, was something of a firebrand himself, but he wanted players who could control their explosive

Norman Whiteside was a triumphant product of United's youth system.

tempers and channel them for the cause. Hence Whiteside was soon written out of the script, and he might have been sold to Everton earlier than August 1989 had he not been blighted by injuries.

Less than two years later, a knee injury prematurely ended Norman's playing career. Still only 26, he was forced into other occupations, including podiatry and matchday entertainment, in order to maintain his links with the game.

CHAPTER TWELVE

FLEDGLING PROGRESS

MANCHESTER UNITED'S RISE UNDER ALEX FERGUSON WAS NO OVERNIGHT SUCCESS STORY. BUT WHILE THE FIRST TEAM STRUGGLED IN HIS EARLY YEARS, FERGUSON'S FAITH IN YOUNG TALENT WOULD LATER PAY RICH DIVIDENDS.

THE NEW MANCHESTER UNITED manager arriving from Aberdeen didn't have a Midas touch, just an acute understanding of the hard work he needed to do before the league championship could return to Old Trafford. His early years in the job were an important period of transition for the club, affecting not only the public face of the first team but also the situation behind the scenes and at grassroots level.

English football's most successful odyssey started in Oxford, a place noted for its scholars of virtually anything but the beautiful game. Despite the fact that accomplished managers like Jim Smith and Ron Atkinson either served or played there, in comparison with Milan, Munich, Madrid, or even a certain city on Merseyside, Oxford does not inspire visitors to think of great football matches or great football players. So it might have come as something of a surprise to Alex Ferguson to lose his first fixture as Manchester United manager there on 8 November 1986.

That afternoon, the Manor Ground in Oxford must have seemed a million miles from Wembley Stadium in London, let alone the Nou Camp in Barcelona or the Maracana in Rio de Janeiro. But Ferguson not only had an awesome responsibility to drag United up from the depths of the First Division, he had sufficient ambition and proven ability to deal with the situation.

Alex Ferguson (far right) watches impassively as United lose 2–0 at Oxford United's Manor Ground.

After losing 2–0 to goals by Oxford's Aldridge and Slatter, the new manager could really only take the team in one direction, and they certainly finished the season higher than they were placed when he took charge. In fact, United finished 11th, comfortably mid-table in a top flight which then had 22 teams.

The highlights of Ferguson's first six months at Old Trafford included a victory over Arsenal, who would emerge as league champions within two years. In the club's end-of-season yearbook, the manager wrote the following words about his team's 2–0 result: "That day we displayed character, guts and a hunger to win which, without doubt, is the least that you as supporters are entitled to expect."

United's hunger to win also helped them to beat defending champions Liverpool both home and away, thrash Newcastle United 4–1 and triumph in two Manchester derbies. But there were no miracles promised or performed by Alex Ferguson, so again the supporters had to swallow some disappointments, notably being knocked out of the FA Cup at home by Coventry City, the eventual winners of the competition. In his notes for the yearbook, the manager admitted that the players were "shell-shocked" by that 3–0 defeat, to the point that their league form also suffered for a while.

"I know that any team can have a shock result," wrote Ferguson, "but for the top teams such results are few and far between. Our problem is that we can beat anyone – we can also be beaten by anyone, and that is not a recipe for winning championships."

The search for greater stability started in earnest during the summer of 1987, Ferguson's first close season as Manchester United manager. His informative, settling-in period had passed and it was time for business in the transfer market. One of the first senior players to leave Old Trafford with his blessing was Frank Stapleton, the very first signed by his predecessor. Stapleton moved to Ajax in July 1987, and was swiftly replaced by Celtic striker Brian McClair. On the same day that McClair met the press at Old Trafford, England defender Viv Anderson was also unveiled as a new signing, arriving from Arsenal.

Both players settled in very well at Old Trafford and helped the evolving team to achieve the club's highest league position since 1979–80. Manchester United finished second, just nine points – or three victories – behind one of the greatest Liverpool teams in history. That was the story told by the final league table, but as Brian McClair points out, the mid-season reality was rather different.

"We were never in touching distance of Liverpool," says McClair. "We had a fantastic run towards the end of the season, when we were unbeaten for three months, but we were playing for second place from Christmas because they were flying."

Alex Ferguson and first signings, Viv Anderson (left) and Brian McClair.

At least McClair and co. could take some delight from delaying Liverpool's title celebrations, when they held the champions elect to a thrilling 3–3 draw at Anfield. Both teams took the lead at one stage in the Easter Monday match, but it was Liverpool who really kicked themselves at the end having been 3–1 up.

"They were showing some arrogance at that point, heading for the title with their supporters really up for it," remembers Brian. "But then Colin Gibson got sent off, Norman Whiteside came on and he terrified them. He caused mayhem for five minutes and disrupted the whole flow of the game."

Bryan Robson's second goal of the game plus one from Gordon Strachan made the final score 3–3.

"We played well and it was a really good game of football," says Brian, "but we'd have sacrificed results like that to win the title. Nobody likes losing, particularly to Liverpool, but ultimately winning the league is more important."

For all their attacking flair and ability to upset the likes of Liverpool, the Reds still finished Ferguson's first full season empty-handed. Their Littlewoods (League) Cup run had ended where the new manager's United career had started, in defeat at Oxford's Manor Ground. Being knocked out of the FA Cup at Highbury was another bitter pill to swallow, especially when Arsenal defender Nigel Winterburn barracked Brian McClair for missing a spot kick that would have levelled the scores.

"I didn't see what the point in haranguing me was," ponders Brian. "I'd missed a penalty in the last minute, which wasn't a nice thing to do. I didn't even know what he was saying, but obviously it wasn't very pleasant!"

192

The unpleasant battle with Arsenal rumbled on into subsequent years. Both clubs were desperate to dismantle Merseyside's monopoly of the league championship. As early as the summer of 1988, it appeared that United would be the team to take on Liverpool in the title race. Alex Ferguson signed two major players, his former Aberdeen goalkeeper Jim Leighton and the club's returning prodigal son, Mark Hughes.

Perhaps the weight of expectation was too great, for the Reds started the new season very poorly. At one stage they went through nine games without a win, a sequence that seemed to stem from United's inability to kill off teams. In eight of those matches, they took the lead only to let it slip again, often in the last 20 minutes. On one occasion, at home to Norwich City, this infuriating habit cost them all three points. McClair missed another penalty and the Canaries scored in the 85th and 86th minutes to win the match 2–1.

After an awful autumn, the Reds required a merry Christmas to help them turn the corner. They duly enjoyed one, beating Nottingham Forest 2–0 on Boxing Day and Liverpool 3–1 on New Year's Day. In the match against the champions, all four goals were scored between the 70th minute, when John Barnes gave Liverpool the lead, and the 77th minute when Russell Beardsmore capped United's amazing, instant comeback.

It was a big day for Beardsmore and the other young players in Alex Ferguson's team, namely the two Lees at right-back and left-back, Martin and Sharpe, and the substitute striker Mark Robins who was called into action in the first half following an injury to Gordon Strachan.

"Lee Sharpe came in at seventeen. He was great," remembers Brian McClair. "Russell also did particularly well. They were a smashing group of players, but for one reason or another they didn't all quite make it. Mark Robins was a natural goalscorer but he was never going to be world class because he didn't have the height or the pace required. Lee Martin was probably the best of them, a two-footed full-back with tremendous physique. He was quick and, had injuries not taken their toll, I think he could have been a top-drawer defender for England."

Martin, Beardsmore, Sharpe, Robins and the goalkeeper Gary Walsh were the leading lights of a larger group which also included Derek Brazil, Tony Gill, Deiniol Graham, Giuliano Maiorana and David Wilson. Collectively, they were known in the media as Fergie's Fledglings, obviously with a nod to the Busby Babes. But while their emergence demonstrated Alex's faith in young talent, the fact they had to play in so many games showed how badly the senior ranks were hit by injury. The defence, in particular, was badly affected with first-choice full-backs Viv Anderson and Colin Gibson starting just seven games between them in 1988–89, while central stalwart Paul McGrath missed almost half of that season's fixtures.

"Paul McGrath went on to play lots of games for Aston Villa and the Republic of Ireland, but he and the manager just didn't have a relationship," says Brian McClair. "Paul didn't want to play, so he couldn't stay, no matter how good he was. He was never going to benefit Alex Ferguson or Manchester United."

Alex Ferguson wondered in hindsight if he'd been a bit hasty in releasing so many senior players, especially the defenders Arthur Albiston, Graeme Hogg and Kevin Moran, who all left the club before the 1987–88 season started. They were later followed through the exit gates by striker

Lee Sharpe was the most successful member of Fergie's Fledglings who broke into the first team in 1988–89.

Lee Martin (white) in action during the 1990 FA Cup final.

Peter Davenport and the midfielders Liam O'Brien, Jesper Olsen and, in the most unpopular departure of all, Gordon Strachan. The latter was sold to Leeds in March 1989, just two days after playing for United in the FA Cup quarter-final at Old Trafford. The Reds were controversially knocked out 1–0 by Nottingham Forest – the referee, Brian Hill, decided what looked a certain goal for United did not cross the line.

The manner of that defeat and the subsequent sale of Strachan sent United spinning into decline. They won two of their last 11 matches, losing seven, and finished in 11th place. Arsenal won the title, pipping Liverpool on goal difference in the most dramatic finale to a league season ever witnessed.

The time for Alex Ferguson to spend some serious money had arrived, and to this end he didn't disappoint the fans. By the end of September 1989, he had splashed out more than £7 million on players, starting with midfielders Mike Phelan from Norwich City and Neil Webb from Nottingham Forest. Both made their debuts on the opening day of the season and they were briefly joined on the field by the wealthy tycoon Michael Knighton, the apparent new owner of Manchester United. He introduced himself to the fans by juggling with the ball. But like the team, the businessman flattered to deceive. After the euphoria of that opening 4–1 win over Arsenal, life soon returned to normal. Knighton's takeover deal fell through and the Reds again fell from grace, losing four of their next six league games.

By far the worst result of that sequence and season – even Fergie's entire career at Manchester United – was the 5–1 defeat by Manchester City on 23 September 1989. Of all the grounds where United could have crumbled, did they really have to do it at Maine Road? That must have been the rhetorical question rattling around in the heads of the Reds fans as they headed home that afternoon, especially those who would have to face working alongside City-supporting colleagues on the Monday morning.

"That was hard because you couldn't just sit in the house and hide," recalls Brian McClair. "I knew people who were City fans, but we just had to take the medicine and get on with it. It was a lesson for all of us."

United were in mourning, not only for the dramatic loss of their supremacy in Manchester but also for the death of their championship chances, even at such an early stage. The midfield dream team of Phelan, Robson and Webb had already been wiped out by a serious injury to the latter, while the other new signings Paul Ince, Gary Pallister and Danny Wallace were struggling to settle in.

"Sometimes you can get away with it, you can come in and change the club around straightaway," says McClair. "But it's difficult to do that at Manchester United because of all the external pressures that new players have to get used to, no matter where they come from."

Gary Pallister (right) outjumps Alan Smith in a heading duel at Highbury.

194

"Every game is a massive one, and that was the case even then," added McClair. "Although United weren't winning the championship at the time, it was likely that our game would draw the other team's biggest crowd of the season. It took a while for some of the new players to get used to that."

Gary Pallister in particular was under the greatest scrutiny, having been signed from Middlesbrough for a British record fee of £2.3 million. Alex Ferguson needed a settled partnership in central defence, and he was hoping that Pallister would form one with Steve Bruce, who was by now in his third season at the club.

Given the raft of personnel changes, consistency was an obvious casualty in the 1989–90 season. The only patterns the Reds could piece together were poor ones – three league defeats in a row in August and September, and the same again in early December. They finished the season in 13th place, their lowest position since being relegated under Tommy Docherty in 1974. Little wonder, then, that Alex Ferguson sought solace in the FA Cup during 1990.

"The Cup games were a relief because there was so much pressure on us to try and stay in the division," admits McClair. "We finished only six places off the bottom and there was a point when we were in real danger of going down. We hadn't won for 11 games and went to Millwall with only a few senior players, the rest were kids or reserves. It was never an easy place to go to but we won, and it turned us in the right direction."

Some observers still maintain that Ferguson would have been sacked had it not been for the face-saving FA Cup run, but Brian McClair, for one, isn't convinced by that argument.

"Only the chairman can answer whether or not the manager would have been sacked," says Brian. "My view was that although the first team was struggling, people were pleased with some of the other things that he'd sorted out, such as the youth set-up that later came to fruition. Somebody once said he was lucky, and I suppose at some point luck carried us through in the FA Cup that year."

The press vultures gathered at Nottingham's City Ground in January 1990, hoping Forest would knock Fergie's men out in the third roumd. But even with the likes of Ince, Robson and Webb injured and watching from the

Steve Bruce was signed from Norwich City in December 1987. Gary Pallister arrived two years later and their partnership improved United's defence.

sidelines, United found the necessary steel and spirit to sneak through 1–0 with Robins on the scoresheet.

Undeterred by that scoop-spoiling result, the news hounds followed the Reds to Hereford in the fourth round, looking for an even bigger banana skin to send Fergie on his way. But United's season was again prolonged by a 1–0 victory, this time courtesy of Clayton Blackmore.

In round five, the Reds were drawn away from home again, to First Division Newcastle United. The live television cameras captured a classic, with the Magpies equalizing twice to keep the

game on a knife-edge. Brian McClair then netted the winner, a feat he repeated against the Blades of Sheffield United in round six in another cagey 1-0 win. The 3–2 tussle at Newcastle had been the exception to the rule, but in the semi-final, the competition caught fire with a glut of goals for the fans to enjoy.

The clash with Oldham Athletic had all the characteristics of a passionate local derby; indeed, it was played at the Maine Road home of Manchester City. The blue-shirted Latics drew first blood when Earl Barrett fired them into an early lead. United's midfield duo of Robson and Webb had recovered from injury in time to play in the match, and after Robson, the captain, equalized in the 29th minute, his partner put the Reds 2–1 up with less than 20 minutes to go.

The strikers in the semi-final had thus far been quiet, but Oldham's number nine, Ian Marshall, made amends when he equalized to force the extra half-hour of action. Late in the April afternoon, the fatigue factor challenged both teams, but both Joe Royle and Alex Ferguson had utilized their substitutes wisely. The two number. 12s, Wallace for United and Palmer for Oldham, both scored in extra time to ensure honours remained even.

After the 3–3 thriller, the teams returned to Maine Road for the replay three days later. This time, the scoring was comparatively sparse, McClair's goal after 50 minutes seemingly sufficient for United to advance to Wembley for the first time during Ferguson's reign. But then, with nine minutes to go, former Old Trafford favourite, Andy Ritchie, popped up to force extra-time again with what was effectively Oldham's fourth equalizer of this epic encounter.

The stage was set for Mark Robins to become the FA Cup hero once again. Brought on as a substitute, he scored to win the tie for United, just as he had done in the third round to save his manager's job. All he had to do now was wait and wonder if that same manager would reward him with a place in the FA Cup final team at Wembley on 12 May against Crystal Palace. In the event, he came on for Pallister in the first half of extra-time. The match ended 3–3 and five days later United won the replay by the only goal of the game.

With the first tangible reward of Alex Ferguson's reign safely locked away in the Old Trafford trophy room, Manchester United were on the march again. Yet not so much in domestic football for the time being as in European competition, to which the team returned in 1990–91.

The five-year ban on all English clubs playing in Europe following the Heysel Stadium tragedy had been a source of frustration for Fergie and his players, especially in 1988, when they would have qualified for the UEFA Cup as league runners-up. That frustration was unleashed on Pecsi Munkas, United's opponents in the first round of the European Cup-Winners' Cup. Within 17

minutes from the first whistle in the first leg, the Reds were 2–0 up and loving every second of their comeback. They were made to wait for the third goal, though. It came as late as the 77th minute of the second leg in Hungary, where McClair made the final aggregate score 3–0 to United.

Brian McClair also scored United's next goal in the competition in the following round, at home to Wrexham. The Welsh Cup holders were to finish the season at the bottom of the entire Football League, but they put up a brave fight before finally surrendering to United 5–0 on aggregate.

Victory over Wrexham booked a place in the quarter-finals, to be played in March 1991. But that wasn't the only thing Reds fans could look forward to as they welcomed in the New Year. The team was through to the last eight of the Rumbelows (League) Cup, having knocked out the two sides who were vying for the title. Beating the champions Liverpool 3–1 in the fourth round was impressive enough, but United achieved an even greater victory in the fifth round.

"We battered Arsenal, when nobody had given us a chance," says McClair. "We were 3-0 by half-time, but when they pulled it back to 3-2, we thought, 'Hang on, we could still lose this.' Fortunately, we scored another three goals to win the match. It was a phenomenal game, but we needed to be capable of doing that week in, week out. The disappointing thing was that we still weren't."

Hence United's final league position of sixth, where they were sandwiched between Manchester City and Wimbledon. The one point deducted by the FA for a mass brawl with Arsenal at Old Trafford had no bearing on this, and the Gunners still won the championship, despite losing two points for the regrettable incident.

With no chance of challenging for the title, and their FA Cup campaign cut short in the fifth round by Norwich, United's hopes of winning domestic honours in 1990–91 rested with the Rumbelows Cup. After beating Leeds United in both legs of the semi-final, the Reds were hot favourites to beat another Yorkshire team in the final. Instead, the underdogs of Sheffield Wednesday won the Cup, thanks to a goal by Manchester-born John Sheridan, and the guidance of ex-United manager Ron Atkinson.

"It was my fault," admits McClair, looking back. "I was supposed to be marking the guy at the edge of the box, so I had to carry the can for it. But really, as a team we didn't play very well. The manager was angry and we were all disappointed."

There was little time to dwell on the Wembley defeat because three days later the Reds had to face Legia Warsaw in the second leg

Overleaf: Jim Leighton and Steve Bruce (4) fail to stop a goal by Mark Bright (right) of Crystal Palace during the 1990 FA Cup final.

Lee Martin stretches to score the winner in the 1990 FA Cup final replay.

Alex Ferguson (right) after the 1991 Cup-winners' Cup final.

of the Cup-winners' Cup semi-final. United had won the first leg in Poland 3–1, the same score by which they had beaten Montpellier over two legs in the quarter-final.

Lee Sharpe gave the Reds a good start to the second leg against Legia when he made the aggregate score 4–1, and even though the Poles forced a draw on the night at Old Trafford, United were not to be denied their place in another final. On 15 May, they beat Barcelona 2–1 in the Feyenoord Stadium, Rotterdam, with Mark Hughes scoring both of United's goals.

Having won the club's first European trophy for 23 years, Alex Ferguson's United seemed to be ready to make a strong challenge for the championship, which had been absent from Old Trafford for an even longer period. The manager himself stuck his neck out and told the press his Reds were ripe for the title race.

Fergie's optimism seemed well-founded when his summer signings, Peter Schmeichel and Paul Parker, galvanized the defence to such an extent that United started the season with four consecutive clean sheets. They joined Bruce, Pallister and Denis Irwin, who had been signed from Oldham in 1990, in a formidable back five. The manager also found fresh impetus for the attack, deploying Andrei Kanchelskis, on the right wing and an emerging youngster named Ryan Giggs on the left.

The new-look team enjoyed an excellent first half to the season, tempered only by their exit from the Cup-winners' Cup at the hands

of Atletico Madrid. There was some degree of compensation for the Reds in the form of the European Super Cup, which they won 1-0 at Old Trafford in November 1991. Brian McClair scored the winning goal against the European champions, Red Star Belgrade.

Prior to New Year's Day, United lost just one league match, 3-2 Sheffield Wednesday. Even then United were unlucky to lose the game, their 13th of the season, after leading 2–1 through McClair's two goals. The points were almost in the bag when substitute Nigel Jemson also scored twice, late in the day.

The team's response to that blip was to win six of their next seven matches, admirably netting 20 goals in the process. McClair scored in four consecutive games, including a double on Boxing Day in the thrilling 6–3 victory at Oldham Athletic. It was a shame he couldn't make it five in a row, because the very next game was against Leeds United, Manchester United's rivals in the title race.

The two sides met three times in three different competitions between 29 December and 15 January, all at Elland Road. The Reds won the mini-series by some measure, knocking the Yorkshire club out of the FA Cup (1–0) and out of the Rumbelows Cup (3–1). But the one match against Leeds that Manchester United didn't win later proved to be the most important result. Had Alex Ferguson's team won 1–0, instead of drawing 1–1, they would have taken a seven-point lead in the league. But a late equalizer from the penalty spot perfectly summed up Leeds's resilience and persistence, qualities

Brian McClair celebrates his Super Cup goal against Red Star Belgrade.

Steve Bruce lifts the Rumbelows Cup aloft at Wembley in April 1992.

that later paid off, at Manchester United's expense, to the tune of one league championship in April 1992.

"We would never take any credit away from Leeds because they stuck at it doggedly all year," says McClair. "But it was interesting that the change in the back-pass law killed them the following season."

It had never been Manchester United's style to take the sting out of the game by playing the ball into their own goalkeeper's hands. They were far too concerned with getting forward and attacking their foes, or as Brian McClair puts it, "We were the more exciting team, trying to batter or steamroller the opposition."

The high-tempo, all-guns-blazing approach eventually took its toll on United's title challenge, not least because they were forced to play their last six league matches in 17 days. In some ways they were victims of their own success, the problem of fixture congestion partly caused by their run in the Rumbelows Cup. This culminated in the Reds winning the competition for the very first time.

"To score in a cup final at Wembley is something that everyone dreams about," says McClair, who netted the only goal of the game against Nottingham Forest. "People might say now that the League Cup doesn't matter, but at the time the club were more than happy to have some more silverware. It was another trophy and that kept the momentum going."

Unfortunately United's momentum in the 1991–92 title race did not continue for much longer. The final furlong started well enough,

with a home win over Southampton followed by an away draw at Luton. But then one or two tired players, perhaps understandably, took their foot off the pedal and the Reds paid dearly for it.

"We lost it because we had to play so many games towards the end of the season," reflects Brian. "We lost at home to Forest at Easter when Giggsy and Sharpey decided to go to Blackpool for the night. Then we just couldn't win a game and by the end of it all, we had nothing left."

Two days after the 2–1 defeat by Forest on Easter Monday, the Reds were beaten 1–0 by West Ham in midweek and then at the end of a miserable seven days, they finally surrendered the title in the most painful manner. Their bitter 2–0 defeat by Liverpool handed the championship to Leeds, who had won their match at Sheffield United earlier that day. The teams still had one fixture left to play and United won theirs, 3–1 against Tottenham, but this was an irrelevance after the agony of losing at Anfield on Sunday, 26 April.

"We had to sit there all summer thinking about what a nightmare it had been," remembers McClair. "People said we'd bottled it, and we just had to take that. In fact, it just gave us more of an identity as a team, and made us all the more determined to ensure it would never happen again. When we returned for pre-season training, the gaffer put to us the same question he asks every year, 'Are you willing to climb back to the top of the mountain?' And we were. We were willing and ready."

1990 FA CUP FINAL

12 MAY 1990, WEMBLEY **MANCHESTER UNITED (1) 3 CRYSTAL PALACE (1) 3 (AET)**

REPLAY, 17 MAY 1990, WEMBLEY **MANCHESTER UNITED (0) 1 CRYSTAL PALACE (0) 0**

THE FIRST FA CUP FINAL OF Alex Ferguson's reign revived memories of the corresponding fixture in Ron Atkinson's career in 1983. Like the Seagulls of Brighton, the Eagles of Crystal Palace had beaten Liverpool on their way to Wembley but they were still considered the underdogs.

If beating Liverpool in the semi-final didn't alone make Crystal Palace dangerous opponents, Manchester United also had to beware the opposition manager, Steve Coppell. The former Reds winger would have played alongside Bryan Robson in the 1983 final had he not been so cruelly injured that year.

Sadly for United, the echoes of '83 didn't end there. Palace scored the first goal in the 18th minute, a mere four minutes later than Brighton had done! Fortunately, the Reds equalized far quicker this time around when Robson headed the ball past Nigel Martyn in the 35th minute. The United captain closed in on his record third FA Cup triumph in the second half when Hughes scored.

Palace refused to be played off the park, however, not even after falling behind for the first time. The tide turned again when Coppell sent on Ian Wright. The live-wire substitute scored just three minutes after making his entrance, and then again just inside extra-time.

"At that point, 3–2 down with not long left in the match, some of us were thinking it's not going to be our year, we're not going to make it," admits Lee Martin, United's left-back. "But with seven or eight minutes to go, Mark Hughes popped up to score the equalizer. It was a big relief, to be given an extra chance in the replay."

One goal-scoring chance in the replay was all Lee Martin needed to make history. The defender, who had only netted one goal for United, chested down a pass from Neil Webb and blasted the ball into the Wembley net, one hour into an otherwise dull encounter.

"Paul Ince said to me at breakfast that morning, 'Just think, you could be a hero tonight,'" remembers Lee. "But I'd never have dreamed in a million years that I'd score the winning goal in a Cup

Dropped goalkeeper Jim Leighton dejectedly makes his way to the United bench, having lost his place in the team for the FA Cup final replay against Crystal Palace. He was replaced by Les Sealey as United won 1–0.

final. Just to play there was a massive achievement, and it didn't get any better than that for me. For three or four days afterwards, the press were at our house, wanting to take pictures of me, the family, even the dog!"

While Martin made most of the headlines, he had to share some of the media glare with Jim Leighton. But the goalkeeper's story was not a happy one. After conceding three goals in the first match, Leighton was lacking in confidence and he was replaced on he team for the replay by Les Sealey.

"Jim was a smashing bloke, but being dropped by the manager just destroyed him," says Lee Martin. "In fact, it was devastating for all of us because he was a friend of ours. We didn't see him for a few days afterwards. Les offered to give him his medal, but he didn't take it."

It was sad that Fergie's first trophy had to be tinged with sadness for one of his loyal servants. But the story suggested, to United's fans at least, that the manager was ruthless enough to raise the team to even greater heights.

Manchester United (manager Alex Ferguson): Leighton, Phelan, Bruce, Pallister (sub Robins 95), Martin (sub Blackmore 87), Webb, Robson, Ince, Wallace, McClair, Hughes.
Scorers: Robson 35, Hughes 62, 113

Crystal Palace (manager Steve Coppell): Martyn, Pemberton, Shaw, Gray (sub Madden 116), O'Reilly, Thorn, Barber (sub Wright 69), Thomas, Bright, Salako, Pardew.
Scorers: O'Reilly 18, Wright 72, 92

REPLAY:
United team changes: Sealey replaced Leighton.
Scorer: Martin 59
Palace team changes: none; substitutes used were Wright (for Barber 64) and Madden (for Salako 80).
Attendances: 80,000 (for both games)

1991 EUROPEAN CUP-WINNERS' CUP FINAL

MANCHESTER UNITED (0) 2 BARCELONA (0) 1

15 MAY 1991, FEYENOORD STADIUM, ROTTERDAM

Mark Hughes breaks clear of the Barcelona defence on a night of vindication for the Welshman.

THE FIRST ENGLISH team to win the European Cup had been missing from the continental honours list for more than two decades. The ban after Heysel excused Manchester United for five years of their barren spell, but before that they had under-achieved overseas while the likes of Liverpool, Nottingham Forest, Aston Villa, Ipswich Town and Spurs had all won trophies on foreign shores.

At least Alex Ferguson had tasted some success in Europe, winning the Cup-winners' Cup with Aberdeen in 1983 against all the odds. His opponents then had been the mighty Real Madrid, so it was something of a coincidence that another Spanish side, Barcelona, blocked his path to glory with Manchester United. His opposite number in May 1991, Johan Cruyff, was a master tactician, so the build-up to the final became a battle of wits.

Fergie, for example, elected to counter the ball-playing abilities of Barcelona's best player, Ronald Koeman. Like his manager Cruyff, the Dutch defender was on home soil in Rotterdam, but he was unable to influence the game as he would have liked with Brian McClair detailed to close him down. Mark Hughes' mission was to seek and destroy his former club, motivated by a desire to prove his Spanish critics well and truly wrong.

With a settled back four of Irwin, Bruce, Pallister and Blackmore protected by the likes of Ince and Robson in midfield, United were in no mood to be broken down by Barcelona and neither side gave anything away in a cagey first half.

When the tempo picked up in the second half, United were in their element. They were better suited to setting the pace than pussy-footing around in midfield, as five minutes of action in the second period were to prove. It started in the 67th minute when Hughes was fouled outside the area by Alexanco, one of his former team-mates. Robson put the ball down and launched his free kick towards the far post, where Bruce sent it towards goal with a towering header. The attacking thrust into Barcelona's box still needed a finishing touch, and nobody was better placed than Hughes to apply it. 1–0 to United!

Sensing that their opponents were now on the ropes, United pressed forward in search of a second goal. It came as soon as the 72nd minute, and although Hughes was again the scorer, his finish differed from the first. This time he had to shoot from what looked like an impossible angle, having run the ball wide to the goalkeeper's left from Robson's precise pass. It was now 2–0 to United and for the second time in 12 months, 'Sparky' Hughes had scored two goals in a cup final.

"Sparky was always the man for the big occasion," says Lee Martin. "He did it throughout his career."

Martin missed playing in the match because of a back injury, but he wouldn't have missed being there for the world. After all, it was his Cup final goal in the previous year that had sent United forward into the competition, and as a boyhood fan, he shared in the anxiety, then the ecstasy, of the 25,000 other Reds in Rotterdam.

Koeman caused anxiety when he made the score 2–1, but Clayton Blackmore prevented calamity when he cleared Michael Laudrup's shot off the line. That narrow escape ended Barcelona's hopes of an equalizer, and completed a momentous win for the men from Manchester. United were back in Europe, and how!

Manchester United (manager Alex Ferguson): Sealey, Irwin, Bruce, Pallister, Blackmore, Phelan, Robson, Ince, Sharpe, McClair, Hughes **Scorer:** Hughes 68, 75

Barcelona (manager Johan Cruyff): Busquets, Nando, Alexanco (sub Pinilla 72), Koeman, Ferrer, Bakero, Goicoechea, Eusebio, Salinas, Laudrup, Beguiristain **Scorer:** Koeman 79

Attendance: 50,000

STEVE BRUCE

DEFENDER (MANCHESTER UNITED 1987–96)

THE THIRD MAJOR SIGNING of Alex Ferguson's reign, Steve Bruce became one of the best central defenders in the history of Manchester United. A natural leader, he was called upon to captain the side when Bryan Robson entered the twilight of his career in the early 1990s. It was a role that Bruce relished, especially when he was lifting trophies towards the sky.

Steve Bruce bore all the hallmarks of the character that Alex Ferguson wanted to instil into the Manchester United team. Enthusiasm, determination, self-belief – all of these attributes and more helped the defender to bounce back from being rejected by several football clubs at the age of 16.

Just before he was due to embark on an alternative career as a trainee plumber, Bruce was given his lucky break in football. Gillingham took him on and 200 league appearances later, they pocketed £135,000 when Norwich City signed him in August 1984. After helping the Canaries to reach the top flight, Bruce caught the eye of Alex Ferguson, who at the time had centre-halves who were either unfit or unwilling to play for Manchester United. The signing of Steve solved the problem, with United paying Norwich £800,000 for his services in December 1987.

In his first season at Old Trafford, the 27-year-old Bruce seemed to have all the knowledge of a veteran player, and he was only too pleased to impart some of this to his younger team-mates.

"He was one of those players whom you look upon as a leader," says Lee Martin, Bruce's fellow defender. "He always wanted to help me. In training, if he saw something that was wrong in my game, he would come over and have a quiet chat with me. He was also great on the pitch. If I made a mistake there, he would encourage me rather than have a go, and that was something I appreciated as a young lad."

Bruce's encouragement paid off when Martin scored the winning goal at Wembley in 1990, to give Steve his first major honour as a United player. This came at the end of the first season for arguably the best defensive pairing ever seen at Old Trafford, formed by Bruce with Gary Pallister. The perfect partners had different specialities; Bruce, for example, could sense danger at an early stage and snuff it out.

"Bruce wasn't the quickest of players, but there was nobody better than him for reading the game," agrees Lee Martin. "He fully deserved to have an England cap, and it was a shame he never received one."

Steve's snub at senior international level was never more obvious than in 1993, when he helped United to end their 26-year wait for the title while England were failing to qualify for the World Cup. April 1993, to be more precise, produced one of his greatest moments in a red shirt when he scored two tremendous headers to beat Sheffield Wednesday 2–1, after the Championship-chasing Reds had trailed 1–0.

In the following year, Steve became the first Englishman in the twentieth century to captain a club to the League and FA Cup double. His bid to repeat the feat failed in 1995 when the Reds missed out in both competitions by a whisker, and in 1996 when they won the trophies again, but this time with Steve on the substitutes' bench. Still, the lows would be as useful as the highs to Steve in his next career. Leaving United to play for Birmingham, he then became Sheffield United boss in 1998. He's also managed Wigan, Huddersfield, Crystal Palace and Birmingham.

Steve Bruce was highly valued by United but overlooked by England.

GARY PALLISTER

DEFENDER (MANCHESTER UNITED 1989-98)

THE OTHER HALF of United's dream defensive partnership cost almost three times the price of Steve Bruce. But since Gary Pallister was so highly rated by Middlesbrough, and so badly needed by Alex Ferguson, it seemed inevitable that his move in August 1989 would break the British transfer record.

The transfer fee was mentioned more than a few times in the early part of Pallister's career at United. The press knew a soft target when they saw one, and after the Reds had lost his debut match 2–0, they inevitably asked – was the defender really worth £2.3 million?

The answer nine years later was a resounding yes, especially when Middlesbrough bought Pallister back from Manchester United for almost the same sum. In the intervening years, he won every major honour in the English game, plus the European Cup-winners' Cup and European Super Cup in 1991. The only pity for Pallister was that he left the club too early for a testimonial year and just prior to United's greatest ever season, although the arrival of Jaap Stam suggests he might have played a cameo role in the Treble triumph.

Although individually a great defender, Stam has not had a partnership to rival the pairing of Pallister and Bruce. That can only be a testament to the consistency of the 1990s duo, who were affectionately dubbed Dolly and Daisy by their manager.

"I think the major success came when Gary Pallister joined Steve Bruce in defence," says Lee Martin, who played alongside the pair in their early years together. "Alex Ferguson bought the two of them as the main base of the team on which he could build. They rarely made mistakes and read the game well. The two of them just seemed to click, they were fantastic."

Despite a slightly rocky start, Pallister was always sure of his own abililty and he settled down to become a player whom United could ill-afford to be without.

"Pallister was good in the air, quick on the ground and could cover behind people if there were problems," adds Martin.

Four different managers picked Pallister for England, and while his United partner was unfortunately frozen out, Gary earned 22 caps to add to his impressive haul of club honours and the PFA Player of the Year award he collected in 1992. That was a disappointing year for the defender, as his first chance of a championship medal was snatched away by Leeds United. Amends were made the following season when the Reds finally won the title, and from that point forward, winning the League became the norm.

However, Pallister never rested on his laurels. He stuck to the task and kept his place in the team while others, such as Hughes, Ince, Kanchelskis and Sharpe, lost theirs. Even when Bruce departed for Birmingham in 1996, Pallister stayed on and formed new partnerships with David May and Ronny Johnsen. When he left in 1998, Gary was the longest-serving player in the squad, having made more than 400 appearances.

Gary Pallister was a graceful defender, capable of bringing the ball forward.

PAUL INCE

MIDFIELDER (MANCHESTER UNITED 1989-95)

AT THE PEAK of his powers in 1993 and 1994, Paul Ince was the embodiment of Manchester United's ambition and spirit. His aggressive advancing movements forced many opponents on to the back foot, as the Reds marched relentlessly to successive championships and what was at the time their greatest ever achievement, the League and FA Cup double.

In Paul Ince, Alex Ferguson polished up a rough-cut diamond. Signed from West Ham United in September 1989, the player was initially too immature to impose himself in the manner which later made him a legend. This immaturity might explain the incident that so incensed the West Ham supporters, when he was foolishly photographed in the red shirt of Manchester United before the deal had been done.

On the field, he was sometimes faulted for being a bit too keen, certainly for the referee's liking, and it took time for the United staff to extract the best from the Essex boy. That said, he collected a medal at the end of his first season, 1989–90, after a determined display in the FA Cup final replay. The following year he featured in another triumph, this time in the European Cup-Winners' Cup final against Barcelona in Rotterdam.

"Paul was a winner through and through," remembers Lee Martin, who played with Ince at the time. "He wanted to win everything that bounced in the middle and if he didn't, he would get upset. He had this real mean streak in him whereby he'd have a go at players after the ball had gone. But after a few years, he learned to calm down and he benefited from that to become a fantastic player. He liked to make driving runs forward and he scored a few goals as well.

Paul Ince was United's midfield driving force.

"He was the ball-winner in the team alongside Robson, and I would have to say that was probably one of the best midfields we'd had for a long time."

While the cup successes in England and Europe were greatly celebrated and appreciated, it was in the league that Ferguson really needed Ince to make an impact, especially against the smaller clubs that had so often thrown spanners in United's works in the past. Nobody needed motivating to face Liverpool or Arsenal, but against the lesser lights of their football world, Paul pulled the team up by the bootlaces. He did so successfully in 1992–93, when Bryan Robson was running out of steam and he found himself playing instead with Brian McClair, who was not a natural midfielder. In the subsequent summer, he became the first black player to captain England, a richly deserved accolade.

Ince was also very influential in 1993–94, when he formed a new partnership with Roy Keane in a team that picked itself week in, week out. Paul, though, did not forget the contributions of the squad at large and in a poignant moment during the 1994 FA Cup final, he selflessly set up substitute McClair for the fourth goal.

Always energetic, Ince exuded arrogance – as if his foes barely deserved to be on the same playing field. Opposition fans loved to hate him, but they were ready to welcome Paul with open arms if their own club ever had the opportunity to sign him.

United's bitter rivals Liverpool did just that in July 1997, to prompt one of the more remarkable U-turns of emotion. It didn't matter to the Old Trafford faithful that Ince had been with Inter Milan for a buffer period of two years, after leaving United in an unpopular transfer in 1995. The fans regarded his transfer to Anfield as betrayal, and revelled in telling him so on more than a few occasions, even when he later joined Middlesbrough and Wolves.

BRIAN McCLAIR

FORWARD (MANCHESTER UNITED 1987-98)

DISCIPLINED, ADAPTABLE and intelligent, Brian McClair was Alex Ferguson's flexible friend during 11 seasons of sterling service. Initially signed from Celtic as a prolific forward, the man known as 'Choccy' later became a midfield general and a guiding light for two or even three generations of Fergie's Fledglings.

As a schoolboy in Scotland, Brian McClair used to doodle the words 'Celtic' and 'United' during technical drawing lessons, so it was a day-dream come true when Alex Ferguson singled him out as the first player he wanted to buy for the club.

"They could have attracted anyone in Europe but Alex decided he wanted me. I thought at the time I couldn't beat that for an endorsement," says Brian. "I believed what Alex Ferguson told me, that I would be part of something that would mushroom and be really special."

The tribunal-fixed transfer fee of £850,000 looked an absolute bargain by the end of McClair's first season, 1987–88. The Scot was ever-present in all three competitions and was named Player of the Year by the club's members, after scoring 31 goals. This total included 24 goals in the First Division, making him the first United player since George Best in 1969 to net more than 20 in one league season.

"At the press conference when I signed, the first question that was addressed to me was about George Best's record," remembers Brian. "I said I couldn't see any point in me scoring 20 league goals if United didn't win the Championship. It's been proved many times since – to win the title, you need a good spread of goals throughout the team."

So it proved in that first season, when Liverpool won the title, and again in 1991–92, when McClair netted 19 but the Reds still finished second to Leeds. In fact, by the time United won the championship in 1992–93, Brian had become a goal-scoring midfielder, running from deep positions behind Eric Cantona and Mark Hughes. That title triumph completed a hat-trick of domestic honours for McClair, whose 100th goal for United won the League Cup in 1992, two years after their FA Cup triumph at Wembley. He also played an important part in the 1991 European Cup-Winners' Cup success, scoring in every round before the final.

Although the arrival of Roy Keane in August 1993 limited Choccy's first-team chances, he still earned three more championship medals (1994, 1996 and 1997) plus another in the FA Cup in 1994 when he scored United's final goal in the 4–0 Wembley win over Chelsea. He was a valued member of the first-team squad, even if he told a tale or two about his comrades in his 'Choccy's Diary' column for the monthly United magazine.

Rarely a man to trouble referees, Brian McClair's temperament was really only rattled by one team, Arsenal. After the Highbury penalty incident, he clashed with Nigel Winterburn in 1989–90 ("I was shaking him by the shirt like a rag doll") and again in the following season, when a mass brawl at Old Trafford resulted in him being fined and both teams losing points.

"I had a go at him for kicking Denis Irwin while he was on the ground," says Brian. "Then it all kicked off."

Encounters with Arsenal aside, McClair's professionalism and discipline made him the perfect role model for United's younger players, especially in the mid-1990s when he played alongside the emerging Paul Scholes and David Beckham in a so-called weakened team in League Cup matches. After spells at Motherwell and Blackburn, McClair rejoined United as a coach in 2001. In his first season, he guided the reserves to their league title. The next season saw his United youth team win the 2003 FA Youth Cup.

Brian McClair (right) was a reliable goalscorer for Manchester United.

BUILDING

The Old Trafford atmosphere is arguably at its best when a match in the UEFA Champions League is played under floodlights.

THE FIRST SIX YEARS of Alex Ferguson's reign did not just witness big changes at Manchester United, they were also a swan-song for some of English football's long-standing traditions. By 1992, it seemed that a simple game enjoyed by thousands on Saturday afternoons had been altered forever.

The biggest change affecting Old Trafford began at the end of the 1991–92 season. After narrowly missing out on winning the last of the old Football League championships, Manchester United removed another of the old bastions of the English game – terracing. This was in keeping with the other top-flight clubs around the country, as recommended by the Taylor Report on the Hillsborough tragedy. For United, it meant demolishing the Stretford End, an emotive decision given the history and significance of that world-famous terrace. In its place, the club built a new stand costing £10 million and containing 10,164 seats.

"When I joined United, football was a pariah. Nobody would touch it," recalls Brian McClair, who signed for the club in 1987. "English clubs were banned from Europe, fans were kept behind fences, and the Government wanted people to carry membership cards. The game seemed synonymous with crowd trouble.

"All-seater stadiums made a difference to that, simply because you're more likely to behave if you sit down and you can't gather in groups. Some people lament that obviously, but after the tragedies at Heysel and Hillsborough, safety had to be the main thing.

"One of the major reasons why United attract such huge crowds now is that all kinds of people can come to Old Trafford and feel safe," adds Brian, reflecting on how the stadium has changed.

The major changes to the Stretford End were completed during the 1992–93 season when United became the inaugural champions of the FA Premier League. Television was to be a major player in this new competition. Led by the satellite broadcasting company BSkyB, television raised the profile of the game and began to exert an influence over how it looked and when it would be played. Names on shirts, fireworks, dancing girls, Monday night matches and an influx of foreign players were just a few features of the new face of English football.

"It was like a new beginning for the game," says McClair. "Football was starting to rise out of the mire it had gone through

BLOCKS

in the 1980s when social problems had blighted it. All of a sudden, the game was sexy and was being promoted everywhere. Now there are daily newspaper supplements, magazines, radio stations and Internet sites devoted to sport, primarily football. Clubs even have their own television channels, such as MUTV."

The rejuvenation of Manchester United under Alex Ferguson coincided perfectly with this explosion of media interest in football. At the end of the first Premier League season, Sky's cameras captured the joyous scenes at Old Trafford when Brian McClair and company paraded the Premiership trophy in front of their ecstatic supporters. Two years later, a simultaneous broadcast of two matches on two Sky channels showed the same players losing their title in the race with Blackburn Rovers. It was high drama and the neutrals around the nation lapped it up.

Yet for all the camera angles, action replays and other benefits offered by television, most football supporters still wanted to experience the real thing. After all, anyone can have a satellite dish rigged up to his or her home in order to see the match, but there remains a certain exclusivity and special excitement in actually purchasing a ticket and walking through the turnstile.

Manchester United have tried to make this real-life experience as accessible as possible by putting Old Trafford through several phases of expansion since it became an all-seater stadium in 1993. First, there was the North Stand. This was constructed from scratch in time to host matches during Euro '96, following the demolition of the old United Road stand in the summer of 1995. The entire project cost in the region of £27 million and raised the capacity to in excess of 55,000, thanks to the three-tiered construction containing 25,300 seats and featuring the largest cantilever roof in the world. The interior of the North Stand was also put to good use, incorporating an impressive £4 million museum and The Red Café, United's own themed restaurant. As a result, Old Trafford is now one of the most visited locations in the north of England; the days of the stadium lying idle for 13 days in a fortnight have long since gone.

After winning the Treble in May 1999, Manchester United decided to increase the stadium's capacity again, this time by adding an extra tier of 6,200 seats to both the East and the West Stands. The new East Stand complex houses the club's main administration block, and for the general public, one of the biggest football club souvenir shops in the world. The project was completed for the start of the 2000–01 season, during which an aggregate audience of 1,810,900 watched United play at Old Trafford in all competitions.

In March 2004, United announced they were considering plans to build in the North-East and North-West corners of the stadium. This would see the addition of 7,500 seats, bringing the overall capacity of Old Trafford to 75,000.

Filling the seats is rarely a problem. In 2000–01, new surveys commissioned by the club calculated there could be as many as 50 million United fans around the world. This staggering figure didn't include the USA, where soccer was still ranked as a minority sport. United have tried to raise their profile by playing friendly matches in the USA on their pre-season tours of 2003 and 2004.

Money-spinning tours and other such ventures initiated by United's commercial team are deemed necessary in order for the football team to continue competing at the highest level. Apart from the stadium, the most expensive asset that the club has to acquire and maintain is the playing staff.

Since 2001, United have broken the British transfer record three times by signing Ruud van Nistelrooy (£19 million), Juan Sebastian Veron (£28 million) and then Rio Ferdinand (£30 million). The deals came ten years or so after the club first became a PLC.

"You can only say that has been a success, when you consider all the things that United have achieved in the years since then." says Brian McClair. "Nobody will know whether the club would have been successful anyway because of the amount of money that has come into the game from television, sponsorship, merchandising and elsewhere."

The Theatre of Dreams awaits another full house for a United home game.

Successful management of the money coming into the game has made United the biggest club on the planet, and its stadium one of the finest in world football – as demonstrated by its hosting of England matches and the UEFA Champions League Final in 2003.

The club may never satisfy the feverish levels of demand for match tickets; consequently, it strives to bring its global fanbase closer in other ways, for example through the official website ManUtd.com and the One United membership scheme. Fans, ultimately, want to feel a connection with their beloved club.

CHAPTER THIRTEEN
THE CANTONA YEARS

AFTER A 26-YEAR ABSENCE, THE LEAGUE CHAMPIONSHIP
FINALLY RETURNED TO OLD TRAFFORD. MANCHESTER UNITED
BECAME THE MOST SUCCESSFUL CLUB IN MODERN BRITISH
FOOTBALL AND THE CATALYST WAS ERIC CANTONA.

Eric Cantona was a surprise signing by Alex Ferguson from Leeds in 1992, but it triggered the most successful era in the club's history.

uccess is a relative term, especially in football and particularly at Manchester United. Despite Cup triumphs at home and in Europe, Alex Ferguson knew that his tenure as United manager would never be considered truly successful unless he achieved the ultimate domestic prize – the league championship. But after 26 years, six managers and several near-misses, it had been so many years coming that some fans despaired of ever seeing United reach the pinnacle again. Under Ron Atkinson, the club had begun a campaign with ten straight victories only to fade away. Even the previous year under Ferguson, the club had had to settle for the role of runners-up after being pipped to the post by Leeds.

"Since Sir Matt Busby last won the championship, it had become an obsession in Manchester," admitted Tommy Docherty, who along with Atkinson, Dave Sexton, Frank O'Farrell and Wilf McGuinness had tried and failed to acquire the elusive trophy. "And the longer the wait, the harder it became for anyone at the club to win it. After coming so close before Leeds United pipped them to it, it became even more difficult."

As the 1992–93 season got under way, there were few signs that this would be the campaign to end the wait for glory. Before it had even begun, there was disappointment for supporters. The country's most successful striker, Southampton's Alan Shearer, had snubbed United by deciding to go to Blackburn Rovers, while popular forward Mark Robins was sold to Norwich City. The arrival at Old Trafford of Dion Dublin proved scant consolation when the former Cambridge striker broke his leg just three games into his United career.

Defeats by Sheffield United, Everton, Wimbledon and Aston Villa in the first third of the season compounded the mood of pessimism as the team slipped to tenth in the table. The lack of goal power didn't bode well. Something spectacular was needed to turn the tide. Fortunately, that something arrived with an unexpected signing.

On Thursday, 26 November, the United chairman Martin Edwards received a call from Bill Fotherby, Leeds United's financial director. Fotherby wanted to know if Denis Irwin was for sale. Edwards forwarded the enquiry to Alex Ferguson, who replied in the negative. On a whim however – probably sparked by United's lack of consistency in front of goal – Ferguson asked if Leeds would consider selling Eric Cantona, their charismatic, if somewhat temperamental, striker. It was a cheeky request. Cantona was a cult figure with the Elland Road faithful, and Ferguson was asking in hope rather than expectation. Unexpectedly, Leeds agreed to discuss the matter and the following day Cantona and Ferguson met at a Holiday Inn in Manchester. One hour-and-a-half later, Cantona was a Manchester United player.

Ironically, the best £1.2 million ever spent in the history of the transfer market was initially considered something of a risk. Cantona came to Old Trafford on the back of a career in France that encompassed half a dozen acrimonious partings. His liaison with Leeds had made him a crowd favourite but a manager's headache and he carried a chip on his shoulder that screamed, "It's me against the world." As Alex Ferguson put it, "It was as though he was born to be a United player."

Former Liverpool captain Emlyn Hughes described the transfer as "a panic buy" and most observers felt that the disciplinarian in Ferguson would struggle with the flamboyant nature of his new signing. Of course, the United manager saw it somewhat differently. "If he's got a temperament, wait until he sees my temperament," he joked.

What few foresaw was just what an impact Cantona would have on the United team. He provided the spark that ignited the longest sustained period of success in United's history.

On 6 December 1992, the new signing made his debut, coming off the bench against Manchester City as a substitute for Ryan Giggs. One defence-splitting crossfield pass later, it was clear that cries of panic buy were somewhat off the mark. Five goals in the next six games reinforced the point and helped United to climb up the table. The victories against Coventry, Tottenham, Queen's Park Rangers, Nottingham Forest and league leaders Norwich not only indicated a new consistency but also a confidence and flair that had not always been evident before the Frenchman's arrival. United were beginning to look like championship contenders.

Off the pitch, Cantona was also making an impression. "He's the best prepared footballer I've ever had," glowed Ferguson. "He's first at the training ground, he does his own warm-up and then he does ours. He trains brilliantly and then he practises after training, and he's the last to leave the car park, signing autographs. He's happy to do hospital visits whenever you ask him to do anything. He's a model pro, an absolute dream footballer."

The work Cantona put in on the training pitch influenced his team-mates, who could soon also be found putting in a few extra hours at the Cliff training ground.

"Eric really changed the way we viewed the game," admitted Mark Hughes. "You see Eric do things and think to yourself, 'Oh, I'll try that.' You can't expect to be as good at it as Eric is, but I think he has just freed us all a little bit."

By the end of January, the newly "freed up" United were in a three-horse title race with Aston Villa, managed by former United boss Ron Atkinson, and Norwich City.

February began in the right way with a 2–1 victory against Sheffield United. Eric was on the scoresheet along with Brian McClair, and United's resilient display provoked Blades boss Dave Bassett to admit, "It wouldn't surprise me if they won the title."

A tough point was secured at Elland Road in a goalless draw with

New signing Eric Cantona applauds the fans after making his debut as a substitute in the 2–1 derby win over Manchester City.

Lee Sharpe played a big part in United's successes in the early 1990s.

Leeds before United returned to winning ways with a 2–1 victory over Southampton. This time, it was Ryan Giggs who was the star, scoring both goals in a virtuoso performance. The 19-year-old winger had already drawn plenty of rave reviews since breaking into the United team at 17, and had inevitably been dubbed "the new George Best". Southampton's keeper Tim Flowers probably summed up the Welshman's talents best, after being on the receiving end of his skills.

"Speaking as a football fan, I thought he was brilliant," said Flowers. "But as a member of the goalkeepers' union, I think he's an absolute nightmare."

Middlesbrough keeper Stephen Pears probably echoed the sentiment the following week as a lightning strike from Giggs left him with no chance and launched United towards a 3–0 victory.

Even better was to come, as United began March with a trip to Anfield and a sweet away victory. Both of United's wingers, Lee Sharpe and Giggs, were on form as the visitors enjoyed a 2–1 win.

Sharpe was another to have endured "the new Best" tag in his early days at United but, after long bouts of illness and injury, the 21 year-old was carving a niche all for himself in the United first team during the 1992–93 season with a series of excellent displays.

If victory at Anfield was a result to savour, United fans were soon brought back to earth with a surprise midweek defeat against relegation-threatened Oldham. The result cost Villa boss Atkinson a few pounds. Before the game he had phoned Oldham manager Joe Royle and claimed Oldham "didn't have the bottle" to beat local rivals United. Royle responded that Atkinson should send him a bottle of champagne if his team proved otherwise. In typically flamboyant mode, the Villa manager promised to send an entire case.

It set the scene nicely for the following weekend, when United played host to Villa at Old Trafford in a top-of-the-table clash. However, despite long periods of domination and a Mark Hughes goal, United had to settle for a point as Villa hung on for a 1–1 draw. It left both teams on 61 points, with only goal difference keeping Ferguson's side top.

Two more draws in quick succession, against Manchester City and Arsenal, meant United slipped to third before a trip to Carrow Road to face league leaders Norwich. Despite the absence of Mark Hughes through suspension, Ferguson decided to make the trip with an attacking line-up that included Giggs, Sharpe, McClair, Kanchelskis and Cantona. It proved to be the right decision as goals in the first 20 minutes from Giggs, Kanchelskis and Cantona secured victory in an enthralling match and put United back on top of the table.

"They had to come here and win it," admitted Norwich manager Mike Walker. "To give them credit, that's exactly what they did. But we are not out of it yet."

United's destiny was now in their own hands. As Steve Bruce put it, "We've seven matches left and if we win them all, no one can stop us." Bruce played a pivotal role in United's next game, at home to Sheffield Wednesday.

With the team closing in on a first title for 26 years, tensions were running high. The Old Trafford crowd were probably more nervous than the players and Ferguson addressed the issue in his programme notes: "I have a two-word message for the players and supporters …enjoy it. We are in a marvellous position and it would be a pity if we all got so full of anxiety and worry that we failed to appreciate what we are watching. I believe it is something very special."

Fine words, but they went out of the window in the 64th minute when Wednesday were awarded a penalty following Paul Ince's challenge on Chris Waddle. The spot-kick was converted by John Sheridan and Wednesday maintained their lead until four minutes from time. By that stage, fingernails had been chewed to the bone as United toiled to get something from the game.

Finally, the break came. Bruce connected with Denis Irwin's corner to bring United level, but there was more drama to come. An injury to the referee had caused a delay during the game and there was some seven minutes of added time to be played. United spent all of it seeking a winner to ensure no points were dropped in this crucial stage of the season. Six minutes and 12 seconds into injury time Old Trafford erupted as Bruce came good again, heading into the top corner from Gary Pallister's chip. Ferguson, supposedly suffering from flu was on the pitch, punching the air. Brian Kidd fell to his knees in pure relief. The mood was euphoric.

Man of the match Bruce compared the game to the Easter Monday fixture the previous season when United lost 2–1 to Nottingham Forest.

"This match was identical in every way," he said. "The sun was boiling down, they got a goal, we weren't playing well and you got a funny feeling. It was like a nightmare coming back, but we dug in, gritted our teeth, got the break and scored twice to come back. I find it hard right now to describe what it all means for me. If we go on to win the championship, it's going to be the highlight of my football life."

Victories over Coventry, Chelsea and Crystal Palace kept United in the driving seat. Ron Atkinson's team had to beat Oldham to prevent United from being crowned champions the following day against Blackburn at Old Trafford. The game was being televised live on Sky Television and the United squad could only sit and wait, hoping for the right result.

"I knew it would be a difficult game for Villa," said Ferguson later. "Every point was life or death for Oldham as far as staying in the Premiership was concerned. I made up my mind that I would not put myself through the mill by watching the match. Instead, I went off to the golf course at Mottram Hall, near my home in Cheshire, with my eldest son, Mark, although it was difficult to concentrate on the course."

Peter Schmeichel managed to avoid the tension for most of the 90 minutes.

"I literally won our first championship medal while I was asleep. We trained on the Sunday and while Villa played Oldham, I was having a nap. When I woke up an hour later, I tuned into Teletext to see the result of the Aston Villa game. There were still five minutes to go but Oldham were winning 1–0. Those were five long minutes for me! I switched off the TV, turned on the radio, turned the radio off again, played for a while on the piano, turned on the TV again, went back to the radio and finally lay down on the floor behind the sofa with my head buried in my arms. And then the final whistle blew. Oldham had won, and we had become champions of England! After 26 years, Manchester United were league champions again, and I was a member of the team that had done it!"

The news soon filtered on to the golf course, where a fan informed Ferguson of the result.

"I heard a car screeching to a halt and footsteps coming up the gravel path by the green," said Ferguson. "A chap appeared with a huge smile on his face. 'Mr Ferguson?' he called, and when I turned to him he shouted, 'Manchester United have won the league.' Mark and I hugged each other, joined by the bearer of this great news. God, what a feeling!"

Steve Bruce and Bryan Robson savour United's first league title for 26 years.

Meanwhile, the first and possibly only example of a pre-match party under Ferguson's reign was in full swing at Steve Bruce's house. Lee Sharpe initially made his way to Old Trafford where he was swamped by celebrating fans, but he eventually arrived at Bruce's house to join the rest of his team-mates.

"It was a tremendous night," said Sharpe. "There was a mixture of pride and relief and just a real sense of achievement."

Serious partying was still going on the next day when the players arrived for the Blackburn match.

"There was a fantastic atmosphere when we got to the ground," said Peter Schmeichel. "Some of us were still bleary-eyed. But among all the jubilation, the manager brought us back down to earth, saying, 'We are the champions now, go out and prove it!'"

After a shaky start, they did, running out 3–1 winners in what was something of a carnival atmosphere at the ground, with fans allowed to bring in flags and making full use of the opportunity. It was one of the greatest days in United's history.

"It was a long time coming," confirmed Bryan Robson. "But from then on, no one could throw the 26-year gap in the faces of the players. It provided the platform for the club to go forward and dominate English football."

In the following season, the team were, if anything, even hungrier

Eric Cantona converts one of two penalties in the 1994 FA Cup final against Chelsea. United's 4–0 win clinched their first Double.

for success. The entire squad re-doubled its efforts. There was also the addition of Roy Keane to the team, a £4 million transfer from Nottingham Forest who quickly became a firm favourite with the fans.

Four wins and a draw in their first five games showed United were stronger than ever and for a large part of the season, they looked like running away with the league title. Meanwhile Cantona's influence continued to grow. There were 24 goals from the Frenchman during the campaign and some of them were truly sublime, such as the effort against Wimbledon in the FA Cup, when he controlled a clearance on the edge of the area with one touch, practically rolling the ball down his leg before imperiously volleying it into the back of the net.

Fans took to heart his comparisons of football and poetry, and his status took on mythic proportions. "What can I say? I love this club," admitted Cantona. "I feel really at home here. I feel good in England, with the people in general, the way they welcome you in the streets. I cannot stress enough how important United fans are to me. They are one of the reasons why I continue doing what I'm doing. The fans here are really special. They make me happy, and when I'm happy, I perform."

The only cloud on the horizon was the media's continued focus on the Frenchman's temper, not helped by Cantona's sendings off at Arsenal and Swindon, which led to a five-match ban. Ferguson was quick to defend his French talisman.

"Some of the players have come under attack," said the United manager, "especially Eric Cantona. He knows that he was basically at fault for what happened at Swindon, but it's just a spark that he's got which can lead to situations like that.

"He's not a tackler, you see. He doesn't know how to tackle and that's his problem. He is a great footballer, but not a tackler.

"But I think at Arsenal and Swindon, he was also a victim of intimidation which didn't help matters. It was inevitable that Eric was going to get slated by the press, but I didn't expect to read some of the things that were written about him. A certain person in the *Daily Express*, the same person who insinuated that my signing of Cantona may have lost me my job, revelled in it all and wrote a load of rubbish about Eric. In this game, you'll always get the backbiters, but some seem to harbour more bitterness than others."

"He's a nutter," bellowed *The Sun*, proving Ferguson's point as the papers had a jingoistic field day over the five-match ban, insisting that United's subsequent loss of form would ensure that the French striker left for pastures new.

It was true that, with Cantona out of the side, results slipped and Blackburn began to put real pressure on United's title challenge. But the Frenchman's return in April steadied the ship. He scored twice in the derby win over City and United went on not only to secure a second Premiership title under Ferguson but also to win the FA Cup against Chelsea. Eric scored with two penalties, typically sending the keeper the wrong way for both.

"Fifteen seconds punctured by a flash of lightning," was the Frenchman's description of the penalty process. "The crowd explodes or crumbles. The penalty is either happiness or sadness, nothing else." It was a fittingly poetic comment to end a stunning season.

Sadly, one United legend did not witness the triumphant climax to the double season. On 20 January 1994, Sir Matt Busby died, aged 84. Fans flocked to Old Trafford to pay tribute to the man who had done so much for the club and the ground was awash with floral tributes and scarves and flags.

Alex Ferguson summed up the thoughts of many when he said, "I found him a wonderful and incredible man, a character of substance and charisma. There have been some outstanding managers in this country, but without doubt he is the greatest there has ever been."

With the memory of the historicd double still fresh in the minds of fans, the 1994–95 campaign began with a keen sense of anticipation. It proved to be a dramatic season, but not in a way anyone foresaw.

On the night of 25 January 1995, Manchester United went to London to play Crystal Palace. It should have been a routine fixture. Palace were fighting what turned out to be a lost cause, avoiding relegation; United were trying to make up ground on Blackburn in the title race. "The build-up to the match could not have been more normal," said Alex Ferguson.

For the first 45 minutes, the game was indeed a typically wintry, blood and guts, midweek Premiership encounter – no goals, few chances but more than a couple of crunching challenges. In particular, Palace's central defenders Richard Shaw and Chris Coleman were struggling to control a rampant Cole and Cantona and their efforts to deal with the striking duo were causing Ferguson some consternation.

"Some of the tackles were disgraceful," he said. "The referee Alan Wilkie's inability to stamp them out made subsequent trouble unavoidable. I spoke to him about it before the second half, but he looked at me as if I had horns on my head."

During the interval, Ferguson warned Eric Cantona not to be tempted into any retaliation, but the advice fell on deaf ears. Not for the first time, an aggrieved Eric decided to take the law into his own hands. And, as was the Frenchman's way, his retaliation was neither subtle nor unnoticed. Four minutes into the second half, he blatantly kicked Shaw, and referee Wilkie decided this was as good a time as any to become an authoritarian. Eric was given his marching orders for the fifth time in a United shirt and the headline writers had their back-page lead. Two minutes later, the story had moved to the front page.

Cantona was being escorted off the pitch by United kitman Norman Davies. "It was part of my job to escort a player off when they got their marching orders," explained Davies. "At first, we were walking along the pitch, but a steward insisted we move over to the touchline. At Selhurst Park, that puts you close to the fans. The abuse Eric was getting was pretty nasty. Then one guy started shouting racist stuff and something about Eric's mother."

Matthew Simmons cascaded down 11 rows of seats to get to the front. "It's an early shower for you, Cantona," was his recollection

of what he said. Even allowing for a blip in translation, the outburst still seems somewhat removed from what Eric claimed to have heard, which was a racist tirade aimed at him and his mother.

In any event, it was too much for the Frenchman. Fouled for 45 minutes, sent off by a referee who hadn't even warned the opposition to cut out the rough stuff and now barracked by a yob with a foul mouth, Eric snapped. He lunged two-footed into the crowd and proceeded to swap punches with a shaken Simmons who had never imagined there might be some payback for his outburst. The police moved in, Paul Ince allegedly offered to take on the entire crowd and Peter Schmeichel dragged Eric away.

"It was incredible," said the Danish keeper. "I'm not saying I would have jumped into the crowd the way Eric did, but I fully understand it. Some of the abuse he had to take was unbelievable."

The second half re-commenced, a 1–1 draw the final result, but behind the scenes, events were still unfolding.

"When Eric got to the dressing-room, he said nothing but you could sense he knew how serious it was," said Ferguson. "All the other players came in after the game and went into the showers and still he sat there in the corner of the room. We were called into the referee's room to talk to the police. The inspector said, 'There are a lot of allegations flying around and we must investigate them thoroughly. But we are not going to get hysterical about this.'"

The media had no such concerns. *The Sun's* 13-page report on "The Shame of Cantona" was just the start. Revelation followed revelation over the next few weeks. Eric was a "kung-fu master with death in his boots", some Palace fans were "still having nightmares about the ordeal" and football, of course, "would never be the same again." Celebrity fans, politicians and other assorted 'experts' were called in to add their two pennies worth and for a while it looked

Eric Cantona (centre) goes to court after his Selhurst Park fight.

Goalkeeper Peter Schmeichel heads home during the UEFA Cup first round second leg match against Rotor Volgograd.

as though Eric would go either into exile or to jail – or maybe join Inter Milan.

When the dust settled, Eric was left with an eight-month ban from football and a jail sentence, subsequently commuted to 120 hours' community service. Without him, United ended the season without a trophy, losing the FA Cup by a single goal and the league by a point. Some said it marked the beginning of the end for Ferguson's team.

During the summer, there was further drama after the FA tried to stop Cantona from joining in training matches. The Frenchman decided enough was enough and went back to France. Fortunately, Alex Ferguson flew to Paris to persuade his player to stay on at United. After a few hours of talks, Eric agreed to do so.

"It was a tremendous boost when Eric decided to stay," admitted Ferguson. "The easiest thing for him to do was leave. But he wanted to stay, and by staying, he's telling everybody he's a courageous person. He's made a bold step and we're going to support that. We hope there is no aggravation towards him. We expect some, but we hope that it dies down eventually, and he can go on to prove he is the best player in England."

The suspension still had a few months to run and Ferguson began the season with a number of his younger squad members

pushed to the forefront. The departures of Hughes, Ince and Kanchelskis created opportunities for the likes of David Beckham, Nicky Butt and Paul Scholes. Defeat in the opening game of the season at Aston Villa did little to show the promise of "Fergie's Fledglings". Television commentator Alan Hansen went so far as to claim, "You'll never win anything with kids."

However, consecutive league wins against West Ham, Wimbledon, Blackburn, Everton and Bolton quickly proved that the manager's faith in his youth system was justified as United moved to their now familiar place at the top of the table.

Sadly, European glory still seemed out of reach with an early exit from the UEFA Cup at the hands of Rotor Volgograd. There was also a shock defeat by York City in the Coca-Cola Cup. But before too much gloom could set in, there was the return of Cantona to look forward to.

On 1 October 1995, after an absence of 248 days, United's French star was back at Old Trafford. He received an enthusiastic reception on his return and the celebrations were to continue for the rest of the season, as a new, improved Eric Cantona cemented his reputation as one of the truly great players. In his first game back, against Liverpool, and wearing his trademark number seven shirt, he created one goal and scored another to salvage a draw.

"You couldn't have asked much more of a man who was under the most intense pressure, but he appeared about as relaxed as someone wandering down to the local shops for a pint of milk," observed an impressed Hansen.

As the title race picked up speed, it was the Frenchman who ensured United finished ahead of the pack. Surrounded by a number of young players with more talent than experience, Eric, now wearing the captain's armband, was to prove a rock of consistency. Thirteen games that season were decided by a Cantona winner or equalizer as he practically dragged the team to a third Premiership title and a Wembley date with Liverpool in the FA Cup final.

He was voted Footballer of the Year by the very journalists who had demanded his departure only a year earlier.

"I am very proud and privileged," said Cantona. "It is a tremendous honour for me and my country. It is also a great tribute to the players at Manchester United."

But the greatest moment of Eric's rehabilitation came at Wembley Stadium in the dying minutes of the Cup final. As though in slow motion, he contorted his body to hit the winning goal

Opposite: The return of the magnificent seven: Eric Cantona celebrates after scoring a penalty against Liverpool. The Premiership match at Old Trafford marked his return to football after an eight-month ban.

David Beckham's 57-yard strike against Wimbledon on the opening day of the 1996–97 season gave an early indication of his exceptional shooting ability.

through a sea of Liverpool players and secure United a historic double Double.

"I couldn't see a goal coming to be honest," admitted Ferguson. "I thought it was an extra-time job. It's the manner in which he scored that people have really been talking about. It took good balance, composure and accuracy. When you see it again, it's such a great goal, incredible. He dropped his shoulder, kept his composure and his eye on the ball … marvellous." Cantona's rehabilitation was complete.

There was to be one final season in a red shirt for Cantona. It began in spectacular fashion for United, courtesy of David Beckham. The youngster who eventually inherited Eric's number seven shirt, decided to win the goal of the season competition early – on the very first day. United had travelled to London to begin their

campaign with a game against Wimbledon. It ended with a comfortable 3–0 win, but the talking point was Beckham's goal, a stunning shot from the halfway line. Overnight, Beckham was a household name.

There were several new faces at Old Trafford. Ferguson had been busy in the transfer market and there were five arrivals – Karel Poborsky, familiar from Euro '96, Jordi Cruyff, Ole Gunnar Solskjaer, Ronny Johnsen and Raimond Van Der Gouw.

The team started the season steadily with a few draws before coming to life in September with a 4–0 thrashing of Leeds United at Elland Road. The result cost Leeds manager Howard Wilkinson his job. Ironically, his former player Cantona was among the scorers who hammered the final nails in his coffin.

In the European Cup, United were defeated twice by Juventus, but did enough against Rapid Vienna and Fenerbahce to ensure qualification for the quarter-finals where they were due to meet Porto.

The home tie decided it; in a 4–0 demolition of the visitors, United truly fulfilled their potential. It was a breathtaking display of counter-attacking football. David May, Ryan Giggs, Andrew Cole and Cantona were the scorers on one of those glorious European nights at Old Trafford.

The Bristish press was also suitably impressed. "Breathtaking" said *The Mirror* while "Inspired" was the word used by *The Guardian* newspaper.

Meanwhile, in the Premiership, despite serious squad rotation to keep players fresh for Europe, United were again dominating. Wins over Coventry, Sheffield Wednesday and Everton ensured that they finished March six points clear at the top of the table.

In April, they consolidated their league position, but there was disappointment in Europe. Borussia Dortmund were United's semi-final opponents and, despite outplaying the Bundesliga champions home and away, poor finishing robbed United of a chance to appear in the European Cup final. It was a bitter pill to swallow, and even the following month's triumph in the league provided little consolation. United were champions again, but still craved the ultimate prize – the European Cup.

It was the end of the road for Cantona, who shocked football by deciding he'd had enough. At 30 years-old, he quit the game for good at the end of the season, deciding his magnificent powers had peaked. "I don't want to be a player who leaves a big club to play in the lower divisions," he once said. "Manchester United will be my last club." Nonetheless, his departure came as a shock, even to his team-mates.

"Jordi Cruyff and I went to London for the weekend with our girlfriends," said Ole Gunnar Solskjaer. "And as we boarded the train back from Euston a British Rail officer told us the news. I didn't believe it at first, neither did Jordi.

"In 30 or 40 years' time, I'll probably boast about having played with Eric. He was a tremendous player. Even before I came to the club, I looked up to him and admired his skills. And I admire him even more now, after I've trained with him and got to know him as a person. He was a huge influence at the club and gave everybody a lift with his presence. That is probably what I'll miss most of all."

Cantona had provided the catalyst to end United's 26-year championship drought and had helped build the foundations of a team that would go on to challenge – and beat – Europe's finest. As a former 'King' of Old Trafford, Denis Law, observed, "Eric was the missing piece of the jigsaw that Alex was searching for. When he arrived everything seemed to fall into place and he was the one who started the success that continues today. He was vital to the current Manchester United team."

Eric was gone, but his legacy lived on, as United would demonstrate two seasons later in the most dramatic fashion imaginable.

Eric Cantona's appearance at Highfield Road in a benefit match for Coventry defender David Busst was his last as a Manchester United player. After four-and-a-half great seasons at United, the Frenchman announced his retirement.

THE DOUBLE
1993-94

Mark Hughes keeps United's Double dream alive with an extraordinary equalizer against Oldham in the 1994 FA Cup semi-final.

WINNING THE LEAGUE CHAMPIONSHIP in 1993 lifted the pressure on Alex Ferguson's team and they started the 1993–94 campaign imbued with enormous confidence. Ferguson's first-choice XI in – Schmeichel, Parker, Bruce, Pallister, Irwin, Kanchelskis, Ince, Keane, Giggs, Cantona and Hughes – is still widely regarded as the most powerful, intimidating and consistent United team of all time. Indeed, from August 1993 to the following May, United were almost permanently lodged at the top of the league table.

Early season highlights included the first home game of the season against Sheffield United when summer signing Roy Keane scored two goals on his Old Trafford debut. Then there was David Seaman's birthday visit to Old Trafford on 19 September. He didn't enjoy helplessly watching a 25-yard rocket shot by Eric Cantona fly past his outstretched hand as Arsenal lost 1–0. United fans were also treated to a miraculous 3–2 comeback win against bitter rivals Manchester City at Maine Road; 2–0 down at half-time, two goals from Cantona (who else?) and an 87th minute winner by Roy Keane completed a sensational reversal of fortunes.

The only blot on the landscape was elimination from the European Cup in the second round by Galatasaray. United had carelessly given away a 2–0 lead in the home leg, finishing with a 3–3 draw. A stormy but goalless second-leg match in Turkey sent the Reds spiralling out of the competition on the away goals rule.

United's stars took out their disappointment on domestic opposition. The league form remained solid and they powered their way to the Coca-Cola Cup final with wins over Stoke City, Leicester City, Everton, Portsmouth and Sheffield Wednesday. But just before

the final against Aston Villa, things started to go wrong. Fiery Frenchman Eric Cantona was sent off in consecutive league games against Swindon Town and Arsenal, matches that both ended in unconvincing 2–2 draws. Cantona wasn't suspended for the final, but he was virtually anonymous as Villa pulled off a shock 3–1 win.

A week later, Blackburn Rovers striker Alan Shearer scored both goals as United went down 2–0 at Ewood Park and their lead over Rovers at the top of the Premiership was reduced to three points. Then a woeful performance against Oldham Athletic in the FA Cup semi-final nearly destroyed the Double dream. Sheffield United, Norwich and Wimbledon had all been dispatched away from home before an Old Trafford victory against Charlton took United into the semi-finals, but Oldham took a 1–0 lead in extra-time. With just 46 seconds of the 120 minutes remaining, Mark Hughes volleyed a brilliant equalizer.

That "stroke of genius", as Oldham manager Joe Royle called it, proved to be the turning point. "Forcing a replay gave us a second chance of reaching the final," said Hughes. "We were not going to let that opportunity slip." United destroyed Oldham 4–1, Cantona returned from suspension and United's league form picked up again. A 2–1 win over Ipswich on 1 May and Coventry's 2–1 win over Blackburn a day later confirmed United as champions again.

But to win the Double, they would have to beat Chelsea in the FA Cup final, the only team to beat the Reds home and away in the league that year. On a rainy day at Wembley, United won 4–0. A stunning second-half display that included two penalties by Cantona, a Mark Hughes goal and a 90th minute tap-in by Brian McClair topped off an historic season.

THE DOUBLE DOUBLE
1995–96

THE SEASON WHEN Manchester United won a second league and FA Cup Double in three years couldn't have started less promisingly. Without Paul Ince, Andrei Kanchelskis and Mark Hughes, all sold during the summer, and Eric Cantona still serving a suspension for his kung-fu folly, Alex Ferguson was pinning his faith on homegrown talent nurtured within United's youth system. But even Reds fans doubted the wisdom of that policy after a comprehensive 3–1 defeat by Aston Villa on the opening day of the season. A certain Dwight Yorke got on the scoresheet for Villa as they romped into a 3–0 lead after just 37 minutes against a United team containing virtual unknowns such as Phil Neville and Paul Scholes. The only consolation was a spirited second-half comeback and a goal by substitute David Beckham, his dipping 25-yard strike giving a glimpse of better times to come.

United's young team bounced back from the defeat with three straight wins including a confidence-boosting 2–1 victory over league champions Blackburn Rovers at Ewood Park. David Beckham scored the 72nd minute winner and people started to realize that the kids were all right after all. Indeed, after youngsters such as Beckham, Terry Cooke and Paul Scholes inspired United to a 3–0 win over Bolton Wanderers in September, Sir Bobby Charlton was moved to say, "I can't remember seeing anything as good as that."

But defeats by York City in the Coca-Cola Cup and Rotor Volgograd in the UEFA Cup (despite Peter Schmeichel scoring a goal!) soon followed, raising questions about whether United had the necessary consistency to win trophies. Then on 1 October, Eric Cantona returned.

It took the Gallic genius 67 seconds to make an impression in his comeback match against Liverpool, setting up Nicky Butt's opening goal; and Cantona's 70th minute penalty clinched a 2–2 draw. Inspired by the Frenchman's mere presence, United won five of their next six games before enduring a distinctly dodgy spell over Christmas. Cantona's lack of match practice appeared to catch up with him as United succumbed to miserable away defeats by Liverpool (2–0), Leeds United (3–1) and Tottenham Hotspur (4–1).

But while form is temporary, class is permanent and it was Cantona who kept United's FA Cup dream alive scoring the late equalizer in a 2–2 third-round tie against Sunderland in January. Much-maligned striker Andrew Cole scored an 89th minute winner in the replay at Roker Park and United were rolling again.

From then on, United's unique blend of youth and experience plus the X-factor of Cantona proved irresistible. In their last 23 Premiership and FA Cup games, United lost just once, scoring 46 goals and conceding 13. The Reds finished off their league campaign in style, demolishing Nottingham Forest 5–0 in the penultimate game at Old Trafford and clinching the title with a 3–0 win at Middlesbrough. A week later, United fans were celebrating again at Wembley as Cantona's sublime 85th minute volley beat Liverpool in the FA Cup final. "You'll never win the Double with kids," sang joyous Reds with heavy irony to herald the team's astonishing achievement – Manchester United had become the first English team ever to do the Double twice.

Eric Cantona celebrates another Double success with his team-mates.

LEE SHARPE

MIDFIELDER (MANCHESTER UNITED 1988-96)

"AT THE TENDER AGE of 17, Lee Sharpe was training with the first team and what a player!" recalls his former United youth team coach Eric Harrison. "What speed! What shooting ability! What crossing ability! He had all the skill of the present-day Manchester United players. I just can't understand why he didn't go

on to better things." Any United fan who saw "Sharpey" play in his short-lived prime will understand Harrison's bafflement.

The gifted left-footer was spotted by United scouts when he was a 16-year-old trainee at Torquay United. He signed for the Old Trafford club in June 1988 and made his debut three months later, playing at left-back against West Ham, but it wasn't until the 1990–91 season that Sharpe pinned down a regular first-team slot in his natural position on the left wing. He made a sensational impact.

In this more attacking role, Sharpe could utilize his electric turn of pace to beat opposition full-backs and whip in fast, accurate crosses for the likes of Mark Hughes and Brian McClair to feed off. Sharpe was also capable of scoring. During United's run to the 1991 League Cup final, he played a spectacular role in United's 6–2 demolition of Arsenal, blasting a hat-trick past David Seaman.

Sharpe made his first England appearance against the Republic of Ireland in March 1991 and 12 days before his 20th birthday he capped a memorable season by playing in United's European Cup-Winners' Cup final victory over mighty Barcelona. Sharpe's status as the most exciting new talent in English football was confirmed when his fellow professionals voted him the PFA Young Player of the Year.

Off the field, the handsome Halesowen lad became a teen pin-up, and a bulging postbag of fanmail prompted him to start his own fan club. An extrovert by nature, he revelled in the attention and even staged parties for his pubescent (predominantly female) fan club members that caused roadblocks in Manchester city centre.

But even as Sharpe hit an early peak, the seeds of his downfall were sown. A pelvic operation caused him to miss the first four months of 1991–92 and while he was recuperating Ryan Giggs burst on to the scene. Sharpe was struck down again at the start of 1992–93 with a serious bout of viral meningitis and by the time he was fit again, Giggs was the first-choice left winger. Rather than mope about his misfortune, Sharpe won a place elsewhere in midfield and contributed an incredible 18 goal assists during the run-in to United's Premiership title win. The following year, Sharpe was the Reds' third top scorer, celebrating 11 goals with his famous Sharpey shuffle or Elvis wiggle as United cruised to a league and FA Cup Double.

The combination of being played out of position and nagging injuries gradually took their toll on Sharpe. Although he picked up his third championship medal in 1996, he could no longer command a regular place and moved to Leeds United for £4.5 million that summer. He later played for Sampdoria (Italy), Bradford City, Portsmouth and Exeter City. It is a shame that this happy-go-lucky character never quite fulfilled his vast potential, but it was fun while it lasted.

Sharpe celebrates in style, using the corner flag as a microphone stand!

RYAN GIGGS

MIDFIELDER (MANCHESTER UNITED 1991–)

IN 2001, MANCHESTER UNITED granted Ryan Giggs a testimonial at the age of 27. No United player has been accorded the privilege so young before, but if anyone deserves such an honour it is Giggs for the thrills he has given millions of Reds over the past decade.

Since the heyday of George Best, United supporters had waited for a player with similar God-given talent. Then Giggs signed schoolboy forms for the club in February 1988 and those who saw him play in United's youth ranks were certain that finally Best's true successor had arrived.

Giggs was just 17 when he made his debut in the first team as a substitute against Everton late on in the 1990–91 season. It was immediately apparent that the whippet-thin winger could cut it at the highest level – his innate sense of balance and ability to run with the ball at lightning speed made him a defender's worst nightmare.

At the start of 1991–92, an injury to United's established left-winger Lee Sharpe gave Giggs a chance to stake his claim for a regular slot and he took it gratefully, playing an important role in United's League Cup-winning run. That season he also broke through at international level, becoming the youngest ever Welsh international at 17 years, 321 days. In May 1992, Giggs was crowned the PFA Young Player of the Year and he completed an extraordinary season by captaining United's youth team to victory in the FA Youth Cup.

The following year, Giggs played his part in United's first league championship success and became the first player ever to win the PFA Young Player of the Year award twice.

By now, Giggs's fame was spreading well beyond football. His football talent allied to good looks gave him what marketing men term "great crossover appeal" and his image helped to shift millions of pounds worth of merchandise from T-shirts to vegetarian Quorn burgers. In 1994, 20-year-old Giggs added to his growing list of "youngest ever" achievements by publishing his autobiography, a book that sold by the lorry-load to his army of teenage admirers.

On the pitch, he has continued to perform heroics ever since. In 1993–94, he supplied 14 assists and 17 goals as United stormed to a league and FA Cup double. Then after a mediocre 1994–95 season, Giggs regained his form and goalscoring touch netting 12 times to help United win the double Double in 1996. He collected his eighth League Championship medal in 2002–03 and his fourth FA Cup winners' medal in 2003–04. But pride of place in his remarkable collection is reserved for the 1999 European Cup.

Over the years, Giggs has developed his all-round game enormously, but it is still his ability to beat defenders with ease that makes him one of the most exciting players in world football. The winning goal he scored against Arsenal in the 1999 FA Cup semi-final replay when he dribbled past four defenders before powering home the ball past David Seaman is arguably the best and most important goal ever scored by a United player. Single-handedly, he had got United's Treble bid back on track. That's Ryan Giggs, a football genius and a natural-born winner.

Ryan Giggs leaves QPR's Ray Wilkins and Darren Peacock (foreground) lying in his wake.

PETER SCHMEICHEL

GOALKEEPER (MANCHESTER UNITED 1991–99)

Alan Shearer was one of many top-class strikers to be denied by Peter Schmeichel's outstanding goalkeeping.

WHEN MANCHESTER UNITED signed Peter Schmeichel from IF Brondby for £500,000 in August 1991, it looked like a good bit of business. After all, Schmeichel was the Danish international goalkeeper and the 1990 Danish Player of the Year. For just half a million pounds, as Sir Alex Ferguson later reflected, "I believe we made the buy of the century."

With his shock of blond hair, massive 6ft 4inch frame and booming voice, it didn't take long for Schmeichel to make his presence felt at Old Trafford. Although Manchester United were pipped for the league title by Leeds in his first season, the big Dane helped the Reds to the best defensive record in the top division, conceding just 33 goals in 42 games. In the summer of 1992, Schmeichel enhanced his reputation by coaxing a distinctly ordinary Denmark team to an unlikely victory in the European championship.

The following season, Schmeichel helped the club he supported as a child to the league title for the first time in 26 years. Although he conceded just 31 goals in 1992–93, Schmeichel proved he was far more than just United's last line of defence. His natural ability to throw the ball great distances with pinpoint accuracy was the perfect complement to United's counter-attacking style and he started off many goalscoring moves.

Schmeichel's good form continued in 1993–94 as United won a Premiership and FA Cup double. His only slight disappointment of the season was missing the Coca-Cola Cup final against Aston Villa through suspension. Defeat in that match cost United the chance of a domestic treble and Schmeichel's absence ended his personal run of 94 consecutive games played, a club record for a goalkeeper.

The 1994–95 campaign was ended without a trophy, despite Schmeichel's best efforts, but his contribution to the double Double success the following year was crucial. His display against title challengers Newcastle in March 1996, a game United won 1–0 despite being under siege for the majority of the game, was unforgettable. At the end of the season, Sir Alex Ferguson highlighted Schmeichel's importance to his team, saying, "He saves us ten to 12 points per season that other 'keepers are not getting for their clubs."

Schmeichel proved Ferguson's point again in December 1996 during a Champions League match against Rapid Vienna, making another remarkable save. He changed direction in mid-air to tip Rene Wagner's header over the bar, conjuring up memories of Gordon Banks's save from Pele in the 1970 World Cup.

However, it appeared Schmeichel would miss out on actually winning the Champions League when he announced his intention to retire from English football in November 1998. Fortunately, he stayed until the end of the 1998–99 season and played a key role in United's Treble success. No United fan will ever forget his last-minute penalty save from Dennis Bergkamp in the FA Cup semi-final replay against Arsenal, nor his mad dash up field to set up United's equalizer in the European Cup final win against Bayern Munich. It was a fitting end to the United career of the club's best-ever goalkeeper.

ERIC CANTONA

FORWARD (MANCHESTER UNITED 1992–97)

ON THE DAY ERIC CANTONA signed from Leeds, 27 November 1992, for a paltry million-pound fee, a TV reporter polled opinion on the shock transfer outside Old Trafford. He asked one United supporter if he would adopt the Leeds fans' favourite chant.

"Ooh Aah Cantona?" came the reply. "It'll never catch on here."

He was wrong, very wrong. Even today, years after Cantona's retirement, fans belt out renditions of "Ooh Aah" to the tune of the "Marseillaise" at Old Trafford, along with a host of other songs the Red Army have dreamt up to honour the great Frenchman. The love and respect for Cantona still borders on worship among United supporters and, in 2001, Cantona was voted United's greatest ever player in a worldwide fans' poll commissioned by the club's official magazine. Some outsiders claim that Cantona is undeserving of such veneration, arguing that he never won the European Cup and didn't make a huge impact at international level. So why is the man Reds often refer to simply as "Le God" still so revered?

First and foremost, he was the catalyst for the most successful period in the club's history. When Cantona arrived at Old Trafford, United hadn't won the league championship for nearly 26 years. It was no coincidence that six months later, the Premiership trophy was safely tucked away in the Old Trafford trophy cabinet. Although United were already brimming with talented players, Cantona made the difference. "When you see Eric Cantona brushing up on his skills, you know that no one can be satisfied with their standard," commented young Ryan Giggs. Eric's work ethic rubbed off on Giggs and other emerging players including David Beckham, who began to stay behind to practise with Eric after official training sessions had ended.

On match days, Eric was equally influential. His record of 80 goals in 180 full appearances for United is incredible for a deep-lying striker, but that statistic takes no account of the many goals he set up for others with visionary passes. During his five-season stay, United lost just 20 matches when Cantona was in the team, won the Double twice and missed out on the league championship once. That was in 1994–95 when, crucially, Cantona was suspended for the second half of the season.

Not only was Cantona a brilliant footballer, he was also the epitome of cool. Who else could get away with wearing his collars up and strutting around with his chest puffed out? How many footballers paint and write poetry and act in movies? And only Cantona could have coined a bizarre "sardine" analogy rather than apologize for his attempt to, literally, kick racism out of football at Selhurst Park in 1995.

Whether he was scoring a goal, misbehaving or simply strolling around, Cantona was a compelling figure, a man who oozed charisma, an icon who appealed to United supporters young and old. He will never be forgotten.

Eric Cantona fires home the winner against Liverpool in the 1996 FA Cup final to clinch United's second Double in three seasons.

CHAPTER FOURTEEN

THE TREBLE AND BEYOND

MANY FANS FEARED THAT ERIC CANTONA'S RETIREMENT IN
MAY 1997 WOULD MARK THE END OF A GLORIOUS ERA. BUT
JUST TWO YEARS LATER, WITHOUT THE KING, MANCHESTER
UNITED REACHED THE PROMISED LAND.

How on earth would United replace Eric Cantona? That was the question every United supporter was asking in the summer of 1997. The charismatic Frenchman had inspired so much success in the previous five seasons and was worshipped like a god by the Old Trafford faithful. His retirement left a gaping hole not only in the team, but also in the hearts of thousands of his Red disciples.

Manager Alex Ferguson was widely expected to look abroad for a world-class successor to Cantona. But while Italian club Internazionale splashed out £16.5 million to buy Ronaldo, Ferguson invested a paltry £3.5 million in Tottenham Hotspur and England star Teddy Sheringham. Sheringham played in exactly the same floating striker's role as Cantona, so in essence Ferguson was replacing like with like. At 31, Sheringham was also the same age as the retired Frenchman, and United fans wondered whether he too was past his peak. The direct comparison between the two was eased slightly when Sheringham was given his favourite No. 10 squad number while the previous incumbent, David Beckham, gratefully slipped into Cantona's No. 7 shirt. Meanwhile, Alex Ferguson handed the captain's armband to his inspirational midfielder, Roy Keane.

United's first league fixture was against Spurs and despite years of loyal service to the club, Teddy Sheringham received a hostile reception on his return to White Hart Lane. With the score poised at 0–0, chants of "Judas" rang out as he stepped up to take a second-half penalty. Sheringham's shot hit the post to the unadulterated joy of home fans, but a late Nicky Butt strike and a Ramon Vega own goal gifted United a 2–0 win.

A day later, United announced the £5 million signing of central defender Henning Berg from Blackburn Rovers. Alex Ferguson was pleased to get his man because previous bids for Berg had been turned down by Rovers and his move to buy Brazilian international centre-back, Celio Silva, had been scuppered when Silva was refused a work permit.

Following the hard-fought win at Spurs, United played solid but generally uninspiring football in the league for the first two months of the season. The most significant incident of this period occurred during a 0–1 defeat by Leeds at Elland Road when captain Roy Keane injured cruciate knee ligaments making a rash challenge on Leeds midfielder Alf-Inge Haaland. That one moment of frustration

put Keane out of action for the rest of the season.

No Cantona and now no Keane – could United cope without two such influential figures? The early signs were positive and in late October the Reds clicked into top gear. Much-maligned striker Andrew Cole proved his critics wrong by firing a hat-trick in the 7–0 demolition of Barnsley. Alex Ferguson's decision to play three strikers in the next match paid off as Sheffield Wednesday were blown away by goals from Cole, Sheringham (two) and Ole Gunnar Solskjaer (two) in a 6–1 drubbing.

By the turn of the year, United were sitting pretty at the top of the Premiership with 46 points from 21 games, five points clear of Blackburn Rovers with Arsenal languishing a distant 12 points behind in sixth place. United's dominant form was confirmed on 4 January when they travelled to Stamford Bridge to play Chelsea in the third round of the FA Cup. On paper, it looked a tough tie against a team then lying third in the Premiership, but Chelsea were simply overpowered as goals from Beckham (two), Cole (two) and Sheringham put United 5–0 up after 75 minutes. Three late goals were no consolation for the Blues and afterwards manager Gianluca Vialli graciously conceded that they had been out-classed.

"This United team is one of the finest Europe has seen," he said.

But Ferguson's men had still to prove it by winning the European Cup. The team's form in the group phase of the Champions League had been encouraging with five wins in six matches, including a confidence-boosting 3–2 win over Juventus at Old Trafford back in October. The only blot on the continental landscape was a 0–1 defeat in the return match at the Stadio Delle Alpi that showed

Opposite: United players congratulate Teddy Sheringham on scoring the goal that put the Reds 5–0 up against Chelsea in the FA Cup.

Right: Teddy Sheringham's debut was against his old club Spurs. To the delight of Tottenham's fans, he hit a penalty against the post. United won 2–0.

United still hadn't discovered the winning formula away from home to top European clubs.

With a Champions League quarter-final against AS Monaco to look forward to in March, United had to concentrate on Premiership and FA Cup affairs in January and February. But rather than build on that sensational win against Chelsea, the Reds form declined markedly. There were surprise single-goal defeats by

Dejection as Denis Irwin (left) Nicky Butt (middle) and Michael Clegg trudge off following their Champions League exit against AS Monaco.

Southampton away and Leicester City at home. Dreams of a Treble were shattered by lowly Barnsley who knocked out a below-strength United side 3–2 in the FA Cup fifth-round replay. Even a 2–0 league victory against Derby County at Old Trafford had a sting in the tail as Ryan Giggs limped off with a hamstring injury that would rule him out of the Monaco tie.

The first leg against Monaco (who had a certain Fabien Barthez in goal) was played on an appalling pitch at the Stade Louis II that stopped either team from playing flowing football. A tedious 0–0 stalemate looked a decent result for United in the circumstances, but the Red attack that had once carried such a potent goal threat now appeared worryingly toothless.

Four days before the return match, United faced a vital league game at home to Arsenal. The resurgent Gunners produced a powerful performance to beat a jaded United side 1–0. Worse still, goalkeeper Peter Schmeichel tore his hamstring after a mad dash upfield for a corner in the final minute.

Alex Ferguson's injury list had reached critical levels. He fielded an 11 against Monaco at Old Trafford minus Schmeichel, Giggs, Keane and Gary Pallister. Ultimately, Monaco striker David Trezeguet's 96mph rocket shot past deputy keeper Raimond Van der Gouw after just five minutes proved vital. Ole Gunnar Solskjaer made it 1–1 on 53 minutes, but Monaco held out to win on away goals.

"It's a bitter pill to swallow," said manager Alex Ferguson. "If we'd had a full side I'm sure we would have gone on, but in retrospect I should have tried harder to find cover for Ryan Giggs. I have never felt so low in football."

Now there was just the Premiership to play for, but by the end of March, Arsenal were six points behind the Reds with three games in hand. The United side continued to battle bravely, but their usual slick passing game had given way to hopeful punts forward – consecutive 1–1 draws at home to Liverpool and Newcastle in April highlighted United's deficiencies.

On 2 May, Arsenal completed an amazing 11-game winning streak with a 4–0 thrashing of Everton at Highbury to claim the Premiership title and render United's two remaining fixtures irrelevant. The Gunners went on to claim their second double, beating Newcastle 2–0 in the FA Cup final at Wembley.

United had ended the season without a trophy, but Alex Ferguson had a warning for anyone who thought Red domination of English football was coming to an end.

"We will all learn from our mistakes," he said. "And don't worry, the players will be up for it again next season."

Although United's failure to win anything in 1997–98 was mainly caused by injuries to key players, Alex Ferguson knew he had to strengthen his squad. Indeed, he'd secured an agreement from PSV Eindhoven to sell Jaap Stam to United before that campaign had even finished. The massive Dutch international central defender officially signed on 1 July for £10.75 million, a world record transfer fee for a defender. Ferguson also fulfilled his promise to buy high-quality cover for Ryan Giggs on the left wing by signing 24-year-old Swedish international Jesper Blomqvist from Parma for £4.5 million.

It was also time to say goodbye to some members of the old guard with Gary Pallister and Brian McClair leaving Manchester United after a combined 20 years of distinguished service.

In summer 1998, United fans got a good chance to see Jaap Stam in action as Holland reached the semi-finals of the World Cup in France. The tournament changed David Beckham's life. He was harshly sent off for a petulant flick at Diego Simeone during England's second-round defeat by Argentina, and returned to England a national hate figure. Beckham had to endure moronic barracking from opposition fans up and down the country for months to come, but United fans backed him all the way.

"There was a lot of stuff in the papers saying I was going to leave after the World Cup," commented Beckham later, "but the way the United fans have been with me, there was no way I'd do that. Their support and the letters they've sent meant a lot to me."

United's pre-season preparations culminated with a chance to gain revenge over league champions Arsenal in the Charity Shield match. Instead, the Reds were soundly thrashed 3–0. The only consolation for United supporters was the sight of captain Roy Keane playing again after a ten month lay-off.

United bounced back with an easy 2–0 home win over LKS Lodz in the Champions League preliminary round. A 0–0 draw in Lodz a fortnight later saw the team through to the group phase.

They began their league campaign with a 2–2 draw against Leicester City at Old Trafford. Before the next fixture away to West Ham, United finally completed the £12.6 million signing of Aston

Dwight Yorke was one of three crucial signings made by Alex Ferguson in the summer of 1998.

Villa striker Dwight Yorke, thus ending months of media speculation. The ever-smiling Tobagan had just one training session with his new team-mates before making his debut against the Hammers, but he was immediately made aware of the standards that would be required of him at his new club.

"On my first day, Roy Keane put in a hard tackle on me to test my touch," recalled Yorke a week later. "I think it was his way of saying, 'Let's see if you really want that money and to play for United.'"

Yorke made little impression against West Ham and the game ended goalless, but he scored two in the 4–1 drubbing of newly promoted Charlton Athletic four days later, which endeared him to home fans. However, Yorke's performance that night was largely over-shadowed by the news that BSkyB's £623 million takeover bid for United had been accepted by the club board. Many fans were against the move and following a Monopolies and Mergers Commission investigation, the Department of Trade and Industry eventually blocked the deal.

United's season warmed up in September with consecutive matches against Barcelona, Arsenal, Liverpool and Bayern Munich. The 3–3 draw against Barcelona at Old Trafford was the first classic of the season. Giggs and Scholes gave United a 2–0 half-time lead. After the interval, Barca launched a fierce comeback and Sonny Anderson's goal and a hotly disputed Giovanni De Olivera penalty made it 2–2. A beautiful Beckham free kick on 64 minutes restored United's advantage, but the visitors earned a deserved draw with a Luis Enrique penalty after Nicky Butt had handled the ball in a goalmouth scramble.

Nicky Butt was sent off for that offence and four days later he was shown another red card as United subsided to an inglorious 0–3 away defeat by Arsenal. There was no respite for the Reds who took on bitter rivals Liverpool next at Old Trafford. The pre-match atmosphere was given extra spice by the screening of a television-documentary in which Alex Ferguson was seen describing Liverpool midfielder and ex-United star Paul Ince as "a big-time Charlie" during a team-talk. United ran out comfortable 2–0 winners and Reds fans delighted in singing, "Charlie, what's the score?" to their former hero.

In the final game of this tough four-game stretch, United performed admirably against Bayern Munich in the Olympic Stadium.

Goals by Dwight Yorke and Paul Scholes gave them a 2–1 lead, but a last-minute mistake by goalkeeper Peter Schmeichel let in Elber to grab an equalizer. United did not let this slight setback worry them though, and thrashed Schmeichel's former club Brøndby IF 6–2 (away) and 5–0 (home) in their next two Champions League outings.

After an inconsistent start, the team's momentum was starting to build in the Premiership, too. A 5–1 thrashing of Wimbledon at Old Trafford and comprehensive away wins against Southampton (3–0) and Everton (4–1) lifted United to second in the table by the end of October. After 10 games, the Reds were on 21 points, one point behind Aston Villa and one ahead of Arsenal.

By now, all of Alex Ferguson's signings appeared to have settled in. Jaap Stam was a colossus in central defence, on the wing Jesper Blomqvist was proving himself to be an excellent stand-in for Giggs, and up front Dwight Yorke had formed a formidable partnership with Andrew Cole. The only worry was the indifferent form of Peter Schmeichel, but the Great Dane's announcement on 12 November

Ryan Giggs leaves Arsenal defenders reeling on his way to scoring *that* goal in the 1999 FA Cup semi-final replay.

1998 that he intended to quit Manchester United at the end of the season still came as a massive shock. Schmeichel cited the physical demands of the Premiership as the main factor behind his decision.

"Playing in goal at my age, it takes time to recover from the bumps and bruises. And when you are playing two or three games a week, it becomes impossible."

Another thrilling 3–3 draw against Barcelona, this time at the Nou Camp, was the highlight of November, but the team's form slumped dramatically during the Christmas period. In December, the Reds record read: one win, five draws and two defeats. The prime reason for this poor run can be traced to the departure of assistant manager Brian Kidd on 4 December. After years of sterling service to the club both as a player and coach, 'Kiddo' decided to try his hand at management with Blackburn Rovers. Kidd had brought through many home-grown players such as Paul Scholes, and initially they clearly missed his presence.

"I never thought I'd see the day when Brian Kidd left United," said a stunned Scholes.

But at a big club like United, life must go on and five wins out of five in January showed the team was back on track. Most memorable of these victories was the 2–1 home win over Liverpool in the FA Cup fourth round. They were 1–0 down to a third-minute goal by Michael Owen and looked destined for defeat with just a few minutes remaining. But an 88th-minute tap-in by the irrepressible Dwight Yorke and a last-gasp winner by substitute Ole Gunnar Solskjaer clinched a remarkable victory.

In February, Sir Alex Ferguson appointed Steve McClaren as his new assistant manager. Ferguson had been impressed by McClaren's work at Derby County under Jim Smith and by his forward-thinking approach. McClaren's United career got off to a good start – his new club battered relegation-bound Nottingham Forest 8–1 at the City Ground in his first game as coach. That day, after watching Andrew Cole and Dwight Yorke score two goals apiece, Ole Gunnar Solskjaer came on as a late substitute and scored four goals in 11 minutes (80, 88, 90, 90). It was the most goals ever scored by a substitute and the quickest four goals ever scored by one player.

By the beginning of March, United were four points clear of Chelsea in the Premiership and attention turned to the Champions League quarter-final match against Milan giants Internazionale. Rumours abounded before the first-leg match at Old Trafford that Brazilian superstar Ronaldo would return from injury to play. In fact, Ronaldo never even got on the plane to Manchester and the stage was clear for Dwight Yorke to give a world-class striking display. Twice in the first half, Yorke capitalized on pinpoint crosses from David Beckham to head in the goals that clinched a 2–0 win.

It was a particularly sweet night for Beckham who was up against Argentinian midfielder Diego Simeone for the first time since Simeone's theatrics cost him a red card in the World Cup the previous summer.

Ronaldo was deemed fit to start the return leg against United and he seemed confident of Inter's chances.

"Tactically, we will have the advantage," said the Brazilian. "I have seen United struggle to contain Italian sides, particularly away."

But in front of an 80,000 capacity crowd at the San Siro, United showed the skill and fighting qualities of true champions. Ronaldo was expertly policed by Henning Berg and substituted after an hour. Inter did create numerous chances, though, and Nicola Ventola finally broke through in the 63rd minute. A mixture of luck and Schmeichel's brilliance stopped Inter grabbing an equalizer before the tension of the 7,000 strong Red Army inside the San Siro was dissipated by Paul Scholes' late goal.

United faced formidable old rivals Juventus in the semi-finals. Trailing 1–0 in the home leg to an Antonio Conte goal, United were struggling, but yet again their never-say-die spirit saved them. With the final whistle imminent, substitute Teddy Sheringham's flick-on set up Ryan Giggs to fire home the equalizer.

United's next game was an FA Cup semi-final against Arsenal which ended 0–0. The replay three days later was an all-time classic. With the score poised at 1–1 after 109 exhilarating minutes of football, it took a wonderful extra-time goal by Ryan Giggs to earn United a place in the final. At the end of the match, the Villa Park pitch was invaded by thousands of happy United fans who were starting to believe the treble could really be on.

That feeling was reinforced a week later, as United produced a miraculous comeback to beat Juventus 3–2 in Turin to reach the European Cup final. After going 2–0 down within 11 minutes, both goals scored by Filippo Inzaghi, captain Roy Keane inspired United to victory with one of the finest performances ever by a player wearing the red shirt. The only sadness on a great night was that bookings for both Keane and Paul Scholes ruled them out of the final against Bayern Munich.

With two Cup finals to look forward to, United had to concentrate on regaining the league title. The run-in included a visit to Anfield, where Liverpool fans waved Bayern flags and celebrated as if they had won the league when Paul Ince scored an 89th-minute goal to snatch a 2–2 draw. A goalless draw in the penultimate fixture at Ewood Park consigned Brian Kidd's Blackburn Rovers team to relegation. A last-day 2–1 win against Spurs meant that United pipped 1998 champions Arsenal by one point and the Premiership trophy returned to Old Trafford.

United were unstoppable and Newcastle were effortlessly dismissed 2–0 in the FA Cup final. Teddy Sheringham came on as a ninth-minute substitute for injured captain Roy Keane and scored 96 seconds later. He also set up Paul Scholes' match-clinching second-half goal. Then, it was off to Barcelona.

On 26 May 1999, 45,000 Reds packed into the Nou Camp to see if United could win the European Cup for the first time since 1968. Bayern were the better side for the majority of the game and it looked as if Mario Basler's sixth-minute strike would prove decisive. But last-gasp goals by substitutes Sheringham and Solskjaer completed another supernatural comeback win. United had become the first English side ever to win the treble. They had reached the Promised Land.

After being presented with the trophy, the celebrations continued for 45 minutes on the pitch as United fans hailed their heroes. Afterwards, the players went to the ballroom at the Arts Hotel and partied until 5 a.m. with friends and family. United fans meanwhile converged on Barcelona's famous Ramblas street and sung the night away. The next day the players flew back with the trophy and were taken on an open-topped bus parade of Manchester. An estimated 750,000 people poured into the city centre to catch a glimpse of arguably the greatest English league team ever.

Alex Ferguson reflected that there was a sense of destiny about that famous night at the Nou Camp.

"It felt like it was meant to be. The fact that it would have been Matt Busby's 90th birthday; the fact that we were playing Munich with everything that means to this club – people who believe in God

Andrew Cole (left) and friends chill out by the pool during the 2000 FIFA Club World Championship in Brazil.

might see a pattern in that. I mean, I believe, I pray a lot. You have that sense that it all has a meaning."

Manchester United were without doubt the best team in Europe once again.

After the greatest season ever, anything else was bound to be an anti-climax, but newly knighted manager Sir Alex Ferguson was determined that his team would continue their unrelenting quest for honours – "Now, we're playing for pride, our place in the history of the game. There are important things at stake. My players understand that."

The United boss's toughest task was to replace goalkeeper Peter Schmeichel who had kept his promise to quit English football by signing for Portuguese club Sporting Lisbon. In the summer, Mark Bosnich was brought in on a free transfer from Aston Villa. Bosnich had started his English football career at United in the late 1980s,

Manchester United's players celebrate their Treble-clinching win over Bayern Munich in the 1999 European Cup final.

but made an unfortunate start to his second spell at Old Trafford. He was injured in United's third league match, a 2–0 win over Leeds United and Raimond Van der Gouw took his place in the team. By the end of August 1999, Bosnich had been relegated to third-choice keeper behind new signing Massimo Taibi (£4.5 million from Venezia) and Van der Gouw.

Taibi made his debut behind another new signing Mikael Silvestre against Liverpool at Anfield in September and produced a man-of-the-match display as United ran out 3–2 winners. But Taibi's embarrassing mistakes in a 3–3 home draw against Southampton and in the 0–5 humiliation by Chelsea at Stamford Bridge allowed Bosnich to regain his first-team place by early October. Bosnich grabbed his chance and a month later his brilliant performance was the key factor behind United's 1–0 victory over Palmeiras in the annual Intercontinental Cup match between the champions of Europe and South America.

"The game meant a lot to me personally," recalled Bosnich later. "I used to watch that game in Australia and it was a big thing. We knew no British team had won it in its 39-year history and we really wanted to be the first."

Despite the unsettled goalkeeping situation, United were the dominant attacking force in domestic football throughout 1999–2000. Highlights included the 5–1 annihilation of Newcastle United (with Andrew Cole scoring four against his old club), the 5–1 demolition of Everton (this time Ole Gunnar Solskjaer poached four goals) and the 7–1 thrashing of West Ham in April (including a Paul Scholes hat-trick). In all, United scored a Premiership record-breaking 97 goals in 38 matches, gathering a total of 91 points to finish a massive 18 points clear of second-placed Arsenal.

Unfortunately, it was impossible for United to repeat their Treble success because the club didn't enter the FA Cup. The controversial decision to play in the inaugural FIFA Club World Championship instead was made under government pressure to support England's 2006 World Cup bid. So while FA Cup third-round matches were being played in the English winter, United travelled to play in the searing heat of Rio de Janeiro. With little time to acclimatize, United drew their opening match with Mexican side Necaxa, lost the second to Brazilian team Vasco Da Gama and were thus eliminated in the group phase. Ultimately, the only real benefit of the trip was that it gave the players the chance to train and relax in warm weather as they prepared for the latter stages of the Champions League in the spring.

United showed the potential to retain their European Cup in the second group-phase match against Fiorentina in mid-March, beating Gabriel Batistuta and co. 3–1 at Old Trafford. But the Reds

Mark Bosnich returned to Old Trafford in 1999 but found that Peter Schmeichel was a tough act to follow.

couldn't sustain their form in the quarter-final tie against Spanish giants Real Madrid. Only a splendid display by Mark Bosnich allowed United to escape from the first leg with a 0–0 draw. But Bosnich wasn't fit to play in the return, and the slack defending which had haunted United all season was exploited to the full by Real who took a 3–0 lead before the hour mark. Despite a valiant fightback in which Beckham and Scholes narrowed the scoreline to 2–3, United were out of the competition. It was of no consolation to the deposed European champions that they lost to the eventual winners.

The following season, United re-asserted their supremacy in English football as Sir Alex Ferguson became the first manager ever

to lead the same team to three consecutive league championship wins. The championship race was effectively over by January – a 3–1 win over West Ham on New Year's Day put the Reds 11 points clear and they never looked likely to surrender their lead. With redevelopment work on Old Trafford completed, capacity 67,000-plus crowds were regularly treated to scintillating displays in that decisive first half of the season. Bradford City (6–0), Leeds United (3–0), Southampton (5–0) and a host of other teams came to Old Trafford and were outclassed as the likes of Teddy Sheringham, Andrew Cole and Ole Gunnar Solskjaer all struck a rich vein of goal-scoring form. But United saved their most savage beating for fierce rivals Arsenal in February. The Gunners were thrashed 6–1, with Dwight Yorke grabbing a hat-trick, to destroy any lingering hopes the Londoners may have had of making a late charge.

The season will also be remembered for the emergence of a new United hero in the shape of World Cup-winning goalkeeper Fabien Barthez. Signed from Monaco in the summer of 2000, the eccentric Frenchman immediately displaced Mark Bosnich from the first team (Bosnich later joined Chelsea) and captured United fans' imagination with his incredible athleticism, ball distribution and penchant for dribbling past opposing forwards!

But although the team looked more assured defensively with Barthez in goal, United could not recapture the glories of 1999. United returned to FA Cup competition, but West Ham produced an excellent display at Old Trafford to knock out the Reds in the fourth round by a 1–0 margin. Meanwhile, in Europe, United's poor away form proved extremely costly. Defeats against PSV Eindhoven (1–3) and Anderlecht (1–2) in the first group phase didn't bode well, and three draws in the second group phase after Christmas against Valencia (0–0 and 1–1) and Panathinaikos (1–1) indicated trouble ahead. When United took on a strong Bayern Munich team, desperate for revenge after 1999, in the quarter-finals, their worst fears were realized. Bayern won 3–1 on aggregate.

In the aftermath of another disappointingly early exit from the European Cup, captain Roy Keane said, "I have seen United players getting complacent, thinking they've done it all and getting carried away by a bit of success. All you have to do is drop your standards slightly and it's obvious, especially in Europe."

If Keane was right and there was a flicker of complacency, the £19 million signing of Dutch striker Ruud Van Nistelrooy from PSV Eindhoven before the season had ended, and Sir Alex Ferguson's promise to strengthen the squad further in the summer (Juan Sebastien Veron joined in a £28m deal), would surely extinguish it.

"This is not by any means the end of this United team," he assured fans after receiving the Premiership trophy at the last home league fixture against Derby County.

Everyone, including the great man himself, expected the 2001–02 season to be Ferguson's final one before retiring from management. Naturally, he was determined to finish his glorious career on a high. He had two particular targets in his sights: a fourth consecutive league title and the European Cup. The final of the latter would be played at Hampden Park in his native Glasgow… it was fate, surely?

Opposite: Flamboyant Frenchman Fabien Barthez shows off his ball skills.

Below: United celebrate their seventh Premiership title in nine years.

Two down, one to go... United's 2–0 FA Cup final win over Newcastle put them within sight of an historic treble.

Towards the end, the 1998–99 season resembled nothing so much as an avalanche for Manchester United as the team's momentum grew towards an historic climax, each game proving more frenzied than the last. These are the five matches that will stick in the mind of any supporter lucky enough to witness them.

FA Cup semi-final replay, 14 April 1999
Manchester United (1) 2 Arsenal (0) 1
Villa Park, Att: 30,223

If a match is judged by the headlines it generates, then 'The Best Match in the World Ever' and 'The Greatest Goal Ever Scored' should tell you something about this epic semi-final replay. Arsenal were United's biggest domestic rivals. The previous season they had won the double, in the process providing United with a rare trophy-less season. Now they stood in the way of the Reds again, in both the League and Cup. Ninety minutes and extra-time had failed to separate the teams at the weekend and so they met again on the Wednesday night. This time United got the break-through, a superb curling shot from David Beckham giving them the lead in the 17th minute. Arsenal struck back through Dennis Bergkamp's deflected shot in the 69th and then disaster struck as Roy Keane was sent off by David Elleray. Down to ten men, and with extra-time looming, it didn't look good for United. Then with just seconds of normal time remaining, Phil Neville brought down Ray Parlour and Elleray pointed to the penalty spot. Arsenal were one kick away from the FA Cup final. Bergkamp stepped up and hit it well only for Schmeichel to save brilliantly. Extra-time arrived and with it the highlight of an astonishing match.

"It was always going to take something special to separate these two teams," said Ferguson afterwards. And how! Picking up a spilt pass from Patrick Vieira in the 109th minute, Ryan Giggs proceeded to dance 70 yards past five defenders before unleashing a ferocious drive into the top of the net. Pandemonium followed; neither fans nor players were able to believe what they'd just witnessed. Arsenal were broken and United were in the Cup final.

European Cup semi-final, 21 April 1999
Manchester United (2) 3 Juventus (2) 2
Stadio delle Alpi, Att: 60,806

After earning a 1–1 draw, and a valuable away goal, at Old Trafford, the mighty Juventus appeared to have one foot in the European Cup final. For Manchester United to reach their first final in 31 years, they would have to get a result in the intimidating atmosphere of the Stadio delle Alpi, an unlikely proposition that looked impossible after the opening 11 minutes of the second leg. Two goals from Filippo Inzaghi put the Italians 2–0 up on the night, and 3–1 on aggregate. United appeared to have committed professional suicide, or so we thought. Fortunately, Ferguson's side were made of sterner stuff. United had never won on Italian soil before this night but if the players were concerned, they didn't let it show. Skipper Roy Keane, out of the final because of a yellow card, led the comeback with a captain's performance that later prompted Ferguson to say, "It is an honour to be associated with such a player." His 24th-minute header pulled United back into the match. Here was a team who simply didn't believe they could be beaten. Dwight Yorke confirmed the point ten minutes later with an adroit header from Andrew Cole's cross. It was 2–2 on the night and United were ahead on away goals. The Italians tried to fight back and came close on several occasions, but Jaap Stam and Peter Schmeichel stood tall to deny them. Six minutes from time, Cole made sure of matters, sliding home from a narrow angle after Yorke had been felled. Manchester United had made it to the final and it was hard not to feel the gods were smiling down on them.

Premiership, 16 May 1999
Manchester United (1) 2 Tottenham Hotspur (1) 1
Old Trafford, Att: 55,189

After all the excitement of the semi-finals, there was the small matter of the league championship. With Arsenal pushing them all the way to the finish line, United's 37 games and 78 goals to date in the League would count for little if they didn't get a result against Tottenham. Despite plenty of possession and attacking football, with both Ryan Giggs and Yorke coming close, the home side were caught out by a Les Ferdinand goal in the 25th minute. Once again, United would have to come back from behind.

David Beckham soothed the fans' nerves just before half-time with an angled drive past Ian Walker. One United goal in the second 45 minutes would secure their fifth title under Alex Ferguson. It was Andy Cole who provided it. Having come on as a substitute, he neatly controlled Gary Neville's pass before beautifully dinking it over Walker. United were champions again – and just two matches away from re-writing football history.

FA Cup final, 22 May 1999
Manchester United (1) 2 Newcastle United (0) 0
Wembley, Att: 79,101

By now the script was set – United find themselves in some sort of adversity and then beat the odds to come good. At Wembley, the adversity was provided after eight minutes when an injured Roy Keane was forced to limp off. Without their inspirational skipper, would United be able to defeat a Newcastle side desperate for victory after a disappointing performance in last year's final? The answer was provided by Teddy Sheringham. The striker came off the bench and provided a man-of-the-match performance. His beautiful strike in the 11th minute put United back in the driving seat. An expert one-two between Sheringham and Ole Gunnar Solskjaer set up the goal, and the just-on substitute finished it perfectly by sliding the ball under the advancing Steve Harper in the Geordies' goal. United dominated the remainder of the half with Sheringham in majestic form. Newcastle tried to make more of a game of it in the second half. Reinforced by Duncan Ferguson, they briefly threatened to equalize but were finished off when

Sheringham's pass in the 52nd minute found Paul Scholes who netted with a low drive from the edge of the penalty box. In the dressing-room afterwards, the team took great delight in singing "Oh Teddy, Teddy, came to Man United and he won the lot!" But for that to be strictly true, there was one more victory required.

European Cup final, 26 May 1999
Manchester United (0) 2 Bayern Munich (1) 1
Nou Camp Stadium, Barcelona, Att: 91,000

Manchester United took out a full-page advert in a national newspaper on the day of the European Cup final. It was one word long and said simply: "Believe". Of course, after the dramatic triumphs of the last few matches, belief in this United team was at an all-time high. Nonetheless, it was still to be tested to the limit in the club's most important game for over three decades.

With both Roy Keane and Paul Scholes suspended, Ferguson was forced to re-arrange his side. David Beckham moved into the centre of midfield, partnering Nicky Butt, while Ryan Giggs moved on to the right wing and Jesper Blomquist played on the left.

The formation didn't seem to suit United with the Germans having the better of the first half and taking the lead from a Mario Basler free kick. Ferguson's side improved in the second half but still lacked penetration and could have gone further behind. Schmeichel made saves to keep out Stefan Effenberg and Mehmet Scholl. Even more alarming was Scholl's chip against the post in the 79th minute. Five minutes later the Germans hit the woodwork again when Carsten Janker's overhead kick crashed against the bar.

UEFA officials had already attached Bayern Munich's colours to the trophy as the final minutes approached. Yorke, Sheringham and Solskjaer had chances but the ball wouldn't go in the net. Still United pushed forward but by now they needed a miracle. It came in injury time. United won a corner and, in desperation, Schmeichel came running up to join the attack. The big goalie's appearance confused the German markers and Beckham's inswinging corner entered a mass of bodies. Ryan Giggs mis-hit a shot that Teddy Sheringham managed to steer into the net.

Suddenly United were back in it. With Bayern still reeling, the Reds won another corner. Again Beckham swung the ball in, again Sheringham got a touch. This time Solskjaer was the player to stick out a foot and, incredibly, the ball was in the Germans' net for a second time in a matter of seconds. Bayern's players and fans were destroyed, United's ecstatic. Neutrals were merely in a state of shock. Club football's biggest prize was heading back to Old Trafford in the most dramatic manner imaginable.

It was a suitably impossible ending to an unbelievable season for Manchester United.

DAVID BECKHAM

MIDFIELDER (MANCHESTER UNITED 1992–2003)

"THERE WAS A TIME when I could walk through the centre of town without any aggravation. But it's changed. I could put on a baseball cap and glasses but I'd still get recognized. I'm not complaining, though. There are nice things about it and you have

to expect a certain amount of attention if you're playing for Manchester United."

So says David Beckham, one of several Manchester United players to capture the public's imagination and make the front pages of newspapers as often as the back pages.

With his photogenic looks and pop star wife, it's little wonder that David has proved ideal tabloid fodder. Haircuts, holidays, houses – there seems little in his life that isn't reported on. None of that should overshadow the more pertinent fact that Beckham is one of the finest footballers of his generation.

The spotlight first turned his way on 17 August 1996, the opening day of the 1996–97 season. United were away to Wimbledon and 2–0 up when Beckham received the ball ten yards inside his own half. A couple of strides later, after a quick look up, he unleashed a long floating ball that beat Dons' keeper Neil Sullivan and found the back of the net. It was an extraordinary start to the season and Beckham followed it up with a series of excellent performances and spectacular goals that helped establish him as an England regular.

Seasoned United watchers were already well aware of his talent. He joined the club as a 16 year-old in July 1991 and was a member of the FA Youth Cup-winning team that season. A senior debut followed in December 1992, although it took a few more years in the reserves before he was ready for a regular first-team place. An excellent performance and well-taken goal against Galatasaray in December 1994 proved to be a sign of things to come and in the 1995–96 double double-winning season Beckham and co. disproved the theory that "you can't win anything with kids".

After his wonder goal against Wimbledon, things were never really the same for Beckham. He has remained resolutely in the public eye ever since, compounded not only by incidents off the pitch but also his infamous sending-off against Argentina in the 1998 World Cup.

Nonetheless, his peers have never forgotten what is really special about the United midfielder. In 1999, he narrowly missed out on winning the European Footballer of the Year award after consistently excellent displays during the treble season, and in 2001 he was named England captain by Sven-Goran Eriksson.

In June 2003, Beckham ended months of speculation by signing for Real Madrid in a deal worth around £25 million to United. Although the England captain failed to win a trophy in his first season, he insisted that he had improved as a player alongside team-mates like Zindedine Zidane and Raul.

"From the first game onwards, I had to prove to people in Spain that I could actually play football instead of just selling shirts. I feel I have done that."

David Beckham's pinpoint crossing is almost unparalleled in world football.

ROY KEANE

MIDFIELDER (MANCHESTER UNITED 1993–)

FROM THE DAY Roy Keane joined Manchester United in 1993, he has constantly proved his worth to the club. Signing for a then British record of £3.75 million, the Republic of Ireland international instantly made an impact, scoring two goals on his home debut as United beat Sheffield Wednesday 3–0.

By season's end, Keane was celebrating his first season at United with a league and Cup double.

Following Paul Ince's departure at the end of the disappointing 1994–95 season, Keane took over the mantle of midfield general. Typically, the Irishman refused to get carried away by his new responsibilities.

"I don't want to be called the new Guv'nor," he said. "I just want to get on and do my job. This club is an institution. It will be around a lot longer than any of the players, whoever they are."

Maybe so, but United fans were certainly grateful to have Keane around during the 1995–96 season as United became double double winners.

"I think Roy Keane is our most influential player," commented Peter Schmeichel at the time. "We've had problems once or twice when he's not in the team." Alex Ferguson clearly agreed with Schmeichel's sentiments and when Eric Cantona retired in 1997, the United manager did not hesitate to give Keane the captain's armband.

"Roy is a natural," said Fergie. "As a captain, he is just like Bryan Robson. He leads the team by example. He's a totally committed, fearless footballer."

A cruciate ligament injury kept Keane out for most of the 1997–98 season – and how United players missed their inspirational captain, finishing the season with no new trophies in the cabinet. Fortunately for all Reds, Keane was back for the next campaign.

The team celebrated by producing the most astonishing run of results ever seen in football. Keane's metronomic passing, his powerful tackling and those energetic tirades against team-mates who fell below his high standards were all in evidence as the United captain led his side to an unprecedented treble – the Premiership title, the FA Cup and, most gloriously of all, the European Cup. Anyone who witnessed that joyous season will have embedded in their memory the glorious sight of Keane rising powerfully to head home in the European Cup semi-final against Juventus. United were on the ropes – 2–0 down – and in need of inspiration. The captain provided it with a display arguably the equal of anything ever seen in a Red shirt. His header made it 2–1 and his constant encouragement led to a 3–2 victory that put United in the European Cup final for the first time in three decades. Keane missed the final because of a suspension, but he had already provided the platform for United to succeed.

A year later, both press and professionals acknowledged as much, as Keane – having added another Premiership title and an Intercontinental Cup medal to his collection – was awarded the Football Writers Footballer of the Year Award and the Professional Footballers Association's equivalent. It was a fitting tribute to a player whom the fans have come to know as 'Massive'.

Perhaps best of all, Keane shows no loss of his appetite for success. Despite having achieved more than most players can dream of, he states unequivocally, "Some live off what they've done in the past. That's not my way and never will be." It's exactly the attitude that has made Roy Keane such a United legend.

Roy Keane has always demanded the highest standards during his career at Manchester United.

TEDDY SHERINGHAM

FORWARD (MANCHESTER UNITED 1997–2001)

WHEN TEDDY SHERINGHAM signed for Manchester United from Tottenham Hotspur for £3.5 million in the summer 1997, he took on a huge challenge – replacing Eric Cantona. At the time, Sheringham didn't appear to be fazed by the prospect. "I've always had comparisons," he commented. "When I came into the England set-up I took over Peter Beardsley's role. Then at Tottenham, I was filling Gary Lineker's shoes."

But with respect to Messrs Beardsley and Lineker, neither were ever worshipped like Cantona was by United fans. For the Red

Army, Cantona was God. Sheringham was trying to replace the irreplaceable and he didn't get off to the best of starts. In his first league outing for United, he missed a penalty against his former club Tottenham Hotspur. A further two penalty misses and he was, in manager Alex Ferguson's words, "on the dole queue as far as penalties are concerned."

Although Sheringham did have his moments in that first season, most notably heading a superb equalizer in United's 3–2 Champions League win over Juventus and scoring in United's sensational 5–3 FA Cup defeat of Chelsea, hardcore United fans didn't warm to him. Ultimately, they made Sheringham their scapegoat for United's failure to win either the European Cup or the Premiership that year. Unfair, yes, but for many fans he wasn't Cantona and that was that.

Sheringham later admitted that he initially found the demands of playing for Manchester United far greater than he had expected, saying, "I've never encountered such intensity before." Another problem he faced was the breakdown in communication between him and his strike partner Andrew Cole. Following an argument during a match against Bolton Wanderers in February 1998, they weren't on speaking terms, and when Dwight Yorke signed for United that summer, Sheringham was the one who lost his place in the team. Yorke and Cole hit it off instantly and Sheringham was reduced to a bit-part player.

Rather than sulk and ask for a transfer, Sheringham was determined to prove he could be an important player for United. He kept working hard in training and bounced back to play a decisive role in the club's treble success. Coming on as an early substitute for the injured Roy Keane in the 1999 FA Cup final, he delivered a man-of-the-match performance, scoring one and setting up a goal for Paul Scholes as United beat Newcastle 2–0. Even better was to come in the European Cup final against Bayern Munich. He came off the bench to score an injury-time equalizer before setting up fellow substitute Ole Gunnar Solskjaer for the winning, history making, goal. The chants of "Oh Teddy, Teddy. Came to Man United and he won the lot" belted out by 55,000 Reds inside the Nou Camp that night showed he had finally won the fans over and become a United legend.

For all his treble heroics, Sheringham remained essentially a squad player and he was widely expected to leave Old Trafford in summer 2000. Instead, he broke back into the first team at the start of the 2000–01 season, didn't stop scoring and stayed there. In his final year at United, Sheringham was a regular again and his brilliance was recognized when, at the ripe old age of 35, he was voted both the Football Writers' Association and Professional Footballers Association Player of the Year.

Teddy Sheringham celebrates his goal in the 1999 FA Cup final.

THE DEADLY DUO: COLE AND YORKE

DURING THE 1998–99 TREBLE SEASON, Andrew Cole and Dwight Yorke formed the deadliest strike partnership in Europe, scoring 63 goals between them in all competitions. For Dwight Yorke, contributing 29 goals and winning three medals in his first season at the club exceeded even his wildest expectations. For Cole, who had been the subject of vicious media criticism throughout his United career despite his phenomenal goalscoring record, the treble success was final, conclusive proof of his top-class ability.

From the time when Newcastle United manager Kevin Keegan surprisingly sold him to Manchester United in January 1995, Andrew Cole was under extreme pressure. The combination of Cole's incredible strike rate at Newcastle (68 goals in 84 games) and the British record transfer fee Manchester United paid for his services meant expectations were sky-high. Although Cole scored 12 goals in 17 games by the end of the 1994–95 season, including a Premiership record of five in one game, against Ipswich Town, he was made the scapegoat for United's narrow failure to win the Premiership title.

This setback knocked Cole's self-confidence. He later described his form in the following season as "nothing short of terrible" even though he ended 1995–96 with both league and FA Cup medals. His partnership with Eric Cantona also failed to gel.

Before the start of the 1996–97 season, Cole contracted pneumonia. His luck got even worse when he sustained two broken legs during a comeback game for the reserves. However, when Cole finally returned to action in the second half of the season, he started to find to his true form. His seven goals helped United to a second successive league title and the following year he netted 24 goals, including the first hat-trick by a United player in the European Cup for 30 years, against Feyenoord.

"I've got rid of the demons in my head," he declared, but when Arsenal overtook United to win the league title, doubts were again raised about his future. Indeed, many observers thought that the signing of Dwight Yorke for £12.6 million in August 1998 would spell the end for Cole. Instead, they immediately bonded as friends and players. Cole helped Yorke to settle into Manchester life and the smiling Tobagan's sunny attitude seemed to rub off on Cole. For most of 1998–99, international-class forwards Teddy Sheringham and Ole Gunnar Solskjaer could only watch from the subs' bench while Cole and Yorke enjoyed themselves on the pitch. A magnificent goal scored by Cole after a lightning combination of passes with Yorke against Barcelona in a Champions League match at the Nou Camp best illustrated their almost telepathic understanding. Yorke finished as the joint top scorer in the Champions League with eight goals and Cole supplied the Premiership-winning goal against Tottenham Hotspur on the last day of the league season.

The following year, Cole and Yorke both broke the 20-goal barrier

again, but in 2000–01, their partnership was broken due to the brilliant form of Teddy Sheringham. So while Cole showed yet again why he was Sir Alex Ferguson's first-choice striker for six years, Yorke was forced to battle for his place in the side. Eventually both men moved on (to Blackburn), following the signing of another goal machine, Ruud van Nistelrooy. But no United fan will ever forget Yorke and Cole's thrilling contribution to the club's greatest-ever season.

Dwight Yorke and Andrew Cole bonded from day one.

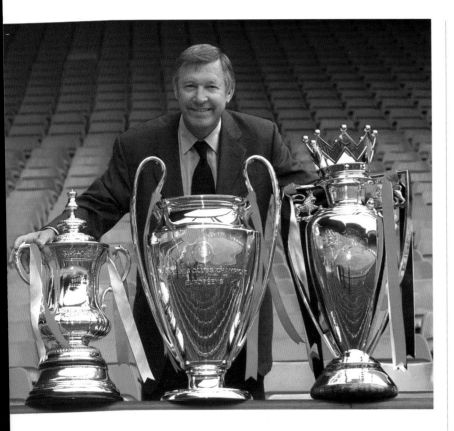

Manchester United's capture of the FA Cup, European Cup and Premiership trophy in 1999 capped Sir Alex Ferguson's remarkable managerial career.

ALEX FERGUSON had already tasted managerial success before he came to Old Trafford, but it was at Manchester United that he secured his status as one of the most successful managers in the history of the game.

Anyone who has ever visited Carrington, Manchester United's training centre, will be aware that the spirit of one man exudes through every corridor of the complex. From the quiet efficiency of the staff to the single-mindedness of the players, there is an insular feeling. It is a tight operation going about its business without distraction. In short, it is Alex Ferguson personified.

Since arriving at Old Trafford in November 1986, Ferguson has made the club in his own image. That should come as no surprise to anyone who has followed the Scotsman's career. Even before football became the centre of his professional life, he was a determined character. Aged 19, he was a union leader at the Clyde shipyard where he worked as a toolmaker, and at one stage he brought his fellow workers out on strike. He has never been one to shirk a big decision.

After a playing career as a centre-forward that took in Queen's Park, St Johnstone, Dunfermline, Rangers, Falkirk and Ayr United, he brought his determined approach to football management. After just three months in charge at East Stirling, he was offered the job

of manager of St Mirren and immediately displayed his now familiar traits of drive and ambition. As former St Mirren star Tony Fitzpatrick recalled, "Alex arrived at a club in a shambles. We used to get crowds of only a thousand. Within 18 months of his arrival, that figure was up tenfold. He used to get someone to drive him around the streets of Paisley before matches, lean out of the passenger window and bellow through a megaphone to let people know there was a game!

"There were also fund-raising bingo nights when Fergie would be in there, ticking his numbers off and shouting 'Bingo' with the rest of them. It was impossible not to be carried away by his enthusiasm."

Ferguson helped St Mirren to the First Division title before moving on to Aberdeen, where he broke the Celtic-Rangers stranglehold on Scottish football. Under his leadership, Aberdeen were crowned Scottish champions three times, they won the Scottish Cup four times (achieving the double in 1984) and the Scottish League Cup once. They also triumphed in Europe, winning the Cup-winners' Cup in 1983.

In 1986, following a sojourn as Scotland's caretaker manager at the Mexico World Cup, Ferguson arrived at Old Trafford. Manchester United were not in great shape. They had finished the previous season in the wrong half of the table and, despite the odd glimpse of flair and some occasional excitement, were really no nearer to winning the title than when Ron Atkinson had taken over. The first few seasons proved difficult, and eye-opening for the man from Govan.

"When I first came here, I thought it was all going to happen the next day," Ferguson admitted. "The club had not won the league for twenty years and I thought it would be dead easy. Well, not exactly that, but I thought it was going to be successful just because of the name Manchester United. It was only when I started analysing why they hadn't won the league for twenty years that I realized history's no good to you."

Those first few seasons created something that would now be unimaginable with the United manager – self-doubt.

"I was questioning everything. We went eight matches without winning and I couldn't understand why. I went through my training selections, my team selections, my team-talks, the lot, and I couldn't find anything wrong. I stopped going out at nights or even weekends. Couldn't face it. Just shut myself off from everything."

Many believe what saved Ferguson from the sack, after three unsuccessful seasons, was the FA Cup victory in 1990, his first trophy at the club. He agrees it was a pivotal moment, but not for the reasons you would think.

FERGUSON

"The Cup run showed me what was wrong with the club," he revealed. "As each round came along, the excitement got greater and I realized what the problem was. United had got used to Cup runs."

The manager set about changing that. Out went a number of Old Trafford favourites and in came new faces, as Ferguson set about creating a championship-winning team. The departures included Neil Webb, Jesper Olsen, Paul McGrath, Jim Leighton, Mark Robins and Arthur Albiston, among others. New arrivals included Steve Bruce, Gary Pallister, Paul Ince, Denis Irwin, Brian McClair and Peter Schmiechel.

The European Cup-Winners' Cup in 1991 was Ferguson's second triumph, but the manager's hunger for trophies just seemed to intensify.

"My job reference when I came here was to win the league," he stated simply. "That was always the priority."

As well as a number of new signings, there were other changes at United. Behind the scenes the club's youth system was undergoing a complete overhaul, the results of which would soon become apparent. However, in 1992 the most significant change at United was probably the arrival of a Frenchman. When a slice of opportunism paid off with the signing of Eric Cantona from Leeds, practically everyone questioned Ferguson's judgement. Debate about the striker's temperament and ability raged. "A panic buy" was the opinion of more than one 'expert' commentator.

Cantona proved to be the catalyst Ferguson needed, the "final piece of the jigsaw" as Denis Law put it. Within months, Ferguson's decision to sign him was completely vindicated as United ended their 26-year barren spell with the 1992–93 championship. Any United fan who has ever had to suffer the abuse and torment regularly served up by opposition fans will be well aware how life-changing an achievement that was. Better still, it was to prove just the beginning.

Next came the double in 1994 and the domination of English football. Some of the Old Trafford faithful were shocked in the summer of 1995, when Ferguson sold Mark Hughes, Andrei Kanchelskis and Paul Ince, but fans didn't know was just how good the crop of youngsters coming through the ranks were. Ferguson did. David Beckham, Paul Scholes, Gary and Phil Neville, Nicky Butt and the already established Ryan Giggs, led by Cantona, proved to be the backbone of a squad that would make history by securing the double Double in 1996.

All bets were off now. Why bother to question anything the manager decided to do? His decisions seemed infallible. Even the departure of Cantona in 1998 couldn't derail this train. In came Teddy Sheringham (another Ferguson decision some tried to query) and in 1999 the greatest season United fans had ever witnessed culminated in the impossible Treble – the league championship, the

FA Cup and the dramatic European Cup final – as Ferguson's team overcame all before them.

"Football, eh? Bloody hell!" said Ferguson minutes after winning the European Cup. It's a sentiment that could equally be applied to the manager. He has gone on to add yet more silverware to an already bulging trophy cabinet and in the process secured his place in the annals of United and football history.

Sir Alex Ferguson makes his point from the Manchester United bench.

CHAPTER FIFTEEN
THE
NEW
MILLENNIUM

SENTIMENT COUNTED FOR LITTLE IN THE SUMMER AND
AUTUMN OF 2001 AS SIR ALEX FERGUSON CONTINUED TO
BUILD WHAT WAS EXPECTED TO BE HIS LAST GREAT TEAM AT
MANCHESTER UNITED.

Sentiment counted for little in the summer and autumn of 2001 as Sir Alex Ferguson continued to build what was expected to be his last great team at Manchester United. From the day in May when he lifted his seventh Premiership trophy to the December night when he celebrated his 60th birthday, the manager allowed four of his Treble-winning heroes to leave Old Trafford.

Teddy Sheringham and Jesper Blomqvist were both released on free transfers, joining Tottenham Hotspur and Everton respectively. Meanwhile, Andrew Cole conceded defeat in the competition for places and joined Blackburn Rovers for an undisclosed transfer fee.

Ferguson's £19 million purchase of Ruud van Nistelrooy and trial of a new 4–5–1 formation had limited Cole's opportunities, just when he needed a regular first-team place to impress Sven-Goran Eriksson and perhaps make the England squad for the 2002 World Cup Finals. "You get to a certain stage in your career where you want to be playing week in, week out and if you're not you find it difficult," admitted Cole.

At least Cole had a few months to realize his Manchester United career was coming to an end. The other Treble-winning star to leave Old Trafford in 2001 had barely 48 hours. One Saturday in August, Jaap Stam was preparing to play in United's second Premiership game of the season, away to Aston Villa. Two days later, he was being introduced to the Italian media as Lazio's surprise new signing.

"It was my decision, it was a football decision and you have to trust me on that," said Ferguson, countering media claims that Stam's revealing autobiography had stirred up trouble at Old Trafford.

"I explained to Jaap that I planned to bring someone in and out of respect to him I didn't want him to sit on the bench."

The mystery "someone" referred to by Sir Alex was revealed, three days later, to be Laurent Blanc. Again there were gasps of surprise from United supporters and reporters alike. The new United defender's credentials were unquestionable. After all, Blanc had won the World Cup with France 12 months previously, playing in front of Fabien Barthez. But at the age of 35, the critics questioned whether Blanc had sufficient pace to pull it off in the Premiership. When United conceded four goals at Newcastle, three at Tottenham and two at home to Bolton, those same critics had a field-day at Blanc and Ferguson's expense.

Luckily for United, the critics weren't the only ones having a field day. Ruud van Nistelrooy was also making the most of the opportunities that were coming his way, following the one-year delay to his dream move. He scored his first goal for the club in the 2–1 Charity Shield defeat by Liverpool; then netted a double on his Premiership debut, the 3–2 home win over Fulham (Ruud's future strike partner Louis Saha twice gave Fulham the lead).

The new signings Blanc, Van Nistelrooy and Veron all scored in a remarkable Premiership match against Tottenham on 29 September 2001. At half-time, United were 0–3 down and destined for slaughter in the newspapers. But at full-time they were 5–3 up after goals by Cole, Beckham and the new trio turned the game on its head.

Many of Manchester United's players had started September by playing back-to-back World Cup qualifiers. Van Nistelrooy and Roy Keane faced up in Dublin where the Republic of Ireland beat Holland. Meanwhile, Gary Neville, Paul Scholes and David Beckham helped England to achieve one of their greatest victories, 5–1 away to Germany.

United were not quite so convincing on the Continent. After scraping a 1–0 win over Lille at Old Trafford, the Reds lost 2–1 away and 3–2 at home to Deportivo La Coruna in the UEFA Champions League. The Spaniards finished the first phase of the competition on top of United's group, with the Reds going through as runners-up.

And then there were 16 teams, all with aspirations of reaching the first European Cup Final to be held in Scotland since 1959. As a teenager, Sir Alex Ferguson had watched in awe as Real Madrid destroyed Eintracht Frankfurt 7–3 at Hampden Park. Now, as a 60-year-old, he had the chance to take his Manchester United team to the same venue for the 2002 final. The omens seemed irresistible. Ferguson's last match as Manchester United manager was to be the Champions League Final, against Real Madrid, in his home city of Glasgow. It was too good to be true, and not only because German underdogs Bayer Leverkusen killed the dream in the semi-finals.

Blanc scores against Boavista in the Champions League.

...en, Ferguson had decided to postpone his retirement anyway. ...least, his wife had decided this for him! "There was a big U-turn ...it only came about through the intervention of my wife Cathy and ...y sons," said Sir Alex. "They colluded between each other to make ...me stay on, but it was the thing I wanted to hear because I was worried ...about what I'd do. I couldn't see myself riding into the sunset."

Confirmation of Sir Alex's U-turn on February 28, 2002 brought an end to the rampant speculation about his successor. Top coaches Fabio Capello, Louis van Gaal and Sven-Goran Eriksson – to name just three – had all been linked with the coveted post by an insatiable press.

However, Ferguson's new contract came too late to save United's season. The Reds had not shown the consistency that had been their hallmark in the previous three campaigns, and Ferguson felt his impending retirement had contributed to this. He vowed never to pre-announce his last season again. (In January 2004, Ferguson signed a one-year rolling contract, making it easier to retire at short notice).

Of course, there were other factors in United's failure to finish in the top two for the first time since 1991. Like Arsenal and Liverpool, for example. Ferguson's men lost at home and away to both of their arch-rivals. The 0–1 home defeat to Liverpool early in the New Year was especially ill-timed; January was often the month when United would start a long unbeaten run.

This time, it was Arsenal who strung together an impressive set of results. Arsene Wenger's side won all of their last 12 domestic matches, including the Premiership decider against United. Sylvain Wiltord's goal gave the Gunners victory at Old Trafford and clinched them the title and the Double; four days earlier, Arsenal had beaten Chelsea in the FA Cup final.

Arsenal also knocked United out of the Worthington (League) Cup in 2001–02. Forced to play the tie the day after losing at Liverpool in the league, Ferguson freshened up his team with reserve-team players; eight who started or came on as substitute were aged 22 or under.

One was John O'Shea, a tall 20-year-old defender from the Irish Republic. Despite the 0–4 scoreline, O'Shea shone sufficiently under the Highbury floodlights to earn a Premiership call-up. He partnered and no doubt learned from Laurent Blanc – 14 years his senior – in the league wins over Middlesbrough and Derby in December 2001.

O'Shea was later named as the club's Reserve Player of the Year, an honour previously bestowed on the likes of Lee Martin and Nicky Butt. O'Shea also picked up a championship medal with the reserves, as they won their league for the first time since 1996–97. Brian 'Choccy' McClair was their coach; Sir Alex Ferguson had invited his former player to join the staff in the summer of 2001 following Steve McClaren's departure and Mike Phelan's promotion.

McClaren's motive for leaving Sir Alex's side was the same as Brian Kidd's in 1998; he wanted to step-up and manage a team. In only his first season as Middlesbrough boss, there were signs that he could make a success of this; not least the defeats he dished out to United in the league and in the FA Cup fourth round.

Ferguson's former assistant was reunited with several Old Trafford stars at the end of the 2001–02 season, as McClaren joined the England set-up for the World Cup Finals in Japan and Korea. Wes Brown, Nicky Butt and the national captain, David Beckham, were also on board. Phil Neville, unfortunately, was overlooked. His brother Gary, meanwhile, missed out with a broken bone, sustained in United's Champions League semi-final against Bayer Leverkusen.

Beckham's last-gasp goal against Greece in October 2001 had ensured England's automatic qualification, and he performed similar heroics in the World Cup itself.

The United midfielder led England to the quarter-finals – where they lost 2–1 to the eventual champions Brazil – and exorcised the ghosts of France '98 by scoring a penalty against Argentina.

But if the World Cup was woeful for Veron and for Fabien Barthez (both were knocked out in the first round) then nobody could rival Roy Keane for negative publicity. The United captain was sent home before a ball had even been kicked, following a row with the Republic of Ireland manager Mick McCarthy.

David Beckham almost missed the World Cup after famously breaking a metatarsal bone.

"When we got to Saipan (Korea) and I saw the facilities, saw how badly organized everything was and saw how poorly we were preparing for the greatest tournament in the world, I decided I'd had enough," said Keane. "Only after I'd spoken to Alex Ferguson and close friends and family did I initially change my mind. Ferguson told me to stick it out." Keane said McCarthy then accused of him being disloyal and a liar, in front of his international team-mates. It was the straw that broke the camel's back and sparked one of the biggest sports news stories of the summer.

"I owed it to myself to respond. I was angry. I told him that as a player, as a manager and as a person, I have no respect for him. I don't regret what I said, but at the same time I agree that Mick had to send me home. A player cannot speak to a manager like that and continue to work under him."

Fortunately, Keane continued to work under Sir Alex Ferguson. With his international career on hold, Roy could now commit himself 110 per cent to United, with whom he had signed a new four-year contract in March 2002. Roy Keane wasn't the only big-name star to sign a lucrative contract with Manchester United in 2002. In May, David Beckham followed his manager's lead and ended months of speculation by putting pen to paper on a new deal.

He took the opportunity to pay tribute to the supporters, saying: "The Manchester United fans are part of my family and they have supported me through all the highs and lows of my career at Old Trafford. I know I owe them a big thank you and if anything the bond between myself and the club and the fans is stronger than ever before. I feel very lucky and privileged to be part of such a fantastic club."

It seems that Beckham's buzz about life at Old Trafford rubbed off on Rio Ferdinand, his England team-mate. By the end of the 2002 World Cup Finals, he was being strongly linked with a move from Leeds to Manchester. Ferdinand to Old Trafford was the only major transfer story the newspapers seemed to be interested in; as it turned out, it was the only major transfer that United completed in the 2002 close season. They also signed a Spanish goalkeeper, Ricardo from Valladolid, but his £1.5 million move was low-key and cut-price compared to United's outlay on Ferdinand.

Rio's excellent performances for England at the World Cup had pushed his price up, to the point that the Yorkshire club pocketed £30 million for the sale of their central defender. The transfer fee beat the previous British record, set by United the previous summer when they signed Veron.

Ferdinand missed the first three games of the season with an injury, eventually making his U debut in the fourth fixture – the 5–0 drubbing Zalaegerszeg in the second leg of a UEFA Champion League qualifier.

After finishing third in the Premiership, the Reds were obliged to play in the preliminary round at the outset of 2002–03. It was a humbling experience for them, especially when they lost the first leg to Zalaegerszeg, 0–1 in Hungary. United experienced another uncomfortable away trip in the first group phase, losing 0–3 to Israeli side Maccabi Haifa. Fortunately, the result was academic; the Reds were already through after winning their opening four games against Haifa, Olympiakos (home and away) and Bayer Leverkusen.

The home thrashing of Haifa was historic for Diego Forlan, the striker signed in January 2002 for £7.5 million from Independiente (Argentina). In his 27th appearance, Forlan finally scored his first goal for United, albeit from the penalty spot and with only a minute to spare! The floodgates didn't quite open but Diego did claim cult hero status by scoring two goals against United's arch-enemies Liverpool at Anfield (2–1). A few more significant goals would follow, including the match-winners in two separate games against Chelsea at Old Trafford (1–0 League Cup, 2–1 Premiership).

If strikers are assessed by the goals they score, then goalkeepers are gauged on the goals they concede. Roy Carroll seemingly did his cause no harm in August 2002 by allowing just four shots to beat him in the first five games. Signed in July 2001 from Wigan Athletic, the Northern Ireland goalkeeper was limited to just ten appearances in his first term at Old Trafford. But Carroll started the 2002–03 season in the number one spot, while the holder of the number one shirt, Fabien Barthez, recovered from a hip injury.

Quality cover and competition for places; spread over two seasons, the signings of Van Nistelrooy, Veron, Blanc and Carroll, Forlan, Ferdinand and Ricardo had given Sir Alex the resources he needed to challenge for the top honours once again. But as impressive and expensive as the United payroll now was, there was still one club on the Continent that could outspend them. Real Madrid had assembled a squad that would previously have been the stuff of fantasy football competitions. France's Zinedine Zidane (£45.62m), Portugal's Luis Figo (£37m) and Brazil's Ronaldo (£28.49m) were all in the Real team that faced Manchester United in the 2002–03 Champions League quarter-finals.

It was a mouth-watering draw – the Kings of Spain against the

Princes of England. And fortunately – for the neutrals – the star players lived up to their price tags and the pre-match hype. Ronaldo, in particular, was awesome, destroying the Reds in the second leg with a world-class hat-trick. The Brazilian became one of the few opposition players to receive a standing ovation from the Old Trafford faithful. The home fans even chorused, "Fergie, Fergie sign him up!" as Ronaldo left the field after 67 minutes, with his work done and the tie all but dusted.

Real Madrid were leading 3–2, and 6–3 on aggregate, when Ronaldo was replaced by Santiago Solari. But if winning the tie and a place in the semi-finals was beyond United, victory on the night was still within reach. And thanks to a substitute scoring twice, they achieved just that, winning 4–3 in front of 66,708 fans inside Old Trafford and millions more watching on TV.

Step forward Ole Gunnar Solskjaer? No. On this occasion, United's European super-sub was none other than David Beckham, the man at the centre of intense transfer speculation. His omission from Sir Alex Ferguson's starting line-up only fanned the flames; the most persistent rumour suggested Beckham would sign for Real Madrid in the summer.

The following morning, the UK's tabloid newspapers devoted most of their back pages to a report on the "incredible, wonderful, glorious" match (*Daily Mirror*). But some sports editors still reserved space for the Beckham saga.

"David Beckham stood in the centre of Old Trafford, Zinedine Zidane's shirt tucked proudly in his shorts, and applauded a mesmerized, capacity audience. Or was Beckham's pointed gesture a goodbye wave from the humiliated England captain? For this extraordinary, pulsating quarter-final was the night United went out of the Champions League and Beckham, possibly, out of Manchester." (Brian Woolnough, *Daily Star*).

The intense speculation about Beckham's future was ignited by an incident on February 15, after United had faced their domestic arch-rivals Arsenal in a bad-tempered FA Cup match at Old Trafford. Losing the match 2–0 was bad enough for the Reds, particularly for Ryan Giggs who extraordinarily missed an open goal when the scores were still level. (Karma, perhaps, for his extraordinary FA Cup goal against Arsenal in 1999.) But worse was to follow. Two days later, *The Sun* newspaper broke the story that Beckham had been injured in the United dressing room.

"David Beckham needed stitches in a head wound after Sir Alex Ferguson kicked a football boot in his face during an amazing dressing room bust-up. Becks, 27, needed two stitches after the Manchester United manager exploded at his players for losing to Arsenal in the FA Cup fifth round…

"There is no suggestion Sir Alex, 61, meant to hurt Beckham… (But) the incident immediately created fears of a major rift between the midfielder and his manager which could wreck United's season." (Neil Custis, *The Sun*).

The manager swiftly denied the rift, referring to the flying boot incident as "a freak occurrence" that he could not repeat if he "tried a hundred, a million times to do it again." And contrary to the conjecture in certain newspapers, United's season wasn't wrecked by the unfortunate episode. If anything, the team was galvanized as they sheltered together from the media storm.

The League Cup was lowest on United's list of priorities, so losing the final 2–0 to Liverpool was hardly a hammer blow. And while it's heartbreaking to bow out of the Champions League, few teams in the world could have lived with Real Madrid on the form they showed in the quarter-finals.

Defeats in the three cup competitions left the Reds with the Premiership to play for. And how they played! From the moment Mikael Silvestre scored a late winner against Leeds on 5 March (2–1), United went on a title-winning run that saw them win nine of their last ten Premiership matches. Highlights included Ruud Van Nistelrooy's solo goal – one of his three – against Fulham (3–0), Ole Gunnar Solskjaer scoring the fourth in a demolition of Liverpool (4–0) and Paul Scholes netting a hat-trick at Newcastle (6–2).

Ironically, it was the other Premiership match – the one that United didn't win – which gave them the upper hand in the title race. On Wednesday 16 April 2003, they travelled to Highbury. It was Arsenal's chance to go back to the top on goal difference, having recently slipped to their fifth league defeat of the season, 0–2 at Blackburn (their fourth was 0–2 at United in December).

Below: Beckham plays against Zidane of Real Madrid – soon to become his team-mate. **Opposite page: Farewell?** David applauds the United faithful.

2003

254

United drew first blood midway through the first half at Highbury when Ruud van Nistelrooy cut inside from the left flank, raced towards goal and slotted the ball low into the net with several Arsenal defenders trailing in his wake. By half-time, the situation looked even better for Sir Alex Ferguson's side; not only were they leading 1–0, but the Gunners had been forced to withdraw their inspirational captain Patrick Vieira with a knee injury.

However, the tide dramatically turned within 18 minutes of the restart as Ashley Cole equalized and then Thierry Henry, from a dubious position, put the Gunners 2–1 up. Had Arsenal defended that lead for more than a minute, the match and the title race might have ended very differently. But before some of the home fans could finish their celebrations, Ryan Giggs grabbed one of the most important goals of his career for the away team.

Ole Gunnar Solskjaer, playing on the right wing in preference to substitute David Beckham, whipped in a cross and Giggs decisively headed it home to make the final score 2–2. The drama didn't end there; Solskjaer was later on the receiving end of Sol Campbell's elbow. The England defender was dismissed and suspended from playing in Arsenal's last three league games.

Prior results rendered two of those matches academic. With Campbell still in the side, the Gunners were held 2–2 at Bolton after leading 2–0. The next day, United won 2–0 at Tottenham thanks to Scholes and Van Nistelrooy.

Then came the decisive weekend. On Saturday 3 May, the Reds thrashed Charlton 4–1, courtesy of another Van Nistelrooy hat-trick and what proved to be David Beckham's last goal for United at Old Trafford. On Sunday 4 May, Sir Alex and his players could only sit back and enjoy the televised scenes from Highbury where Leeds beat Arsenal, now minus Campbell, 3–2.

Manchester United were champions – again! Sir Alex Ferguson described the eighth Premiership title as his team's "greatest achievement," given the number of points they had trailed Arsenal by at one stage in the race.

Sir Alex added, "They have shown great determination, perseverance and ability. I think they are the qualities that have won the title for us."

The Reds collected the Premiership trophy at Everton's Goodison Park, after wrapping up the campaign with another victory (2–1). Beckham scored, with a superb free-kick, and as he trooped off the field with another medal around his neck, it seemed the perfect end to his 12-year United career.

The end was duly confirmed at 9pm on Tuesday 17 June. In a statement, United confirmed they had "reached agreement for the transfer of David Beckham to Real Madrid for a fee of €35 million (approximately £25m)."

United chief executive Peter Kenyon commented: "While we are sad to see David go after so many great years at Old Trafford, we believe this is a good deal for the club. We now look forward to building on the success of our championship title."

Djemba-Djemba makes his debut in the Community Shield against Arsenal.

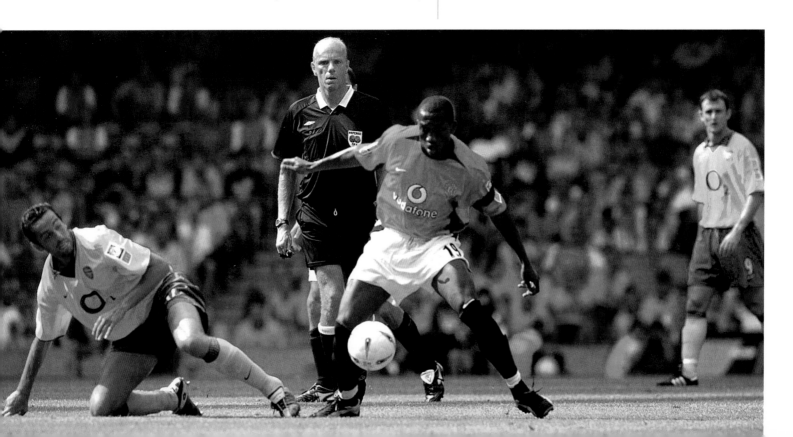

There was considerable building work at United during the summer of 2003. Not where the stadium was concerned – Old Trafford had just proved it was capable of hosting one of the biggest games in world football, the 2003 Champions League Final (AC Milan defeated Juventus on penalties).

The restructuring work, in fact, took place within the club's personnel. In United's busiest close season since 1996, five first-team players were recruited and three were allowed to leave.

Many fans thought Beckham's departure would enable Juan Sebastian Veron to at last express his creative qualities in United's midfield. Instead, the Argentine star was sold to Chelsea for £15m (representing a loss of £13.1m).

The other senior player to depart was David May; the central defender joined Burnley on a free transfer, following an injury-blighted few years.

The farewells were not confined to the playing staff, however. Sir Alex Ferguson's talented assistant, Carlos Queiroz, followed Beckham to Real Madrid where he replaced Vicente Del Bosque as manager. (Del Bosque's 'crime' was failing to retain the Champions League in 2003!)

Ferguson accepted the exit of his influential coach after just one season, saying: "This is a wonderful opportunity for Carlos, too big a chance to turn down. We won't be in a rush to appoint a new coach. I have been very satisfied with the job that Mike Phelan has been doing."

Another shock lay just around the corner. The 2003–04 season was barely underway when, on September 8, Kenyon quit his high-profile post as United's chief executive to take on a similar role at Chelsea. The London club was shaping up to be a major threat, following the arrival of a wealthy new owner, oil billionaire Roman Abramovich. The Russian's investment enabled Chelsea to sign eleven new players during the summer of 2003 at a total cost of £111.25 million (and Charlton's Scott Parker followed in January 2004 for £10 million).

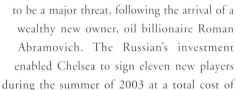

Cynics suggested a new-look team that was thrown together like Chelsea's was doomed to fail. Certainly, it wasn't the way that United had achieved success under Sir Alex Ferguson, who generally introduces new players to his team in ones, twos or threes. That was still the case at the dawn of 2003–04; Ferguson may have made five summer signings, but only one or two were expected to establish themselves in the line-up straightaway.

Tim Howard, the American goalkeeper signed for £2.3 million from New York/New Jersey Metrostars, was the only United new boy who kicked off the season's curtain-raiser – the 2003 Community Shield match against Arsenal at the Millennium Stadium. However, Cameroon international Eric Djemba-Djemba, signed for £3.5 million from French club Nantes, eventually made his debut in the second half as a substitute for Nicky Butt.

It proved to be a good first day at the office for all the United boys, new and old. Silvestre opened the scoring and although Henry beat Howard with a free-kick equalizer, the American saved two spot-kicks from Pires and Van Bronckhorst as the Reds won the Shield 4–3 on penalties. The 2003–04 season had started for United as they hoped it would end – with silverware.

Rio Ferdinand, seen here leaping above Everton's Kevin Campbell, was sorely missed by Manchester United in the second half of the 2003–04 season.

The next player to make his debut was Cristiano Ronaldo, the Portuguese teenager signed for £12.24m from Sporting Lisbon. His close control and dribbling skills created a wave of excitement when he helped United to beat Bolton 4-0 in the first Premiership game of the season. "There's only one Ronaldo," sang the Stretford End, after witnessing one of the most memorable debuts in a red shirt.

Ronaldo was introduced at the same press conference as another new acquisition – Kleberson, from Atletico Paranaense in Brazil. Despite being the third World Cup winner to join United in as many years, he didn't cost the earth – just £5.93 million in total. Ferguson said his arrival had paved the way for Juan Sebastian Veron's departure; the fans hoped Kleberson would prove more successful.

Completing the quintet of senior summer signings was Sunderland striker David Bellion, born in the suburbs of Paris and educated at the same football academy (Cannes) as Patrick Vieira and Zinedine Zidane.

Ferguson again used his lowest-priority competition to blood some new talent – not just the new signings but also the latest academy graduates – including Hertfordshire-born winger Chris Eagles and the future Scotland captain, midfielder Darren Fletcher.

The youthful United's adventure sadly ended at the second hurdle. After winning a five-goal thriller at Leeds (Djemba-Djemba scored in the 119th minute!), the Reds were knocked out of the Carling Cup away to West Brom (0–2), despite second-choice goalkeeper Roy Carroll saving a penalty.

Fabien Barthez was by now Fergie's third-choice shot-stopper after falling out of favour. The Frenchman failed to make an appearance in 2003–04 – at least for United anyway. He joined Marseille, initially on loan and then permanently, after helping them to beat Liverpool and Newcastle en route to losing the UEFA Cup Final.

With Barthez off the wage bill, United could afford to make another dip into the transfer market in January 2004. They signed Fulham's French striker Louis Saha at a total cost of £12.825 million. For the first time in United's history of conducting transfers, the press release announcing the deal broke down the total fee. It stated that £11.5m was payable to Fulham, £0.575m was the levy payable to the Premier League and £0.75m was payable to agents.

The disclosure of the agents' fee was particularly significant as the club's major shareholders, JP McManus and John Magnier, had recently expressed concerns about the role of agents in United's negotiations. In response, new chief executive David Gill and his board not only disclosed the details of the Saha deal; they also conducted an internal review into the club's transfers between January 2001 and January 2004. The review found that all payments to clubs and agents had been made in accordance with the rules.

Five days after announcing the Saha deal, Gill made another major signing. Sir Alex Ferguson signed a new contract on 28 January 2004; effective from 30 June 2005, it would be an open-ended one-year rolling contract. Gill said: "Sir Alex considers this arrangement to offer distinct advantages over a long and fixed-term contract in that he feels it will keep him even more motivated every season and hungry for more success over the future years."

"We believe it [the rolling contract] reflects our total confidence in the manager and also reduces speculation about his possible retirement date." The announcement of Ferguson's new contract also countered any speculation that his job was imminently under threat. For months, he had been embroiled in a row with the afore-mentioned Magnier over the ownership of a successful racehorse, Rock of Gibraltar. Some United fans and conspiracy theorists feared Magnier would mount a takeover bid for the club and subsequently sack Ferguson. But the bid never materialized, the gentlemen settled their dispute, and life at United returned to normal. Well, relatively normal. The team's form was not at its usual high standards in the latter part of the 2003–04 season and the Reds suffered some damaging results.

FC Porto took United's place in the Champions League quarter-finals after beating them 2–1 in Portugal and scoring a dramatic late equalizer in the second leg at Old Trafford (1–1). Meanwhile, league losses away to Wolves, Manchester City, Blackburn and Portsmouth, plus home defeats by Middlesbrough and Liverpool saw United finish outside the top two again. Chelsea were second; United were third, 15 points adrift of Arsenal who claimed the title without losing a game.

In an end-of-season brochure for the club's One United members, Ferguson commented: "Any serious look at our season will show you that there was little wrong before Christmas and that it was only in the New Year that we began to lose our way. What was the difference between the two halves of the season? Simply the blow of losing Rio Ferdinand, compounded by a run of injuries and suspensions that wreaked havoc with our defensive stability."

The Ferdinand situation was certainly a body blow for both club and player. Rio's failure to attend a routine drugs test at United's training ground on 23 September 2003 eventually led to him being fined £50,000 by the FA and suspended for eight months from 20 January 2004.

Not only did Rio miss Euro 2004 with England, he also missed out on his second trophy with the Reds – the 2004 FA Cup. But with Ferguson standing by Ferdinand and signing exciting new players like Alan Smith (from Leeds) and Liam Miller (from Celtic), Manchester United could surely look forward to more success in the future.

Ronaldo made a big impression in his first season at Manchester United.

2004

22 MAY 2004, MILLENNIUM STADIUM, WALES

Roy Keane holds up an old friend – the FA Cup.

Manchester United collected their record eleventh FA Cup at the end of a season that was otherwise blighted by disappointing results in the Premiership and UEFA Champions League.

The final itself was something of a formality, a one-sided mismatch between the recently deposed Premiership champions and Millwall, an average Division One side that had failed to even reach the promotion play-offs.

Not that anyone should have begrudged Millwall their big day out at the Millennium Stadium. Finalists are always there on merit; it certainly wasn't the fault of player-manager Dennis Wise that his team had avoided playing a Premiership side in every one of their five previous rounds.

The closest Millwall came to facing a big gun was playing Sunderland in the semi-final at Old Trafford; Mick McCarthy's side had been relegated from the top flight only twelve months

previously. They had knocked out one Premiership club, Birmingham, in the same fifth round that saw United win the all-Manchester tie against City 4–2, Arsenal beat 2000 winners Chelsea 2–1 and Portsmouth shock 2001 winners Liverpool with a 1–0 win in a replay.

Arsenal, holders for the past two years, then thrashed Portsmouth 5–1 at Fratton Park in the quarter-final, while United came back from 1–0 down to see off Fulham 2–1. The neutrals hoped the arch-rivals would be kept apart in the semi-final draw and meet in the mother of all finals. It wasn't to be, and so United faced favourites Arsenal with the pundits predicting that the winners of their match would march on to lift the trophy in Cardiff.

The semi-final at Villa Park opened with Arsenal in the ascendancy; the Reds needed Roy Carroll to make two great saves inside the first four minutes to thwart Dennis Bergkamp and then

FA CUP FINAL

MANCHESTER UNITED (1) 3 MILLWALL (0) 0

United scorers Ronaldo and Van Nistelrooy celebrate the win.

Kolo Toure, who almost converted the rebound when Edu's free-kick struck the United crossbar.

Such moments can turn big matches; after seeing the Gunners create and miss the best chances for half an hour, Sir Alex Ferguson's men scored with one of their own. Created by Giggs, finished by Scholes, the 32nd minute strike was enough to settle the semi-final in United's favour. The Reds went through to their sixteenth final, spoiling Arsenal's sole ownership of that particular record. They also wrecked Arsenal's hopes of winning the Treble – the Premiership champions elect also bowed out of Europe a few days later.

With the hard work of beating Arsenal, Manchester City, Fulham, Aston Villa and Northampton(!) behind them, United were odds-on favourites to complete the easier task of beating Millwall in the Millennium Stadium. Especially with Ruud van Nistelrooy now back in the starting line-up – after missing the semi-final with injury, the Dutchman was hotly tipped to score the first hat-trick in a final since Stan Mortensen netted three in 1953.

The Reds' number ten was denied this piece of history by Darren Ward, the Millwall defender who blocked his shot in the 86th minute. Ruud had reached the brink of it only five minutes earlier, tapping in his second goal after a great run and perfect ball from Giggs. His first strike of the final – a penalty – came in the 65th minute when the same provider was brought down in the box by David Livermore's desperate challenge.

Much of Millwall's defending was desperate and they were

Ronaldo celebrates his opening goal with Wes Brown.

grateful to their goalkeeper and to Ward (yes, him again) for keeping United out for 44 minutes. Andy Marshall produced a world-class save to push Roy Keane's firecracker over the bar; Ward was on hand to head the ball off the line when Ronaldo's shot squirmed through Marshall's grasp.

Neither Millwall man could stop Ronaldo's last attack of the half, however. The Portuguese youngster ghosted in at the far post to head home from Gary Neville's perfect right-wing cross and that, effectively, was it – game, set and match to United. They may have added two more after the break but with Millwall hardly managing a shot all afternoon, that opening goal from the real man-of-the match Ronaldo (Ruud received the official award) was enough to give United their silver lining at the end of a cloudy season.

Manchester United (manager Sir Alex Ferguson): Howard (sub Carroll 84), Neville G., Brown, Silvestre, O'Shea, Ronaldo (sub Solskjaer 84), Fletcher (sub Butt 84), Keane, Giggs, Scholes, Van Nistelrooy. Scorers: Ronaldo 44, Van Nistelrooy 65 pen., 80.

Millwall (player–manager Dennis Wise): Marshall, Elliott, Lawrence, Ward, Ryan (sub Cogan 75), Wise (sub Weston 89), Ifill, Livermore, Cahill, Sweeney, Harris (sub McCammon 75).

Attendance: 71,350

PAUL SCHOLES

MIDFIELDER (MANCHESTER UNITED 1991–)

Some of the best crowd songs in football are the simplest ones, those that describe their subject's special talent succinctly. For example, "Giggs… Giggs will tear you apart, again." Another is, "Paul Scholes, he scores goals." And that has certainly been true of the former United trainee, since the day in September 1994 when he netted twice on his first team debut. United actually lost the match, 3–2 at Ipswich Town, but this was hardly the norm; usually when Scholes scores, the Reds benefit to the tune of three more points or a place in the next round of a competition.

One of the best examples of this was the 2004 FA Cup semi-final when Scholes scored the only goal of a crucial match against Arsenal. Another is the 1999 Champions League quarter-final in Milan; Scholes took the wind out of Inter's sails, when they were threatening to level the tie on aggregate.

Paul's best ever season for goals – so far – was in 2002–03 when he made a significant contribution to United winning the title. He scored twenty in all competitions, including a burst of six goals in six league games when the campaign was nearing its thrilling climax. He fired in a magnificent hat-trick against Newcastle at St James Park, a 6–2 win that really underlined United's determination to catch Arsenal and snatch the championship.

Scholes is also the proud owner of a Wembley match-ball, after scoring a hat-trick there for England against Poland in March 1999. The feat forced him to undertake one of his least favourite tasks – talking to the media. "That was the best feeling I've had in football," said Scholes at the time.

"I have scored some important goals for United in the Champions League, but that was something else. To come off with that match-ball under my arm and have all the (England) fans cheering for me felt great."

England managers from Glenn Hoddle, who capped him first, to Sven-Goran Eriksson have regarded Scholes, quite rightly, as one of the country's key players. Peers and TV pundits have done the same – former Liverpool captain and now BBC summarizer Alan Hansen once said: "Scholes is the only English player with world-class technical ability. He is superb."

Hansen's words seem ironic when you recall his statement about United at the start of the 1995–96 season, "You'll never win anything with kids." He was referring to the United team which featured Scholes, Butt and Beckham, Ferguson's choice of young replacements for Hughes, Ince and Kanchelskis.

With Cantona as their inspirational skipper, Scholes and co proved Hansen and other critics wrong. They won United's second League and FA Cup Double at the end of the 1995–96 season, and later went on to achieve the unprecedented Treble in 1999. Scholes scored in the FA Cup Final that year but missed the European Cup Final in Barcelona through suspension. To finally play in and win a Champions League Final is just one of the goals which continues to drive Scholes in the peak years of his United career.

Paul Scholes has been a firm favourite with United fans for many years.

RUUD VAN NISTELROOY
FORWARD (MANCHESTER UNITED 2001–)

"Van The Man." "Van-tastic." "Reds in Ruud health." Ruud van Nistelrooy's name and goal-scoring ability have been gifts for the headline writers on Britain's national newspapers since his United debut in August 2001.

But before all the back-page platitudes, we had headlines of a different kind where Ruud was concerned. "Van on the road to recovery" would have told the story of the striker's fight back to fitness after a knee injury that threatened to wreck not only his dream move to Manchester but his entire career. It occurred at the worst possible time, towards the end of 1999–2000 when he was originally supposed to have signed for the Reds from PSV Eindhoven. United even hosted a press conference at Old Trafford in his honour; Ruud's chair remained empty when his medical revealed a problem.

Ruud returned to Holland and patiently went through the rehabilitation process while United pushed towards their third consecutive title in 2000–01 with their existing strike-force of any two from Andy Cole, Ole Gunnar Solskjaer, Teddy Sheringham and Dwight Yorke.

When Ruud recovered and joined United for a then record transfer fee of £19 million, he proved to be well, well worth the wait. Teddy took the hint and left for Tottenham; Andy Cole soon followed him through the exit door. Dwight dug his heels in, in the hope that he could partner the new man at Old Trafford. But with Ferguson playing a new system, especially in Europe, there was really only room for one striker – and what a striker!

Van Nistelrooy netted 36 goals in all competitions during 2001–02. In December and January, he set a new Premiership record by scoring in eight consecutive league games – including a 6–1 thrashing of Southampton on 22 December, in which he claimed his first United hat-trick. The perfect Christmas present! Ruud in fact scored in fourteen consecutive league and cup matches; early in the New Year, he was the two-goal hero as the Reds came back from 2–0 down to beat Aston Villa in the FA Cup.

It was a crying shame that his first season's efforts went unrewarded in terms of trophies and medals. The closest Ruud came to silverware in 2001–02 was when he scored in the Champions League semi-final against Bayer Leverkusen, but the Germans won on the away goals rule.

The disappointment of missing out only made the Dutchman more determined in his second campaign. This time he grabbed 44 goals, including 15 in his last ten matches. And although the European, FA and League Cups again proved elusive, the Premiership trophy was brought home to Old Trafford on the back of another great scoring run by Ruud. This run continued into the first two matches of 2003–04, resulting in a new record for United as well as the Premiership – Ruud's goals in ten successive games beat the standard of eight set by the late Liam Whelan in the 1950s.

The 2003–04 season also ended with silverware – the FA Cup – after Van Nistelrooy scored twice against Millwall in the final. Ruud also rounded off his third term with a warning for any club wanting to lure him away. Referring to his extended contract, due to expire in June 2008, he said:

"I'm now sentenced for life with United – but that is not a punishment. The manager is building a new team and I trust him. I don't need to go to Spain or another country. When I stop playing, I will quit the game for good and never come back into football. I will finish my career in Manchester."

Van Nistelrooy is one of the most feared strikers in the game.

APPENDIX

EUROPEAN TRIUMPHS, DOMESTIC LEAGUE CHAMPIONSHIPS, MAJOR CUP VICTORIES AT HOME AND ABROAD HAVE HELPED TO MAKE MANCHESTER UNITED ONE OF THE MOST SUCCESSFUL AND POPULAR FOOTBALL CLUBS IN THE WORLD. DETAILED ON THE FOLLOWING PAGES ARE THE CLUB'S TOP HONOURS, RECORD IN LEAGUE FOOTBALL AND THE TEAM LINE-UPS FOR EVERY MAJOR COMPETITIVE MATCH INCLUDING EUROPEAN FINALS, FA CUP FINALS, FOOTBALL LEAGUE CUP FINALS AND FA CHARITY SHIELD. ALL THE GREAT NAMES AND GREAT GAMES FROM MANCHESTER UNITED'S FASCINATING HISTORY ARE LISTED HERE FOR EASY REFERENCE.

THE MAJOR HONOURS

EUROPEAN CHAMPION CLUBS' CUP
Winners: 1968, 1999

EUROPEAN CUP-WINNERS' CUP
Winners: 1991

FA PREMIER LEAGUE
Champions: 1993, 1994, 1996, 1997, 1999, 2000, 2001, 2003

FOOTBALL LEAGUE DIVISION ONE
Champions: 1908, 1911, 1952, 1956, 1957, 1965, 1967

FA CHALLENGE CUP
Winners: 1909, 1948, 1963, 1977, 1983, 1985, 1990, 1994, 1996, 1999, 2004

FOOTBALL LEAGUE CUP
Winners: 1992

INTER-CONTINENTAL CUP
Winners: 1999

UEFA SUPER CUP
Winners: 1991

FA CHARITY SHIELD
Winners: 1908, 1911, 1952, 1956, 1957, 1965*, 1967*, 1977*, 1983, 1990*, 1993, 1994, 1996, 1997, 2003 *Joint winners

MANCHESTER UNITED'S RECORD IN THE FOOTBALL LEAGUE

Season	Div.	P	W	D	L	F	A	Pts	Pos.
1892–93	One	30	6	6	18	50	85	18	16th
1893–94	One	30	6	2	22	36	72	14	16th
1894–95	Two	30	15	8	7	78	44	38	3rd
1895–96	Two	30	15	3	12	66	57	33	6th
1896–97	Two	30	17	5	8	56	34	39	2nd
1897–98	Two	30	15	9	6	64	35	38	4th
1898–99	Two	34	19	5	10	67	43	43	4th
1899–1900	Two	34	20	4	10	63	27	44	4th
1900–01	Two	34	14	4	16	42	38	32	10th
1901–02	Two	34	11	6	17	38	53	28	15th
1902–03	Two	34	15	8	11	53	58	38	5th
1903–04	Two	34	20	8	6	65	33	48	3rd
1904–05	Two	34	24	5	5	81	30	53	3rd
1905–06	Two	38	28	6	4	90	28	62	2nd
1906–07	One	38	17	8	13	53	56	42	8th
1907–08	One	38	23	6	9	81	48	52	Champions
1908–09	One	38	15	7	16	58	68	37	13th
1909–10	One	38	19	7	12	69	61	45	5th
1910–11	One	38	22	8	8	72	40	52	Champions
1911–12	One	38	13	11	14	45	60	37	13th
1912–13	One	38	19	8	11	69	43	46	4th
1913–14	One	38	15	6	17	52	62	36	14th
1914–15	One	38	9	12	17	46	62	30	18th
1919–20	One	42	13	14	15	54	50	40	12th
1920–21	One	42	15	10	17	64	68	40	13th
1921–22	One	42	8	12	22	41	73	28	22th
1922–23	Two	42	17	14	11	51	36	48	4th
1923–24	Two	42	13	14	15	52	44	40	14th
1924–25	Two	42	23	11	8	57	23	57	2nd
1925–26	One	42	19	6	17	66	73	44	9th
1926–27	One	42	13	14	15	52	64	40	15th
1927–28	One	42	16	7	19	82	98	39	18th
1928–29	One	42	14	13	15	66	76	41	12th
1929–30	One	42	15	8	19	67	88	38	17th
1930–31	One	42	7	8	27	53	115	22	22nd
1931–32	Two	42	17	8	17	71	72	42	12th
1932–33	Two	42	15	13	14	71	68	43	6th
1933–34	Two	42	14	6	22	59	85	34	20th
1934–35	Two	42	23	4	15	76	55	50	5th
1935–36	Two	42	22	12	8	85	43	56	1st
1936–37	One	42	10	12	20	55	78	32	22nd
1937–38	Two	42	25	7	10	73	35	57	2nd
1938–39	One	42	11	16	15	57	65	38	14th
1946–47	One	42	22	12	8	95	54	56	2nd
1947–48	One	42	19	14	9	81	48	52	2nd
1948–49	One	42	21	11	10	77	44	53	2nd
1949–50	One	42	18	14	10	69	44	50	4th
1950–51	One	42	24	8	10	74	40	56	2nd
1951–52	One	42	23	11	8	95	52	57	Champions
1952–53	One	42	18	10	14	69	72	46	8th
1953–54	One	42	18	12	12	73	58	48	4th
1954–55	One	42	20	7	15	84	74	47	5th
1955–56	One	42	25	10	7	83	51	60	Champions
1956–57	One	42	28	8	6	103	54	64	Champions
1957–58	One	42	16	11	15	85	75	43	9th
1958–59	One	42	24	7	11	103	66	55	2nd
1959–60	One	42	19	7	16	102	80	45	7th
1960–61	One	42	18	9	15	88	76	45	7th
1961–62	One	42	15	9	18	72	75	39	15th
1962–63	One	42	12	10	20	67	81	34	19th
1963–64	One	42	23	7	12	90	62	53	2nd
1964–65	One	42	26	9	7	89	39	61	Champions
1965–66	One	42	18	15	9	84	59	51	4th
1966–67	One	42	24	12	6	84	45	60	Champions
1967–68	One	42	24	8	10	89	55	56	2nd
1968–69	One	42	15	12	14	57	53	42	11th
1969–70	One	42	14	17	11	66	61	45	8th
1970–71	One	42	16	11	15	65	66	43	8th
1971–72	One	42	19	10	13	69	61	48	8th
1972–73	One	42	12	13	17	44	60	37	18th
1973–74	One	42	10	12	20	48	48	32	21st
1974–75	Two	42	26	9	7	66	30	61	1st
1975–76	One	42	23	10	9	68	42	56	3rd
1976–77	One	42	18	11	13	71	62	47	6rd
1977–78	One	42	16	10	16	67	63	42	10th
1978–79	One	42	15	15	12	60	63	45	9th
1979–80	One	42	24	10	8	65	35	58	2nd
1980–81	One	42	15	18	9	51	36	48	8th
1981–82	One	42	22	12	8	59	29	78	3rd
1982–83	One	42	19	13	10	56	38	70	3rd
1983–84	One	42	20	14	8	71	41	74	4th
1984–85	One	42	22	10	10	77	47	76	4th
1985–86	One	42	22	10	10	70	36	76	4th
1986–87	One	42	14	14	14	52	45	56	11th
1987–88	One	40	23	12	5	71	38	81	2nd
1988–89	One	38	13	12	13	45	35	51	11th
1989–90	One	38	13	9	16	46	47	48	13th
1990–91	One	38	16	12	10	58	45	59	6th
1991–92	One	42	21	15	6	63	33	78	2nd
1992–93	Prem.	42	24	12	6	67	31	84	Champions
1993–94	Prem.	42	27	11	4	80	38	92	Champions
1994–95	Prem.	42	26	10	6	77	28	88	2nd
1995–96	Prem.	38	25	7	6	73	35	82	Champions
1996–97	Prem.	38	21	12	5	76	44	75	Champions
1997–98	Prem.	38	23	8	7	73	26	77	2nd
1998–99	Prem.	38	22	13	3	80	37	79	Champions
1999–2000	Prem.	38	28	7	3	97	45	91	Champions
2000–01	Prem.	38	24	8	6	79	31	80	Champions
2001–02	Prem.	38	24	5	9	87	45	77	3rd
2002–03	Prem.	38	25	8	5	74	34	83	Champions
2003–04	Prem.	38	23	6	9	64	35	75	3rd

FA CUP FINALS

Saturday, 24 April 1909
(Crystal Palace)
Manchester United 1
Bristol City 0
Moger, Stacey, Hayes, Duckworth,
Roberts, Bell, Meredith, Halse,
Turnbull J., Turnbull A., Wall
Scorer: Turnbull A.
Attendance: 71,401

Saturday, 24 April 1948
(Wembley)
Manchester United 4
Blackpool 2
Crompton, Carey, Aston, Anderson,
Chilton, Cockburn, Delaney, Morris,
Rowley, Pearson, Mitten
Scorers: Rowley 2, Pearson,
Anderson
Attendance: 99,000

Saturday, 4 May 1957
(Wembley)
Aston Villa 2
Manchester United 1
Wood, Foulkes, Byrne, Colman,
Blanchflower, Edwards, Berry,
Whelan, Taylor, Charlton, Pegg
Scorer: Taylor
Attendance: 100,000

Saturday, 3 May 1958
(Wembley)
Bolton Wanderers 2
Manchester United 0
Gregg, Foulkes, Greaves, Goodwin,
Cope, Crowther, Dawson, Taylor,
Charlton, Viollet, Webster
Attendance: 100,000

Saturday, 25 May 1963
(Wembley)
Manchester United 3
Leicester City 1
Gaskell, Dunne, Cantwell, Crerand,
Foulkes, Setters, Giles, Quixall,
Herd, Law, Charlton
Scorers: Herd 2, Law
Attendance: 100,000

Saturday, 1 May 1976 (Wembley)
Southampton 1
Manchester United 0
Stepney, Forsyth, Houston, Daly,
Greenhoff, Buchan, Coppell,
McIlroy, Pearson, Macari, Hill
Substitute: McCreery (Hill)
Attendance: 100,000

Saturday, 21 May 1977 (Wembley)
Manchester United 2
Liverpool 1
Stepney, Nicholl, Albiston, McIlroy,
Greenhoff B., Buchan, Coppell,
Greenhoff J., Pearson, Macari, Hill
Substitute: McCreery (Hill)
Scorers: Pearson, Greenhoff J.
Attendance: 100,000

Saturday, 12 May 1979 (Wembley)
Arsenal 3
Manchester United 2
Bailey, Nicholl, Albiston, McIlroy,
McQueen, Buchan, Coppell,
Greenhoff J., Jordan, Macari, Thomas
Substitute: Greenhoff B.
Scorers: McQueen, McIlroy
Attendance: 100,000

Saturday, 21 May 1983 (Wembley)
Manchester United 2
Brighton & Hove Albion 2 (aet)
Bailey, Duxbury, Albiston, Wilkins,
Moran, McQueen, Robson, Muhren,
Stapleton, Whiteside, Davies
Substitute: Grimes
Scorers: Stapleton, Wilkins
Attendance: 100,000

Thursday, 26 May 1983 replay
(Wembley)
Manchester United 4
Brighton & Hove Albion 0
Bailey, Duxbury, Albiston, Wilkins,
Moran, McQueen, Robson, Muhren,
Stapleton, Whiteside, Davies
Substitute: Grimes
Scorers: Robson 2, Muhren,
Whiteside
Attendance: 100,000

Saturday, 18 May 1985 (Wembley)
Manchester United 1
Everton 0 (aet)
Bailey, Gidman, Albiston, Whiteside,
McGrath, Moran, Robson, Strachan,
Hughes, Stapleton, Olsen
Substitute: Duxbury (Albiston)
Scorer: Whiteside
Attendance: 100,000

Saturday, 12 May 1990 (Wembley)
Manchester United 3
Crystal Palace 3 (aet)
Leighton, Ince, Martin, Bruce,
Phelan, Pallister, Robson, Webb,
McClair, Hughes, Wallace
Substitutes: Robins (Pallister),
Blackmore (Martin)
Scorers: Hughes 2, Robson
Attendance: 80,000

Thursday, 17 May 1990 replay
(Wembley)
Manchester United 1
Crystal Palace 0
Sealey, Ince, Martin, Bruce, Phelan,
Pallister, Robson, Webb, McClair,
Hughes, Wallace
Substitutes: Robins, Blackmore
Scorer: Martin
Attendance: 80,000

Saturday, 14 May 1994 (Wembley)
Manchester United 4
Chelsea 0
Schmeichel, Parker, Irwin, Bruce,
Kanchelskis, Pallister, Cantona,
Ince, Keane, Hughes, Giggs
Substitutes: Sharpe (Irwin), McClair
(Kanchelskis), Walsh
Scorers: Cantona 2 pens, Hughes,
McClair
Attendance: 79,634

Saturday, 20 May 1995 (Wembley)
Everton 1
Manchester United 0
Schmeichel, Neville G., Irwin,
Bruce, Sharpe, Pallister, Butt, Ince,
McClair, Hughes, Keane
Substitutes: Giggs (Bruce), Scholes
(Sharpe), Walsh
Attendance: 79,592

Saturday, 11 May 1996 (Wembley)
Manchester United 1
Liverpool 0
Schmeichel, Neville P., Irwin, May,
Beckham, Pallister, Cantona, Butt,
Cole, Keane, Giggs
Substitutes: Sharpe, Neville G.
(Beckham), Scholes (Cole)
Scorer: Cantona
Attendance: 79,007

Saturday, 22 May 1999 (Wembley)
Manchester United 2
Newcastle United 0
Schmeichel, Neville G., Neville P.,
May, Johnsen, Keane, Beckham,
Scholes, Cole, Solskjaer, Giggs
Substitutes: Stam (Scholes),
Sheringham (Keane), Blomqvist,
Van der Gouw, Yorke (Cole)
Scorers: Sheringham, Scholes
Attendance: 79,101

Saturday, 22 May 2004 (Millennium
Stadium, Cardiff)
Manchester United 3
Millwall 0
Howard, Neville, G., Brown,
Silvestre, O'Shea, Ronaldo,
Fletcher, Keane, Giggs, Scholes,
van Nistelrooy.
Substitutes: Carroll (Howard), Phil
Neville, Djemba-Djemba, Butt
(Flecher), Solskjaer (Ronaldo)
Scorers: Ronaldo, van Nistelrooy 2
Attendance: 71,350

FOOTBALL LEAGUE CUP FINALS

Saturday, 26 March 1983 (Wembley)
Liverpool 2
Manchester United 1
Bailey, Duxbury, Albiston, Moses,
Moran, McQueen, Wilkins, Muhren,
Stapleton, Whiteside, Coppell
Substitute: Macari (Moran)
Scorer: Whiteside
Attendance: 100,000

Sunday, 21 April 1991 (Wembley)
Sheffield Wednesday 1

Manchester United 0
Sealey, Irwin, Blackmore, Bruce,
Webb, Pallister, Robson, Ince,
McClair, Hughes, Sharpe
Substitutes: Donaghy, Phelan (Webb)
Attendance: 77,612

Sunday, 12 April 1992 (Wembley)

Manchester United 1
Nottingham Forest 0
Schmeichel, Parker, Irwin, Bruce,
Phelan, Pallister, Kanchelskis, Ince,
McClair, Hughes, Giggs

Substitutes: Webb, Sharpe (Kanchelskis)
Scorer: McClair
Attendance: 76,810

Sunday, 2 March 2003
(Millennium Stadium, Cardiff)
Liverpool 2
Manchester United 0
Barthez, G. Neville, Brown,
Ferdinand, Silvestre, Beckham,
Keane, Veron, Giggs, van
Nistelrooy, Scholes.
Substitutes: Carroll, P Neville, Butt,

O'Shea, Solskjaer (Brown).
Attendance: 74,500

Sunday, 27 March 1994
(Wembley) **Aston Villa 3**
Manchester United 1
Sealey, Parker, Irwin, Bruce,
Kanchelskis, Pallister, Cantona,
Ince, Keane, Hughes, Giggs
Substitutes: Sharpe, McClair
(Bruce), Walsh
Scorer: Hughes
Attendance: 77,231

FA CHARITY SHIELD

Monday, 27 April 1908
(Stamford Bridge)
Manchester United 1
Queen's Park Rangers 1
Moger, Stacey, Burgess, Duckworth,
Roberts, Bell, Meredith, Bannister,
Turnbull J., Turnbull A., Wall
Scorer: Meredith
Attendance: 6,000

Saturday, 29 August 1908
(Stamford Bridge)
Manchester United 4
Queen's Park Rangers 0
Moger, Stacey, Burgess,
Duckworth, Roberts, Bell, Meredith,
Bannister, Turnbull J., Picken, Wall
Scorers: Turnbull J. 3, Wall
Attendance: 60,000

Monday, 25 September 1911
(Stamford Bridge)
Manchester United 8
Swindon Town 4
Edmonds, Hofton, Stacey,
Duckworth, Roberts, Bell, Meredith,
Hamill, Halse, Turnbull, Wall
Scorers: Halse 6, Turnbull, Wall
Attendance: 10,000

Wednesday, 6 October 1948
(Arsenal Stadium)
Arsenal 4
Manchester United 3
Crompton, Carey, Aston, Anderson,
Chilton, Warner, Delaney, Morris,
Burke, Rowley, Mitten
Scorers: Burke, Rowley, Smith (og)
Attendance: 31,000

Wednesday, 24 September 1952
(Old Trafford)
Manchester United 4
Newcastle United 2
Wood, McNulty, Aston, Carey,
Chilton, Gibson, Berry, Downie,
Rowley, Pearson, Byrne
Scorers: Rowley 2, Downie, Byrne
Attendance: 11,381

Wednesday, 24 October 1956
(Maine Road)
Manchester United 1
Manchester City 0
Wood, Foulkes, Byrne, Colman,
Jones, Edwards, Berry, Whelan,

Taylor, Viollet, Pegg
Substitute: Gaskell (Wood)
Scorer: Viollet
Attendance: 30,495

Tuesday, 22 October 1957
(Old Trafford)
Manchester United 4
Aston Villa 0
Wood, Foulkes, Byrne, Goodwin,
Blanchflower, Edwards, Berry,
Whelan, Taylor, Viollet, Pegg
Scorers: Taylor 3, Berry
Attendance: 27,923

Saturday, 17 August 1963
(Goodison Park)
Everton 4
Manchester United 0
Gaskell, Dunne, Cantwell, Crerand,
Foulkes, Setters, Giles, Quixall,
Herd, Law, Charlton
Attendance: 54,840

Saturday, 14 August 1965
(Old Trafford)
Manchester United 2
Liverpool 2
Dunne P., Brennan, Dunne A.,
Crerand, Cantwell, Stiles, Best,
Charlton, Herd, Law, Aston
Substitute: Anderson (Best)
Scorers: Best, Herd
Attendance: 48,502

Saturday, 12 August 1967
(Old Trafford)
Manchester United 3
Tottenham Hotspur 3
Stepney, Brennan, Dunne, Crerand,
Foulkes, Stiles, Best, Kidd,
Charlton, Law, Aston
Scorers: Charlton 2, Law
Attendance: 54,106

Saturday, 13 August 1977 (Wembley)
Manchester United 0
Liverpool 0
Stepney, Nicholl, Albiston, McIlroy,
Greenhoff B., Buchan, Coppell,
Greenhoff J., Pearson, Macari, Hill
Substitute: McCreery (Greenhoff J.)
Attendance: 82,000

Saturday, 20 August 1983 (Wembley)
Manchester United 2
Liverpool 0
Bailey, Duxbury, Albiston, Wilkins,
Moran, McQueen, Robson, Muhren,
Stapleton, Whiteside, Graham
Substitute: Gidman (Muhren)
Scorer: Robson 2
Attendance: 92,000

Saturday, 10 August 1985 (Wembley)
Everton 2
Manchester United 0
Bailey, Gidman, Albiston, Whiteside,
McGrath, Hogg, Robson, Duxbury,
Hughes, Stapleton, Olsen
Substitute: Moses (Duxbury)
Attendance: 82,000

Saturday, 7 August 1993 (Wembley)
Manchester United 1
Arsenal 1
Schmeichel, Parker, Irwin, Bruce,
Kanchelskis, Pallister, Cantona,
Ince, Keane, Hughes, Giggs
Substitutes: Robson (Giggs),
Sealey, McClair, Sharpe,
Ferguson
Scorer: Hughes
United won 5–4 on penalties.
Penalty scorers: Ince, Bruce,
Keane, Cantona, Sharpe
Attendance: 66,519

Sunday, 14 August 1994 (Wembley)
Manchester United 2
Blackburn Rovers 0
Schmeichel, May, Kanchelskis,
Bruce, Sharpe, Pallister, Cantona,
Ince, McClair, Hughes, Giggs
Substitutes: Butt, Dublin, Casper,
Gillespie
Scorers: Ince, Cantona pen.
Attendance: 60,402

Sunday, 11 August 1996 (Wembley)
Manchester United 4
Newcastle United 0
Schmeichel, Neville P., Irwin, May,
Keane, Pallister, Cantona, Butt,
Scholes, Beckham, Giggs
Substitutes: Neville G. (Irwin),
McClair, Cruyff (Scholes), Poborsky
(Butt), Van der Gouw, Johnsen,
Solskjaer

Scorers: Cantona, Butt, Beckham,
Keane
Attendance: 73,214

Sunday, 3 August 1997 (Wembley)
Manchester United 1
Chelsea 1
Schmeichel, Neville P., Irwin,
Keane, Johnsen, Pallister, Scholes,
Butt, Cole, Sheringham, Giggs
Substitutes: Neville G., Beckham
(Giggs), McClair, Cruyff
(Sheringham), Poborsky, Van der
Gouw, Thornley
Scorer: Johnsen
United won 4–2 on penalties.
Penalty scorers: Scholes, Irwin,
Keane, Butt
Attendance: 73,636

Sunday, 9 August 1998 (Wembley)
Arsenal 3
Manchester United 0
Schmeichel, Neville G., Irwin,
Keane, Johnsen, Stam, Beckham,
Butt, Cole, Scholes, Giggs
Substitutes: May, Sheringham
(Cole), Neville P. (Scholes), Cruyff
(Giggs), Solskjaer (Butt), Berg
(Keane), Culkin
Attendance: 67,342

Sunday, 1 August 1999 (Wembley)
Arsenal 2
Manchester United 1
Bosnich, Neville P., Irwin, Berg,
Scholes, Stam, Beckham, Butt,
Cole, Yorke, Cruyff
Substitutes: May (Stam),
Sheringham (Butt), Curtis, Solskjaer
(Cruyff), Culkin, Wilson, Greening
Scorer: Yorke
Attendance: 70,185

Sunday, 13 August 2000 (Wembley)
Chelsea 2
Manchester United 0
Barthez, Neville G., Irwin, Keane,
Johnsen, Silvestre, Beckham,
Scholes, Solskjaer, Sheringham,
Giggs
Substitutes: Yorke (Sheringham),
Cole (Solskjaer), Butt, Stam
(Silvestre), Fortune (Giggs), Neville
P., Van der Gouw
Attendance: 65,148

FA COMMUNITY SHIELD

Sunday, 12 August 2001
(Millennium Stadium, Cardiff)
Liverpool 2
Manchester United 1
Barthez, Irwin, Neville, G., Stam,
Silvestre, Beckham, Butt, Keane,
Giggs, Scholes, van Nistelrooy.

Substitutes: Carroll, Brown,
Chadwick, Neville, P., Johnsen,
Solskjaer, Yorke (Butt).
Scorer: van Nistelrooy
Attendance: 72,500

Sunday, August 10 2003
(Millennium Stadium, Cardiff)
Manchester United 1
Arsenal 1
Howard, Neville, P., Ferdinand, Keane,
Silvestre, Solskjaer, Butt, Fortune,
Giggs, Scholes, van Nistelrooy.

Substitutes: Carroll, Bellion,
Djemba-Djemba (Butt), Forlan
(Neville, P.), O'Shea (Fortune),
Richardson, Fletcher.
Scorer: Silvestre
United won 4–3 on penalties
Attendance: 59,923

EUROPEAN CHAMPION CLUBS' CUP FINALS

Wednesday, 29 May 1968
(Wembley)
Manchester United 4
SL Benfica 1 (aet)
Stepney, Brennan, Dunne, Crerand,
Foulkes, Stiles, Best, Kidd,
Charlton, Sadler, Aston
Substitute: Rimmer
Scorers: Charlton 2, Best, Kidd
Attendance: 92,225

Wednesday, 26 May 1999
(Nou Camp, Barcelona)
Manchester United 2
Bayern Munich 1
Schmeichel, Neville G., Irwin,
Blomqvist, Johnsen, Stam,
Beckham, Butt, Cole, Yorke, Giggs
Substitutes: May, Sheringham
(Blomqvist), Neville P., Van der Gouw,
Solskjaer (Cole), Brown, Greening
Scorers: Sheringham, Solskjaer
Attendance: 90,045

EUROPEAN CUP-WINNERS' CUP FINAL

Wednesday, 15 May 1991
(Feyenoord Stadium, Rotterdam)
Manchester United 2
Barcelona 1
Sealey, Irwin, Blackmore, Bruce,
Phelan, Pallister, Robson, Ince,
McClair, Hughes, Sharpe
Substitutes: Donaghy, Walsh,
Webb, Robins, Wallace
Scorer: Hughes 2
Attendance: 50,000

INTER-CONTINENTAL CUP

Wednesday, 25 September 1968 –
first leg (Bombonera Stadium,
Buenos Aires)
Estudiantes de la Plata 1
Manchester United 0
Stepney, Dunne, Burns, Crerand,
Foulkes, Stiles, Morgan, Sadler,
Charlton, Law, Best
Attendance: 55,000

Estudiantes de la Plata won 2–1 on aggregate

Wednesday, 16 October 1968 –
second leg (Old Trafford)
Manchester United 1
Estudiantes de la Plata 1
Stepney, Brennan, Dunne, Crerand,
Foulkes, Stiles, Morgan, Kidd,
Charlton, Law, Best
Substitute: Sartori (Law)
Scorer: Morgan
Attendance: 63,428

Tuesday, 30 November 1999
(Olympic Stadium, Tokyo)
Manchester United 1
SE Palmeiras 0
Bosnich, Neville G., Irwin, Keane,
Silvestre, Stam, Beckham, Butt,
Solskjaer, Scholes, Giggs
Substitutes: Sheringham (Scholes),
Neville P., Yorke (Solskjaer),
Fortune, Taibi, Higginbotham,
Wallwork
Scorer: Keane
Attendance: 53,372

UEFA SUPER CUP

Tuesday, 19 November 1991
(Old Trafford)
Manchester United 1
Red Star Belgrade 0
Schmeichel, Martin, Irwin, Bruce,
Webb, Pallister, Kanchelskis, Ince,
McClair, Hughes, Blackmore
Substitutes: Donaghy, Walsh,
Beardsmore, Robins, Giggs (Martin)
Scorer: McClair
Attendance: 22,110

Friday, 27 August 1999
(Stade Louis II, Monaco)
SS Lazio 1
Manchester United 0
Van der Gouw, Neville G., Neville P.,
Keane, Berg, Stam, Beckham,
Scholes, Cole, Sheringham, Solskjaer
Substitutes: Giggs, Curtis (Stam),
Cruyff (Beckham), Yorke, Culkin,
Wilson, Greening (Cole)
Attendance: 14,461

INDEX

PICTURE CREDITS